Autonomy, Oppression, and Gender

Studies in Feminist Philosophy is designed to showcase cutting-edge monographs and collections that display the full range of feminist approaches to philosophy, that push feminist thought in important new directions, and that display the outstanding quality of feminist philosophical thought.

STUDIES IN FEMINIST PHILOSOPHY

Cheshire Calhoun, Series Editor
Advisory Board

Harry Brod, University of Northern Iowa
Claudia Card, University of Wisconsin
Lorraine Code, York University, Toronto
Kimberle Crenshaw, Columbia Law School/UCLA School of Law
Jane Flax, Howard University
Ann Garry, California State University, Los Angeles
Sally Haslanger, Massachusetts Institute of Technology
Alison Jaggar, University of Colorado, Boulder
Helen Longino, Stanford University
Maria Lugones, SUNY Binghamton
Uma Narayan, Vassar College
James Sterba, University of Notre Dame
Rosemarie Tong, University of North Carolina, Charlotte
Nancy Tuana, Penn State University
Karen Warren, Macalester College

Recently Published in the Series:

Visible Identities: Race, Gender, and the Self
Linda Martín Alcoff

Women and Citizenship
Edited by Marilyn Friedman

Women's Liberation and the Sublime: Feminism, Postmodernism, Environment
Bonnie Mann

Analyzing Oppression
Ann E. Cudd

Ecological Thinking: The Politics of Epistemic Location
Lorraine Code

Self Transformations: Foucault, Ethics, and Normalized Bodies
Cressida J. Heyes

Family Bonds: Genealogies of Race and Gender
Ellen K. Feder

Moral Understandings: A Feminist Study in Ethics, Second Edition
Margaret Urban Walker

The Moral Skeptic
Anita M. Superson

"You've Changed": Sex Reassignment and Personal Identity
Edited by Laurie J. Shrage

Dancing with Iris: The Philosophy of Iris Marion Young
Edited by Ann Ferguson and Mechthild Nagel

Philosophy of Science after Feminism
Janet A. Kourany

Shifting Ground: Knowledge and Reality, Transgression and Trustworthiness
Naomi Scheman

The Metaphysics of Gender
Charlotte Witt

Unpopular Privacy: What Must We Hide?
Anita L. Allen

Adaptive Preferences and Women's Empowerment
Serene Khader

Minimizing Marriage: Marriage, Morality, and the Law
Elizabeth Brake

Out from the Shadows: Analytic Feminist Contributions to Traditional Philosophy
Edited by Sharon L. Crasnow and Anita M. Superson

The Epistemology of Resistance: Gender and Racial Oppression, Epistemic Injustice, and Resistant Imaginations
José Medina

Simone de Beauvoir and the Politics of Ambiguity
Sonia Kruks

Identities and Freedom: Feminist Theory Between Power and Connection
Allison Weir

Vulnerability: New Essays in Ethics and Feminist Philosophy
Edited by Catriona Mackenzie, Wendy Rogers, and Susan Dodds

Sovereign Masculinity: Gender Lessons from the War on Terror
Bonnie Mann

Autonomy, Oppression, and Gender
Edited by Andrea Veltman and Mark Piper

Autonomy, Oppression, and Gender

Edited by Andrea Veltman
and
Mark Piper

OXFORD
UNIVERSITY PRESS

Oxford University Press is a department of the University of Oxford.
It furthers the University's objective of excellence in research, scholarship,
and education by publishing worldwide.

Oxford   New York
Auckland   Cape Town   Dar es Salaam   Hong Kong   Karachi
Kuala Lumpur   Madrid   Melbourne   Mexico City   Nairobi
New Delhi   Shanghai   Taipei   Toronto

With offices in
Argentina   Austria   Brazil   Chile   Czech Republic   France   Greece
Guatemala   Hungary   Italy   Japan   Poland   Portugal   Singapore
South Korea   Switzerland   Thailand   Turkey   Ukraine   Vietnam

Oxford is a registered trademark of Oxford University Press
in the UK and certain other countries.

Published in the United States of America by
Oxford University Press
198 Madison Avenue, New York, NY 10016

© Oxford University Press 2014

All rights reserved. No part of this publication may be reproduced, stored in a
retrieval system, or transmitted, in any form or by any means, without the prior
permission in writing of Oxford University Press, or as expressly permitted by law,
by license, or under terms agreed with the appropriate reproduction rights organization.
Inquiries concerning reproduction outside the scope of the above should be sent to the
Rights Department, Oxford University Press, at the address above.

You must not circulate this work in any other form
and you must impose this same condition on any acquirer.

Library of Congress Cataloging-in-Publication Data
Autonomy, oppression, and gender / edited by Andrea Veltman and Mark Piper.
pages cm.—(Studies in feminist philosophy)
Includes bibliographical references.
ISBN 978-0-19-996910-4 (hardcover : alk. paper)—
ISBN 978-0-19-996911-1 (pbk. : alk. paper)
1. Autonomy (Philosophy)   2. Feminist theory.   I. Veltman, Andrea.
B808.67.A985 2014
126—dc23
2013044775

1 3 5 7 9 8 6 4 2
Printed in the United States of America
on acid-free paper

{ CONTENTS }

Notes on Contributors   vii

1. Introduction   1
   ANDREA VELTMAN AND MARK PIPER

PART I Autonomy and Independence

2. Three Dimensions of Autonomy: A Relational Analysis   15
   CATRIONA MACKENZIE
3. Relational Autonomy and Independence   42
   MARILYN FRIEDMAN
4. Autonomy? Or Freedom? A Return to Psychoanalytic Theory   61
   NANCY J. HIRSCHMANN

PART II Autonomy and Normative Commitments

5. Feminist Commitments and Relational Autonomy   87
   PAUL BENSON
6. The Feminist Debate over Values in Autonomy Theory   114
   DIANA TIETJENS MEYERS
7. A Commitment to Autonomy Is a Commitment to Feminism   141
   MARINA OSHANA

PART III Autonomy, Reasons, and Care

8. Emotions, Reasons, and Autonomy   163
   CHRISTINE TAPPOLET
9. Autonomy and Self-Care   181
   ANDREA C. WESTLUND

PART IV Autonomy, Oppression, and Adaptive Preferences

10. Coping or Oppression: Autonomy and Adaptation to Circumstance   201
    JOHN CHRISTMAN
11. Autonomy and Adaptive Preference Formation   227
    NATALIE STOLJAR

PART V Autonomy in Social Contexts

12. Raising Daughters: Autonomy, Feminism, and Gender
    Socialization   255
    MARK PIPER
13. Autonomy and Oppression at Work   280
    ANDREA VELTMAN
14. The Right to Bodily Autonomy and the Abortion Controversy   301
    ANITA M. SUPERSON
15. Choosing Death: Autonomy and Ableism   326
    ANITA HO

Index   351

{ NOTES ON CONTRIBUTORS }

Paul Benson is professor of philosophy and dean of the College of Arts and Sciences at the University of Dayton. He works in the areas of moral psychology, action theory, and social philosophy. He has published on autonomy, free agency, oppressive socialization, and moral responsibility in journals such as *Journal of Philosophy, Hypatia, Canadian Journal of Philosophy, Philosophical Studies,* and *Journal of Social Philosophy.* He has also published in edited volumes on autonomy including *Autonomy and the Challenges to Liberalism* (Cambridge, 2005, ed. Christman and Anderson), *Personal Autonomy* (Cambridge, 2005, ed. Taylor), *Moral Psychology: Feminist Ethics and Social Theory* (Rowman & Littlefield, 2004, ed. DesAutels and Walker), and *Relational Autonomy* (Oxford, 2000, ed. Mackenzie and Stoljar).

John Christman is professor of philosophy, political science, and women's studies at Pennsylvania State University. His is the author of various essays and books, including *The Myth of Property: Toward an Egalitarian Theory of Ownership* (Oxford, 1994), *Social and Political Philosophy: A Contemporary Introduction* (Routledge, 2002), and most recently *The Politics of Persons: Individual Autonomy and Socio-historical Selves* (Cambridge, 2009). He is editor of *The Inner Citadel: Essays on Individual Autonomy* (Oxford, 1989) and *Autonomy and the Challenges to Liberalism: New Essays* (Cambridge, 2005, with Joel Anderson), and *Contemporary Debates in Political Philosophy* (Basil Blackwell, 2009, with Thomas Christiano).

Marilyn Friedman is W. Alton Jones Professor of Philosophy and professor of political science at Vanderbilt University. She works in the areas of political philosophy, feminist theory, and ethics and has published extensively in those areas. Her authored books include *Autonomy, Gender, Politics* (Oxford, 2003), and her edited collections include *Women and Citizenship* (Oxford, 2005). She has also published articles in journals such as *Ethics, Journal of Philosophy*, and *Hypatia*, as well as numerous book chapters in edited collections.

Nancy J. Hirschmann is professor of political science at the University of Pennsylvania. Her books include *The Subject of Liberty: Toward a Feminist Theory of Freedom* (Princeton University Press, 2003), which won the 2004 Victoria Schuck Award for the best book on women and politics from the American

Political Science Association; *Gender, Class and Freedom in Modern Political Theory* (Princeton University Press, 2008); and *Rethinking Obligation: A Feminist Method for Political Theory* (Cornell University Press, 1992). She is also co-editor of several volumes including *Revisioning the Political: Feminist Reconstructions of Traditional Concepts in Western Political Theory* (Westview Press, 1996) and *Feminist Interpretations of Thomas Hobbes* (University of Pennsylvania Press, 2013). She is also the author of many articles and has held fellowships from the National Endowment for the Humanities, Institute for Advanced Study, American Council of Learned Societies, and Princeton University Center for Human Values.

Anita Ho is associate professor at the W. Maurice Young Centre for Applied Ethics at the University of British Columbia and director of ethics services at Providence Health Care. She specializes in bioethics, social/political philosophy, and disability studies she has published on themes such as autonomy, informed consent, disability, and trust in journals including *American Journal of Bioethics, Journal of Medical Ethics,* and *Journal of Bioethical Inquiry*. She has also co-edited an anthology titled *The Reflective Woman* (Coply, 2002) and an issue of *Teaching Philosophy* (Special Issue on Disability in the Classroom, 2007, with Anita Silvers). She is currently working on a project on trust and autonomy in clinical and research medicine, supported by a research grant from the Social Sciences and Humanities Research Council of Canada, and another project on supportive decision making in health care, funded by the Canadian Institutes of Health Research.

Catriona Mackenzie is associate dean (research), professor of philosophy, and director of the Research Centre for Agency, Values and Ethics at Macquarie University, Sydney. She is co-editor of several volumes, including *Relational Autonomy: Feminist Perspectives on Autonomy, Agency, and the Social Self* (Oxford, 2000, with Natalie Stoljar), *Practical Identity and Narrative Agency* (Routledge, 2008, with Kim Atkins), and *Vulnerability: New Essays in Ethics and Feminist Philosophy* (Oxford, 2013, with Wendy Rogers and Susan Dodds). Mackenzie has published widely in moral psychology, ethics, applied ethics, and feminist philosophy in a variety of edited collections and in journals including *Australasian Journal of Philosophy, Hypatia, Journal of Applied Philosophy, Journal of Social Philosophy,* and *Philosophical Explorations*.

Diana Tietjens Meyers is emerita professor of philosophy at the University of Connecticut. She has held the Ellacuría Chair of Social Ethics at Loyola University, Chicago, and the Laurie Chair in Women's and Gender Studies at Rutgers University. She works in four main areas of philosophy—philosophy of action, feminist ethics and aesthetics, and human rights theory. Her monographs are *Inalienable Rights: A Defense* (Columbia University Press, 1985), *Self, Society, and Personal Choice* (Columbia University Press, 1989), *Subjection and Subjectivity: Psychoanalytic Feminism and Moral Philosophy* (Routledge, 1994), and *Gender in the Mirror: Cultural Imagery and Women's Agency* (Oxford University Press, 2002). *Being Yourself: Essays on Identity, Action, and Social Life* (Rowman & Littlefield, 2004) collects some of her previously published essays as well as presenting one new one. She is at work on a new monograph, *Victims' Stories and the Advancement of Human Rights*, and a new edited collection, *Poverty, Agency, and Human Rights* (Oxford University Press, 2014).

Marina Oshana is professor of philosophy at the University of California, Davis. Her research focuses on issues in personal autonomy, responsible agency, and self-identity. She teaches classes in normative ethics, moral psychology, philosophy of law, political philosophy, and feminism. Her publications include *Personal Autonomy in Society* (Ashgate, 2006) and *The Importance of How We See Ourselves: Self-Identity and Responsible Agency* (Rowman & Littlefield, 2010).

Mark Piper is assistant professor of philosophy at James Madison University. His principal research interests are in normative ethical theory, with a special concentration on the topics of autonomy and well-being. He has published articles and book chapters on autonomy, virtue ethics, well-being, justice, and the value of education in venues such as *Journal of Value Inquiry*, *International Journal of Philosophical Studies*, and *Southwest Philosophical Review*. He is also the author of "Autonomy: Normative" in the *Internet Encyclopedia of Philosophy*. He is currently working on a monograph on the principle of respect for autonomy.

Natalie Stoljar is associate professor in the Department of Philosophy and the Institute for Health and Social Policy at McGill University. She is co-editor of the collection *Relational Autonomy: Feminist Perspectives on Autonomy, Agency and the Social Self* (Oxford University Press, 2000, with Catriona Mackenzie). She is the author of many articles on the philosophy of law, feminist philosophy, and autonomy, in journals and edited collections including *Philosophical Topics*, *Legal Theory*, and *Journal of Political Philosophy*. She is working on a book on self-government under conditions of oppression.

Anita M. Superson is professor of philosophy at the University of Kentucky. She specializes in ethics, including metaethics, moral psychology, normative and applied ethics, and feminism. Her recent books include *The Moral Skeptic* (Oxford University Press, 2009) and *Out from the Shadows: Analytical*

Feminist Contributions to Traditional Philosophy (Oxford University Press, 2012, co-edited with Sharon Crasnow). She is working on a book on bodily autonomy.

Christine Tappolet is full professor in the Department of Philosophy at the Université de Montréal. Her research interests lie mainly in metaethics, normative ethics, moral psychology, and emotion theory. She has edited a number of volumes, including *Weakness of Will and Practical Irrationality* (Oxford University Press, 2003, with Sarah Stroud), *The Modularity of Emotions* (*Canadian Journal of Philosophy*, 2008, with Luc Faucher). She is the author of numerous articles on themes such as values, normativity, weakness of will, procrastination, autonomy, and emotions and of two books, *Émotions et valeurs* (Presses Universitaires de France, 2000) and *Les concepts de l'éthique. Faut-il être conséquentialiste?* (Hermann Éditeurs, 2008, with Ruwen Ogien). She is currently working on a book manuscript titled *Emotions, Values, and Agency*.

Andrea Veltman is associate professor of philosophy at James Madison University. She has edited *Social and Political Philosophy* (Oxford University Press, 2008), *Oppression and Moral Agency* (Special Issue of *Hypatia*, 2009, with Kathryn Norlock), and *Evil, Political Violence and Forgiveness* (Rowman & Littlefield, 2009, with Kathryn Norlock). She is also author of articles on feminist ethics and on Simone de Beauvoir, Hannah Arendt, Jean-Paul Sartre, Kant, Plato, and Aristotle in journals such as *Hypatia* and *Journal of Value Inquiry*. She is currently working on a monograph on meaningful work and human flourishing.

Andrea C. Westlund is associate professor of philosophy and women's studies at the University of Wisconsin, Milwaukee. She works in ethics, moral psychology, and feminist philosophy and has published in journals including *Hypatia, Monist, Philosopher's Imprint, Philosophical Studies*, and *Philosophical Review*. Her research focuses on relational autonomy, authority, and self-regarding attitudes, and she is currently working on a series of papers on narrative, meaning, and the self.

Introduction

Andrea Veltman and Mark Piper

If feminism is a response to the oppression of women, and if resistance and emancipation include living according to one's own lights, then autonomy is central to issues in feminist philosophy. Classically defined as self-determination, autonomy includes the ability to shape our own lives and to live authentically rather than being directed by external forces that manipulate or distort us.[1] Some influential accounts define autonomy as requiring a process of critical self-reflection, whereas others emphasize several agential competencies, values, or self-regarding attitudes. Still others argue that autonomy requires control over one's circumstances, a range of options that one can hope to achieve in the development of her life, and a lack of severe constraint, coercion, or subordination in which one would be subject to the dictates of others.[2] Each of these kinds of accounts of autonomy can recognize the social and relational character of human agency, and each can acknowledge that autonomous abilities can be undermined by severely oppressive social forces, for instance by stifling the development of critical intellectual faculties or by blocking life options among the oppressed.

Autonomy provides not only an emancipatory ideal for those who cope with systemic abuse, degradation, domination, or other forms of oppression but also a lens for illuminating philosophical issues surrounding women's desires, choices, and identities. Feminist philosophers working in this area ponder, for instance, whether women can freely or authentically accept conditions that support their own oppression. Should we give credence to reflectively endorsed desires and choices that are the result of socially subordinate positions? Is the pursuit of desires that issue from patriarchal norms consistent with autonomous agency? What do we say about women who are willingly self-abnegating or wholly deferential to the interests of others? An analysis

---

[1] As characterized by John Christman, "Autonomy in Moral and Political Philosophy," in *The Stanford Encyclopedia of Philosophy*, August 2009.

[2] Marina Oshana, "Personal Autonomy in Society," *Journal of Social Philosophy* 29:1 (Spring 1998): 81-102; Oshana, *Personal Autonomy in Society* (Aldershot, UK: Ashgate, 2006).

of autonomy serves crucially in illuminating these and related questions, informing evaluations of women who adopt symbols of gender oppression, who define themselves through unequal personal relationships, or who harm themselves or others in conforming to cultural norms.

Autonomy plays an important role not only in feminism but also, more broadly, in ethical theory, applied ethics, political philosophy, and the philosophy of education. In the area of ethical theory, it has been argued that autonomy is integral in living well—that is, that autonomy is one primary good among others that a person needs to lead a good life or to achieve human flourishing. Autonomy also supports such basic human values as dignity, respect, truthfulness, and moral responsibility: in the vein of Kant, mature and rational human beings are seen as free and responsible moral agents in virtue of our capacities to control ourselves through the exercise of our autonomous wills. In applied ethics, autonomy informs ever-bourgeoning debates on issues surrounding, for example, abortion, birth, physician-assisted suicide, and same-sex marriage. A principle of respect for autonomy also lies at the core of liberal democracies, and political philosophers often invoke autonomy in evaluating social and political principles and political power as well as in grounding individual rights or in criticizing paternalistic policies or practices. Since enhancing autonomy ranks among the most important goals of a free society, some also argue that promoting autonomy is among the most important goals of a liberal education.[3] These branches of philosophical interest in autonomy intertwine with feminist work on autonomy, as issues involving gender and oppression deeply permeate ethical and political philosophy.

Insofar as liberal democracies value individual autonomy, ideals of autonomy provide norms for critiquing oppressive practices that stifle agency and limit opportunities. If living autonomously requires an agent to have "a significant array of opportunities to act in ways that reflect what deeply matters to her," as Marilyn Friedman writes, then social conditions "should not so limit her options that she cannot choose or act for the sake of any of her deep values and commitments."[4] Oppression not only limits opportunities and life options, thus preventing an oppressed person from acting autonomously in ways that reflect her values and commitments, but also deforms desires and infects "the conditions under which growing persons are socialized."[5] Oppressive socialization can damage a person's concern for herself and stifle the development of cognitive capacities, such as those employed in self-reflection or the critical appraisal of social norms.

---

[3] For more on the importance of autonomy in normative philosophy, see Mark Piper, "Autonomy: Normative," in the *Internet Encyclopedia of Philosophy*, December 2010.

[4] Marilyn Friedman, *Autonomy, Gender, Politics* (New York: Oxford University Press, 2003), 18.

[5] Friedman, *Autonomy, Gender, Politics*, 19.

Classically defined as a weighing down or as harsh dominion, oppression is characterized in contemporary feminist philosophy as structural or systemic in nature. In her landmark feminist analysis of oppression, Marilyn Frye writes that it encompasses "a system of interrelated barriers and forces which reduce, immobilize and mold people who belong to a certain group, and effect their subordination to another group."[6] Others add that oppression presents multiple faces, including marginalization, exploitation, and powerlessness, and extends beyond economic and political forces to include psychological barriers that reduce, limit, or mold people as members of certain groups.[7] Ann Cudd also clarifies that, by means of physical violence, economic domination, and psychologically coercive forces, oppression is essentially "an institutionally structured harm perpetrated on groups by other groups," in which a privileged social group benefits from the harm endured by the oppressed.[8]

Oppression can distort or damage the self-conception of an oppressed person, alienating her from her authentic self and further molding her into subordinate positions. As Sandra Bartky highlights in her work on the psychological dimensions of oppression, an oppressed person can come not only to adopt desires and values that are not her own but also to hold beliefs about herself that reflect social positions of inferiority: "to be psychologically oppressed is to be weighed down in your own mind; it is to have a harsh dominion exercised over your self-esteem."[9] The oppressed internalize a message of inferiority, as when, for instance, women are regarded by others and come to regard themselves as childlike, as cheap labor, or as objects for the gaze or sexual pleasure of others.[10] As Michael Walzer writes in conveying another example from working life, "When a garbage-man feels stigmatized by the work he does…the stigma shows in his eyes. He enters 'into collusion with us to avoid contaminating us with his lowly self.' He looks away; and we do too. 'Our eyes do not meet. He becomes a non-person.'"[11] To feel oneself inferior or to feel oneself worthless as a person poses a threat to autonomy by undermining self-respect, which is necessary for the realization of autonomous agency on some accounts.[12]

---

[6] Marilyn Frye, *The Politics of Reality: Essays in Feminist Theory* (Freedom, CA: Crossing Press, 193), 33.

[7] Sandra Bartky, "On Psychological Oppression" and Iris Marion Young, "Five Faces of Oppression" reprinted in *Feminist Theory: A Philosophical Anthology*, edited by Ann Cudd and Robin Andreasen (Malden, MA: Blackwell, 2005).

[8] Ann Cudd, *Analyzing Oppression* (New York: Oxford University Press, 2006), 26, cf. 23–27.

[9] Bartky, "On Psychological Oppression," 105.

[10] Bartky, "On Psychological Oppression," 106, 112.

[11] Michael Walzer, *Spheres of Justice: A Defense of Pluralism and Equality* (New York: Basil Blackwell, 1983), 176. Walzer here cites Stewart E. Perry's *San Francisco Scavengers: Dirty Work and the Pride of Ownership* (Berkeley: University of California Press, 1978), 7.

[12] As Joel Anderson and Axel Honneth write, practices that confer denigration or humiliation threaten "self-esteem by making it much harder (and, in limit cases, even impossible) to think of oneself as worthwhile. The resulting feelings of shame and worthlessness threaten one's sense that there is

In thinking about autonomy and gender oppression, it is important to recognize at the start that autonomy has "long been coded masculine," as Jane Dryden writes.[13] Given historical and ideological exclusions of women from ideals of autonomy, some feminist philosophers have looked askance at conceptions of autonomy, at times rejecting the value altogether. One classic criticism, in circulation since the 1980s, is that autonomy is drawn from male biographies and bound up with socially atomistic and individualistic conceptions of human beings, such that autonomy is antithetical to the personal connections and social bonds around which many women reflectively form self-identities. In this earlier wave of feminist scholarship on autonomy, basic questions asked by philosophers concern whether autonomy requires self-sufficiency at the expense of human connections, whether women find the ideal of autonomy alienating, and whether feminine or feminist moral concerns require different conceptions of autonomy, relative to those that have been dominant in the history of philosophy or in contemporary moral and political philosophy.

This skeptical stance toward classic ideals of autonomy forms part of the starting point for work on relational conceptions of autonomy, in which feminist philosophers rehabilitate autonomy to accommodate the social character of human agency. Accounts of relational autonomy draw attention to the social, cultural, and historical contexts in which agents are embedded and to the fact that autonomy is a capability of human agents who are not only rational but also "emotional, embodied, desiring, creative and feeling."[14] Those who offer accounts of relational autonomy also analyze the effect of oppressive socialization upon human agency and underscore that autonomy should not be cast as antithetical to human connections, including those manifested in love, friendship, appropriate care, and even loyalty and devotion.

Feminist accounts of relational autonomy have now changed the landscape of autonomy studies, shifting philosophical thinking about autonomy toward the social and interpersonal dynamics that shape agency, desires, and choices.[15] Feminist scholarship has focused attention on the need for a finer and richer account of agency, and there is now a fair amount of agreement that autonomous agency is saturated with self–other relations. As Friedman notes,

---

point to one's undertakings. And without that sense of one's aspirations being worth pursuing, one's agency is hampered." Anderson and Honneth, "Autonomy, Vulnerability, Recognition and Justice," in *Autonomy and the Challenges to Liberalism: New Essays*, edited by John Christman and Joel Anderson (Cambridge: Cambridge University Press, 2005), 131.

[13] Jane Dryden, "Autonomy: Overview," in *The Internet Encyclopedia of Philosophy*, November 2010.

[14] Catriona Mackenzie and Natalie Stoljar, "Introduction: Autonomy Refigured," in *Relational Autonomy: Feminist Perspectives on Autonomy, Agency and the Social Self*, edited by Mackenzie and Stoljar (New York: Oxford University Press, 2000), 21; Natalie Stoljar, "Feminist Perspectives on Autonomy," in *Stanford Encyclopedia of Philosophy*, Summer 2013.

[15] See, e.g., John Christman, "Autonomy in Moral and Political Philosophy."

philosophical conceptions of autonomy—as opposed to conceptions of autonomy that may be culturally dominant—now seldom suggest that autonomy requires a self-sufficient or self-made person.[16] Adaptive preferences formed in the context of oppressive circumstances, such as preferences for subservience or for iconic symbols of gender oppression, also now serve as formidable potential counterexamples to purely proceduralist accounts of autonomy, which typically hold that an agent's autonomy in relation to a commitment is secured merely by the agent's endorsement of it, assuming the agent's reflection is suitably independent.

Since the publication of the landmark collection *Relational Autonomy* in 2000, feminist philosophers and autonomy scholars have continued debate over the conditions necessary for autonomous choice, the satisfactoriness of value-neutral accounts of autonomy, and the respect-worthiness of preferences formed in adaptive contexts, among other issues. For instance, in developing feminist accounts of autonomy, some theorists maintain that women who act subserviently or upon preferences formed in oppressive circumstances are not autonomous.[17] Others, however, argue that respecting the agency and deliberative capacities of oppressed women requires that we not characterize such women as "compliant dupes of patriarchy"[18] and that women living in severely oppressive conditions find outlets for the exercise of autonomy.[19] Both lines of argument initially appear plausible: as Diana Meyers observes, value-neutral accounts of autonomy, in which autonomy does not require choosing particular values, such as equality or independence, appear attractive partly on account of showing respect for women who choose subservience or deference. On the other hand, value-saturated accounts appear attractive on account of highlighting the autonomy-subverting costs of living under oppressive systems.[20]

In *Gender in the Mirror*, Meyers notes that both value-neutral and value-saturated accounts of autonomy are troubling: value-saturated accounts appear to stigmatize some women as victims, to homogenize autonomous and

---

[16] Marilyn Friedman, "Autonomy, Social Disruption and Women," in *The Feminist Philosophy Reader*, edited by Alison Bailey and Chris Cuomo (New York: McGraw-Hill, 2008). See also Friedman's chapter "Relational Autonomy and Independence" in this volume.

[17] Natalie Stoljar, "Autonomy and the Feminist Intuition," in Mackenzie and Stoljar, *Relational Autonomy*.

[18] Uma Narayan, "Minds of Their Own: Choices, Autonomy, Cultural Practices and Other Women," in *A Mind of One's Own: Feminist Essays on Reason and Objectivity* (Boulder, CO: Westview Press, 2002).

[19] John Christman, "Relational Autonomy, Liberal Individualism, and the Social Construction of Selves," *Philosophical Studies* 117 (2004): 143–164; Andrea Westlund, "Rethinking Relational Autonomy," *Hypatia* 24 (2009): 26–49; Serene J. Khader, *Adaptive Preferences and Women's Empowerment* (New York: Oxford University Press, 2011).

[20] Diana Tietjens Meyers, *Gender in the Mirror: Cultural Imagery and Women's Agency* (New York: Oxford University Press 2002), 11.

authentic lives, and to overlook the agency women exercise even in contexts of oppressive circumstances. Yet value-neutral accounts serve poorly as tools of social critique and suffer on account of packing autonomy into purely procedural processes of reflection that effectively "neglect the possibility that a well-integrated, smoothly-functioning self could be in need of rigorous scrutiny and drastic overhaul."[21] In light of potential pitfalls of both approaches, Meyers argues that a compelling feminist account of autonomy "must acknowledge that oppression impedes autonomy without stripping women of that autonomy which they have managed to wrest from a patriarchal, racist, heterosexist, ageist, class-stratified world."[22] In her contribution to this volume, she further distinguishes ways values enter autonomy theories, demarcating new conceptual axes along which to position accounts of autonomy.

In this collection of new papers, leading scholars carry forward examinations of central theoretical and practical issues at the intersection of autonomy studies and feminist philosophy. Contributors examine fundamental components and commitments of autonomy, examining for instance the role of reflective deliberation, reasons, values, cares, emotions, self-worth, self-care, adaptive preferences, social and political commitments, and norms of independence in accounts of autonomy. Some papers pursue the question of whether autonomy is compatible with subordination, including forms of gender subordination and class-based subordination. Others examine how ideals of autonomy are affected by capitalism, political commitments to inclusivity, and feminist emphases on the relationality of human agency. In looking at autonomy amid oppression, the volume represents a plurality of perspectives about autonomy. Some contributors examine the agency of women and oppressed persons through the lens of value-neutral accounts of autonomy, whereas others utilize dialogical accounts, capabilities accounts, or thicker value-saturated accounts. Still others make meta-arguments about the merits of different kinds of approaches relative to feminist ambitions. A number of papers focus on assessing autonomy in social contexts in which agents form adaptive preferences or internalize gendered norms, and some focus on how autonomy bears in social and personal contexts of raising girls, working, pregnancy and abortion, and end-of-life decisions.

We have organized the papers in the volume into five sections, beginning with an initial cluster that explores key dimensions of the concept of autonomy, especially in regards to its relational character and associated notions of independence and freedom. In Chapter 2, Catriona Mackenzie focuses on the concept of autonomy itself. According to Mackenzie, one of the key reasons that autonomy remains a contested value is because philosophers have tended to

---

[21] Meyers, *Gender in the Mirror*, 16.
[22] Meyers, *Gender in the Mirror*, 16.

view autonomy as a unitary concept. She argues that autonomy ought instead to be understood as a multidimensional concept consisting of three logically distinct but causally related dimensions: self-determination, self-governance, and self-authorization. In addition, Mackenzie provides a relational analysis of each of these dimensions of autonomy and argues that what is required to satisfy the conditions of autonomy in particular contexts will often fluctuate. The result of her work is to provide philosophers with a more nuanced understanding of autonomy, one that will allow debate on autonomy to proceed with greater clarity, precision, and sensitivity to context.

Chapter 3, by Marilyn Friedman, explores ways the concept of autonomy can combine relational and individualistic elements. Focusing on the discussion of liberal individualism in Jennifer Nedelsky's book *Law's Relations: A Relational Theory of Self, Autonomy, and Law,* Friedman contends that relational and individualistic aspects of autonomy need not be irreconcilable: acknowledging the constitutive relationality of human selves is consistent with maintaining boundaries among individuals, such as occurs when the state serves to protect individuals from threats posed by one another. She argues further that the popular notion of the self-made man—valorized by some but criticized by others—is not relevant to discussions of autonomy so much as to debates about capitalism. Freidman concludes her paper with a defense of independence as an ideal for subordinate persons: not only does an ideal of independence provide a useful goal for liberatory movements, partly because it protects against some forms of vulnerability, but it also serves a classic feminist goal of freeing women to shape their own lives rather than accepting confining definitions imposed by others.

Chapter 4, by Nancy Hirschmann, further explores the theme of independence. Hirschmann registers skepticism about relational autonomy, arguing provocatively that the concept originates from a pathology in feminine psychoanalytical development: in sexist and heteronormative practices of childrearing, girls and women emerge with relational self-identities oriented toward care and empathy that undermine the need to cultivate an independent self. She suggests that if we retain the concept of relational autonomy, then we also need a feminist concept of freedom in which a person remains an individual responsible for her own choices. Whatever desires and abilities we cultivate through relationships with others, she argues, "we need to act by and for ourselves."

The volume continues with a second cluster of papers focusing on the normative and social commitments of relational approaches to autonomy. In Chapter 5, Paul Benson contends that many of the ongoing disagreements about the normative commitments of relational autonomy can be overcome by considering the practical question of how a conception of autonomy can best advance the ethical, social, and political aims of feminism. He argues that a conception of autonomy that focuses on autonomous agents' authority to speak or answer to others for their choices and actions affords a preferred way to understand autonomy's relational character. Such a conception is especially congenial to advancing the practical goals of feminism, according to Benson, because it captures the importance of women's attitudes toward their own experience and because it accurately takes account of the social conditions that inform that experience. Chapter 6, by Diana Meyers, also discusses the issue of the normative commitments of autonomy. Taking as her starting point the ongoing disputes between those who defend substantive accounts of autonomy and those who defend content-neutral accounts, Meyers argues that values may be implicated in autonomy theories in two distinct ways. On one hand, an autonomy theory may prescribe or proscribe certain types of behavior or allow that any sort of behavior might be autonomously chosen; she calls this the *Directivity Axis*. On the other hand, an autonomy theory may utilize or invoke background values to elucidate the process of autonomous choice; she terms this the *Constitutivity Axis*. According to Meyers, this Double Axis Thesis has the benefit of making room for autonomy theories that are both value neutral and value utilizing. Echoing the practical concerns addressed in Benson's paper, Meyers ends her paper by arguing that value-neutral positions on the Directivity Axis serve feminist purposes well.

In Chapter 7, by contrast, Marina Oshana sees feminist purposes served well with a thicker conception of autonomy in which autonomy requires authority over certain choices, a lack of domination and exploitation in social relationships, and enough economic security to maintain control over important aspects of our lives. Without meaningful economic security, she points out, a person cannot maintain control over fundamental choices, such as choices concerning family or life partners. Broadly, Oshana also argues biconditionally that a commitment to autonomy entails a commitment to feminism and that a commitment to feminism entails a commitment to autonomy. For Oshana, respecting autonomy entails opposing forms of social domination and thus respecting autonomy entails the core demands of feminism, which mutually entails respecting the abilities of persons to make their own decisions and engage in action by means of their own authority.

A third cluster of papers in the volume attends particularly to care, emotion, and reason in accounts of autonomy and challenges certain influential notions about autonomy. In Chapter 8, Christine Tappolet rebuts a notion found in both historical and contemporary philosophical sources that emotional agents (and by extension women) cannot be autonomous. She draws on an account of emotions she develops elsewhere to show not only that emotions are integral in autonomous agency but also that emotions and reason-responsiveness are not at odds. In addition to dismantling a ludicrous argument that women cannot be autonomous, Tappolet's paper thus constitutes a powerful challenge to autonomy accounts that are predominantly rationalistic in character. This paper dovetails with our ninth chapter by Andrea Westlund, who argues that autonomy requires an attitude of self-care, which involves taking care with one's reasons and decisions as well as taking responsibility for one's judgments. Clarifying distinct conceptions of care at play in the philosophical literature, she utilizes a finessed conception of care to augment answerability accounts of autonomy, which, for Westlund, involve maintaining an open-minded disposition to explain one's reasons and cares and to engage in potentially self-transformative deliberation with others. Westlund sees the relational character of autonomy as being at least partially grounded in the autonomous agent's attitude of self-care: it is precisely the autonomous agent's attitude of care for her self that leads her to take seriously reflective deliberation with qualified others about reasons for action.

The fourth cluster of papers in the volume engages with issues surrounding the relation among autonomy, oppression, and adaptive preferences. In Chapter 10, John Christman addresses the question of how to distinguish between (1) cases in which agents respond to changing life circumstances while retaining their autonomy and (2) cases in which agents adapt to new circumstances in an autonomy-undermining way. He examines this distinction by considering not only different sources of serious life constraints, including human trafficking and paralysis through disability, but also different judgments about these constraints that can be supported with various accounts of autonomy. He argues ultimately that a proceduralist account of autonomy is best able to account for the difference between self-governing adaptation and loss of agency in response to oppressive constraints. In so doing he refines the procedural account of autonomy developed in his earlier work, incorporating a new condition he calls reflexive self-affirmation.

Chapter 11, by Natalie Stoljar, continues a focus on autonomy and adaptation to oppressive social circumstances. Tackling the claim that some philosophers have made that desires formed under oppressive circumstances are deformed and hence autonomy undermining, Stoljar defends a two-sided thesis. On one hand, she argues that adaptive preferences *per se* are not incompatible with autonomy. Yet on the other hand, she contends that many of the cases of adaptive preference formation of concern to feminists are autonomy undermining insofar as they fail to satisfy criteria contained in both proceduralist and substantive theories of autonomy. Like that of Christman, Stoljar's discussion offers both an illuminating analysis of preferences formed in oppressive contexts and a substantive engagement with the important recent work of feminist philosopher Serene Khader.

A final fifth cluster of papers deals with autonomy as it relates to particular social and personal contexts. In Chapter 12, Mark Piper raises the question of how parents ought to gender socialize their daughters, given a commitment both to feminism and to enhancement of the development of daughters' future autonomy. He joins other feminist theorists in observing that traditional female gender socialization tends to subvert the autonomy of women, such as by teaching girls to favor subordinate roles or by undermining girls' confidence in themselves. In light of a need for alternative forms of gender socialization, Piper examines a variety of forms of gender socialization in light of commitments to autonomy and feminism, ultimately favoring an inclusive form of feminist gender socialization that retains a positive valuation of the category of womanhood.

Whereas Piper addresses the impact that parents and others can have on the development of autonomy in girls and women, Andrea Veltman, in Chapter 13, turns attention to the impact that work can have on the development and exercise of autonomous capabilities. Drawing on empirical and philosophical literatures on work and well-being, she argues that working extensively at eudemonistically meaningless work undermines autonomy and self-respect and that promoting autonomous agency entails respecting the agency and skills people exercise at work. In part, Veltman also examines autonomy in relation to economic independence, writing in agreement with Friedman, Oshana, and others that economic independence is a condition of personal autonomy that women have good reason to seek. Although some feminist theorists highlight morally problematic implications of a social ethos of economic independence (particularly for women whose need to raise young children renders ideals of independence and self-sufficiency unattainable), Veltman says that an appreciable dimension of the oppression of many women workers is that they labor extensively at jobs that do not enable a meaningful measure of financial independence.

A final pairing of papers in our fifth cluster examines autonomy and embodiment with attention to pregnancy, abortion, disability, and physician-assisted suicide. Chapter 14, by Anita Superson, concerns the place of a right to bodily autonomy in relation to the abortion controversy. Drawing centrally on the work of Judith Jarvis Thomson,[23] Superson argues that the right to bodily autonomy is even stronger than Thomson supposed, and she underwrites powerful arguments in favor of women's right to abortion. Although focusing the majority of her essay on the abortion debate, Superson concludes by noting that the right to bodily autonomy has crucial normative weight in many other debates that are of importance to women, including rape, female genital manipulation, and woman battering. Finally, in Chapter 15, Anita Ho discusses the influence of ableist social ideology on the autonomy of those facing end-of-life decisions. According to Ho, even if the influence of ableist social ideology is not directly coercive, it can inform people's deliberations about their alternatives in an autonomy-undermining way. The upshot of her work is a call for greater attention to the broader societal assumptions about the value

---

[23] Judith Jarvis Thomson, "A Defense of Abortion," *Philosophy and Public Affairs* 1:1 (Autumn 1971): 47–66.

of life with impairments and an appreciation of how these assumptions may negatively affect people's quality of life, the autonomy of their decision-making processes, and their end-of-life decisions.

This collection is a collaborative endeavor, and we would like to express our sincere thanks to all our contributing authors, who have been a pleasure to work with and whose papers we are proud to bring together in this volume. We especially thank Natalie Stoljar and Catronia Mackenzie for supporting this collection by organizing a workshop called Relational Autonomy: Ten Years On, at which our contributors had an invaluable opportunity to present and discuss drafts of papers for the volume. We would also like to thank the Department of Philosophy and Religion at James Madison University for supporting our work on the project and our research assistant, Sara Scherer, for assistance in helping us prepare and streamline the collection. Thanks also to our acquisitions editor at Oxford University Press, Lucy Randall, for her support and assistance with the project from its inception and to the anonymous reviewers of our book project for valuable recommendations for the project. We hope that readers of this volume will benefit from the efforts of all who have contributed and will find the papers as important and as richly stimulating as we do.

{ PART I }

Autonomy and Independence

{ 2 }

Three Dimensions of Autonomy: A Relational Analysis

Catriona Mackenzie

It is no secret that although respect for individual autonomy is a foundational principle of liberal and democratic theory, just what this principle means and how the concept of autonomy should be interpreted and applied in specific contexts are highly contested. For example, in many debates in bioethics, it is not uncommon for disputants on both sides of a debate to invoke the concept of autonomy in support of their position. One way to interpret what is at stake in these disputes is to appeal to Rawls's concept/conception distinction. While the disputants both invoke the *concept* of autonomy, they are in fact appealing to different *conceptions* of individual autonomy, and these different conceptions arise from different normative theoretical frameworks and from different value orientations and political commitments.

I think this suggestion goes part of the way toward explaining why autonomy is such a contested value. However, I don't think that the concept/conception distinction provides a full diagnosis of the problem. Another aspect of the problem is that in both bioethics and debates about autonomy in the philosophical literature there is a lot of talking at cross-purposes because there is a lack of clarity about what kind of *concept* the concept of autonomy is. Is it a unitary concept or a multidimensional concept? And is it a context-invariant concept or a context-sensitive concept that is employed for different purposes in different contexts? Related to this second question, there is a lack of clarity about what is at issue in debates about autonomy. Is the aim of such debates to analyze the concept, or is it to clarify the role the concept plays in our social and normative practices?

My aims in this chapter are twofold. First, I seek to address the question of what kind of concept the concept of autonomy is. My response to this question is that autonomy is a multidimensional, rather than a unitary, concept. In developing this response, I propose a taxonomy that distinguishes three distinct, but causally interdependent, dimensions or axes of autonomy: self-determination, self-governance, and self-authorization. Each dimension involves distinct conditions, which may be satisfied to varying degrees. I suggest further that autonomy is not a context-invariant concept. Rather, it is employed for different purposes in different social and normative contexts, and in these different contexts it may be appropriate to set different thresholds for satisfying the conditions for autonomy.

The second aim of the chapter is to develop a relational interpretation or *conception* of the three axes of self-determination, self-governance, and self-authorization. Although relational conceptions of autonomy have become increasingly influential in feminist theory, relational autonomy is often invoked in support of feminist commitments rather than analyzed in detail, particularly in feminist bioethics. By developing a relational interpretation of the three dimensions or axes of autonomy, I seek to provide a more detailed analysis of the commitments and aims of relational autonomy. In doing so, I point to interesting conceptual connections between relational autonomy theory and capabilities approaches to justice, which have not hitherto been identified in the literature.[1]

The chapter is in five sections. In the first section, I provide a brief overview sketch of my proposed multidimensional analysis of the concept of autonomy. In the second section, I provide an overview of the main motivations and commitments of relational autonomy. In sections 3 to 5, I propose a specific relational interpretation of each autonomy axis and its relevant conditions. It is important to clarify at the outset that this is a big picture project, an exercise in conceptual mapping. Each of the three axes of autonomy, with their specific conditions, refers to a large and complex literature, which I cannot discuss in any great detail. So my conceptual map is an outline of the terrain. Filling in its topographical details is a much bigger project than could be undertaken in a single chapter.

1. Three Dimensions of Autonomy

A unitary concept is a concept for which there is a single set of necessary and sufficient conditions for the correct application of the concept. Natural kind terms such as water, gold, and elephant are unitary concepts. Ethical concepts, such as goodness, trust, and autonomy, are also often treated as unitary concepts. In the case of individual autonomy, the kernel of what is taken to be the unitary concept of autonomy is the notion of self-governance, the idea that to be autonomous is to be capable of making decisions and acting on the basis of

---

[1] I also explore these connections in Mackenzie, "The Importance of Relational Autonomy and Capabilities for an Ethics of Vulnerability," in *Vulnerability: New Essays in Ethics and Feminist Philosophy*, edited by Catriona Mackenzie, Wendy A. Rogers and Susan Dodds (New York: Oxford University Press, 2014). For a related discussion, see Marina Oshana's contribution to this volume.

motives, values, or reasons that are "one's own" in some relevant sense. Different conceptions of autonomy aim, in part, to analyze the necessary and sufficient conditions for a motive, value, reason, or action to be "one's own."

In the literature two broad kinds of condition for self-governance have been identified: competency conditions, which spell out the cognitive, volitional, normative, or other competences deemed necessary to act effectively on one's motives, values, or reasons; and authenticity conditions, which spell out what it means for these elements of one's motivational structure to be genuinely one's own. Much debate about autonomy in philosophical moral psychology, including debate among theorists of relational autonomy, has focused on advancing differing interpretations of these conditions, with debate proceeding by way of examples and counterexamples designed to test the necessity or sufficiency claims of rival interpretations. Not surprisingly, no agreement on a single, definitive interpretation of the competence or authenticity conditions for autonomy has emerged from the debate. I think there are two connected reasons for this. First, the concept of autonomy is employed for different purposes in different social and normative contexts. This is one reason why we need a multidimensional analysis of the concept. Second, the unitary notion of self-governance, which identifies conditions for autonomy that relate to agents' practical identities and the skills and competences required for autonomy, is inadequate to capture the multidimensional nature of the concept of autonomy.

My suggestion is that the concept of autonomy involves three distinct but causally interdependent dimensions or axes: self-determination, self-governance, and self-authorization. *Self-determination* involves having the freedom and opportunities to make and enact choices of practical import to one's life, that is, choices about what to value, who to be, and what to do. The self-determination axis identifies external, structural conditions for individual autonomy, specifically *freedom* conditions and *opportunity* conditions. Freedom conditions identify the kind of social and political constraints that interfere with the exercise of self-determination and the kind of political and personal liberties that enable it. Opportunity conditions specify the kinds of opportunities that need to be available to agents in their social environments for them to have choices about what to value, who to be, and what to do. Gerald Dworkin, Joseph Raz, and Marina Oshana have all emphasized the importance of freedom and opportunity conditions for autonomy.[2]

Self-governance involves having the skills and capacities necessary to make choices and enact decisions that express, or cohere with, one's reflectively constituted diachronic practical identity. Following Korsgaard,[3] I understand

---

[2] Gerald Dworkin, *The Theory and Practice of Autonomy* (New York: Cambridge University Press, 1988); Joseph Raz, *The Morality of Freedom* (Oxford: Clarendon Press, 1986); Marina Oshana, *Personal Autonomy in Society* (Aldershot, UK: Ashgate, 2006).

[3] Christine Korsgaard, *The Sources of Normativity* (Cambridge: Cambridge University Press, 1996).

practical identity as a normative self-conception, which embodies a person's sense of self-identity and her commitments, values, and beliefs. The self-governance axis identifies internal conditions for autonomy, specifically competence and authenticity conditions. Competence conditions are central to many accounts of autonomy in bioethics. Beauchamp and Childress, for example, understand competence in medical decision making in terms of capacities to understand relevant information, make a judgment about that information in light of one's values, and communicate the decision to caregivers.[4] Within philosophical moral psychology, there is quite a range of different accounts of competence, including reason-responsiveness views (e.g., Wolf), normative competence views (e.g., Benson and Stoljar), and skills-based views (e.g., Meyers).[5] Predominantly, however, debates about autonomy within philosophical moral psychology have focused on authenticity conditions. For example, the early work of Harry Frankfurt on identification with one's will, care-based analyses of autonomy that develop themes in Frankfurt's later work on caring[6], and John Christman's nonalienation analysis of critical reflection all provide different articulations of authenticity.[7]

The third axis, *self-authorization*, involves regarding oneself as having the *normative authority* to be self-determining and self-governing. In other words, it involves regarding oneself as authorized to exercise practical control over one's life, to determine one's own reasons for action, and to define one's values and identity-shaping practical commitments. The self-authorization axis has emerged as a central concern of recent social and relational theories of autonomy. This axis identifies several conditions for autonomy, relating to *accountability, self-evaluative attitudes*, and *social recognition*. These conditions are discussed, with different inflections and emphases, in recent work by a range of theorists. Paul Benson and Andrea Westlund, for example, ground

---

[4] Tom Beauchamp and James Childress, *Principles of Biomedical Ethics*, 7th ed. (New York: Oxford University Press, 2012).

[5] For reasons-responsiveness views, see Susan Wolf, *Freedom within Reason* (New York: Oxford University Press, 1990); for normative competence views, see Paul Benson, "Autonomy and Oppressive Socialization," *Social Theory and Practice* 17 (1991): 385–408; Natalie Stoljar, "Autonomy and the Feminist Intuition," in *Relational Autonomy: Feminist Perspectives on Autonomy, Agency and the Social Self*, edited by C. Mackenzie and N. Stoljar (New York: Oxford University Press, 2000), 94–111; for skills-based views, see Diana Meyers, *Self, Society and Personal Choice* (New York: Columbia University Press, 1989).

[6] For the notion of identification, see the essays in Harry Frankfurt, *The importance of what we care about* (Cambridge: Cambridge University Press, 1988); for care-based analyses, see, e.g., Frankfurt, "On Caring," in Frankfurt, *Necessity, Volition and Love* (Cambridge: Cambridge University Press, 1999), 155–180; Agnieszka Jaworksa "Caring and Internality," *Philosophy and Phenomenological Research* 74:3 (2007): 529–568; Jaworksa, "Caring, Minimal Autonomy, and the Limits of Liberalism," in *Naturalized Bioethics: Towards Responsible Knowing and Practice*, edited by H. Lindemann, M. Verkerk, and M. Walker (Cambridge: Cambridge University Press, 2009), 80–105.

[7] John Christman, *The Politics of Persons: Individual Autonomy and Socio-historical Selves* (Cambridge: Cambridge University Press, 2009).

autonomy in an agent's attitudes or dispositions to hold herself accountable and answerable to others for her reasons.[8] Carolyn McLeod emphasizes the importance of agents' self-evaluative attitudes, in particular self-trust, for autonomous decision making in health-care contexts.[9] And Joel Anderson argues that autonomy is a constitutively social capacity, in the sense that it is constituted within normative social practices of mutual recognition.[10]

Two clarifications are in order at this point. First, the aim of this taxonomy is to map out the different dimensions or axes of the concept of autonomy in a way that makes sense of our complex, and sometimes conflicting, intuitions about autonomy and our diverse autonomy-related social practices. Of course, the map by itself doesn't resolve debates about how best to understand the different conditions I have identified as relevant to each axis. Different theories of autonomy will continue to conceptualize these conditions in different ways, and in later sections I propose a relational conception of each of the conditions. But I hope the map will help to resolve some of the talking at cross-purposes in the literature that arises from understanding autonomy as the unitary concept of self-governance.

Second, it is important to recognize that the exercise of autonomy along these different dimensions can be assessed at different levels: locally, with respect to specific decisions or choices; programmatically, with respect to domains of a person's life, such as with respect to her finances, at work, or in her family or intimate relationships; or globally, with respect to a person's life overall.[11] So it is possible that a person might exercise a high level of autonomy in one domain, such as at work, while being subject to domination in another domain, such as in her family life. It is also possible that a person might be able to exercise local autonomy with respect to a particular decision, such as the choice to accept or refuse a particular medical treatment, even though his global autonomy may be seriously impaired, for example because he is an addict. Within bioethics, autonomy is usually understood as local, that is, as

---

[8] Paul Benson, "Feminist Intuitions and the Normative Substance of Autonomy," in *Personal Autonomy: New Essays on Personal Autonomy and Its Role in Contemporary Moral Philosophy*, edited by James Stacey Taylor (Cambridge: Cambridge University Press, 2005), 124–142; Paul Benson, "Taking Ownership: Authority and Voice in Autonomous Agency," in *Autonomy and the Challenges to Liberalism*, edited by J. Christman and J. Anderson (Cambridge: Cambridge University Press, 2005), 101–126; Andrea Westlund, "Rethinking Relational Autonomy," *Hypatia* 24:4 (2009): 26–49.

[9] Carolyn McLeod, *Self-Trust and Reproductive Autonomy* (Cambridge, MA: MIT Press, 2002).

[10] Joel Anderson and Axel Honneth, "Autonomy, Vulnerability, Recognition and Justice," in Christman and Anderson, *Autonomy and the Challenges to Liberalism*, 127–149; Joel Anderson, "Vulnerability and Autonomy Intertwined," in *Vulnerability: New Essays in Ethics and Feminist Philosophy*, edited by Catriona Mackenzie, Wendy A. Rogers, and Susan Dodds (New York: Oxford University Press, 2014).

[11] For discussions of the distinctions between local, programmatic, and global autonomy, see especially Meyers, *Self, Society and Personal Choice*; Oshana, *Personal Autonomy in Society*.

applying to a specific decision at a specific time.[12] Feminist bioethicists, however, who are influenced by relational theories of autonomy, tend to hold the view that the exercise of local autonomy needs to be understood in the context of a person's capacity to exercise programmatic or global autonomy.[13]

2. Why "Relational" Autonomy?

Relational theories of autonomy were originally motivated by three central convictions. First, in spite of feminist critiques of autonomy as a masculinist and excessively individualist ideal, it is a mistake for feminists to jettison the value of autonomy because the exercise of some threshold level of self-determination, self-governance, and self-authorization is crucial for women's emancipation. Second, gender oppression, in different ways in different contexts and to different degrees, constrains women's abilities to lead self-determining lives and thus can impair their capacities for self-governance and can undermine their sense of being self-authorizing agents. Gender oppression is here understood as a system or pattern of hierarchically structured social relations, institutions, and practices of gender-based domination and subordination. Third, we need a refigured conception of autonomy that is responsive to feminist critiques of overly individualistic conceptions of autonomy. Relational theories aim to provide this refigured conception.[14]

As a conception of individual autonomy, relational autonomy is committed to a form of normative individualism—that is, to the view that the rights, welfare, dignity, freedom, and autonomy of individuals matter and impose normative constraints on the claims of social groups or collectives.[15] Capabilities theory is also committed to normative individualism in this sense.[16] In what

---

[12] See the discussion of autonomy in Beauchamp and Childress, *Principles of Biomedical Ethics*. See also UK Department for Constitutional Affairs, *Mental Capacity Act 2005 Code of Practice* (Norwich: Stationery Office, 2007).

[13] For further discussions of this claim and of the significance of relational autonomy for bioethics, see Susan Sherwin, "A Relational Approach to Autonomy in Health Care," in *The Politics of Women's Health: Exploring Agency and Autonomy*, edited by S. Sherwin and the Feminist Health Care Ethics Research Network (Philadelphia: Temple University Press, 1998), 19–47; Catriona Mackenzie, "Autonomy," in *Routledge Companion to Bioethics*, edited by John Arras, Elizabeth Fenton, and Rebecca Kukla (New York: Routledge, forthcoming).

[14] For more extended discussion of these claims, see Mackenzie and Stoljar, "Introduction: Autonomy Refigured," in Mackenzie and Stoljar, *Relational Autonomy*.

[15] A stronger version of normative individualism is proposed by Elizabeth Anderson, "Towards a Non-Ideal, Relational Methodology for Political Philosophy," *Hypatia* 24:4 (2009): 132. She holds that the claims of individuals have normative priority over the claims of social groups or collectives. Relational autonomy need not be committed to this stronger form of normative individualism, although some relational theorists might endorse the stronger view.

[16] See. e.g., Martha Nussbaum, *Creating Capabilities* (Cambridge, MA: Harvard University Press, 2011).

sense, then, is the theory "relational"? I suggest it is relational in several ways that can be articulated in the form of three premises or starting assumptions to which relational theories are committed. It should be noted that, with respect to these assumptions, there is much common ground between relational autonomy theory and capabilities theory.

The first premise is that an adequate conception of autonomy must be responsive to the facts of human vulnerability and dependency rather than assuming a conception of persons as self-sufficient, independent, rational contractors. It follows that the conditions for self-determination, self-governance, and self-authorization cannot be specified in such a way that these dimensions of autonomy are inconsistent with human vulnerability, dependency, or social relations of care.[17] Because relational autonomy theory starts from a conception of persons as vulnerable and dependent to varying degrees, I want to suggest that it is highly relevant to health-care contexts, where obligations to respond to vulnerability must be balanced with respect for patient autonomy. It should also be noted that Nussbaum's capabilities theory, in particular, emphasizes the importance for a theory of justice to be premised on the facts of human vulnerability.[18]

The second premise is that persons are embodied and socially, historically, and culturally embedded and that their identities are constituted in relation to these factors in complex ways. Thus, although relational autonomy theory is committed to normative individualism, it is also committed to a social ontology of persons—that is, a conception of persons that emphasizes the role of embodied social practices (including linguistic and cultural practices), social group identities, and historical contingencies in the formation of our individual practical identities. This premise is particularly relevant to the way the self-governance dimension of autonomy should be understood. It suggests, first, that an adequate analysis of authenticity conditions must account for the complex social constitution of individual identity. Second, this premise suggests that an adequate analysis of competence conditions must acknowledge

---

[17] This is not to deny that some sources of vulnerability (e.g., abusive interpersonal relationships, or political repression) may undermine autonomy. For more detailed analysis of vulnerability, see Catriona Mackenzie, Wendy A. Rogers, and Susan Dodds, eds., *Vulnerability: New Essays in Ethics and Feminist Philosophy* (New York: Oxford University Press, 2014). For reflections on the complex relationship between autonomy and vulnerability, see especially the essays in that volume by Joel Anderson, Catriona Mackenzie, and Jackie Leach Scully. For extended discussion of the way that some social relationships, including relations of care, can undermine autonomy, see especially Marilyn Friedman, "Autonomy and Social Relationships: Rethinking the Feminist Critique," in *Feminists Rethink the Self*, edited by Diana Tietjens Meyers (Boulder, CO: Westview Press, 1997), 40–61; Friedman, "Autonomy, Social Disruption, and Women," in Mackenzie and Stoljar, *Relational Autonomy*, 35–51; Friedman, *Autonomy, Gender, Politics* (New York: Oxford University Press, 2003).

[18] See especially Martha Nussbaum, *Frontiers of Justice: Disability, Nationality, Species Membership* (Cambridge, MA: Harvard University Press, 2006).

the extensive interpersonal, social, and institutional scaffolding necessary for the development and ongoing exercise of the complex cognitive, volitional, imaginative, and emotional skills involved in self-governance. As I argue in the following sections, the extent of this scaffolding also points to the causal interdependence between self-governance and the self-determination and self-authorization dimensions of autonomy.

The third premise is that social conditions restricting the exercise of self-determination are unjust. These include social conditions that deny members of social groups fundamental political or personal liberties or restrict the opportunities available in their social environments, that thwart the development and exercise of autonomy competences, or that sanction social relations of misrecognition, thereby excluding some individuals or social groups from the status markers of autonomy and compromising their sense of themselves as self-authorizing agents.[19] A socially just society therefore has an obligation to develop social, legal, and political institutions that foster the autonomy of all citizens, particularly those from historically oppressed or marginalized social groups.

It is worth clarifying two points about the understanding of justice that underlies this third premise. First, this account of justice assumes that injustice is not just a function of inequality in the distribution of resources; rather, it is also a function of inequalities in opportunities, and in social relations, institutions, norms, and practices. These inequalities constitute forms of domination and subordination that track social group identities and that operate through hierarchies of social standing, power, authority, and esteem.[20] These hierarchies operate at multiple levels within a society, for example within the family and in the context of intimate relationships; in the institutions of civil society, for example in workplaces, educational institutions, hospitals and clinics, religious institutions, clubs, sporting teams, the media (including the Internet); and through the institutions of the state, such as the police force, the army,

---

[19] This third premise is implicit rather than explicit in many accounts of relational autonomy. Theorists who have explicitly discussed the social justice implications of relational autonomy are Anderson and Honneth, "Autonomy, Vulnerability, Recognition and Justice"; Catriona Mackenzie, "Autonomy: Individualistic or Social and Relational?" in *Risk, Welfare and Work*, edited by G. Marston, J. Moss, and J. Quiggin (Melbourne: Melbourne University Press, 2010), 107–127; Mackenzie, "Conceptions of Autonomy and Conceptions of the Body in Bioethics," in *Feminist Bioethics: At the Center, on the Margins*, edited by Jackie Leach Scully, Laurel Baldwin-Ragaven, and Petya Fitzpatrick (Baltimore: Johns Hopkins University Press, 2010); Marina Oshana, "Personal Autonomy and Society," *Journal of Social Philosophy* 29:1 (1998): 81–102; Oshana, *Personal Autonomy in Society*.

[20] The way I have formulated this point is influenced by Elizabeth Anderson's analysis of relational inequality in Anderson, "What Is the Point of Equality?" *Ethics* 109:2 (1999): 287–337; Anderson, "Towards a Non-Ideal, Relational Methodology for Political Philosophy," *Hypatia* 24:4 (2009): 130–145; Anderson, "Justifying the Capabilities Approach to Justice," in *Measuring Justice: Primary Goods and Capabilities*, edited by Harry Brighouse and Ingrid Robeyns (Cambridge: Cambridge University Press, 2010), 81–100.

the judiciary, and the legislature. Relational theories aim to develop analyses of autonomy that are responsive to the effects of such inequalities on agents' abilities to lead self-determining, self-governing, and self-authorizing lives.

Second, I see relational autonomy as a form of non-ideal theorizing about autonomy, which is aligned with non-ideal approaches to justice.[21] It does not assume that persons are ideally, or even hypothetically, fully rational agents or that their motivational structures are transparent to themselves. Nor does it take as its starting point a model of an ideally just society and assess the extent to which current social relations fall short of this model. Rather, its starting point is the individual as situated in, shaped, and constrained by her sociorelational context in all its complexity; that is, its starting point is non-ideal agents in a non-ideal world, characterized by social oppression, injustice, and inequality. Given this starting point, the aim of relational autonomy theory is to theorize the kind of autonomy that is possible for non-ideal human agents; to diagnose how social domination, oppression, stigmatization, and injustice can thwart individual autonomy; and to hypothesize possible solutions, in the form of proposing how specific social relations, practices, and institutions might be reformed in such a way as to protect and foster individuals' autonomy.

In the following three sections of the paper I elaborate the three axes of autonomy in more detail and develop a specifically relational conception of each axis and its distinct conditions.

3. Self-determination: A Relational Conception

The notion of self-governance, as I have already suggested, is the core or kernel of what is taken to be a unitary concept of individual autonomy and has been the central focus of debates in bioethics and philosophical moral psychology. One problem with this focus, and with analyzing autonomy in terms of necessary and sufficient conditions for self-governance, is that it makes it difficult to explain how structural (social and political) constraints can undermine or impair individual autonomy and to identify the enabling structural conditions for autonomy.

In the recent literature, theorists of autonomy have attempted to try to explain the importance of these constraints and conditions in different ways. One approach is that of Oshana, who develops a global analysis of self-governance as having de facto power and authority to exercise effective practical control

---

[21] In his critique of ideal theory, Charles Mills describes relational autonomy as a form of non-ideal theorizing about autonomy. Mills, "Ideal Theory as Ideology," *Hypatia* 20:3 (2005): 165–184. For a related discussion of non-ideal theory, see Ingrid Robeyns, "Ideal Theory in Theory and Practice," *Social Theory and Practice* 34:3 (2008): 341–361. For a different kind of critique of ideal theory, see Amartya Sen, *The Idea of Justice* (Cambridge: Cambridge University Press, 2009).

over one's life.²² Oshana argues that certain structural sociorelational conditions must be in place for an agent to be genuinely self-governing in this sense. Agents who stand in relations of subordination, subservience, deference, or economic or psychological dependence, for example, cannot be self-governing because they do not enjoy practical control over their lives. This is the case even if the agents in question endorse (or are not alienated from) their subordinate, subservient, or dependent position and even if they seem to satisfy the competence and authenticity requirements for self-governance. Oshana uses an array of examples—voluntary slaves, prisoners, women subject to extreme forms of gender oppression, members of restrictive religious orders—to support the guiding intuition behind her account—namely, that a person cannot lead a self-governing life if her options are severely restricted and she is effectively under the control of others.

I am very sympathetic to Oshana's guiding intuition, but I also think that she is forced into an overly strong position because she attempts to articulate this intuition in terms of necessary and sufficient conditions for self-governance. Her view is overly strong because it is easy to devise counterexamples or to find real-life examples of persons who are subject to severe constraint but who are nevertheless clearly self-governing. Moreover, as John Christman and others have argued, the view seems to impugn the autonomy of persons who, despite being subject to crushing forms of oppression, nevertheless struggle to make plans, set goals, and have clear identity-defining commitments that are genuinely their own.²³ For this reason, I think a better way to articulate Oshana's guiding intuition is by distinguishing self-governance and self-determination as two distinct, but causally interdependent, axes or dimensions of autonomy.

I develop this argument in what follows. Before doing so, however, I want briefly to discuss Christman's way of accounting for the structural constraints on and enabling conditions for autonomy. I refer here to his autonomy-based conception of justice as democratic legitimacy, as developed in *The Politics of Persons*.²⁴ Christman's account of the competence and authenticity conditions for self-governance is premised on a thick, sociohistorical conception of the person, and he is highly sensitive to the way that social group memberships and historic and ongoing injustice shape and constrain individual practical identities. But, contra Oshana, he does not think that structural conditions should be included in the conditions for self-governance.²⁵ Instead, he includes these

---

²² Oshana, "Personal Autonomy and Society," Oshana, *Personal Autonomy in Society*.

²³ See, e.g., his critique of Oshana's position in Christman, *Politics of Persons*, 167–173.

²⁴ Christman, *Politics of Persons*.

²⁵ Christman's reason for excluding structural conditions from the conditions for self-governance is that he thinks including them involves unacceptable perfectionism. Christman criticizes Oshana's view on these grounds, claiming that her account requires "that autonomous agents must have certain value commitments and/or must be treated in certain normatively acceptable ways," even if the agents in question do not endorse those value commitments. Christman, *Politics of Persons*, 171. For a detailed response to Christman's perfectionism argument, see Oshana, *Personal Autonomy in*

conditions as part of the requirements of democratic justice. Thus, Christman claims that an adequate description of the background circumstances of justice must include reference to the fact that specific social groups have been subject to historical and ongoing forms of social domination, inequalities of power, and "systematic exposure to unique forms of violence."[26] Christman also argues that his account of democratic legitimacy would support, as a basic claim of justice, constitutionally guaranteed access to the basic capabilities and to the basic rights and liberties because of their role in enabling autonomy. I agree with Christman that claims of justice are distinct from the conditions for self-governance. However, autonomy as self-determination is typically a practical precondition for autonomy as self-governance, and securing the conditions for self-determination is a matter of basic justice.

I have defined *self-determination* as having the freedom and opportunity to make and enact choices of practical import to one's life, that is, choices about what to value, who to be, and what to do. I have also suggested that the self-determination axis identifies external, structural (social and political) conditions for individual autonomy, specifically *freedom* conditions and *opportunity* conditions.[27] Let me now say more about how I think these conditions should be understood.

Freedom conditions specify the political and personal liberties that are necessary for leading a self-determining life. Political liberties include the kinds of liberties that all liberal, democratic, and feminist theorists think should be protected, such as freedom of thought and expression, freedom of association, freedom of conscience and religious exercise, freedom to engage in political participation, and freedom from arbitrary arrest. Nevertheless, among theorists of autonomy and political philosophers, there will inevitably be substantive disputes about the extent of the liberties that are necessary for self-determination. A salient example in the context of international debates about immigration is whether freedom of international movement should be included among the basic liberties.[28] I won't take a stand on this issue here.

Society; Mackenzie, "Relational Autonomy, Normative Authority and Perfectionism," *Journal of Social Philosophy* 39 (2008): 512–33.

[26] Christman, *Politics of Persons*, 224.

[27] The distinction between freedom conditions and opportunity conditions overlaps to some extent with Isaiah Berlin's distinction between negative and positive liberty in Berlin, "Two Concepts of Liberty," in *Four Essays on Liberty* (Oxford: Oxford University Press, 1969). As I explain in the following text, theorists who understand the freedom conditions for autonomy in terms of negative liberty construe the freedom required for autonomy primarily as freedom from the undue interference of other persons or the state. Theorists who understand the freedom conditions for autonomy in terms of substantive freedom or opportunity think that although some degree of negative liberty is a necessary condition for autonomy it is insufficient. What matters for autonomy is the extent of a person's substantive opportunities to be and to do. Autonomy-enabling opportunities require a lot more than freedom from interference; they require substantial support by other persons and by state agencies.

[28] Joseph Carens and Phillip Cole are examples of theorists who argue that liberal political principles entail that freedom of international movement should be included among the basic liberties.

With respect to the personal liberties, again I think there is likely to be substantial agreement among liberal, democratic, and feminist theorists about the basic personal liberties that are preconditions for self-determination. These liberties include freedom of movement (if not international movement), freedom of sexual expression, and freedom from all forms of coercion, manipulation, exploitation, and violence, including sexual exploitation and assault. However, again, there will be substantive disputes about what counts as coercion or exploitation. In bioethics, the question of how exploitation should be understood is at the core of debates about the commodification of reproductive tissue, body parts, and blood products. Bioethicists of a more libertarian persuasion, for example, insist that commodification—that is, markets in tissue, body parts, and blood products—need not be exploitative and that if properly regulated such markets enable individual self-determination. Their critics argue that in the constrained and often oppressive social contexts in which such markets operate, commodification is inherently exploitative.[29] Similarly, while liberal, democratic, and feminist theorists support the principle of reproductive freedom, there are substantive disputes about how far this liberty should extend. Bioethicists of a more libertarian persuasion think it extends to a right to determine the sex or to enhance the characteristics of one's offspring. Their critics respond that the libertarian position equates autonomy with negative liberty and mere preference satisfaction, fails to account for the social influences on and social impacts of individual choice, and trivializes the responsibilities and obligations attendant upon the exercise of reproductive autonomy, in particular parental responsibilities for the well-being and future autonomy of children.[30]

Carens, "Aliens and Citizens: The Case for Open Borders," *Review of Politics* 49:2 (1987): 251–273; Cole, "Open Borders: An Ethical Defense," in *Debating the Ethics of Immigration: Is There a Right to Exclude?*, edited by Christopher Heath Wellman and Phillip Cole (New York: Oxford University Press, 2011). Liberal theorists who reject this claim and who seek to defend the rights of nation states to exclude immigrants include Michael Blake, "Immigration," in *Companion to Applied Ethics*, edited by R. Frey and Christopher Heath Wellman (Malden, MA: Blackwell, 2005), 224–237; David Miller, "Immigrants, Nations and Citizenship," *Journal of Political Philosophy* 16:4 (2008): 371–390. This is of course a complex debate that I cannot enter into here, and I refer to it purely for illustrative purposes.

[29] Theorists who appeal to the right to self-determination to defend markets in body parts, tissues, and eggs, include, e.g., J. Radcliffe-Richards, "Selling Organs, Gametes and Surrogacy Services," in *The Blackwell Guide to Medical Ethics*, edited by R. Rhodes, L. Francis, and A. Silvers (Malden, MA: Wiley-Blackwell, 2007), 254–268; David Resnik, "Regulating the Market for Human Eggs," *Bioethics* 15:1 (2001): 1–25; James Stacey Taylor, "Autonomy, Constraining Options, and Organ Sales," *Journal of Applied Philosophy* 19:3 (2002): 273–285. For critiques, see, e.g., Margaret Jane Radin, *Contested Commodities: The Trouble with the Trade in Sex, Children, Body Parts and Other Things* (Cambridge, MA: Harvard University Press, 1996); N. Scheper-Hughes, "Illegal Organ Trade: Global Justice and the Traffic in Human Organs," in *Living Donor Organ Transplants*, edited by Rainer Gruessner and Enrico Benedetti (New York: McGraw-Hill, 2007), 106–121; Tamara Zutlevics, "Markets and the Needy: Organ Sales or Aid?" *Journal of Applied Philosophy* 18:3 (2001): 297–302.

[30] The most well-known advocates of the libertarian position on genetic enhancement are Nicholas Agar, "Designing Babies: Morally Permissible Ways to Modify the Human Genome," *Bioethics* 9:1 (1995): 1–15; John Harris, *Clones, Genes and Immortality* (Oxford: Oxford University Press, 1998);

With respect to both these issues, I disagree with the libertarian position. Although I cannot engage in a detailed discussion of these specific normative issues here, hopefully the basis for my stance will become clearer in what follows. What these debates point to is that although the freedom and opportunity conditions for self-determination overlap and often converge they can also be in tension. Theorists who understand freedom in terms of negative liberty are likely to give more weight to freedom conditions than to opportunity conditions and hence to interpret the freedom conditions quite expansively. Theorists who emphasize the importance of substantive equality of opportunity think that what is important is not the promotion of freedom per se, since not all kinds of freedom are either important or desirable, but those freedoms that enable equality of opportunity.[31] According to this view, which freedom conditions count as important will be determined by the opportunity conditions for self-determination. On my interpretation, theories of relational autonomy prioritize opportunity conditions and hence fall into this latter category of theory.

Opportunity conditions specify the personal, social, and political opportunities that are preconditions for individual self-determination. Among theorists of autonomy, Raz is the most prominent exponent of the view that self-determination, as I have defined it, requires access to an adequate array of significant opportunities, or what he refers to as options.[32] Although access to options requires certain freedoms, in the form of basic rights and liberties, Raz rejects the libertarian conception of freedom as minimally constrained freedom of choice, arguing that this conception conflates self-determination with license.[33] Raz develops a nuanced analysis of options as those complex and multidimensional activities, practices, and relationships that make our lives meaningful, such as pursuing a career in a particular profession, being a parent, being a member of a religious community, or participating in sport, cultural activities, or politics. Options, in other words, are ways of life, "dense webs of complex actions and interactions," which depend on social practices, with their implicit rules, conventions, and shared meanings. Specific options are available only to those who have developed the relevant skills, as "embodied in social practices and transmitted by habituation."[34] A culture,

---

Julian Savulescu, "Procreative Beneficence: Why We Should Select the Best Children," *Bioethics* 15:5–6 (2001): 413–426.

I develop critiques of the libertarian position with respect to debates in bioethics in Mackenzie, "Autonomy: Individualistic or Social and Relational?"; "Conceptions of Autonomy and Conceptions of the Body in Bioethics"; "Autonomy," in Arris et al., *Routledge Companion to Bioethics*.

[31] This is clearly Nussbaum's position as well, and it is on these grounds that she criticizes Sen's interpretation of capabilities theory as concerned with promoting freedom. See, e.g., Nussbaum, *Creating Capabilities*, 69–76.

[32] Raz, *Morality of Freedom*.

[33] Raz, "Multiculturalism: A Liberal Perspective" in Raz, *Ethics in the Public Domain: Essays in the Morality of Law and Politics* (Oxford: Clarendon Press, 1994) 17–191.

[34] Raz, 'Multiculturalism, 177.

in Raz's view, is a complex network of interlocking social practices, and it is only by being socialized in a culture that the range of options that constitute that culture are made available to a person. Thus, "by and large one's cultural membership determines the horizon of one's opportunities."[35] Raz's analysis of options highlights the importance of the social environment for self-determination. As he puts it, autonomy depends "not on the availability of one option of freedom of choice. It depends on the general character of one's environment and culture."[36] An autonomy-supporting culture, in his view, is one that makes available to its citizens an adequate range of significant options, by providing the institutional infrastructure—legal, educational, economic, political—that supports a wide array of significant options and by developing social policy measures aimed at making these options genuinely accessible to members of marginalized, disadvantaged, or historically oppressed social groups.

In developing her sociorelational account of autonomy, Oshana endorses Raz's view of the importance of significant options for autonomy, and this is why I think her concern with the structural conditions for autonomy is best characterized as a concern with the self-determination dimension of autonomy.[37] While I am broadly sympathetic to Raz's view, I have come to think that capabilities theory provides a better vocabulary for articulating the opportunity conditions for self-determination, both because it helps to make explicit the link between basic justice and self-determination and because I think there are fruitful connections, still to be explored, between relational autonomy theory and feminist interpretations of capabilities theory, such as those of Elizabeth Anderson, Martha Nussbaum, and Ingrid Robeyns.[38] I cannot explore these connections in any detail here, but I do want to provide a few reasons as to why I think capabilities theory provides a useful vocabulary for articulating the opportunity conditions for self-determination.

Capabilities theory provides a fine-grained comparative metric of equality, which disaggregates distinct dimensions of well-being and human development. The metric aims to focus attention on what a person is actually able to be and do in her life (her achieved functionings) and on the

---

[35] Raz, 'Multiculturalism,' 177.

[36] Raz, *Morality of Freedom*, 391.

[37] Oshana, *Personal Autonomy in Society*, 84–86.

[38] Elizabeth Anderson, "What Is the Point of Equality?"; Anderson, "Justifying the Capabilities Approach to Justice"; Martha Nussbaum, *Women and Human Development: The Capabilities Approach* (Cambridge: Cambridge University Press, 2000); Nussbaum, *Frontiers of Justice*; Nussbaum, *Creating Capabilities*; Ingrid Robeyns, "Sen's Capability Approach and Gender Inequality: Selecting Relevant Capabilities," *Feminist Economics* 9:2–3 (2003): 71–84; Robeyns, "Gender and the Metric of Justice," in Brighouse and Robeyns, *Measuring Justice*, 215–235.

extent of her substantive opportunities (capabilities) to achieve valuable functionings. It also aims to focus attention on the factors that affect an individual's ability to convert the resources available to her into valuable functionings.[39] Such factors include both individual differences in natural endowments, personal characteristics, and values and the external circumstances of people's lives, such as their natural, social, cultural, and political environments. Because it attends to the particularities of individual circumstance and context, capabilities theory also enables a fine-grained analysis of the different sources of social injustice, inequality, and disadvantage within a society and their impact on people's opportunities and capacities to lead self-determining lives.

There is some disagreement among capability theorists as to how valuable capabilities should be identified. Sen has resisted the development of a list of valuable capabilities, arguing that this should be settled via mechanisms of social choice, although it is evident from his writings that he thinks education, political participation, health, and gender equality are central capabilities.[40] Nussbaum, as is well known, has developed a universal list of ten central human capabilities.[41] Other feminist capability theorists argue that such lists should be context specific and should be developed and refined through processes of democratic deliberation. For example, Elizabeth Anderson proposes a set of functionings necessary for equality of democratic citizenship, which includes "adequate safety, health and nutrition, education, mobility and communication, the ability to interact with others without stigma, and to participate in the system of cooperation."[42] Ingrid Robeyns suggests a more extensive list of fourteen capabilities necessary for gender equality in Western societies, which includes life and physical health, mental well-being, bodily integrity and safety, social relations, political empowerment, education and knowledge, mobility, domestic and paid work, time-autonomy, respect, and religion.[43] I do not propose to discuss the details of these lists here or to weigh into the debate about the appropriate method for arriving at any such list, although I do favor a more context-specific, deliberative approach. However, I would argue that lists of capabilities such as those of Anderson and Robeyns help to identify the kinds of opportunity conditions required for self-determination. Furthermore, the idea that a just society is one that ensures access, above a certain minimum threshold, to the valuable capabilities, however they are defined, shows

---

[39] See Amartya Sen, *Inequality Reexamined* (Cambridge: Cambridge University Press, 1992) for a detailed analysis of the notions of capability and functioning.
[40] See the chapter on social choice in Sen, *Idea of Justice*.
[41] For a recent version of this list, see Martha Nussbaum, *Creating Capabilities*.
[42] Anderson, "Justifying the Capabilities Approach to Justice," 83.
[43] Robeyns, "Sen's Capability Approach."

why ensuring the opportunity conditions for self-determination is a matter of social justice.

A further reason for thinking that capabilities theory provides a useful vocabulary for articulating the opportunity conditions for self-determination is that it marries a focus on the importance of individual self-determination with attention to the social and political constraining and enabling conditions of self-determination. Thus, on the one hand, the theory recognizes that different people will value different capabilities, and hence argues that a just society ought to ensure equality of access to a wide range of opportunities but leave it to individuals to choose which particular capabilities to realize beyond the threshold. On the other hand, capability theorists, like theorists of relational autonomy, are sensitive to the role of the social environment and social, political, legal and economic institutions in enabling or constraining individual self-determination. Of particular concern to both theories is the phenomenon of adaptive preference formation—the phenomenon whereby persons who are subject to social domination, oppression, or deprivation adapt their preferences (or goals) to their circumstances, eliminating or failing to form preferences (or goals) that cannot be satisfied, and even failing to conceive how their preferences might differ in different circumstances.[44] In social situations characterized by oppression or deprivation, the problem then is not just that restricted opportunities constrain self-determination but also that the internalization of these constraints can shape individuals' sense of who they are and what they can be and do. Here, the causal interdependence between the opportunity conditions for self-determination, the competence and authenticity conditions for self-governance, and the conditions for self-authorization become evident.

My aim in this section has been to provide a brief characterization of autonomy as self-determination and its two conditions: freedom and opportunity. I have argued that relational autonomy theorists prioritize opportunity conditions, in the sense that the freedoms that count as important are those that promote substantive opportunity. I have also suggested that capabilities theory provides a vocabulary for articulating the kinds of opportunity conditions for self-determination that is particularly amenable to the concerns of relational autonomy theorists.

---

[44] For the original formulation of the problem of adaptive preferences, see Jon Elster, *Sour Grapes: Studies in the Subversion of Rationality* (Cambridge: Cambridge University Press, 1983). For its relevance in motivating capabilities theory, see Sen, *Inequality Reexamined*; Nussbaum, *Women and Human Development*; Nussbaum, "Adaptive Preferences and Women's Options," *Economics and Philosophy* 17 (2001): 67–88. For a recent discussion of its relevance for gender oppression, see Serene Khader, *Adaptive Preferences and Women's Empowerment* (New York: Oxford University Press, 2011). For discussion of its relevance to relational autonomy theory, see Natalie Stoljar's contribution to this volume.

4. Self-governance: A Relational Conception

Self-governance, as I have defined it, involves having the skills and capacities necessary to make choices and enact decisions that express or cohere with one's reflectively constituted diachronic practical identity. The self-governance dimension of autonomy picks out autonomy conditions (competence and authenticity) that are in some sense internal to the person, whereas the self-determination axis identifies external, structural conditions. However, from a relational perspective, the distinction between internal and external conditions is complicated. If persons are socially constituted, then external conditions, including our social relations with others, shape the process of practical identity formation—the *self* of self-governance—and the development of the skills and competences required for *governing* the self. On the one hand, this is not necessarily problematic from a relational perspective—it points to the facts of developmental and ongoing dependency and to the extensive interpersonal, social, and institutional scaffolding necessary for self-governance. On the other hand, in contexts of social oppression, as is shown by the phenomenon of adaptive preference formation, severely limited opportunity conditions can deform the process of practical identity formation and impair the development and exercise of autonomy competence.

Authenticity conditions specify what it means to be self-governing with respect to one's motivational structure—that is, what it means for a choice, value, commitment, or reason to be one's own. Relational autonomy theorists are critical of conceptions of self-governance, such as hierarchical or endorsement conceptions, which analyze authenticity in terms of structural features of an agent's will at the time of choice or action. The argument, in brief, is that such synchronic accounts and criteria for authenticity that appeal to relations of internal coherence within the agent's will (e.g., identification, endorsement) fail to account for the historical processes of practical identity formation.[45] In particular, they fail to account for the internalized effects of psychological oppression, that is, the way oppression shapes agents' practical identities and motivational structures, for example their preferences, values, and cares.[46] Furthermore, criteria for coherence, such as identification, wholeheartedness, or endorsement, seem to rule out any kind of ambivalence or internal

---

[45] Examples of synchronic hierarchical theories include Dworkin, *Theory and Practice of Autonomy*; Frankfurt, *Importance of What We Care About*. Endorsement theories include Gary Watson, "Free Agency," *Journal of Philosophy* 72 (1975): 205–220; Korsgaard, *Sources of Normativity*.

[46] For the first critique along these lines, see Marilyn Friedman, "Autonomy and the Split-Level Self," *Southern Journal of Philosophy* 24:1 (1986): 19–35. For a more detailed overview, see Mackenzie and Stoljar, "Introduction: Autonomy Refigured." Christman is the best-known proponent of the historical approach, first articulated in Christman, "Autonomy and Personal History," *Canadian Journal of Philosophy* 21 (1991): 1–24 and developed in its most sophisticated form in Christman, *Politics of Persons*.

psychic conflict or fragmentation as inconsistent with self-governance.[47] But this is both normatively problematic and unrealistic, since ambivalence and some degree of inner psychic conflict or fragmentation seem to be inescapable aspects of practical identity formation.

On the basis of these criticisms, some relational theorists have rejected any kind of authenticity condition for autonomy, arguing that the concept of autonomy should be uncoupled from notions of practical or self-identity and understood in terms of other conditions, such as sociorelational structural conditions, normative (or some other) competence conditions, or accountability and answerability.[48] As I said at the outset, if we think of autonomy as the unitary concept of self-governance, requiring a single set of necessary and sufficient conditions, then these other conditions all need to be understood as additional or competitor conditions for self-governance. My proposal is to think of these conditions as identifying different dimensions or axes of the multidimensional concept of autonomy. In my view, the concept of self-governance cannot be uncoupled from the *self* who is supposed to govern itself, and I think the notion of practical identity provides a plausible conception of the self. For this reason, I don't think the authenticity condition should be rejected. Rather, I favor adopting a more nuanced analysis of authenticity, such as that proposed by John Christman, which is responsive to the criticisms that relational theorists have raised against standard accounts of authenticity. Christman understands authenticity as "non-alienation upon (historically sensitive, adequate) self-reflection, given one's diachronic practical identity and one's position in the world" or as reflective self-acceptance.[49]

Competence conditions specify the range of competences or skills a person must possess, to some degree at least, to be self-governing. These include cognitive skills, ranging from minimally specified capacities to understand and process information, to more complex capacities for critical reflection and reasons responsiveness as well as volitional skills, such as self-control, and

---

[47] For critiques along these lines, see Benson, "Taking Ownership"; Oshana, "Autonomy and Self-Identity," in Christman and Anderson, *Autonomy and the Challenges to Liberalism*, 77–97.

[48] For sociorelational structural conditions see Oshana, *Personal Autonomy in Society*. For normative (or some other) competence conditions see Benson, "Autonomy and Oppressive Socialization." For accountability and answerability see Benson, "Feminist Intuitions and the Normative Substance of Autonomy"; Benson, "Taking Ownership: Authority and Voice in Autonomous Agency"; Westlund, "Rethinking Relational Autonomy."

[49] Christman, *Politics of Persons*, 155. Much more needs to be said of course to flesh out Christman's analysis of authenticity. For detailed discussion see Christman, *Politics of Persons*, 149–163, and his contribution to this volume. It is important to stress that Christman's reflection condition is hypothetical; an agent is not required to reflect on every aspect of her practical identity, that is, every value, commitment, preference, trait, and characteristic to be authentic with respect to that aspect of her motivational structure. Rather, the requirement is just that were she to so reflect she would not feel alienated from it. Note that in his contribution to this volume Christman weakens the requirement of reflection further, now preferring to talk of *reflexive* rather than *reflective* self-acceptance.

decisiveness. These skills have been extensively discussed in the philosophical literature, along with the ways self-governance can be compromised by a range of mundane volitional or cognitive failings—such as weakness of will, self-deception, failures of self-control, and prudential irrationality—as well as by less common but more severe, volitional, and cognitive threats, such as compulsions, phobias and neuroses, addictions, and delusions and other forms of psychosis.

Relational autonomy theorists concur that such skills are certainly important for self-governance. However, relational approaches extend the philosophical understanding of autonomy competence by developing a more complex and capacious analysis of the skills involved in self-governance. Relational theorists argue that philosophers have overly rationalized the competences required for critical reflection while neglecting an array of other skills, including emotional skills, such as emotional responsiveness, and being able to interpret one's own and others' emotions; imaginative skills, which are necessary for envisaging alternative possible courses of action, or "imagining oneself otherwise" and engaging in self-transformative activities; and social or dialogical skills required for self-understanding or self-knowledge.[50] On a relational view, although self-governance does require a degree of self-knowledge, self-knowledge is not necessarily developed primarily through introspection. This is not only because we are not motivationally self-transparent but also because self-knowledge, indeed the self itself on this view, is constituted through ongoing social or dialogical interaction with others. This focus on the dialogical dimensions of self-governance echoes Charles Taylor's dialogical conception of the self.[51] This kind of dialogical approach does recognize, of course, that some kinds of social interaction can thwart self-understanding and deform the formation of a self-governing practical identity. But the corrective is not to think that we can be self-governing only if we are freed from social influence. It is rather to promote social relationships that foster self-governance.

It is worth noting here that the autonomy skills identified by relational theorists and the relational emphasis on the constitutive role of social interaction overlap with four of the items on Nussbaum's list of capabilities:[52]

1. Senses, imagination and thought, which she characterizes as "being able to use the senses, to think, imagine and reason—and to do these things in a 'truly human' way, a way cultivated by an adequate education."

---

[50] For discussion of the importance of these skills for autonomy, see especially Meyers, *Self, Society and Personal Choice*; Mackenzie, "Imagining Oneself Otherwise," in Mackenzie and Stoljar, *Relational Autonomy*, 124–150; Mackenzie, "Critical Reflection, Self-Knowledge, and the Emotions," *Philosophical Explorations* 5:2 (2002): 186–206.
[51] Charles Taylor, *Sources of the Self* (Cambridge: Cambridge University Press, 1989).
[52] Nussbaum, *Creating Capabilities*, 33–34.

2. Emotions, which she characterizes as "being able to have attachments to people and things outside ourselves.... Not having one's emotional development blighted by fear and anxiety."
3. Practical reason, which she characterizes as "being able to form a conception of the good and to engage in critical reflection about the planning of one's life."
4. Affiliation, which involves two components: (a) "Being able to live with and towards others, to show concern for other human beings, to engage in various forms of social interaction; to be able to imagine the situation of another"; and (b) "Having the social bases of self-respect and non-humiliation; being able to be treated as a dignified being whose worth is equal to that of others."

Although I would include affiliation (b) under the axis of self-authorization, the overlap between these four items on Nussbaum's list and the autonomy skills identified by relational theorists suggests that these items are centrally focused on the capabilities required for self-governance. Nussbaum also claims that practical reason and affiliation play an architectonic role in organizing and pervading the other capabilities.

This overlap raises a puzzle about why Nussbaum insists that her capabilities approach does not assume the value of autonomy and why she is at pains to distinguish the capability of practical reason from autonomy. She gives two reasons for this position.[53] First, although she regards the capability of practical reason as central to a dignified human life and thinks that this capability raises claims of justice against the state to provide the kind of educational opportunities that enable the development of this capability, she argues that individuals who have acquired the capability may choose not to exercise it. Autonomy, on the other hand, is an exercise concept.[54] Nussbaum does concede that it is difficult to develop the capability for practical reason without exercising it, but she seems to think that this is possible. I think this is implausible and that it makes more sense to say that individuals may exercise the capacity for practical reason, or self-governance, to greater or lesser degrees, sometimes by choice, but often because their social environment has not supported the development of the relevant competences.

---

[53] Nussbaum provides the most extensive discussion of these reasons in Nussbaum, "Political Liberalism and Respect: A Response to Linda Barclay," *SATS: Nordic Journal of Philosophy* 4:2 (2003): 25–44.

[54] Nussbaum also seems to think that those who support the value of autonomy, such as Raz, think that a life in which a person does not exercise this capacity is less valuable and less worthy of respect. I don't think that Raz holds a derogatory view of persons whose lives are not autonomous. His view is rather that individual autonomy is crucial for living a decent human life in contemporary democratic societies and that therefore the state has an obligation to support its development and exercise by ensuring that individuals have an adequate range of significant opportunities.

Nussbaum's second reason, which I think underpins the first, concerns the relationship between autonomy and epistemic and normative authority. I take up this issue in the following section.

5. Self-authorization: A Relational Conception

Self-authorization, as I have defined it, involves regarding oneself as having the *normative authority* to be self-determining and self-governing. In other words, it involves regarding oneself as authorized to exercise practical control over one's life and to determine one's own values and identity-defining commitments. In the recent literature on social and relational autonomy, a number of theorists (myself included) have characterized what I am here calling self-authorization as a necessary condition for self-governance.[55] I now think this is a mistake and that self-authorization is a separate axis or dimension of autonomy, which involves three conditions: that the person regards herself as the kind of agent who can be held accountable and answerable to others for her reasons—call this the *accountability* condition; that the person stands in certain self-affective relations to herself, in particular relations of self-respect, self-trust, and self-esteem—call this the *self-evaluative attitudes* condition; and that such attitudes in turn presuppose that the person is regarded by others as having the social standing of an autonomous agent—call this the *social recognition* condition.

In explaining the accountability condition it is helpful to contrast it with one way in which the notion of self-authorization might be interpreted. Self-authorization is sometimes understood as requiring substantive epistemic and normative independence from authority. That is, the self-authorizing person does not look to any external authority—whether another person or God—in determining what to believe, value, or commit herself to. I think Nussbaum equates autonomy with such a conception of self-authorization, as does Oshana. This is the second reason why Nussbaum insists that the capability of practical reason is different from autonomy: because she thinks a commitment to the value of autonomy is inconsistent with religious commitment. So she says: "Autonomy thus means something positive, that one gives oneself laws and engages in critical reflection; but it also means something negative, that one denies that God is a necessary part of the justification of moral claims."[56] In my view, this is a mistaken interpretation of self-authorization,

---

[55] See, e.g., Benson, "Feminist Intuitions and the Normative Substance of Autonomy"; Benson, "Taking Ownership"; Mackenzie, "Relational Autonomy, Normative Authority and Perfectionism"; Westlund, "Rethinking Relational Autonomy."

[56] Nussbaum, "Political Liberalism and Respect," 41.

and in fact Nussbaum's capability of affiliation is centrally concerned with self-authorization, as I characterize it.

Self-authorization involves, first, regarding oneself as responsible to oneself and as answerable and accountable to others, for one's beliefs, values, commitments, and reasons. Taylor's notion of autonomy as involving responsibility for self articulates this kind of accountability condition, as does Stephen Darwall's second-person standpoint.[57] In the recent literature on autonomy, Benson and Westlund are its most eloquent exponents.[58] The basic idea is that as social agents we are subject to others' demands that we account for our decisions, explain the reasons for them, and take responsibility for those decisions. To be self-authorizing, a person must not only be capable of understanding and responding to this social demand but must also regard herself as a valid source of self-authorizing claims.

It is important to clarify that being accountable does not mean that we must be accountable to certain specific others or that others must agree with our beliefs, values, commitments, reasons, or decisions. Nor does it mean that we must actually be held to account for each and every belief, value, and so on. What it requires is what Westlund refers to as a disposition to be answerable: that we are prepared to take responsibility as agents, for our beliefs, values, and commitments. This means being responsive to others' requests for explanation, being prepared to provide reasons for our beliefs and values, and being willing to defend or revise them in light of others' critical questioning. It also requires, in turn, that we regard ourselves as authorized to hold others accountable in the same way. I want to stress that the accountability condition is fundamentally social and dialogical, not only because its structure is dyadic or second-personal but also because our reasons, values and commitments, indeed our sense of our selves, emerge only through this kind of dialogical interaction. I would also suggest, contra Nussbaum, that accountability, thus understood, is not inconsistent per se with religious commitment. But it is inconsistent with dogmatic forms of religious commitment, or any other form of dogmatism, for that matter, which involve appeals to authority that bypass a person's reflective agency.

Regarding oneself as accountable involves having a sense of one's epistemic and normative authority with regard to one's life and one's practical commitments. This in turn seems to require the agent to have certain self-evaluative attitudes, in particular attitudes of appropriate self-respect, self-trust, and

---

[57] See Taylor's distinction between strong and weak evaluation in "What Is Human Agency?" in Taylor, *Human Agency and Language: Philosophical Papers 1* (Cambridge: Cambridge University Press, 1985), 15–44; Taylor, *Sources of the Self*. For Darwall's account of the second-person standpoint, see Darwall, *The Second-Person Standpoint: Morality, Respect and Accountability* (Cambridge, MA: Harvard University Press, 2006).

[58] Benson, "Taking Ownership"; Westlund, "Rethinking Relational Autonomy."

self-esteem. This second condition for self-authorization has been articulated in different ways in the literature on social and relational autonomy.[59] I mention here Joel Anderson and Axel Honneth's version of the claim, which brings out the connections between self-authorization and self-governance.[60] Anderson and Honneth characterize *self-respect* as "an affectively laden self-conception that underwrites a view of oneself as the legitimate source of reasons for acting."[61] To regard oneself with appropriate self-respect is to regard oneself as the moral equal of others, as having equal standing to have one's views and claims taken seriously. *Self-trust* or "basic self-confidence" is the capacity to trust one's own convictions, emotional responses, and judgments. Anderson and Honneth argue that this attitude underpins the kind of reflexive self-interpretation that is central to self-governance. Because our practical identities are complex and dynamic, deliberating about what to do involves self-interpretation—for example, working out which desires should constitute reasons for us, which commitments are most important, which emotional responses we should attend to, and how to reconcile conflicts arising from different social roles. The attitude of *self-esteem* or self-worth is a fundamentally evaluative stance toward oneself; it involves thinking of one's life, one's commitments, and one's attitudes as meaningful, worthwhile, and valuable.

It is always possible to find or think up examples of heroic persons who hold appropriate self-evaluating attitudes even in situations where they are despised and humiliated by others. However, psychologically these self-evaluative attitudes are typically dependent on intersubjective social relations, that is, on whether a person is regarded as a respect-worthy, autonomous agent by others. These attitudes are also constituted within normative structures and practices of *social recognition*.[62] Hence, they are vulnerable to others' failures, or refusals, to grant the person appropriate recognition in a range of different spheres: for example, in her interpersonal relations; at work and in the institutions of civil society; and as a citizen. Such failures of recognition are quite typical in social relations involving domination or inequalities of power, authority, or social and economic status, especially when these are inflected by gender, race, ethnicity, or disability. Relational autonomy theorists claim that the internalization of non- or misrecognition can corrode an agent's sense of self-regard,

---

[59] For different variants, see, e.g., Trudy Govier, "Self-Trust, Autonomy, and Self-Esteem," *Hypatia* 8 (2003): 99–120; Paul Benson, "Free Agency and Self-Worth," *Journal of Philosophy* 91 (1994): 650–668; Carolyn McLeod, *Self-Trust and Reproductive Autonomy*; Mackenzie, "Relational Autonomy, Normative Authority and Perfectionism."

[60] Anderson and Honneth, "Autonomy, Vulnerability, Recognition and Justice."

[61] Anderson and Honneth, "Autonomy, Vulnerability, Recognition and Justice," 132.

[62] See Anderson, "Vulnerability and Autonomy Intertwined" for a detailed analysis of the interrelation between the psychological and normative dynamics of social recognition with respect to the self-evaluative attitudes.

thereby undermining her sense of herself as self-authorizing. For example, unless she is incredibly resilient, an employee who is subject to constant sexist and racist abuse by her boss and co-workers may find it very difficult to maintain an appropriate sense of self-regard.[63]

It might be thought that the self-authorization axis of autonomy is unduly demanding and likely to be met by relatively few people. For example, the accountability condition for self-authorization may seem to assume an unrealistically high level of articulacy and open-mindedness, while the self-evaluative attitudes condition may seem to assume an unrealistically high level of confidence in oneself. Who among us, for example, does not doubt the worth or meaningfulness of our commitments? And if we did not would that make us more autonomous or just arrogant and insufferable? In response, it is important to emphasize that this condition requires that a person have "appropriate" self-evaluative attitudes.[64] I would also reiterate that each of these conditions should be understood as a matter of degree rather than an all-or-nothing affair. Different persons are likely to meet these different conditions to different degrees. Indeed any one individual is likely to meet them to different degrees in different contexts and domains.

It is also important to counter here a common, but I think misguided, charge against supposedly overdemanding conceptions of autonomy, namely, that they can be used to sanction objectionable forms of paternalistic interference with the choices of persons who may already be socially marginalized: those with limited capacities for self-governance or who do not regard themselves and are not recognized by others as self-authorizing agents.[65] In response I would argue that if the social relations, institutions, norms, and practices to which a person is subject fail to recognize her social standing as a self-authorizing agent and that if this kind of misrecognition impairs her capacities for self-governance it does not follow at all that paternalistic interference is warranted. Rather, first, it provides grounds for criticizing those social structures as unjust and reforming them, and second, it provides reasons for providing targeted social support and resources to scaffold the person's capacities for self-governance.[66]

---

[63] The impact of work on personal autonomy has been curiously neglected in the literature. This neglect is a serious omission, given the importance of work for our lives. For valuable analyses of work and autonomy, see Beate Roessler, "Meaningful Work: Arguments from Autonomy," *Journal of Political Philosophy* 20:1 (2012): 71–93; Andrea Veltman's contribution to this volume.

[64] The question of how to distinguish appropriate from misplaced self-evaluative attitudes raises complex psychological and normative issues that do need to be addressed by theorists who emphasize the importance of these attitudes for autonomy. However, it is beyond the scope of my discussion in this chapter to address this question.

[65] For criticisms along these lines, see, e.g., John Christman, "Relational Autonomy, Liberal Individualism, and the Social Constitution of Selves," *Philosophical Studies* 117 (2004): 143–164; Jules Holroyd, "Relational Autonomy and Paternalistic Interventions," *Res Publica* 15:4 (2009): 321–336.

[66] For a more detailed argument for this claim, see Mackenzie, "Importance of Relational Autonomy and Capabilities for an Ethics of Vulnerability."

The conditions for self-authorization, then, although they may be met to varying degrees, are underpinned by a fundamentally normative conception of persons as moral equals who ought to be treated as respect-worthy, or dignified beings, and as self-authorizing sources of valid claims. This notion of persons as respect-worthy or dignified beings is categorical; it is neither context specific nor a matter of degree.[67]

Conclusion

I have argued that autonomy should be understood as a multidimensional concept, with three distinct but causally interdependent axes—self-determination, self-governance, and self-authorization—each with its distinct conditions, which may be realized to different degrees. There are two obvious objections to this multidimensional analysis. One objection might be to insist that there must be a unitary idea underlying these different dimensions of autonomy. The other objection might be to suggest that if my analysis is correct, then it is not clear why we should hold onto the concept of autonomy at all. Why not just stop talking about "autonomy" and start talking instead about self-determination, self-governance, and self-authorization?

In response to the first objection, my reply is that if our goal is to understand the role played by the concept of autonomy in our social and normative practices, then insisting on the necessity of an underlying unitary idea is mistaken. Although philosophers are attracted to tidy conceptual boundaries, and for that reason are also attracted to the project of determining the necessary and sufficient conditions for the correct application of our concepts, many social concepts, such as the concept of autonomy, are not readily amenable to such analyses.

In response to the second objection, my reply is that although I have argued that the concept of autonomy is multidimensional rather than unitary, it would be a mistake to stop talking about autonomy and just talk instead about self-determination, self-governance, and self-authorization. This is because the concept of autonomy plays an important role in diverse social and normative practices. The advantage of the multidimensional analysis is that it enables us to tease apart the different dimensions of the concept while still holding onto the term *autonomy*.

---

[67] This categorical notion of respect is what Stephen Darwall refers to as recognition respect, as distinct from appraisal respect, which involves positive evaluation of a person's character or accomplishments and attributes and which is context dependent, earned, and a matter of degree. Darwall, "Two Kinds of Respect," *Ethics* 88 (1977): 36–49. It should be noted that having appropriate self-evaluative attitudes seems to be dependent on both recognition and appraisal respect.

There are several further advantages of the multidimensional analysis. First, distinguishing self-determination from self-governance and self-authorization enables us to give due weight to the social and political preconditions for autonomy and to underscore that securing these conditions is a matter of social justice. But it also accounts for our important intuitions about autonomy—namely, that a person may be self-governing and self-authorizing to some degree even in situations of crushing oppression where these preconditions are severely curtailed, and conversely that a person may enjoy all the freedoms and opportunities necessary for self-determination but nevertheless fail to be self-governing or have a sense of herself as a self-authorizing agent. I think many of the examples and counterexamples in the literature on relational autonomy appeal to these conflicting intuitions and that the unitary concept of self-governance is inadequate to account for them. Rather than devoting our energies to thinking up yet more examples and counterexamples, theorists of autonomy should instead focus our attention on analyzing in more detail and depth the different dimensions of autonomy and the interrelations between them.

Second, in doing so, we may find that in different contexts certain dimensions of autonomy, and the conditions that fall under them, may be more salient than others. Further, since the conditions for autonomy may be satisfied to differing degrees, it may be important to set different thresholds for meeting these conditions in different contexts. For example, with respect to democratic citizenship, it might be important to set high thresholds for self-determination, in the form of requiring extensive opportunities and the liberties that enable them, but quite low thresholds for an agent to count as self-governing. It might also be important to place a great deal of emphasis, in interpersonal relations, in civil society, and at the level of the state, on ameliorating the social conditions that undermine self-authorization. In the context of medical decision making it may be the case that the most salient dimensions of autonomy are self-governance and self-authorization. Thus, health professionals ought to focus on whether patients meet the competence and authenticity conditions for self-governance to a sufficiently high degree and whether they seem capable of meeting the accountability condition. In cases where individuals do not meet the required threshold for one or other of these conditions, then extensive social scaffolding in the form of support and resources provided by carers may be required to enable autonomous decision making, except in cases where it is more appropriate for a legally appointed guardian or family members to make the decision on the patient's behalf.

Third, even if it is the case that the salience of the different dimensions and conditions varies with context, the importance of the multidimensional analysis is that it also draws attention to the interrelations among these distinct dimensions and conditions. For example, even if the self-governance and self-authorization dimensions of autonomy are most relevant to making specific decisions in medical contexts, it is nevertheless crucial, both in medical ethics and in bioethics more generally, to be attentive to the self-determination dimension of autonomy. In particular, we need to be attentive to the ways that constrained opportunities and restricted liberties may increase people's vulnerability, making them more open to exploitation, coercion, and manipulation and less able to regard themselves as self-authorizing agents.

Acknowledgments

I would like to thank the editors, Mark Piper and Andrea Veltman, for extremely helpful comments on an earlier version of this chapter. Thanks also to Natalie Stoljar for extensive and ongoing discussions about autonomy. Earlier versions of the chapter were presented at the conference on Thick (Concepts of) Autonomy, Institute for Advanced Study in Bioethics, University of Muenster, and to a seminar at the University of Amsterdam. Thanks to audiences on both occasions for helpful comments.

{ 3 }

Relational Autonomy and Independence
Marilyn Friedman

As Catriona Mackenzie and Natalie Stoljar write in their introduction to *Relational Autonomy*, a relational approach to autonomy involves emphasizing the social nature of the self and the social relations and conditions that are necessary for the realization of autonomy.[1] Defenders of a relational account might think their approach rules out any individualistic claims about autonomy. That would be a mistake. In this chapter, I explore how conceptions of autonomy can combine relational and individualistic aspects.

These possibilities are worth exploring because individualistic aspects of autonomy, such as independence, can form worthwhile goals and should therefore not be disregarded. I frame my discussion with special reference to the discussion of liberal individualism by Jennifer Nedelsky in her recent book *Law's Relations: A Relational Theory of Self, Autonomy, and Law*.[2] Nedelsky champions a relational account of autonomy and strongly disavows liberal individualism. Yet her own account of autonomy includes numerous ideas that seem individualistic. Section 1 summarizes key ideas in Nedelsky's approach.

In the second section, I discuss what Nedelsky regards as a popular, liberal individualist model of autonomy, namely, "self-made men" and women. According to relational autonomy theorists such as Nedelsky, self-made persons are a myth and an illusion. I argue by contrast that the debate over "self-made persons" is not relevant to the question of how to conceptualize autonomy. Instead, it is better understood as part of the debate over capitalism. Furthermore, in the debate over capitalism, "self-made" persons are not necessarily mythic or illusory. They can be interpreted as genuine empirical possibilities so long as the term is taken nonliterally. This is not to deny that self-made persons are controversial. However, as I shall suggest, even in

---

[1] Catriona MacKenzie and Natalie Stoljar, eds., *Relational Autonomy: Feminist Perspectives on Autonomy, Agency, and the Social Self* (New York: Oxford University Press, 2000), 4.

[2] Jennifer Nedelsky, *Law's Relations: A Relational Theory of Self, Autonomy, and Law* (New York: Oxford University Press, 2011). Some parts of this essay draw on my review of Nedelsky's book in the *University of Toronto Law Journal*, Volume 63, Number 2 (April 2013).

popular discourse, the controversy has to do with economic possibilities in capitalism, not with personal possibilities of autonomy.

In the third section, I delve more deeply into the concept of independence. I discuss ways in which the concept of independence can cohere with an otherwise relational account of autonomy. I also explain reasons why members of subordinated or dominated groups might want to retain independence as an aim of action.

1. Liberal Individualism

Some of the defenders of a relational conception of autonomy are avid critics of individualistic interpretations of autonomy, which they regard as antithetical to relational interpretations. Jennifer Nedelsky, for example, particularly targets liberal individualist conceptions of autonomy in her recent book *Law's Relations*.[3] This prevalent Anglo-American mode of thought, according to Nedelsky, conceptualizes human beings as essentially disconnected from one another and fails to treat relationships as constitutive of persons. Nedelsky maintains that, for liberalism, human beings are "fundamentally independent rational agents."[4]

Nedelsky does not completely reject liberalism. She accepts some liberal goals, such as equality. However, she thinks that "egalitarian projects will be better advanced in relational terms." What she challenges is the dominance of liberal individualism. She insists that her relational approach offers a deeper and more insightful way of considering what liberals may value, such as equality. Nedelsky emphasizes that relationships enable individuals to develop the capacities valued by liberalism, such as reason, autonomy, and liberty.[5]

Nedelsky acknowledges that *egalitarian* liberals such as Joseph Raz, Jeremy Waldron, and Will Kymlicka have already paid attention to the social nature and conditions of human beings.[6] Yet Nedelsky maintains that, in the work of "academic political theory and philosophy," attention to the social "co-exists with a still powerful individualism." She claims that the liberal attention to relationships remains peripheral, and relationships are not treated as constitutive of things like cognitive capacities. Nedelsky sometimes treats liberal

---

[3] Nedelsky, *Law's Relations*, e.g., 7.

[4] Nedelsky, *Law's Relations*, 3, 86. I have argued by contrast that mainstream theorists of autonomy, whether specifically liberal or not, do not generally reject, and often mention, relational or social connections in their accounts of personal autonomy. See Marilyn Friedman, "Autonomy and Social Relationships: Rethinking the Feminist Critique," in my *Autonomy, Gender, Politics* (New York: Oxford University Press, 2003), 81–97.

[5] Nedelsky, *Law's Relations*, 7, 9, 86.

[6] Nedelsky, *Law's Relations*, 382, note 14. Nedelsky also lists Ronald Dworkin, Owen Fiss, Frank Michelman, and Cass Sunstein.

individualism and relationality as if they were mutually exclusive. Yet at other times she treats them as mutually compatible, the theoretical difference being a matter of which one is more heavily emphasized.[7]

Nedelsky writes that liberal individualism is exemplified by the liberal conception of autonomy as independence. Nedelsky regards independence as "mythic" and an "illusion." Models of autonomy as independence are not really possible for human beings. In her view, the possibility of autonomy always requires dependence on others. Dependence and interdependence are pervasive throughout all human lives. A relational approach "denies most conventional claims to independence" and "denies that autonomy is fundamentally about independence."[8] Nedelsky thus writes:

> Relations (at all levels) are then not simply conditions under which a freestanding self emerges. It is the very nature of human selves to be in interaction with others. In important ways, they do not exist apart from these relations…. Autonomy is a mode of interacting with others. Relations, including those with collectives of all sorts, become not just potential threats to autonomy but its source.[9]

Nedelsky claims, in addition, that when people strive to be independent, this can happen "only… at the cost of subordinating the others who do the (unacknowledged) work made necessary by dependence."[10]

It is not always clear what Nedelsky is rejecting under the rubric of "independence" although, at one point she gives what sounds like a definition of independence: "the capacity to make decisions without being subject to anyone else's preferences, judgments, or choices…."[11] Yet Nedelsky often construes autonomy in ways that sound very similar to this idea. For example, she writes that autonomy is about "finding one's own law." The laws in question are to include commitments to oneself that will foster one's capacity for creative interaction with others, a capacity that Nedelsky regards as encompassing autonomy. For Nedelsky, autonomy captures that aspect of creative interaction that involves acting on new patterns of engagement that alter received patterns. Laws are one's own when they involve values and demands that arise from within each person and are not imposed from outside. Nedelsky writes that an autonomous person shapes her own life and does not accept a definition of herself that is conferred by other persons. Individual values should not be superseded by "collective powers." The essence of autonomy, according to

---

[7] Nedelsky, *Law's Relations*, 9, 36, 86–87.
[8] Nedelsky, *Law's Relations*, 5, 118, 43, 45, 46, 134.
[9] Nedelsky, *Law's Relations*, 55.
[10] Nedelsky, *Law's Relations*, 45.
[11] Nedelsky, *Law's Relations*, 142. Nedelsky claims that in a 1964 essay Charles Reich associates this sort of "autonomy" with property. Reich, "The New Property," *Yale Law Journal* 73(5): 733–787.

Nedelsky, may well be norms that a person recognizes as stemming from the significance or aims of the life she is living.[12]

What is noteworthy is that Nedelsky gives all of these individualistic sounding claims a relational interpretation. As quoted already, she asserts that autonomy is "a mode of interacting with others." She argues that, for a relational self, nothing is ever simply one's own. She holds that the capacity to find one's own law must be nurtured by relationships and that the content of one's own law is meaningful with reference to shared norms, values, and concepts. Indeed, her whole project includes giving a relational interpretation to key concepts that liberalism supposedly interprets individualistically, concepts such as autonomy, equality, dignity, individuality, and individuation. For Nedelsky, all of these values arise out of community and constitutive relationships.[13]

Also significant is Nedelsky's insistence that her relational interpretation does not deny "the significance of the experience of making or claiming something as one's own...." As well, recognizing the centrality of relationships does not entail denying the value of privacy or solitude. Rather, it reveals how these values are sustained by practices of allowing people to step back from each other in certain ways.[14] In general, Nedelsky insists that her approach is

> very attentive to and concerned with the particular individual. Indeed, I would say that I have insisted on such attention. Much of the relational approach is a call to attend to the individual in her particularity, which must include her particular context.[15]

Nedelsky writes that her approach

> participates in the vision of self-defining interiority as the core of what is human, the ground and purpose of the liberal commitment to freedom. At the same time, I urge a return to relationality as constitutive of self.... One might say that I am trying to claim the best of both worlds, to propose a kind of synthesis. I embrace the notion of the unique, infinite value of each individual, and the value of interiority, and the value of the ability of individuals to shape their own lives. But I reject the liberal variants of these values that fail to see the central role relation plays in each of them.[16]

Thus, Nedelsky's relational interpretation, by her own account, does not undermine the apparent individualism of many of her own claims about autonomy. Instead she accommodates their apparent individualism. She either reconceptualizes those claims in relational terms or simply combines them as they stand with relational ideas. This prompts a question: Why not treat

---

[12] Nedelsky, *Law's Relations*, 46, 166–167, 123–124, 121, 33.
[13] Nedelsky, *Law's Relations*, 55, 49, 124, 36.
[14] Nedelsky, *Law's Relations*, 49, 33.
[15] Nedelsky, *Law's Relations*, 374.
[16] Nedelsky, *Law's Relations*, 36.

independence in the same inclusive manner? If autonomy can be thought of as "a mode of interacting with others,"[17] why not think of *independence* as a mode of interacting with others? In that way, individualistic claims about autonomy would take their place alongside relation claims as two aspects of the same underlying reality.

However, we might wonder whether a simple juxtaposition of individualistic and relational claims wouldn't be self-contradictory. How could both be true together? Nedelsky recognizes this puzzle and regards it as one that she must solve or dissolve. The puzzle, as she puts it, is that autonomy seems to be both grounded in and opposed to relationality.[18] Let us consider how Nedelsky resolves this apparent inconsistency.

Nedelsky notes that there are indeed cultural narratives in which autonomy seems to involve opposing one's community and changing or rising above its traditional roles and practices. Her examples include stories that honor women for exerting nontraditional, heroic efforts. Nedelsky thinks that such oppositional accounts would make it self-contradictory to regard autonomy also as being inseparable from relationships and requiring relationships over the course of one's life. Nedelsky argues that if the prevalent conception of autonomy is as opposition to the collective, a relational approach will remain puzzling and seem exceptional. Nedelsky claims that her approach involves changing the framework that treats autonomy in this oppositional manner. She asserts that her changes make the self-contradiction disappear.[19]

Sometimes, Nedelsky's solution seems to be simply to deny certain individualistic sounding claims. For example, she frequently simply rejects independence as a conception of autonomy. Yet such claims are in tension with Nedelsky's "synthesis" between individualistic and relational ideas. In her synthesizing mode, Nedelsky herself expresses individualistic ideas such as "the value of the ability of individuals to shape their own lives."[20] Granted, she interprets these ideas relationally. Nedelsky thus often retains both individualistic and relational ideas in her account, although the deepest level of understanding is relational. Individual selves are individuals, but they are constitutively relational in the last analysis. Autonomy can be described individualistically, say, as resisting collective norms, but those feats can be realized only in virtue of relational aspects of selves.

Does this synthesized approach succeed as an account of autonomy? I believe it does and, in fact, will rely in Section 3 on the method of synthesis to argue against Nedelsky that independence, too, can be retained in accounts of autonomy. However, some reservations about Nedelsky's exact position seem

---

[17] Nedelsky, *Law's Relations*, 55.
[18] Nedelsky, *Law's Relations*, 52.
[19] Nedelsky, *Law's Relations*, 51–52.
[20] Nedelsky, *Law's Relations*, 36, 52.

called for at the outset. First, Nedelsky is mistaken to suggest that the "dominant" picture of autonomy is "opposition to the collective." That is not the dominant picture among philosophers, at any rate.[21] No major philosophical account of autonomy holds that autonomy requires opposition to any collective norms, roles, or practices. Philosophical accounts generally include procedural requirements that a person reflect on her choices, values, or commitments. When philosophical accounts specify the sorts of commitments a person must hold to be autonomous, these commitments usually have to do with valuing autonomy or regarding oneself in a certain way, such as trusting oneself.[22] Opposition to collective norms or traditions is not typically a philosopher's defining feature of autonomy. Also, although philosophical accounts do not always emphasize the collective origin of an individual's perspective, this is usually not precluded either.[23]

It is possible that Nedelsky is aiming her critique at popular conceptions of autonomy rather than those in academic philosophy. However, philosophical works are still legitimate sources of counterexamples since there is a substantial amount of work in philosophy on autonomy and, especially, on liberal theories in which autonomy figures as a fundamental value. Also, Nedelsky makes clear that academic philosophy is among her targets; for example, she points to "a still powerful individualism within academic political theory and philosophy."[24]

A second reservation about Nedelsky's combined individualized and relational approach is this. There is need for clarification of how the individualism that remains in Nedelsky's account coheres with the relationality that she claims as fundamental. It seems that, on Nedelsky's account, individualistic ideas about autonomy arise when one first thinks about autonomy, ideas such as finding "one's own law." Relationality seems to enter Nedelsky's account when those starting points are explained. One interpretation of Nedelsky's approach is that the relational explanations of autonomy replace and thereby eliminate the individualism of the initial understandings of autonomy. On this interpretation of Nedelsky, the deeper explanatory understanding gets at what is "really" true about autonomous selves. Individualistic appearances of autonomy would turn out to have been *mere* appearances without any deeper reality.

---

[21] This is important because it is not clear that many people outside philosophy actually deal in any depth with the concept of autonomy.

[22] On self-trust, see, e.g., Joel Anderson and Axel Honneth, "Autonomy, Vulnerability, Recognition, and Justice," in *Autonomy and the Challenges to Liberalism: New Essays*, edited by John Christman and Joel Anderson (Cambridge: Cambridge University Press, 2005), 127–149.

[23] Nedelsky seems to direct her critique toward at least three different social sectors: academic theorists (including philosophers), law, and government. My comments deal with academic theorists unless otherwise indicated.

[24] Nedelsky, *Law's Relations*, 9.

However, another interpretation is possible according to which the deeper relational explanations of autonomy do *not* necessarily undermine individuality but rather explain how it emerges. On this interpretation, the deeper relational understanding of autonomy need not undermine the apparent individualism of notions such as finding "one's own law."[25] Both relational and individualistic claims would be simultaneously true of autonomy on this interpretation because they would be regarded as applying to different modes or levels of understanding. Consider, for example, Nedelsky's claim that the capacity to find one's own law (an individualistic attribution) must be nurtured by relationships[26] (a relational, causal explanation). Both relationality and individuality can thus be (different) aspects of autonomy, expressing different modes of understanding it.

Nedelsky does not clarify whether her relational account of autonomy is meant to eliminate its initially apparent individuality or to explain and preserve it. This is an issue that merits further elaboration in regard to what we might call the metaphysics of her account.

A third reservation regarding Nedelsky's combined account is that she exaggerates the problem that arises when autonomy is construed as opposition to one's collective. Opposition to a collective to which one belongs is not necessarily individualistic. Opposition to a collective of one's own does not entail that one must be free of affiliation with any and all collectives. For one thing, there are usually multiple collectives in anyone's life. Someone may gain the perspective to defy the conventions of her own limited community by associating with another collective that is committed to differing values or norms. The relationships that enable a particular person's autonomy need not be the very same ones she defies. Even if they were the same relationships, there is nothing contradictory in a person's criticizing or repudiating, say, the very people or doctrines that endowed her with the capacity for critical reflection that she now exercises against them. Why think that a "master's tools" are necessarily so effectively master oriented that they cannot be used by their own community members to destroy the "master's house"?[27] Both opposing and reaffirming the norms of a collective to which one belongs each constitute a relational engagement with one's collective.

In the next section, I take a temporary detour around what Nedelsky considers to be a particularly troubling exemplar of liberal individualist accounts of autonomy, namely, the idea of "self-made men" and women. I argue that this idea does not in fact challenge the conception of relational autonomy, as Nedelsky thinks, but instead plays a different role in popular debate. Because

---

[25] Nedelsky, *Law's Relations*, 124.
[26] Nedelsky, *Law's Relations*.
[27] Cf. Audre Lorde, "The Master's Tools Will Never Dismantle the Master's House," in Audre Lorde, *Sister Outsider: Essays and Speeches* (Berkeley, CA: Crossing Press, 1984), 110–113.

of that different role, challenges to the idea of self-made persons do not undermine any particular conceptions of autonomy. My conclusion to the next section will be that the idea of self-made persons should be dropped from debates over autonomy.

2. Self-made Men and Women

As part of her critique of liberal individualism, Nedelsky directs attention to "the liberal vision of human beings as self-made and self-making men." She rejects the idea of the self-made man as an exemplar of autonomy. This image of autonomy provides an "ugly caricature" of autonomy. People are not simply self-made, writes Nedelsky; they are constituted socially.[28]

One drawback of Nedelsky's rejection of self-made men is that she does not take account of what is meant by those who invoke this image. In ignoring its defenders, Nedelsky risks attacking a straw person. In this section, I attend to what some ordinary people mean by *self-made person* and to what some social thinkers have written about this image. Some of its defenders in particular use the image in an empirically plausible manner. However, this usage does not vindicate any particular conception of autonomy, for, as I will suggest, the debate over self-made men or women is not really a debate about autonomy in any of the usual philosophical senses of autonomy. Instead, it is part of a debate over capitalism. The self-made person, I argue, is supposed to exemplify an important kind of success in a capitalist economy that, if it can really be achieved by participants in the economy, would undermine certain criticisms of capitalism. Most importantly, even a successful critique (or defense) of the idea of the self-made person would contribute nothing to an account of autonomy.

Are self-made persons empirically possible? One of my maternal uncles was regarded as a self-made man by my mother's family. The uncle I have in mind, like the rest of my mother's generation in her family, was a Lithuanian–Jewish immigrant to the United States. My uncle had had little formal education in Lithuania and had arrived in the United States with few resources. Also, he was partially disabled by the loss of sight in one eye due to a childhood illness. Once he arrived in the United States, he got a job as a cutter in a clothing factory, a ground-floor-level job that involved some physical danger. Cutters in the garment industry sometimes lost fingers using power tools to cut long, stacked rows of fabric. My uncle worked hard, went to night school, and attracted the attention of the factory owner, who eventually promoted my uncle up the ranks. After several decades, he reached the position of vice

---

[28] Nedelsky, *Law's Relations*, 120, 49.

president of the company. From this position, he eventually bought out the original owner. At the time of his death in 1967, my uncle was a millionaire (when that was still a lot of money!) who owned the company in which he had started out as a low-ranking laborer. He reached his successful position from humble origins that involved no inherited wealth, immigrant status, English as a second language, and few if any special privileges.

Nedelsky claims that terms such as *independent* and *self-made man* refer to myths and illusions. In her view, no one is really independent or a self-made person.[29] Nedelsky would be right about self-made man if this expression were taken literally. A literal interpretation would treat a self-made man as one who created himself out of *nothing*. This idea is, of course, metaphysically ridiculous. (I can assure you that my family did not think my uncle created himself out of nothing. My grandmother would have had a thing or two to say about that.)

There is another interpretation of self-made person that may not be metaphysically impossible but would come very close to it. According to this second interpretation, a self-made man is one who depended on *no other persons* in any way on his path toward workplace success. This notion would also be wrong because any successful career person had to have depended on other persons and on social institutions for the care, support, technology, means of communication, and so on that allowed the successful person to grow from childhood and do what he or she did to succeed.

To be sure, several contemporary social commentators agree with Nedelsky in rejecting the image of the self-made person. Brian Miller and Mike Lapham's book *The Self-Made Myth: The Truth About How Government Helps Individuals and Businesses Succeed*[30] shows the central role played by government in creating the conditions that enable people to gain economic prosperity. The government provides public education, a regulatory environment that protects businesses, copyright and intellectual property laws, an infrastructure including roads and airports, and support for the Internet. Miller and Lapham also observe that success is partly due to luck, fortunate timing, and sources of social capital such as race, gender, appearance, and upbringing.[31] Social capital is obviously relational.

---

[29] Nedelsky, *Law's Relations*, 43, 118, 120. A similar position is defended by Iris Young, "Autonomy, Welfare Reform, and Meaningful Work," in *The Subject of Care: Feminist Perspectives on Dependency*, edited by Eva Feder Kittay and Ellen K. Feder (Lanham, MD: Rowman & Littlefield, 2002), 40–60.

[30] Brian Miller and Mike Lapham, *The Self-Made Myth: The Truth About How Government Helps Individuals and Businesses Succeed* (San Francisco: Berrett-Koehler Publishers, 2012); cited favorably by Sara Robinson, "Self-made men debunked," http://www.salon.com/2012/04/30/self_made_men-debunked_salpart/print/.

[31] Miller and Lapham, *Self-Made Myth*, 2–3.

Also Mike Myatt, contributing to *Forbes Magazine* online, disparages the concept of the self-made man or woman.[32] He regards as obviously false and ridiculous the "'self-made man' propaganda floating around business circles." He agrees that there are inspiring stories such as that of Bill Gates but believes that every success involves the contributions of many people, such as family, friends, advisors, and teachers. Myatt writes that "mature" leaders tend to recognize and seek out the contributions of others.[33]

Yes, a self-made person would be a ridiculous idea if interpreted literally or close to it. It is possible that some defenders of self-made persons do understand this idea in the impossible, literal sense. However, to criticize only this weakest version of the idea is to attack a straw person.

It is more worthwhile to search for a defensible, nonliteral version of the idea of self-made person and see where that idea leads. This figurative version of the idea turns up in some defenses of it. A self-made man or woman figuratively is one who entered the workforce with minimal resources, few special privileges, and few or no influential contacts but who nevertheless worked his or her way up to a position of economic or career success. A self-made person is the main author of her successful labors; her success is not thought to be due merely to luck. My uncle's narrative fits this picture. He entered the workforce at a working-class level with few resources and the difficulties of an immigrant trying to survive in a foreign language and culture, and he ended his work life as a wealthy business owner.

On the interpretation I identify as plausible, to call someone self-made is to assert not a near impossibility but rather an empirically possible narrative of a distinctive sort. It is a narrative that credits someone with a life of hard work at an income-producing job, starting with few if any special privileges and ultimately achieving economic success. To be sure, this narrative is a debatable one (see note 46); however, the debate is not about autonomy.

A noteworthy feature of self-made persons in the empirically plausible sense is that, even though this idea is not about autonomy, it is still compatible with a relational analysis. The person without special economic advantages doubtless acquired habits of hard work from family, teachers, and friends. She entered an economy created by others using means of technology and communication also created by others. And so on. Defenders of the plausible conception of self-made persons rely on the fact that, while everyone's life depends on relationships, not everyone has a life story that conforms to the self-made narrative in its empirically possible sense.

The empirically possible conception of self-made persons that I have identified appears in a nineteenth-century essay called "Self-Made Men" by the

---

[32] Mike Myatt, "Self-Made Man—No Such Thing," http://www.forbes.com/sites/mikemyatt/2011/11/15/self-made-man-no-such-thing/print/.

[33] Myatt, "Self-Made Man," 1, 2.

ex-slave Frederick Douglass.[34] Douglass interpreted self-made man in a relational manner yet still believed the concept had a legitimate use. Relationally, he wrote that

> Properly speaking, there are in the world no such men as self-made men. That term implies an individual independence of the past and present which can never exist.... [N]o possible native force of character, and no depth of wealth and originality, can lift a man into absolute independence of his fellow men, and no generation of men can be independent of the preceding generation.[35]

Thus, Douglass rules out the existence of *literally* self-made men. However, he still insists that the expression 'self-made men' is "eminently descriptive of a class."[36] He explains:

> Self-made men are the men who, under peculiar difficulties and without the ordinary helps of favoring circumstances, have attained knowledge, usefulness, power and position and have learned from themselves the best uses to which life can be put in this world, and in the exercises of these uses to build up worthy character. They are the men who owe little or nothing to birth, relationship, friendly surroundings, to wealth inherited or to early approved means of education, who are what they are, without the aid of any favoring conditions by which other men usually rise in the world and achieve great results.[37]

Douglass surely has ex-slaves in mind when he adds that self-made men sometimes rise in the world in "defiance of all the efforts of society and the tendency of circumstances to repress, retard and keep them down."[38]

Douglass's initial explanation of why some men succeed in unfavorable circumstances while other men do not is this: "allowing only ordinary ability and opportunity, we may explain success mainly by one word and that word is WORK! WORK!! WORK!!! WORK!!!!" Douglass later qualifies this point to take account of the changed nature of work under slavery: "Men cannot be depended upon to work when they are asked to work for nothing."[39] With a few qualifications such as these, however, Douglass states his final message thus:

---

[34] Frederick Douglass, "Self-Made Men," in *The Frederick Douglass Papers*, Series One, vol. 4, edited by John Blassinghame and John McKivigan (New Haven, CT: Yale University Press, 1992), 545–575. See also http://www.monadnock.net/douglass/self-made-men.html. References here are to the online version.
[35] Douglass, "Self-Made Men," 4.
[36] Douglass, "Self-Made Men," 4.
[37] Douglass, "Self-Made Men," 5.
[38] Douglass, "Self-Made Men," 5.
[39] Douglass, "Self-Made Men," 12, 14.

> My theory of self-made men is, then, simply that they are men of work....
> [H]onest labor faithfully, steadily and persistently pursued, is the best, if not
> the only, explanation of their success.... Other agencies co-operate, but this
> is the principal one and the one without which all others would fail.[40]

Douglass is clear that self-made men need relationships with others. However, this need for relationships does not prevent "self-made man" from having a qualified, nonliteral meaning, namely, as that of a man (today: person) who comes from humble origins and achieves great success due principally to her or his own hard work.

Another example of my interpretation of self-made persons can be found in an article on an otherwise objectionable website on "The Art of Manliness." The article is entitled "25 of the Greatest Self-Made Men in American History" and is coauthored by Brett McKay and Kate McKay.[41] The authors explain what they mean by "self-made man":

> anyone who attains far greater success than his original circumstances would
> have indicated was possible. The self-made man often has to overcome great
> obstacles to achieve his goals. Self-made men attain their success through
> education, hard work, and sheer willpower. While no man is an island, it's
> not external help or special relationships that make the crucial difference in
> the self-made man's rise.... Nor is luck the deciding factor.... While there
> are always many factors to success, all are subordinate to work, which is the
> great key to success.[42]

McKay and McKay do not deny that education, relationships ("no man is an island"), and luck play a role; what they claim is that the deciding factor, the great key to success is how hard the self-made man works. The concept of a self-made person is, in their view, the concept of someone who achieves career success that is unusual in light of his humble origins and is based, among other things, most importantly on his hard work. Their qualified terminology again allows that relationships could be included among the conditions that together explain success in these cases. However, the authors single out hard work as the most important factor. Understood in this way as a comparative concept, the idea of a self-made person becomes harder to dismiss as mythic or illusory.[43]

---

[40] Douglass, "Self-Made Men," 17.

[41] Brett McKay and Kate McKay, "25 of the Greatest Self-Made Men in American History," http://artofmanliness.com/2008/12/28/self-made-men/print.

[42] McKay and McKay, "25 of the Greatest Self-Made Men," 1.

[43] Readers might disagree with the twenty-five examples of self-made men that McKay and McKay, "25 of the Greatest Self-Made Men," list. However, the list does span something of a political and economic range. It includes Clarence Thomas, Barack Obama, Ronald Reagan, Harry Truman, Harry Reid, Frederick Douglass, Booker T. Washington, Henry Ford, Ralph Lauren, Sean Combs, and Ben & Jerry (3–26).

Recall that Miller and Lapham challenge the concept of the self-made person on a very specific point. They are not making a general claim that everyone is dependent on other persons in many ways. They are instead making the more specific claim that every successful businessperson depends on *government*.[44] Their argument is with those who reject government programs and regulations in particular. At least two sorts of government programs and regulations are relevant: those that intervene in business activities and those that provide welfare services for the poor and needy.[45] Let us consider welfare programs more specifically.

Critics of welfare programs might agree that everyone is dependent on some others in various ways but argue that we are not all dependent on "government handouts"; they might cite self-made persons as examples of those who do not depend on government programs. Miller and Lapham, as noted already, argue specifically that successful business people *are* dependent on government support in one form or another. This argument makes it even clearer that debates over self-made persons are irrelevant to the debates over autonomy because relational theorists of autonomy are *not* trying to make the case that autonomy requires dependence on government in particular.

However, Miller and Lapham's argument is very relevant to what I believe the concept of self-made person is really about. As I argued earlier, a "self-made person," as understood by those who defend the concept in a plausible way, is a person who achieves great career success despite humble origins and principally by hard work. If people can be self-made in this sense, then being self-made is not humanly impossible, and human impossibility would be the wrong reason for excluding the idea of self-made persons from accounts of autonomy.

However, there is a *right* reason for excluding the image of self-made person from debates over autonomy. The right reason is that the image of self-made persons is not an image of *autonomy*—at least not an image that necessarily meets philosophical definitions of autonomy. For example, it is not about self-reflection or acting authentically according to one's own values. Defenders of the concept of self-made person are not assuming that a self-made person reflects on her own values or commitments in any way, let alone endorses them. A self-made person may or may not exemplify autonomy in any philosophical definition of the term.

A self-made person is one who is (presumed to be) a success in conventional capitalist terms. The debate over self-made persons, I suggest, is

---

[44] Miller and Lapham, *Self-Made Myth*, 7–8.
[45] For a discussion of the concept of dependency in relation to welfare programs, cf. Nancy Fraser and Linda Gordon, "A Genealogy of *Dependency*: Tracing a Keyword of the U.S. Welfare State," in Kittay and Feder, *Subject of Care*, 14–39.

implicitly part of debates over the nature and value of capitalism and the related debate over the justification of welfare programs. Praise for a self-made person tends to reflect a capitalist, anti-welfare-program mentality. A successful businessperson who started her work life in the paid labor force with few resources (and no friends in high places) and "worked her way up" the business ladder is an epitome of what capitalist defenders say is possible in capitalism.[46]

Perhaps there could be a sense of self-made person that is relevant to autonomy. If so, we should not simply speculate on what that sense would be like. We should first find expressions of such an account by those who would actually defend it. Otherwise, we would risk conjuring up, and then attacking, a straw person. Thus far, my admittedly nonsystematic researches into public debates over the idea of self-made persons do not reveal any important meanings that are relevant to the concept of autonomy.

It thus appears that the insistence that self-made persons are a mythic illusion fails to discredit either capitalism or autonomy. It fails to discredit capitalism because there *are* examples of self-made persons, in the nonliteral sense its defenders have in mind. If a self-made person is someone who starts her income-producing work life from humble origins, works hard in that capacity, and becomes successful in conventional capitalist terms, then there do seem to be some of those persons around. I believe my uncle was an example. McKay and McKay, as noted earlier, give famous contemporary examples. However, and more importantly for this essay, even if self-made persons are genuine possibilities, this tells us nothing about how to understand autonomy. As I have been arguing, the idea of self-made persons, even in the plausible, nonliteral sense, is not about autonomy.

---

[46] The economically successful person who rose up from humble origins is supposed to be evidence that the inequalities of capitalism are not absolute barriers to success in the workplace. If some people can be "self-made," that is, can achieve economic success principally by hard work even from humble origins, then, so the story goes, *anyone* who works hard can do so as well; poverty is no necessary barrier to workplace success. From this perspective, welfare programs serve only those who refuse to work hard or to work at all at an income-producing job. Refuting this claim is part of the significance of the argument in Miller and Lapham, *Self-Made Myth*, that all businesspeople depend on government in particular.

Thus, the existence of self-made persons does not bring the *critique* of capitalism to an end. Far from it. Those who oppose capitalism have various options. They can argue that, even if a few people can achieve career success from humble origins by working hard, such successes are so few in number that their existence does not show that the system is inherently fair. They can debate the extent to which such lives are *still* possible today. They can ask what costs and trade-offs are imposed on those who don't succeed, and, especially, on their young children and other dependents? Critics of capitalism do not yield any ground by conceding the possibility of self-made persons, in the sense that Douglass and others define them.

3. Independence

As noted in Section 1, Nedelsky criticizes the notion of independence as a misguided model of autonomy. However, as in the case of the idea of self-made person, the idea of independence also can be used in a nonliteral sense that is genuinely possible for people to achieve. To understand this plausible sense of independence, let us begin by noting that *dependence* is a scalar notion, a matter of degree in some specific mode of acting or interrelating with others. One can be more or less dependent on others in some particular way. I suggest that independence be understood as a relatively low degree of dependency, but one that is still humanly possible.[47] Also, my proposed notion of independence allows for varied forms, just as there are varied ways in which people can be dependent. Accordingly, *independence* should be understood as referring to relatively low levels of *dependency* in some particular form of dependence. I suggest that this notion is reasonable and empirically plausible. Furthermore, it is consistent with relational approaches such as that of Nedelsky.

Nedelsky generally rejects theories and concepts that deny or disregard relationships that are *constitutive* of human beings and lives. While Nedelsky does not define *constitutive relationship*, she does make clear at least two things about what it means. First constitutive relationships shape people, both in childhood and throughout life; they are formative relationships. Nedelsky's examples include relationships with parents, teachers, friends, and neighbors but also relationship patterns such as gender norms and employment practices. Second, constitutive relationships are not determinative. Nedelsky appears to mean that constitutive relationships do not *exhaustively* determine what people are or how they behave. Constitutive relationships, she insists, leave room for freedom and autonomy.[48]

The meaning of independence that I propose, namely, that of being a relatively low but still humanly possible form of dependence is consistent with Nedelsky's idea of selves as the product of constitutive relationships. Consider someone who is said to be financially independent in virtue of having wealth of her own and not needing to depend on financial support from someone else. This person exhibits a low degree of financial dependence on others, but her financial dependence is not nonexistent. She may rely on a bank or financial institution to protect her wealth, and she probably depends on a functioning economy to sustain her wealth. However, she legally owns resources that are uncontested under her name, and these resources are more than sufficient

---

[47] The idea that independence is a form of relationship involving dependency appears in Nancy Chodorow, *The Reproduction of Mothering: Psychoanalysis and the Sociology of Gender* (Berkeley: University of California Press, 1978), e.g., 187–188.

[48] Nedelsky, *Law's Relations*, 19–20, 31.

to cover her financial needs. Why be reluctant to say that she is financially independent?

This notion of financial independence leaves open the possibility that the person in question is relatively dependent in nonfinancial ways. The financially independent woman may rely on other persons to grow her food, build her dwelling, and provide her health care. Also the notion of financial independence is quite consistent with the idea that the person in question was constituted by early relationships with parents and teachers and continues in adulthood to be constituted by relationships with friends and by gender norms and employment practices. Thus, my proposed use of "independent" is easily consistent with a relational approach to selves and to autonomy. On my proposal, independence, interpreted as a relatively low form of some type of dependency, need not be a myth or an illusion.

Why does the idea of independence matter to an account of autonomy? Are there any special reasons for wanting to reclaim the idea of "independence"? I believe there are such reasons. Independence can identify a useful ideal for disadvantaged or subordinated persons to aim at. It can constitute one legitimate goal among many for emancipatory movements. Onora O'Neill, for one, cites financial independence as a valuable attribute for women worldwide.[49] Poor women worldwide are often dependent on the economic terms and conditions set by others. As O'Neill writes:

> They are vulnerable not only to low wages, low standards of industrial safety, endemic debt and disadvantageous dependence on those who provide credit, but also to disadvantageous patterns of entitlement within the family. Debtors who need further loans for survival cannot make much fuss about the terms creditors offer for purchasing their crops; the most dependent women—daughters-in-law and younger daughters in some societies—are acutely vulnerable both to market forces and to more powerful kin.[50]

The term "independence" can serve to stand for a capacity that Nedelsky herself lauds, namely, the "human capacity for creation in the shaping of one's life and self." It can serve to guide a feminist concern that Nedelsky cites, namely, "freeing women to shape their own lives" and to define *themselves* "rather than accepting the definition given by others (men and male-dominated society, in particular)."[51]

---

[49] See Onora O'Neill, "Justice, Gender, and International Boundaries," in Onora O'Neill, *The Bounds of Justice* (Cambridge: Cambridge University Press, 2000), 162–167. See also my discussion of O'Neill on these issues in Marilyn Friedman, "Independence, Dependence, and the Liberal Subject," in *Reading Onora O'Neill*, edited by David Archard, Monique Deveaux, Neil Manson, and Daniel Weinstock (Abingdon: Routledge, forthcoming), 111–129.

[50] O'Neill, "Justice, Gender, and International Boundaries," 164.

[51] Nedelsky, *Law's Relations*, 121.

To be sure, Nedelsky worries about independence for several reasons. She worries that the use of the idea of independence is not only illusory but also positively harmful. She writes that when people strive to be independent, this can happen "only...at the cost of subordinating the others who do the (unacknowledged) work made necessary by dependence."[52] We are familiar with the idea that, for example, successful careerpeople, usually men, are highly dependent on family partners, usually women, whose domestic work is crucial for allowing the career people to concentrate on building their careers. However, if, say, a woman's job outside the home requires her husband to do more housework than he did before, this might not cause his subordination at all. And if the woman must hire someone to do child care—often a working-class woman—she (the employer) can pay a decent wage, social security, and workers' compensation as well as providing fair conditions of employment, thus minimizing the subordinating effects of paid child-care labor.

If subordination were "made necessary by dependence," as Nedelsky states, then *all dependency* relations would subordinate someone. Independent strivings would not be any different from dependent strivings in that respect. The argument has yet to be made, however, that either people's dependencies or their strivings to be independent necessarily result in subordinating others. A relationship to someone who is striving to be independent might make someone more vulnerable to subordination. Or it might not; it is a contingent matter whether subordination actually occurs in any given case. When it does, this probably means that the person striving to be independent has actually become more exploitative and thus more dependent in some ways on the now more subordinate other person, so the problem is not independence per se. Thus, these complex outcomes should not discourage oppressed persons from seeking relatively greater independence in those areas in which their own independence would reduce their vulnerabilities to subordination or abuse by others.

Nedelsky claims a second way the cultural esteem for independence can be harmful. She suggests that when independence is culturally celebrated, people who do not fit the image are devalued.[53] Because different groups have unequal abilities to maintain the "illusion" of autonomy conceptualized as independence,[54] some groups will probably be stigmatized whenever autonomy is revered as independence. Nedelsky is right to worry about scorn directed against persons regarded as dependent. Those who fail to become independent, that is, to reduce dependency to a relatively low level, may have lacked the appropriate, constitutive relationships or material circumstances that could have promoted their independence. They should therefore not be stigmatized—just

---

[52] Nedelsky, *Law's Relations*, 45.
[53] Nedelsky, *Law's Relations*, 42–43. On this point, Nedelsky cites Margaret Walker, *Moral Contexts* (Lanham, MD: Rowman & Littlefield, 2003), 192.
[54] Nedelsky, *Law's Relations*, 43.

as people should not be stigmatized for failing to develop *any* capability for which they lacked appropriate relationships or material circumstances.

However, the faulty *application* of an ideal of independence does not entail that independence is a faulty *ideal*.[55] The key point for discussions of autonomy is that if independence is defined as the lesser form of some specific type of dependence, then independence is humanly possible. In addition, persons can be independent in some ways while being (more) dependent in other ways.

We can also ask whether any sort of independence is especially important for autonomy. The notion of independent-mindedness comes to mind. Saying that someone is independent-minded seems highly relevant to saying she is an autonomous person, even if it is not the only relevant consideration.[56] Independent-mindedness need not be interpreted as a narrow kind of rationality or rational agency. Mindedness can encompass reason, emotion, desire, will, and so on.[57] Nedelsky's own conception of autonomy fits well with a notion of independent-mindedness. As discussed earlier, Nedelsky writes that autonomy involves "finding one's own law," which consists of values and commitments that arise from within the self and are not imposed by others.[58] Nedelsky does not use the term independent-mindedness for her account, but there is no need for her to reject it. As I have been suggesting, independence can be understood consistently with a relational account of autonomy, and it offers a valuable aspirational ideal for women and other subordinated persons.

One final point about liberalism, independence, and autonomy: Nedelsky criticizes liberalism for focusing on the way people are threats to each other and ignoring the positive or constructive ways they affect each other relationally. Nedelsky suggests that regarding individuals as independent and as threats to each other is at odds with regarding them as constitutive of each other.[59]

However, the two perspectives are not incompatible at all. First, an emphasis on the threats posed by (some) others does not entail a belief that all others are

---

[55] One widely scorned sort of dependency is dependency on government programs by those who are poor and need those programs to meet their basic needs. Nedelsky is concerned that the esteem for "independence" becomes part of a discrediting of the poor for their (welfare) dependency. Nedelsky's strategy for contesting this approach is to discredit the standard of independence so that it is not available for condemning people who depend on welfare services.

However, criticizing the idea of independence does not succeed in defending welfare programs. One key question is whether welfare programs are required or justifiable as a matter of justice. Unfortunately, discrediting "independence" does not make a positive case for the justice of social welfare programs. Arguing that no one is literally independent and everyone is dependent does not by itself justify government programs that redistribute wealth to those dependents who are poor.

[56] For a strong defense of the importance of favorable external social conditions, see Marina Oshana, *Personal Autonomy in Society* (Aldershot, UK: Ashgate, 2006).

[57] The notion of independent mindedness may seem to exclude embodiment. This could be remedied, however, by building embodiment into the accounts of reason, emotion, desire, and will. Most scientific accounts of mindedness today are accounts of brain function.

[58] Nedelsky, *Law's Relations*, 46, 123.

[59] Nedelsky, *Law's Relations*, 121.

nothing more than threats to the self. An emphasis on persons as (sometimes) threats is consistent with regarding persons also as (sometimes) constitutive of each other.[60] Second, the notion of protecting individuals from the threats of others does not presuppose that individuals are completely independent of all other individuals. Indeed, if individuals were completely independent of each other, they would not need any protections against each other. Only someone in some sort of relation to another person can be a threat to that other person. Regarding individuals as (sometimes) threats to each other thus exemplifies a relational approach. Nothing about a relational approach requires us to deny that some relations are harmful.

Third, it is obvious that people *sometimes* harm each other, and stopping these harms is a legitimate purpose of the state. A large part of feminist theory and practice consists of opposition to harms inflicted on women. It is therefore odd for feminists such as Nedelsky to dismiss the liberal concern with preventing interpersonal harm. Indeed, most of Nedelsky's examples throughout her book, as she herself states, "focus on harm suffered by women."[61] Chapters 5 and 8 in particular focus on violence against women and against children. Nedelsky writes that women are "always at risk of violence and...the violence is tolerated, condoned, and not taken seriously."[62] Perhaps Nedelsky should have said that liberalism has not paid *enough* attention to threats to persons—especially to women.[63] At any rate, the focus on persons as threats to each other and as independent does not undermine liberalism's account of autonomy and is consistent with a relational approach to autonomy.

I have argued that a relational approach does not preclude the ideas of self-made person and independence. The idea of independence can easily be incorporated into a relational account of autonomy. However, the idea of self-made person is not really relevant to debates about autonomy. Instead, it picks out a humanly possible sort of career narrative that should be assessed in debates about the injustice of capitalist systems.

Acknowledgments

I am grateful to the editors, Andrea Veltman and Mark Piper, for helpful suggestions on an earlier draft of this chapter.

---

[60] People are no more *always constitutive* of each other than they are always *threats* to each other. Also, lives can vary in the proportions of each sort of relationships.
[61] Nedelsky, *Law's Relations*, 6.
[62] Nedelsky, *Law's Relations*, 211.
[63] Nedelsky, *Law's Relations*, 22, does say, at one point, that liberalism has not paid the right *kind* of attention to threats to persons.

{ 4 }

Autonomy? Or Freedom? A Return to Psychoanalytic Theory

Nancy J. Hirschmann

The idea of autonomy as developed by Kant, pertaining to the lone independent self who is able to deduce and follow universal moral principles through the use of a priori reasoning, has been the subject of much feminist critique, even leading some feminists to argue that we should reject the idea of autonomy altogether as a relic of a sexist, racist, and classist liberal individualism.[1] But relational autonomy feminists have brought attention to the need to reconfigure autonomy rather than reject it. By recognizing that the problem with autonomy is not the concept itself but rather the conception of it that follows from the individualist and "naturally free and equal" self that dominates Enlightenment liberal thought, feminists have contributed to an important rethinking of the concept.

The basic idea of relational autonomy may appear to be commonsensical to most feminists: the powers, capabilities, talents, life plans, and visions of self that are essential to our abilities to guide and shape our own lives come from relationships. We are not isolated individuals but acquire our very sense of self, our self-understandings, through living in relationship with others. I have been an advocate of relational autonomy ever since my first book, in which I traced the idea of relational autonomy to object relations theory, a school of psychoanalysis made popular by Nancy Chodorow's *The Reproduction of Mothering* and embraced by Carol Gilligan as a foundation for the gendered dimensions of her "care model" in *In a Different Voice*.[2] Chodorow's theory was similarly deployed by feminist political theorists Nancy Hartsock, Jane Flax, and Christine DiStefano as well as feminist philosophers like Sandra

---

[1] See particularly Martha Fineman, *The Autonomy Myth: A Theory of Dependency* (New York: New Press, 2004). But also see Sarah Lucia Hoagland, *Lesbian Ethics: Toward New Values* (Palo Alto, CA: Institute of Lesbian Studies, 1989); Catharine Keller, *From a Broken Web: Separation, Sexism, and Self* (Boston: Beacon, 1986).

[2] Nancy J. Hirschmann, *Rethinking Obligation: A Feminist Method for Political Theory* (Ithaca, NY: Cornell University Press, 1992).

Harding and Evelyn Fox Keller, not to mention social theorists like Dorothy Dinnerstein and Jessica Benjamin.[3] This feminist deployment of object relations theory arguably ushered in a revolution within the ongoing revolution of feminist theory by kick-starting the argument that, rather than rejecting the traditional work of care and relationship that women have historically been assigned to, we should value its contributions and importance to the human condition.

Yet I have become more ambivalent about the concept of relational autonomy in recent years. Part of this ambivalence stems from the work on the concept of freedom that I have done, in which I have increasingly come to believe that whatever desires, preferences, and abilities our relationships may have led us to have, we need to act by and for ourselves. Even when we act wrongly, perhaps even against our own interests, we must be free to so act. I believe that this position diverges from the views of many (though not all) relational autonomy theorists because freedom is still relevant even if an agent fails a variety of autonomy tests and measures. Consider, for instance, a driver who causes an accident while drunk: even if we excuse her decision to drive (on the argument that her judgment was impaired), the choice to drink in the first place when she knew that she had to drive home afterward clearly fails various autonomy tests of self-reflective judgment and rational self-interest. But we consider her action free, which is why we hold her responsible for the harm she causes. I may want to act recklessly, irrationally, even self-destructively, but the freedom to choose to act in such ways is nonetheless important to our conception of a person: we want to be able to make our own choices.

Part of my ambivalence, however, stems from going back to where relational autonomy started: object relations theory. The psychoanalytic origin of relational autonomy is something that we tend to forget about, and this forgetting suppresses the dark side of relational autonomy, a suppressing that I have been as guilty of as anyone.

That worry is the starting point for this paper. I begin by describing object relations theory's account of relational autonomy and why I think it is problematic for feminism. I then turn to the ways feminist accounts of freedom and agency can help us get beyond this problematic point of origin. My goal is not to argue against autonomy per se, much less against relational autonomy. Indeed,

---

[3] Nancy Hartsock, *Money, Sex and Power: Toward a Feminist Historical Materialism* (Evanston, IL: Northeastern University Press, 1983); Jane Flax, "Political Philosophy and the Patriarchal Unconscious: A Psychoanalytic Perspective on Epistemology and Metaphysics," in *Discovering Reality: Feminist Perspectives on Epistemology, Metaphysics, Methodology, and Philosophy of Science*, edited by Sandra Harding and Merrill B. Hintikka (Dordrecht: D. Reidel, 1983); Christine DiStefano, *Configurations of Masculinity: A Feminist Perspective on Modern Political Theory* (Ithaca, NY: Cornell University Press, 1991); Sandra Harding, *The Science Question in Feminism* (Ithaca, NY: Cornell University Press, 1986); Evelyn Fox Keller, *Reflections on Gender and Science* (New Haven, CT: Yale University Press, 1985); Dorothy Dinnerstein, *The Mermaid and the Minotaur: Sexual Arrangements and Human Malaise* (New York: Harper and Row, 1976); Jessica Benjamin, *The Bonds of Love: Psychoanalysis, Feminism, and the Problem of Domination* (New York: Pantheon, 1988).

feminists such as Drucilla Cornell, Wendy Brown, Linda Zerilla, and I have developed many shared concerns and features between autonomy and conceptions of freedom, even as different as those theories are from one another.[4] Rather, I want to suggest that recognizing the problems of relationality may lead us to the view that it is appropriate to conceive of autonomy only in tandem with a theory of freedom. Indeed, perhaps *relational autonomy* should be better thought of as *relational freedom*. As a more open-ended concept, I suggest that freedom may allow for more flexibility in how we theorize the choice-making subject, and I close the paper with some speculative notes on that suggestion.

1. The Origins of Relational Autonomy

Object relations theory is a school of post-Freudian psychoanalytic theory holding that boys experience different psychosexual development from girls because women, rather than men, are the primary caretakers of children. This psychosexual development entails different gender identification and self-identification, which results in different conceptualizations of the self–Other relationship. The central tenet of object relations theory is one that seems self-evident to feminist theorists and philosophers today, namely, that "human beings are created in and through relations with other human beings."[5] The object in object relations is the caretaker, usually the mother; the mother is called the object both in the sense that the mother is objectified by the infant and in the sense that the self is formed by the other—the subject by the object.

In contrast to Freud's focus on the oedipal period, object relations theory focuses on the first three years of life, the pre-oedipal period. When it begins life outside of the womb, an infant is not conscious of its existence as an entity distinct from those who care for it. This realization of distinction—and along with that, the realization of its complete helplessness—comes at approximately three months, as the infant starts to recognize its caretaker in recognizing its own dependence. This means that the infant forms an intense attachment—a symbiotic one, from its perspective—to the caretaker. Margaret Mahler, in fact, names this first stage of life, from birth to six months, symbiosis.[6] It is common in this work to use "it" to refer to infants of both genders, and I follow that custom here. Formation of this attachment is "the most important task" of infants' first three years.[7]

---

[4] Drucilla Cornell, *At the Heart of Freedom: Feminism, Sex, and Equality* (Princeton, NJ: Princeton University Press, 1999); Wendy Brown, *States of Injury: Power and Freedom in Late Modernity* (Princeton, NJ: Princeton University Press, 1995); Linda Zerilli, *Feminism and the Abyss of Freedom* (Chicago: University of Chicago Press, 2005); Nancy J. Hirschman, *The Subject of Liberty: Toward a Feminist Theory of Freedom* (Princeton, NJ: Princeton University Press, 2003).

[5] Flax, "Political Philosophy and the Patriarchal Unconscious," 250.

[6] Margaret Mahler, *On Human Symbiosis and the Vicissitudes of Individuation* (New York: International University Press, 1968).

[7] Flax, "Political Philosophy and the Patriarchal Unconscious," 251.

In this period, infants form their primary identification, which involves their growing perception of a demarcation between the self and the other. "An essential task of infantile development, it [primary identification] involves the development of ego boundaries (a sense of personal psychological division from the rest of the world) and of a bounded body ego (a sense of the permanence of one's physical separateness and the predictable boundedness of one's own body, of distinction between inside and outside)."[8] Since in most societies caretakers of infants tend to be women, this primary attachment is almost always to a woman, and "the infant develops its sense of self mainly in relation to her."[9]

As infants develop motor skills, begin to interact with the world around them, and most importantly learn language, they start to develop a secondary identity, which is their adult identity as an individual person. This is also when the acquisition of gender and sexual identity takes place, which are "with rare exception firmly and irreversibly established for both sexes" by age three and often as early as eighteen months.[10] The acquisition of gender identity overlaps and coincides with the acquisition of received language, as Merleau-Ponty calls it—a language that already embodies sexist understandings of gender difference.[11] As children learn how to assign the abstract concept of *boy* and *girl* to different persons, such as the self and the mother, they learn about what gender *is*, as a concept and category in the structuring of family relations.[12]

The reason that this is important is that when children learn "which" gender they are, they also learn which gender their mothers are. In the process, their primary identity (again, usually with their mother) is retroactively assigned a gender (at the subconscious level, of course). This creates a different set of problems for girls and boys as they emerge from the pre-oedipal to the oedipal period. The bottom line—skipping over a great deal of the theory—is that when children learn gender identity, girls learn that they are "the same as mother" and boys that they are "different from mother." Experienced up to this point in an intense and exclusive relationship as an ungendered entity who supplies all of the infant's needs and wants, the mother represents all things outside the self to the infant. But once children learn that their mother is a

---

[8] Nancy Chodorow, "Feminism and Difference: Gender, Relation, and Difference in Psychoanalytic Perspective," *Socialist Review* 46 (July–August 1979): 54.

[9] Nancy Chodorow, *The Reproduction of Mothering: Psychoanalysis and the Sociology of Gender* (Berkeley: University of California Press, 1978), 78.

[10] Chodorow, *Reproduction of Mothering*, 150; Mahler, *Human Symbiosis*; see also Flax, "Political Philosophy," 251; Jane Flax, "The Conflict between Nurturance and Autonomy in Mother–Daughter Relationships and within Feminism," *Feminist Studies* 4:2 (1978): 171–189.

[11] Maurice Merleau-Ponty, *The Prose of the World*, edited by Claude Lefort, translated by John O'Neill (Evanston, IL: Northwestern University Press, 1968).

[12] Again, operating within a heteronormative framework in which there are only two genders.

woman, girl infants see themselves as the same as, or connected to, the entire outside world, whereas boy infants sees themselves as separate from, or even opposed to, that world.

That is, as a girl identifies with her mother and perceives a basic definitional connection and continuity between herself and her mother, she also sees the world itself, as represented by her mother, as continuous and connected with her. Her "other"—the not-me, the boundary of the self—is very much connected to and part of the self. Self and other constitute a continuum, a movement from the core self to external objects that she perceives as connected to her core self. The self, to a significant degree, *is* the other.[13] In contrast, for the boy, self and other constitute a dichotomy; since gender is viewed as a mutually exclusive category and it is culturally forbidden for him to identify as female, he is culturally and psychically forced to expel that part of himself that is embodied by his mother. But that is an impossible task. Under conditions of patriarchy, the boy copes with this task "by denial (of having been related), by projection (women are bad; they cause these problems), and by domination (mastering fears and wishes for regression by controlling, depowering, and/or devaluing the object [viz. women])."[14] The other is radically separated and different from the self: "other" is female; self is male. In doing this, masculinity is defined by the boy in negative terms, that is, "as that which is not feminine and/or connected to women."[15]

This gender difference leads to two different models of autonomy. For the boy, autonomy is conceptualized reactively, as a reaction against the mother. According to Evelyn Fox Keller, reactive autonomy "confuses autonomy with separation and independence from others."[16] Reactive autonomy is static, according to Keller, because it is locked into a reductive and negative conception of the self as non-mother. If autonomy is defined as, in her terms, "the psychological sense of being able to act under one's own volition instead of under external control" and turns on individuality and the integrity of the self, then reactive autonomy is self-defeating. In fact, it robs the individual of self-creative agency, for such autonomy is premised on an artificial separateness that cannot be sustained without repression and on abstract roles and rules, which are

---

[13] Chodorow, *Reproduction of Mothering*, 93.

[14] Flax, "Political Philosophy and the Patriarchal Unconscious," 253. Other feminists, like Hartsock in *Money, Sex and Power*, further maintain that violence is another tool men use to establish their distinction from the mother. Indeed, erotic violence and the linkage of sex with domination is, Hartsock argues, the logical outcome of this situation, a conclusion with which other object relations theorists at least implicitly agree, such as Dinnerstein, *Mermaid and the Minotaur;* Benjamin, *Bonds of Love;* Harding, *Science Question in Feminism.*

[15] Chodorow, *Reproduction of Mothering*, 174, 175. By "negative" I do not imply a normative judgment; I mean only that it is defined as *not* female.

[16] Keller, *Reflections on Gender and Science*, 97.

external to the self.¹⁷ In David Bakan's words, reactive autonomy "manifests itself in self-protection, self-assertion and self-expansion...in the formation of separateness...in isolation, alienation and aloneness...in the repression of thought, feeling, and impulse."¹⁸ This is the conception of autonomy that coheres with the dominant notion that we find in the philosophical literature beginning with Kant.¹⁹

By contrast, the girl cannot engage in the sort of repression and denial that the boy engages in—even if she wants to—because it is precisely at this age that recognition of her female gender identity becomes important. She thus depends on a close psychic tie with her mother even as the boy's identity depends on severing that tie. Moreover, because her identity with the mother is ongoing, concrete, and continuous, the girl retains—and is encouraged to retain—her close psychic connection with the mother. The girl's gender identity grows out of a personal, concrete relationship involving a diffuse identification with someone else's general personality; primary and secondary identity become merged.

It is out of this deep psychic connection that relational autonomy develops: the self is conceived in terms of, and draws strength from, relationships with others. Bakan says this notion of the self gives rise to a communal personality; in his words, girls exhibit "the sense of being at one with other organisms...the lack of separateness...contact, openness, and union...noncontractual cooperation."²⁰ This is seen by feminist object relations theorists as a preferred model, a source of strength, what Keller even calls "the true self"²¹ and clearly superior to masculine experience. Boys and men are seen as incapable of genuine love, empathy, and relationship: because boys are pushed out of the preodedipal relationship and forced to curtail the empathic tie with the mother, their understanding of love between two people becomes confused with the fear of loss of self. Indeed, Chodorow goes so far as to claim that men "look to relationships with women for narcissistic-phallic reassurance rather than for mutual affirmation and love."²² Women, by contrast, can maintain genuine, deep, empathic relations. Indeed, according to the theory, that is why they become mothers.

---

[17] Ibid.

[18] David Bakan, *The Duality of Human Existence: Isolation and Communion in Western Man* (Boston: Beacon Press, 1966), 55.

[19] Though not all readers of Kant interpret his conception of autonomy in this way; see Nancy J. Hirschmann, *Gender, Class and Freedom in Modern Political Theory* (Princeton, NJ: Princeton University Press, 2008), chap. 4, for my views of Kant on freedom and autonomy.

[20] Bakan, *Duality of Human Existence*, 56.

[21] Keller, *Reflections on Gender and Science*, 99.

[22] Chodorow, *Reproduction of Mothering*, 196.

2. What's Wrong with Relational Autonomy?

This valorization of the "feminine" model of development has particularly characterized work that brought this psychoanalytic framework into political and moral philosophy. Political theorists and philosophers such as Jane Flax, Nancy Hartsock, Christine DiStefano, and I all deploy object relations theory to critique central figures in canonical political philosophy as well as the conceptual frameworks that emerged out of Enlightenment thought in the structure of concepts such as obligation, freedom, and power.[23] Other feminist philosophers such as Sandra Harding and Evelyn Fox Keller used object relations theory to develop feminist philosophies of science and epistemology.[24] All of these figures, including myself, made value judgments about the superiority of the feminine model of relational autonomy. It is arguably the case that Keller was the first in this group to focus on the notion of autonomy; she offered an extremely positive, perhaps even romantic, vision of girls' relational autonomy as far superior to boys' reactive autonomy, which cohered more to the rule-governed conception that we have learned from Kant. But Keller's ideas came from Chodorow, who in turn got them from David Bakan's *The Duality of Human Existence* as well as other object relations psychoanalysts such as D. W. Winnicott and Melanie Klein. In these sources, the further back one goes, the less "feminist friendly" the ideas underlying relational autonomy appear.

One might well ask: so what? Why cannot philosophers today adopt the idea and reject its baggage? As a political theorist, I believe that history matters, and particularly the history of a concept like relational autonomy, because I am worried that this uncritical favoring of the feminine model unconsciously persists. Feminists have still failed to acknowledge that relational autonomy stems from a pathology exhibited by feminine development operating within a sexist model of childrearing. If the boy's problem is fear of connection and the need to differentiate the self radically from the other, the girl's difficulty comes from an inability to separate adequately, which she needs to do to form an adult identity. If the mother represents her infantile, primary self, the development of a secondary, adult self is compromised by the need to "shift" her identity back to the very same person it is *from*. Just as the theory posits that the boy's reaction against the mother and identification with an abstraction makes it difficult for him to maintain connection and trust in later life, so does the girl's difficulty in breaking away from her primary identification inhibit her sense of separateness. In Bakan's notion of the feminine *communal self*, the individual as such becomes merged with the other and never realizes a sense

---

[23] Flax, "Political Philosophy and the Patriarchal Unconscious"; Hartsock, *Money, Sex and Power*; DiStefano, *Configurations of Masculinity*; Hirschmann, *Rethinking Obligation*.

[24] Harding, *Science Question*; Keller, *Reflections on Gender and Science*.

of individual identity. Mahler and Winnicott similarly show how the girl's inability to separate adequately from the mother creates serious problems of developing self-confidence, self-awareness, and even an understanding of the self as an individual.[25] And Flax notes that girls have the most serious difficulty in psychically separating themselves from their mothers, a difficulty that carries through into adulthood and into their own roles as mothers. She cites clinical evidence that female therapy patients commonly express a lack of "sense where they end and their mothers begin, even in a literal, physical way."[26] This finding is supported by Macoby and Jacklin's work on the gender-specific ways mothers discipline boys and girls.[27]

As Chodorow put it in probably the most famous passage from *The Reproduction of Mothering*: "Girls emerge from this period with a basis for 'empathy' built into their primary definition of self in a way that boys do not. Girls emerge with a stronger basis for experiencing another's needs or feelings as one's own *(or of thinking that one is so experiencing another's needs and feelings)*."[28] I have added emphasis to that conditional phrase because it is significant that Chodorow puts it in parentheses, as if to obscure it for the reader. But what it describes is the pathology of the lack of separation, the notion that we *think* we experience others' feelings as our own. We know that I cannot literally feel what you feel; even Hume acknowledged that sympathetic vibrations were less pronounced in the string next to the one plucked.[29] Parents who have had a seriously ill or injured child and who have desperately wished or prayed that they could take on their child's suffering know that we cannot feel the other's feelings; we can only imagine and mourn. We suffer at the suffering of others, but it is of a qualitatively different nature. Believing that you literally feel another's feelings as your own, as Flax's clinical patients reported, is a sign of pathology called borderline personality syndrome.[30]

But many relational autonomy theorists tend to forget—or indeed perhaps were never aware—that this is where the idea of relational autonomy

---

[25] Bakan, *Duality of Human Existence*; Mahler, *Human Symbiosis*; D. W. Winnicott, *The Family and Individual Development* (New York: Tavistock, 1965).

[26] Flax, "Conflict between Nurturance and Autonomy," 174.

[27] Eleanor Macoby and Carol Jacklin, *The Psychology of Sex Difference* (Stanford: Stanford University Press, 1975).

[28] Chodorow, *Reproduction of Mothering*, 167.

[29] David Hume, "An Enquiry Concerning Human Understanding," in *Enquiries Concerning Human Understanding and Concerning the Principles of Morals*, edited by L. A. Selby-Bigg, 3rd ed., revised by P. H. Nidditch (Oxford: Clarendon Press, 1975); Nancy J. Hirschmann, "Sympathy, Empathy, and Obligation: A Feminist Rereading," in *Feminist Interpretations of David Hume*, edited by Anne Jacobsen (University Park: Pennsylvania State University Press, 1999).

[30] Jane Flax, *Thinking Fragments: Psychoanalysis, Feminism, and Postmodernism in the Contemporary West* (Berkeley: University of California Press, 1990). Dinnerstein, *Mermaid and the Minotaur*, which I have not brought into the discussion because even I find it too gloomy in its portrayal of the disastrous gender inequality that women's mothering produces, provides an even stronger account of this pathology.

originates. Even those who have never read this literature, however, should be aware that the idea of relational autonomy emerged out of this trajectory, from nonfeminist analysts like Mahler and Winnicott to feminist nonphilosophers such as Chodorow, Dinnerstein, Gilligan, and Benjamin, to feminist philosophers and political theorists such as Keller, Harding, and Hartsock. From there, the concept of relational autonomy was taken up by feminist theorists and philosophers who may not have even read this literature, despite the effective critiques that leading feminist philosophers, such as Diana Meyers, have made of it.[31]

None of this is to deny that there are valid objections to object relations theory. It is often difficult to recognize the family forms it depends on, namely, the heterosexual two-parent family where the woman has primary responsibility for child care. It may at times seem more appropriate to an episode of *Mad Men* than to the complicated lives we live today. After all, feminists have struggled for the past three decades to change this family structure, and many of us are very proud of the fact that, in our own families, male and female partners share equally (more or less) in childrearing. We are also rightly proud of the fact that different family forms, such as gay and lesbian families, have succeeded in part because of our political advocacy.

But let me offer a reminder: we are not the majority or the mainstream. Studies show that although the sexual division of labor has shifted somewhat, women still perform the bulk of labor associated with childrearing, and particularly early childrearing (the first six months of life).[32] Although some women have male partners who also took parental leave, it is still rare, even among feminists, for men to be as actively engaged in early infant care as women.[33]

---

[31] Diana T. Meyers, "The Subversion of Women's Agency in Psychoanalytic Feminism: Chodorow, Flax, Kristeva," in *Revaluing French Feminism: Critical Essays on Difference, Agency, and Culture*, edited by Nancy Fraser and Sandra Lee Bartky (Bloomington: Indiana University Press, 1992). I disagree with her that Chodorow deploys a "traditional feminine tendency to reduce care and nurturance to conflict minimization and uncritical support" (140), because I think Meyers downplays the role of capitalism in Chodorow's argument. However, I think she is correct that Chodorow ends up valorizing feminine pathology in spite of herself. See also Meyers, *Gender in the Mirror: Cultural Imagery and Women's Agency* (New York: Oxford University Press, 2002), esp. chap. 1.

[32] Rhona Mahoney, *Kidding Ourselves: Breadwinning, Babies, and Bargaining Power* (Boston: Basic Books, 1996). According to research funded by the National Science Foundation, women are still doing two to three times more household work: seventeen to twenty-eight hours per week for women versus seven to ten hours per week for men. Bobbie Mixon, "Chore Wars: Men, Women and Housework," http://www.nsf.gov/discoveries/disc_summ.jsp?cntn_id=111458.

[33] See, e.g., the symposium on Nancy J. Hirschmann, "Mothers Who Care Too Much," *Boston Review*, July–August 2012, particularly the response of Lane Kenworthy, "Time for Public Childcare," and my response to him, "The Sexual Division of Labor is the Problem." Particularly relevant to readers of this volume is an American Association of University Women study showing that among tenure-track faculty, parental leave is associated with positive outcomes at tenure for men but negative outcomes for women, the implication being that many men use such leaves to advance their scholarship whereas women use them to care for their infants exclusively. Mary Ann Mason, "Title IX and Babies: The New Frontier?" *Chronicle of Higher Education*, November 29, 2012.

But even so, object relations theory posits that the "solution" to patriarchy is precisely what feminists strive for today—shared parenting and redistributing the sexual division of labor. That is, although object relations theory may describe a natural process of human development—in the sense that the developing infantile brain responds to the external stimuli of its relationships with other people who shape its encounter with the physical world—the particular form those reactions take will differ by the specific cultural practices of childrearing. Within the profoundly sexist late-capitalist Western sexual division of labor, we end up with gender dichotomy. Object relations theory shows that the sexual division of labor is not just unfair to women: it is damaging to boys and men's psychic and emotional well-being as well. Accordingly, feminists who mother in heterosexual relationships where men share equally, as well as gay and lesbian shared parenting families that radically break the heteronormative pattern, offer significant hope for the feminist future we all seek. This does not disprove the theory but rather supports it.

It is also important to remember that psychoanalytic theory is best understood not as a series of reductive empirical claims about infantile psychology but is rather an interpretive framework. Certainly, part of the logic of psychology and psychoanalysis entails the attempt to understand the meaning that adheres to real social relations, hence its reliance on case studies and interviews. But gender psychology also provides a symbolic language that can help us understand these meanings in a new way by offering a larger theoretical framework: larger because it allows questions that a liberal individualist framework forbids; symbolic because the unconscious gains its most important expression at the cultural level, in the symbols and structures that a culture adopts. As Chodorow says, psychoanalysis is "a deeply embedded cultural discourse," not simply a scientific one.[34] Indeed, given that this literature was a response to the decidedly sexist tendencies of Freudian psychoanalysis, its primary contribution from a feminist theoretical perspective is precisely to point out that what has been taken to be true—such as the classic Freudian concept of penis envy—in fact represents a particular masculinist reading of masculine experience. Yet it is out of the sexist, heteronormative model of childrearing that relational autonomy arises.

The grounding of the idea of relational autonomy in this pathology of feminine development is what worries me. In our arguments critiquing Kantian individualist morality we are at least tacitly endorsing the feminist object relations view that masculine individuation and separation is less valuable than women's connectedness. I believe that this is problematic. For all our attention to the need to stress relationship and connection, we have failed to stress the

---

[34] Nancy Chodorow, *Feminism and Psychoanalytic Theory* (New Haven, CT: Yale University Press, 1989), 179.

need for individuation and separateness, at which girls and women too often fail. It is because of my unease about these aspects of relational autonomy, particularly the critique of individualism, that I think that freedom needs to be an important part of the discussion. Its greater stress on individuality, combined with its more flexible and perhaps less well-defined conception of the subject, can usefully complement theories of relational autonomy.

3. The Role of Freedom

The meaning of freedom might seem to be fairly straightforward: doing what I want without interference from anybody else, or as John Stuart Mill put it, "pursuing our own good, in our own way."[35] This is clearly the dominant conception of freedom we find in both law and political philosophy since at least the seventeenth century. Thomas Hobbes famously declared, "By liberty, is understood, according to the proper signification of the word, the absence of external impediments: which impediments, may oft take away part of man's power to do what he would."[36] John Locke similarly noted that "we must consider what State all Men are naturally in, and that is *a State of perfect Freedom* to order their Actions, and dispose of their Possessions, and Persons as they think fit, within the bounds of the Law of Nature, without asking leave, or depending upon the Will of any other Man."[37]

Early feminists similarly followed this line of thought: as Mary Astell acerbically asked in reference to Locke, "if all Men are *born free*, how is it that all Women are *born slaves*"?[38] Mary Wollstonecraft argued for the abolition of laws restricting women's control of property as well as for increased access to education, urging Talleyrand to expand his new proposal for national education to girls, whom he excluded. And Harriet Taylor argued not merely for women's enfranchisement and for their control of property but also for the extreme liberalization of divorce laws and even the abolition of marriage, all in the interest of enhancing women's freedom from control by men.[39]

---

[35] John Stuart Mill, "On Liberty," in *On Liberty and Other Essays*, edited by John Gray (New York: Oxford University Press, 1991).

[36] Thomas Hobbes, *Leviathan*, edited by C. B. Macpherson (New York: Penguin, 1985), 189.

[37] John Locke, *Two Treatises of Civil Government*, edited by Peter Laslett (New York: New American Library, 1963), sec. 2.4.

[38] Mary Astell, "Reflections on Marriage," in *Astell: Political Writings*, edited by Patricia Springborg (New York: Cambridge University Press, 1996), 18. See also Astell, *A Serious Proposal to the Ladies, for the Advancement of Their True and Greatest Interest*, edited by Patricia Springborg (Brookfield, VT: Pickering and Chatto, 1997).

[39] Mary Wollstonecraft, *A Vindication of the Rights of Women*, edited by Miriam Brody (New York: Penguin Books, 1992); Harriet Taylor, "The Enfranchisement of Women" and "Marriage and Divorce," in *Essays on Sex Equality*, John Stuart Mill and Harriet Taylor, edited by Alice Rossi (Chicago: University of Chicago Press, 1970).

In the mid-twentieth century, Isaiah Berlin labeled this freedom *negative liberty* to communicate that freedom entails an absence of interference or constraints.[40] But he noted that another conception of liberty also pervaded the history of philosophy, namely, positive liberty. Positive liberty entails the positive provision of resources to help the individual take advantage of negative liberties—such as education for girls, which would enable them to support themselves economically. More significantly, however, positive liberty also involves the assessment of desire. Is my desire "the mere impulse of appetite," responding to which is "slavery" as Rousseau maintained? True freedom, according to Rousseau, consists in "obedience to a self-prescribed law."[41] Berlin, following this line of argument, maintained that positive liberty entails the foundational premise that pursuing rational desires is freedom but pursuing irrational ones is not. According to this view, we can and should make qualitative assessments among various desires.

This might sound to some like autonomy, for as Kant noted autonomy involves the following of imperatives that I lay down for myself but that are universal in application—the categorical imperative.[42] But Berlin maintains that positive liberty is something less than autonomy. If I am in the grip of irrational desires and *others* prevent me from acting on those desires—thereby interfering with my negative freedom—those others are actually preserving my positive freedom by preventing me from acting on a desire that is irrational, false and therefore not what I really want. As innocent as this may sound—after all, when I stop you from engaging in harmful addictive behavior, am I not helping to liberate you?—Berlin argued that it led to something more, even something ominous: because who decides what desires are "rational" or "irrational"? What Charles Taylor called "second guessing" means that others claim to know what my "true" interests and preferences are better than I know myself.[43] Rather than autonomy, however, this coheres with the classic definition of heteronomy: doing what another wills, because they will it—even if they will it because they want you to will it.

Shaded by the Cold War, Berlin sought to align negative liberty with Western democracies and positive liberty with communist totalitarianism. And feminists, aware of the long history of men's deciding for women what is in their true interests, have reason to be wary of this form of freedom as well. But Berlin's account of positive liberty was not accurate. What he misses is that positive liberty's

---

[40] Isaiah Berlin, "Two Concepts of Liberty," in *Four Essays on Liberty*, Isaiah Berlin (New York: Oxford University Press, 1971).

[41] Jean-Jacques Rousseau, *The Social Contract and Discourses*, translated by G. D. H. Cole (London: J.M. Dent and Sons, 1973), bk. 1, chap. 8.

[42] Immanuel Kant, *Groundwork of the Metaphysics of Morals*, translated by H. J. Patton (New York: Harper and Row, 1964).

[43] Charles Taylor, "What's Wrong with Negative Liberty?" in *The Idea of Freedom: Essays in Honor of Isaiah Berlin*, edited by Alan Ryan (New York: Oxford University Press, 1979).

attention to internal barriers to liberty, the possibility of conflicting desires within an individual self, and even the notion of second guessing that Berlin despises all tie to an idea that most feminists today take for granted: namely, the idea that many of our desires and preferences are socially constructed and that we often need the help of others to see how that has happened. The desires and preferences we have as well as the choices we make must be understood in and seen as coming out of the particular society, culture, and time in which we live as well as out of the specific locations of gender, sexuality, race, and class that we occupy within those contexts. Women's choices—as well as their ability to make the choices and pursue their preferences—all need to be understood within these contexts that shape options, and even shape desires themselves. These social contexts determine which barriers or obstacles we will face, and which enabling structures and supports we may have at our disposal. In other words, these social contexts provide the conditions for both negative and positive freedom.

But because those contexts are importantly shaped by patriarchy, sexism, racism, classism, and heterosexism, social construction is not simply innocent or neutral: as feminist theorists have shown, cultural norms and social practices can produce desires within women that arbitrarily limit their abilities to engage in the world. Women may appear to be "free" in negative liberty terms, but our own desires may restrict us. Social constructivism thus presents a paradox, for the very social structures that limit women are the same structures that produce us and our abilities to choose. Feminists want to be able to claim that some contexts produce greater freedom for women than others; but social construction turns that desire back on itself, because the framework for evaluating contexts, and the values that inform our judgments, are themselves constructed by and through a patriarchal context. So how can feminists judge which choices are "better" or "worse" for women?

A feminist theory of freedom needs aspects of both positive and negative liberty to analyze this paradox of the choosing subject. Indeed, from a feminist perspective, the opposition between negative and positive liberty is mistaken. For key to social constructivism is the idea that what is "inside" the self (i.e., desire, preference, will) is to a significant degree produced by what is "outside" the self (i.e., social relations, including institutions, customs, practices, and laws). Indeed, language, the essential tool for thinking about who I am and what I want, operates at this very juncture of inner and outer, for it comes to me from others. It is received: I do not invent it but learn it as a way to communicate with others who already have it. Yet I process it through and incorporate it into my conscious and unconscious mind to form and express my desires, will, and identity. This interaction of inner and outer realms, and of positive and negative liberty, extends through the history of modern political thought.[44]

---

[44] I document this at considerable length in the theories of Hobbes, Locke, Rousseau, Kant, and Mill in Hirschmann, *Gender, Class and Freedom*.

But it is my view that, just because the inner self, "the individual," is socially constructed does not mean that it is not real.[45] And fundamental to the very concept of "the individual" is that she is able to exercise choice: she is able to make choices that affect, shape, and direct her own life. This is the essential value that the Enlightenment bequeathed to us, a value that has been vitally important to feminists throughout history.

Rather than proving the superiority of negative liberty over positive, however, recognizing the value of individual choice leads us to the need to consider the two conceptions together. Both positive and negative liberty share the notion that choice is central to freedom: both conceptions of liberty have at their heart the ability of the self to make choices and act on them. The contested terrain between them generally covers differences about what constitutes the process and activity of choosing and what constitutes the product or an "actual" choice. For both models, choice is constituted by a complex relationship between so-called internal factors of will and desire—the preferences one has, which of the available options one prefers, and how one chooses among them—and factors "outside" the self that may inhibit, enable, or enhance one's ability to pursue one's preferences, including the kind and number of choices available, the obstacles to making the choice one prefers, and the variable power that different people have to make choices.

The terms internal and outside, however, point out that implicit in these debates is the more fundamental question of what or who the self is that makes these choices—a question particularly relevant to relational autonomy. The social constructivist thesis posits that what is internal to the self, such as desire, is socially produced through culture, practice, law, custom, history, and language—all ostensibly external to the individual. Yet those very cultures, practices, laws, customs, history, and language are themselves produced by individuals who participate in them every day. Social constructivism challenges the duality of inner and outer, and I believe that this challenge is illustrated in the concept of freedom. Social construction shows that a feminist conception of freedom is as relational as autonomy is.

Yet this understanding of freedom that feminist social constructivism yields us allows more space for the individual and for the indefinable, undetectable (to others), and perhaps even incommunicable aspects of human existence than do many versions of relational autonomy. Feminist freedom does not require an essential core self, but it does require an *identifiable* self who is

---

[45] Nancy J. Hirschmann, "Feminist Standpoint as Postmodern Strategy," in *The Feminist Standpoint Theory Reader*, edited by Sandra Harding (New York: Routledge, 2003); Hirschmann, *Subject of Liberty*, chap. 3. See also Judith Butler, *Bodies that Matter: On the Discursive Limits of "Sex"* (New York: Routledge, 1994) for a critique of "linguistic monism" and the possibilities of "the real" coming out of social constructivism.

the final arbiter of her own choices.[46] That is, even if my desires are ultimately opaque to myself, in that I cannot truly know where they came from or why I have them, it is important for me to be able to identify them as "mine" and there is value in my being able to assert and pursue them. In keeping with negative liberty, a feminist theory of freedom demands that the individual self must make her own choices. Yet that self, its status and content, is continually in doubt and requires context and relationship with others to provide and sustain its meaning. The relational aspects of freedom mean that others may see me, or at least think they do, better than I see myself, much like positive liberty. And this in turn means that my freedom may in part depend on their engagement with my understanding of my own desires.

Understanding the relationality of freedom requires a subtle distinction. Specifically, granting that positive liberty's second guessing must be rejected by a feminist conception of freedom as antithetical to women's agency and self-determination does not mean that the interrogation of desire—which is what often *leads to* second guessing—should itself be avoided. On the contrary, it is vitally important to freedom that critical questioning about desire, about who we are and what we want, be engaged. The issue is where we draw the line between asking questions and providing answers. Autonomy theorists, like positive liberty theorists, may often provide external standards for what answers are legitimately autonomous.[47] Feminist freedom holds that others can, and indeed should, ask me questions. However, only I can come up with the answers; nobody else can answer those questions for me. Indeed, freedom does not even require that I come up with any reasoned answers at all; I can say "I don't really know, I just want to do it" and still be free, even if doing so fails the autonomy test. If you don't like or disagree with my answers—as a shelter worker might when a battered woman decides to return to her abuser—you can only persist in asking more questions, which I may refuse to answer.[48] Feminist freedom requires relationship, much as autonomy does, but

---

[46] Admittedly, my assertion may point to a disciplinary fracture in the concept of autonomy, pertaining to the methodologies and modes of inquiry that we engage in as philosophers; as an internationally known colleague in an English department said in response to a draft of this paper, "in my field, the subject who is opaque to herself is simply a given, we don't even argue about that anymore." By contrast, philosophers—as well as many political theorists, including myself—do not wish to give over entirely to the claim of opacity. Many of us still believe that the point of philosophy is to clarify our understanding of ourselves. But the social construction thesis requires us to acknowledge that the project of knowing ourselves, not to mention knowing others, is ongoing, in process, always partial, and never complete.

[47] Procedural autonomy theorists suggest that autonomy is measured not by the outcome of a decision but rather by the procedures that the decision maker follows. However, these theorists, too, must indicate the standards that the decision maker must meet. See Diana T. Meyers, *Self, Society, and Personal Choice* (New York: Columbia University Press, 1989); Gerald Dworkin, *The Theory and Practice of Autonomy* (New York: Cambridge University Press, 1988).

[48] I discuss this theory in relation to domestic violence at greater length in *The Subject of Liberty*, chap. 4.

the obligations of critical engagement lie on others, not on the self, for the self must be free to reject such engagement at all times.

Such rejection does not mean that I have somehow placed myself outside of the processes of social construction, of course, like the abstract individual often associated with negative liberty. As Foucault suggests in one of his last interviews, freedom is not simply resistance or liberation. Nor is freedom a quality one possesses or a condition that one could attain by meeting preset criteria. Rather, freedom is a mode of activity in which people participate by partaking in practices that create the self. That self is both passive and active; we are produced through social formations over which we have little control, yet we act upon these formations in daily and ongoing processes through specific actions. Such actions involve individuals—in some ways intentionally, directly, consciously, in some ways not—in the creation of who they are. Central to the "practices of freedom" is the "exercise of self upon self by which one tries...to transform one's self and to attain a certain mode of being."[49] But this "care for the self...implies also a relationship to the other...in order to really care for self, one must listen to the teachings of a master. One needs a guide, a counselor, a friend—someone who will tell you the truth."[50] Given that Foucault is most well known for his rejection of the idea of truth,[51] not to mention his attention to the ways relations of power can produce oppression,[52] this claim may sound odd, but I believe he means only critical observation. The "counselor" is to ask hard questions that challenge the answers we have come up with for ourselves in defining the self. The point of this questioning is to engage the process of social construction, to entangle oneself in the messy paradox of desires that are constituted and produced through social formations, out of which one often needs someone to help pull one out in order to understand and express the self.

4. What Does Freedom Add?

I suggested earlier in this paper that relational autonomy should be considered in tandem with freedom. If feminist freedom is relational, however, requiring others to help produce and articulate the self and its desires, how does this differ from relational autonomy and what does it add?

---

[49] Raùl Fornet-Betancourt, Helmut Becker, and Alfredo Gomez-Müller, "The Ethic of Care for the Self as a Practice of Freedom: An Interview with Michel Foucault on January 20, 1984," translated by J. D. Gauthier, *Philosophy and Social Criticism* 12:2–3 (1987): 124, 123, 114.

[50] Fornet-Betancourt et al., "Ethic of Care," 118.

[51] See, e.g., Michel Foucault, "Two Lectures," in *Power/Knowledge: Selected Interviews and Other Writings, 1972–1977*, edited by Colin Gordon (New York: Pantheon Books, 1980).

[52] Michel Foucault, *Discipline and Punish: The Birth of the Prison*, translated by Alan Sheridan (New York: Vintage, 1979).

The first thing my account of freedom adds is the relationship of the passive subject to the active subject, both of which Foucault insists on. Autonomy primarily involves an active subject; as Raz says, autonomy is "a kind of achievement."[53] Relational autonomy theorists suggest that autonomy requires "some kind of conscious work," as Nedelsky argues. Friedman defines autonomy as "acting and living according to one's own choices, values, and identity within the constraints of what one regards as morally permissible."[54] Autonomy particularly involves "reflective judgment," "the critical evaluation of desires," "self-discovery, self-definition, and self-direction," "living life from the inside."[55] Meyers puts it best: "Since one must exercise control over one's life to be autonomous, autonomy is something that a person accomplishes, not something that happens to persons."[56] All of these ideas cohere with the "active self."

But a key feature of freedom is that it involves a combination of what individuals do and what happens *to* them: both the active and the passive. As Foucault notes, even if "the subject constitutes himself in an active fashion, by the practices of self, these practices are nevertheless not something that the individual invents by himself. They are patterns that he finds in his culture and which are proposed, suggested and imposed on him by his culture, his society and his social group."[57] As I read Foucault, because we are situated in such "patterns" that preexist us, what is relevant to understanding freedom is not simply the act of making choices within these patterns but rather the degree to which a choosing subject has the capacity to participate in the creation of the options from which she must choose. This is essential for feminism, because the choices that women make every day are constituted—to varying but always important degrees—by and through patriarchal social relations that define even the terms of relationships between women. The paradox of relational autonomy is that autonomy is defined by relationships that are created and shaped by patriarchy—which has women's nonautonomous status as one of its foundations. According to social constructivism, women cannot "just say no" to patriarchy and form "new" relationships because the "new" is constituted by and through the "old."[58] Instead, women need to be able to participate in the

---

[53] Joseph Raz, *The Morality of Freedom* (Oxford: Clarendon Press, 1986), 204.

[54] Jennifer Nedelsky, *Law's Relations: A Relational Theory of Self, Autonomy, and Law* (New York: Oxford University Press, 62); Marilyn Friedman, "Autonomy, Social Disruption, and Women," in *Relational Autonomy: Feminist Perspectives on Autonomy, Agency, and the Social Self*, edited by Catriona Mackenzie and Natalie Stoljar (New York: Oxford University Press, 2000), 37.

[55] Robert Young, *Personal Autonomy: Beyond Positive and Negative Liberty* (New York: St. Martin's Press, 1986), 42; John Christman, "Introduction," in *The Inner Citadel: Essays on Individual Autonomy*, edited by John Christman (New York: Oxford University Press, 1989), 10; Emily R. Gill, *Becoming Free: Autonomy and Diversity in the Liberal Polity* (Lawrence: University Press of Kansas, 2001), 29.

[56] Meyers, *Self, Society, and Personal Choice*, 96.

[57] Foucault, "Ethic of Care," 122.

[58] See, e.g., The Milan Women's Bookstore Collective, *Sexual Difference: A Theory of Social-Symbolic Practice*, translated by Patricia Cicogna and Teresa de Lauretis (Bloomington: Indiana University Press, 1990). I discuss this work at greater length in *The Subject of Liberty*, chap. 7.

social formations that structure, both actively and passively, the framework within which relationships are formed and exist, options are made available, and desire is formed. They need to participate in the processes of social construction that produce their freedom and restraint.

A second contribution that freedom can make to relational autonomy involves a shift in the dynamics of relationship. That is, in my previous account I said that freedom requires engagement with others and critical questioning, which might seem to be identical to the requirements of autonomy. Autonomy theorists, including many relational autonomy theorists, stress the importance of the subject's ability to articulate reasons for choice: Dworkin defines autonomy as a "capacity...to reflect critically upon...preferences, desires, wishes," an idea Raz echoes.[59] And many of the passages I cited to demonstrate the role of the "active" subject in autonomy theory also involved critical thinking and reflective judgment. Moreover, relational autonomy theorists maintain that such judgment cannot be an isolated activity. Nedelsky, for instance, maintains that although "one can exercise freedom simply by choosing," choosing "autonomously" requires the exercise of "judgment." But judgment emerges out of relations of dependency: "We are dependent on others for the social world that enables us to develop all of our core capacities," including "reason" and "judgment."[60] We must critically engage and interrogate our own desires within a context of relationship because relationship does not merely make it possible to exercise those capacities: it is also *part of* those capacities.

By contrast, note that my formulation requires *others* to ask questions, not the self. Questioning by others operates from a position outside my particular context and therefore potentially challenges the assumptions and givenness that experience has produced in my self. It is such challenges that open up possibilities for my thinking and choosing differently. At the same time, however, because I am the one who has the experience, I must be the filter and arbiter of such questions, challenges, and information, even to the point of deciding to reject them. Also, I must be the one to come up with the answers, no matter how imperfect or imperfectly formulated they might be. Autonomy theorists might agree with that. However, where a theory of freedom diverges is that, as I said earlier, I do not have to answer others' questions at all: I can simply say "this is what I want," I do not need to engage in the kind of critical self-reflection that autonomy usually requires. Nedelsky suggests that what this means is that "people can 'choose' to use their freedom in a weakly autonomous manner,"[61] but I think that even that is too strong. The value judgment

---

[59] Dworkin, *Theory and Practice of Autonomy*, 20; Raz, *Morality of Freedom*, 204.

[60] Jennifer Nedelsky, "Reconceiving Autonomy: Sources, Thoughts and Possibilities," *Yale Journal of Law and Feminism* 1:1 (1989): 24; Nedelsky, *Law's Relations*, 62, 28.

[61] Nedelsky indeed says this explicitly in response to a similar point I made in *Subject of Liberty*; see *Law's Relations*, 61.

that that imposes on my freedom, it seems to me, echoes the paradox of positive liberty's forcing you to be free. The choices that we make are not necessarily self-conscious, objectively rational, or even well thought out, but to deny or devalue the role and power that individuals have to make choices and that help constitute the self is equally mistaken. Freedom must lie in the self's ability to make choices and act on them, regardless of what others—including philosophers—think of those choices.

This leads to the third, and perhaps most important, contribution that thinking of freedom in tandem with relational autonomy can make: namely, helping us rethink the role of the self. Because a feminist theory of freedom requires us to hang on to negative liberty and not just positive liberty, it reminds us of the value of the liberal individual. Relational autonomy theory is built on a rejection of the classical model of the isolated self thought to sit at the heart of traditional autonomy theory from Kant onward. The rejection of the idea of a true or strong core self may have been gradual among some relational autonomy theorists (who nevertheless argued for a different, relational way of understanding that core),[62] but the relational self that others promote seeks to reject altogether the liberal, atomistic self. Nedelsky, for instance, spends much of her excellent book *Law's Relations* struggling with the idea of the self at the heart of relational autonomy. She explicitly targets liberalism as the model that she wishes to reject.[63] Although she claims to acknowledge human difference, self-creation, and individual choice, she spends much of the book arguing for a conception of relationality that is so all-encompassing, and so deep, as to allow very little room for individuality.[64] Indeed, she says that well-known communitarian Alistair MacIntyre "*understates* the nature of our dependence and interdependence" claiming that relationships are *part of* autonomy, rather than simply providing the *condition* for autonomy.[65] Indeed, she draws on object relations theory explicitly, particularly Jessica Benjamin and to a lesser degree Chodorow and Evelyn Fox Keller, to shore up her critique of the idea of "autonomy as control" that is associated with the male model of reactive autonomy.[66] Moreover, in a section titled "Understanding and Overcoming Pathology," she says "the most promising model, symbol, or

---

[62] In *Self, Society, and Personal Choice*, e.g., Diana Meyers said not only that one must be able to offer reasons but also that what guides those reasons must be "firm goals or moral views" rather than "feelings, intuitions, and arguments of the moment," for autonomy "expresses the true self" a view that she no longer shares according to her essay in the present volume. See also Diana T. Meyers, "Personal Autonomy and Feminine Socialization," *Journal of Philosophy* 84:11 (1987): 619.

[63] Nedelsky, *Law's Relations*, esp. chap. 3.

[64] In this, although I agree with much of Marilyn Friedman's critique of Nedelsky in the present volume, I disagree that Nedelsky is sympathetic to some aspects of liberalism. Rather, Nedelsky seeks to claim some concepts that liberalism first gave us, such as equality, to transform them for her own project.

[65] Nedelsky, *Law's Relations*, 28 (emphasis added), 41.

[66] Nedelsky, *Law's Relations*, 296–298, 48.

metaphor for autonomy is... child rearing" and identifies liberal individualism as the pathology in question.[67]

Yet in a curious moment, she approvingly quotes Richard Flathman, one of the strongest contemporary advocates of liberal individualism this side of Robert Nozick, regarding individual creativity as coming from a space beyond relationship.[68] I say this not to disparage Nedelsky's book as incoherent but as a testimony to the book's complexity and the intractability of the subject matter. However, this last invocation of one of my own mentors crystalized some of my dissatisfaction with her argument, and my anxiety about relational autonomy more generally, which attention to freedom can help address, namely, that the liberal self needs to be recuperated. Decades of scholarship refining our readings of canonical Enlightenment thinking have shown that "abstract individualism" is not an accurate representation of the canonical texts.[69] The liberal self may be exaggerated, an exaggeration made possible in part by the oppression of women in the private sphere but it is nonetheless vital to the feminist project.[70]

What a feminist perspective on freedom suggests is that the liberal individual could be treated as a metaphor for the dimensions of human life that make social relations less important. That is, rather than taking the liberal individual as a literal ideal for us to emulate, we should take it as a theoretical signpost and reminder that autonomy needs to be formulated not just in relationship with others but also *against* others. Taking it as a metaphor is made possible by the fact that freedom tolerates a less well-defined self than

---

[67] Nedelsky, *Law's Relations*, 124.

[68] Nedelsky, *Law's Relations*, 62. Since the days when Flathman advised my doctoral dissertation, he has been in strong disagreement with feminist arguments for relationality. See particularly Richard Flathman, *The Philosophy and Politics of Freedom* (Chicago: University of Chicago Press, 1984), where he endorses a strongly individualist conception of negative liberty as the only philosophically and politically coherent conception; *Reflections of a Would-Be Anarchist* (Minneapolis: University of Minnesota Press, 1998), which, to quote the publisher, "warns of the individualism-limiting potential of even liberal efforts to promote social justice"; *Thomas Hobbes: Skepticism, Individuality, and Chastened Politics* (Lanham, MD: Rowman and Littlefield, 2002), where he holds up Hobbesian individualism as a model for contemporary political theorists to follow. He thus opposes almost everything Nedelsky's book argues for.

[69] See, e.g., Quentin Skinner, *Hobbes and Republican Liberty* (New York: Cambridge University Press, 2008); John Dunn, *The Political Thought of John Locke: An Historical Account of the Argument of the "Two Treatises of Government"* (New York: Cambridge University Press, 1983); Gordon Schochet, *The Authoritarian Family and Political Attitudes in Seventeenth Century England: Patriarchicalism in Political Thought* (New Brunswick, NJ: Transaction, 1988); Joanne H. Wright and Nancy J. Hirschmann, "Introduction: The Many Faces of 'Mr. Hobs,'" in *Feminist Interpretations of Thomas Hobbes*, edited by Nancy J. Hirschmann and Joanne Wright (University Park: Pennsylvania State University Press, 2013).

[70] In *Rethinking Obligation*, I linked the liberal subject of social contract theory to the male model of object relations theory. I still believe my analysis of the masculinism of the "natural self" in obligation theory is correct, because contemporary theories deploy an abstract model that the historical theories did not. However, I also believe that I should have attended to the greater subtleties of relationship in those canonical theories, a failure I believe I addressed in *Gender, Class and Freedom*.

autonomy requires. In keeping with the idea that it is important to view the passive self in conjunction with the active self and that freedom is a function not just of what the subject does but what happens to the subject, the self necessary to freedom theory is more fluid and porous. Yet it is decidedly present.

Granting that nothing escapes social relations, a feminist theory of freedom reminds us that some things at the least make relations beside the point. If everything and everyone is always already socially constructed, if there is no way *not* to be socially constructed, there is no way to exist outside social relations, outside social contexts, outside language. We can grant that. But then relationality becomes so expanded as to make it almost meaningless: even reactive autonomy is relational because it entails a reaction against the mother.

In other words, if we take the concept of relationality and social construction to its logical end, we are led to an impasse, and autonomy itself starts to look incoherent. This is not a problem I attribute to any of the arguments in the present volume as much as it is a conceptual problem that exceeds the grasp of all of us. Autonomy is fundamentally about capabilities—as several papers in the present volume suggest—specifically the ability to assess one's choices, to reflect critically about them, and to make choices that allow one to exert some control over one's life. Thus, there must be a self. But if we are always and already socially constructed, then how can autonomy actually exist? What purpose does the notion of "self rule" really serve if the "self" is always already constructed and produced through complex webs of relationships, which were in turn constructed by other social relations, "all the way down"? Indeed, how can there be a "self" necessary to the idea of "self rule?" We always insist that the self exists, yet that acknowledgment is a challenge for the logic of relationality. Our alternative, to reject social construction, can return us only to the naturalism of social contract theory that gave birth to the liberal individual.

Treating that liberal individual as a metaphor, however, can help us recognize that this deep embeddedness in relationship that social construction gives us does not forestall self-definition and acting for the self by acting against context. Returning to where I began this paper, my anxiety about relational autonomy is that relationship is not only complex, as many relational autonomy theorists note, but also is as problematic for autonomy as it is helpful. Surely, can some relationships be harmful, as many relational autonomy feminists acknowledge. However, even the "good" relationships—like that between mother and daughter in object relations theory—can harm us, by hiding the ways in which oppressive power relations of patriarchy are replicated and reinforced in our daily interactions.

By calling for a recuperation of the liberal self as a metaphor, I am in a sense suggesting that feminist autonomy theorists should reassess the importance and value of reactive autonomy. What reactive autonomy can contribute is the recognition that autonomy importantly must develop *against* others and against prevailing norms and customs, such as Hirsi Ali discussed in Marina

Oshana's essay for this volume. I agree with Oshana and Friedman that it may be time for the liberal self to be recuperated, though, I would argue, recuperated within a context of freedom, specifically "relational freedom."[71]

5. Conclusion: Recuperating the Liberal Self

Perhaps ironically, I find a model for what I am suggesting in John Stuart Mill, with whom I opened my discussion of freedom. Often seen as the icon of classical liberalism and of negative liberty—not to mention a problematic feminist[72]—Mill actually deployed both negative and positive liberty elements as well as the idea of social construction in his theory. In the chapter "Of Liberty and Necessity" in his *System of Logic* Mill agrees with determinists that a person's character determines his desires and causes him to act on his preferences: "given...the character and disposition of the individual, the manner in which he will act might be unerringly inferred."[73] In turn, an individual's "character is formed by his circumstances:" by the experiences he has, how he was brought up, the kind of influences and education he was exposed to, and so forth. In true social constructivist fashion, Mill says that we cannot stand outside of ourselves to create ourselves ab initio, because we are who we are through the social conditions, institutions, practices, relationships, language, and frameworks in which we come to be.

However, this does not foreclose the power of self-creation or free action. That a person's character is "formed for him, is not inconsistent with its being, in part, formed *by* him as one of the intermediate agents." That is, "he has, to a certain extent, a power to alter his character." He does this by changing his circumstances: "We, when our habits are not too inveterate, can, by similarly willing the requisite means, make ourselves different. If [others] could place us under the influence of certain circumstances, we, in like manner, can place ourselves under other circumstances. We are exactly as capable of making our own character, *if we will*, as others are of making it for us."[74] When the

---

[71] I think it is significant that Oshana draws on Nussbaum's capability approach, which is a theory of *freedom*, to develop her own theory of *autonomy*. This is a point that would require another paper, but I offer the provocative suggestion that a number of the essays in this volume are writing about freedom rather than autonomy or at least are developing a theory of autonomy that tacitly depends on the understanding of freedom that I am articulating here.

[72] See Nancy J. Hirschmann, "Mill, Political Economy, and Women's Work," *American Political Science Review* 102:2 (May 2008): 199–213, on Mill's ambiguity over married women's participation in paid labor that, for all but women of property, was essential to their independence and equality.

[73] John Stuart Mill, *A System of Logic Ratiocinative and Inductive, Being a Connected View of the Principles of Evidence and the Methods of Scientific Investigation* (Books IV–VI), in *The Collected Works of John Stuart Mill*, edited by J. M. Robson, vol. 8 (Toronto: University of Toronto Press, 1974), 836–837.

[74] Mill, *System of Logic*, 840.

determinist asks where the desire to change our character comes from, Mill responds that the desire to alter our character, and thereby our circumstances, comes from the "experience of the painful consequences of the character we previously had; or by some strong feeling of admiration or aspiration, accidentally aroused."[75] In other words, experience is not only backward-looking, to consider how we got to be the way we are, but also forward-looking, to possibilities of what we could be.

Despite his strong social constructivism, then, his argument also invokes a strong sense of self that produces its own construction: the self-made man that Friedman discusses in this volume becomes literally self-made, in that he (to continue the metaphor) engages in the construction of his self. What Mill gives us, I think, is a sense of how freedom depends on a notion of the self that, although deeply constructed and socially related, is nevertheless independent, capable of rejecting specific relationships, and capable of forging the self in and through new contexts. The passive subject, who is formed by his context, can act to change that context.

When one is considering the kind of wide-ranging "circumstances" that feminists confront, however—patriarchy, including the heterosexism, classism, and racism that it is in part built on—this task becomes proportionately more difficult. But that is why feminism is so vital to freedom and autonomy: if we are socially constructed by our contexts, and if those contexts are oppressive to women, then the only way for women to achieve freedom is by participating in the processes of social construction to change that context to produce new meanings and possibilities. Greater participation in the processes of social construction allow greater freedom not for self-imagining per se but for group imagining within which individuals can define and construct themselves. Without the discursive categories defining the larger context, the individual has no vocabulary with which to imagine the self. But changing those categories, and the struggle to change the context of patriarchy, is beyond the grasp of any given individual; it is multigenerational and ongoing.

In a sense, of course, this notion of relational freedom can be taken to suggest that autonomy is a fiction after all, as some postmodern theorists assert. But I believe that the picture of relational freedom I have put forth supports relational autonomy by recognizing that, insofar as we are produced by relationships, we can participate in those relationships in ways that are shaped by our feminist beliefs—beliefs that have come from relationships both positively and supportively and negatively and reactively. That is, relational freedom can help us see that we need not just relational autonomy; we may also need a little reactive autonomy as well to achieve the sense of individual selfhood that many autonomy theorists desire.

---

[75] Mill, *System of Logic*, 841.

Acknowledgments

Thanks to the editors of this volume, the other contributors who participated in the Montreal conference related to this volume, and participants in the Gender, Sexuality, and Women's Studies Faculty Works-in-Progress workshop at the University of Pennsylvania for their comments and suggestions, particularly Sally Scholz and Heather Love.

{ PART II }

Autonomy and Normative Commitments

{5}

Feminist Commitments and Relational Autonomy
Paul Benson

One of the notable features of Catriona Mackenzie and Natalie Stoljar's influential volume *Relational Autonomy*[1] was the contributors' clear commitment to investigate personal autonomy from explicitly feminist perspectives. Mackenzie and Stoljar announced this commitment on the opening pages of the volume, asserting that the collection's aim was to challenge feminist theorists' suspicion of the ideal of personal autonomy and to affirm that "the notion of autonomy is vital to feminist attempts to understand oppression, subjection, and agency."[2] Mackenzie and Stoljar employed the term *relational autonomy* as a "refiguring" of the concept of personal autonomy in the wake of feminist concerns about the concept's allegedly masculinist, individualist, and rationalist baggage.[3] In particular, they saw feminists' attention to "the intersubjective and social dimensions of selfhood and identity" as offering fruitful standpoints from which refiguration of individual autonomy could proceed.[4]

Thus, the dual aims of the broad set of projects to construct relational conceptions of autonomy were, at the start, (1) to craft theories of personal autonomy that could do the work that feminist ethical and social theories need from accounts of autonomy without succumbing to the pitfalls that seem to lurk in many contemporary accounts of autonomy and, thereby, (2) to make important, new contributions to the philosophical literature on autonomy, a literature that had undergone significant resurgence in the wake of Harry Frankfurt's and Gerald Dworkin's groundbreaking scholarship in the 1970s and 1980s. This latter aim of bringing feminist investigation of autonomy into active dialogue with so-called mainstream theorizing about autonomy was especially noteworthy and has been particularly fruitful.

---

[1] Catriona Mackenzie and Natalie Stoljar, eds., *Relational Autonomy: Feminist Perspectives on Autonomy, Agency, and the Social Self* (New York: Oxford University Press, 2000).

[2] Mackenzie and Stoljar, *Relational Autonomy*, 3.

[3] Mackenzie and Stoljar, *Relational Autonomy*, 3–4. Mackenzie and Stoljar attribute the first such feminist articulation of relational autonomy to Jennifer Nedelsky, "Reconceiving Autonomy: Sources, Thoughts and Possibilities," *Yale Journal of Law and Feminism* 1 (1989): 7–36.

[4] Mackenzie and Stoljar, *Relational Autonomy*, 4.

My purpose in this chapter is to examine more carefully the relationship between some of the accounts of autonomy that have been proposed since Mackenzie and Stoljar's volume and the feminist normative commitments that have shaped those accounts. One of the interesting developments in the literature on relational autonomy over the past decade has been the emergence of what appear to be increasingly sharp and unbridgeable boundaries among different conceptions of autonomy and their respective evaluative commitments. As conceptions of autonomy influenced by feminist commitment have flourished, we have seen at the same time that more disputes have opened up about the relational and normative dimensions of autonomy and that the grounds for disagreement among competing accounts seem to be hardening.

This is hardly a surprising development in philosophy, of course. Yet many of us would have supposed at the time of *Relational Autonomy*'s publication that the sharing of some fundamental feminist convictions about the nature of women's subordination and the constriction of women's agency in patriarchal modern societies, as well as about the character of the harms sustained through such domination, would go a long way toward overcoming philosophical disagreement about the constituents of personal autonomy. The bearings afforded by feminist moral and political solidarity, it was hoped, would make for deeper and more ready agreement on the ways previous accounts of autonomy should be refigured. One sign of such hope was Natalie Stoljar's appeal to "the feminist intuition" regarding the poisonous relationship between the influence of oppressive social norms of femininity and the autonomy of women so influenced.[5] Stoljar's important paper implied that widespread feminist critiques of norms of femininity could afford a philosophically powerful platform on the basis of which prevalent procedural, or content-neutral, accounts of autonomy could be found wanting. In other words, it appeared that familiar and widely shared feminist convictions could, in a straightforward manner, be put in the service of establishing a more adequate understanding of personal autonomy—and that the emerging understanding would involve intrinsically relational constituents.

Yet progress among feminist philosophers working to develop and refine relational accounts of autonomy has not been so straightforward. Numerous distinct camps have emerged, and the lines of argument that separate them appear, if anything, to be solidifying, making it increasingly less likely that strong substantive accounts of relational autonomy, such as Stoljar's or Marina Oshana's, or largely procedural, value-neutral accounts, such as Marilyn Friedman's or John Christman's (constitutively) nonrelational theories or Andrea Westlund's relational (and value-neutral) conception, will eventually

---

[5] Natalie Stoljar, "Autonomy and the Feminist Intuition," in Mackenzie and Stoljar, *Relational Autonomy*, 94–111.

be able to present arguments that hold sway decisively among most feminist theorists of autonomy. The ensuing discussion seeks to diagnose this polemical situation by drawing critical attention to some of the appeals to feminist normative commitments that various influential theories of autonomy have made recently. The diagnoses proposed here will suggest that some of the primary disagreements concerning relational accounts of personal autonomy can be understood and addressed effectively by considering how a conception of personal autonomy can best advance feminist ethical, social, and political commitments. Future progress in work on relational autonomy, I shall suggest, will depend in large measure on greater attention to what feminists really need a conception of personal autonomy to do in relation to the normative social purposes of confronting and overcoming women's subordination.

Our discussion will begin by analyzing the ways Marina Oshana and Natalie Stoljar, respectively, invoke feminist normative commitments to construct their particular accounts of autonomy's constitutively relational character. I then examine Marilyn Friedman's and John Christman's respective appeals to certain feminist principles of social and political inclusion to support their nonrelational theories of autonomy. While Friedman and Christman both appreciate ways in which social relations influence persons' capabilities for autonomous agency, neither accepts, as do Oshana and Stoljar, that certain kinds of interpersonal or social relation are conceptually requisite components of personal autonomy. Consideration of the difficulties that arise with the ways these four theorists envisage personal autonomy to function within feminist social theory leads me to contend that a conception of personal autonomy may best serve feminist commitments by integrating considerations of autonomous agents' *voices*, which nonrelational theories characteristically highlight, with considerations of the sort of agential *authority* that distinguishes autonomy, which relational theories characteristically highlight. I use this contention to propose that conceptions of autonomy that focus on autonomous agents' authority to speak or answer to others for their choices and actions afford a preferred way to understand autonomy's relational character. Such conceptions may take a value-laden form (as I have argued elsewhere), or they may offer purely formal conditions of autonomy (as Andrea Westlund has argued).[6]

I conclude by surveying some of the primary lessons that this approach affords about the role that personal autonomy should serve within accounts of social and political life informed by feminist commitments. As will become clear, this paper does not aim to present a detailed account of the necessary and sufficient conditions of autonomous action.

---

[6] As explained in Section 5, this chapter does not seek to resolve the debate between substantive and formal, or content-neutral, theories of autonomy.

1. Autonomy and Social-Relational Power and Authority

I begin diagnosing the relationship between relational theories of autonomy and feminist commitments by considering Marina Oshana's important efforts to develop a substantive, "social-relational" theory of personal autonomy.[7] Oshana's theory offers a useful starting point, as she is more explicit than are many autonomy theorists about the relationship of her understanding of personal autonomy to wider normative commitments in social and political theory. Oshana's work regularly appeals to core intuitions she has about the kinds of power and authority that personal autonomy demands. First, "autonomous persons are beings in *actual* control of their own choices, actions, and goals.... The person is in possession of the *de facto* power to govern herself. Here we find the familiar idea that a self-determining person faces minimal interference in her actions and choices.... The autonomous individual is not forced to do the will of another."[8] Second, Oshana continues, "autonomous persons are in a kind of *authoritative* control of their own choices, actions, and goals. To have authoritative control is to 'own' the management of one's choices, actions, and goals.... Having the relevant kind of authority guarantees that a person's life is free of the domination of others."[9] Elsewhere she states, "autonomy guarantees that will and action exist under the de facto authority and de jure entitlement of the agent."[10] Oshana believes that the power and authority that constitute autonomy require both procedural independence and negative liberty. But the sort of self-governance in which autonomy consists entails much more, she argues. Among other things, autonomy requires that the person is substantively independent so that she enjoys minimum social and psychological security as well as a certain level of material self-sufficiency and is empowered to pursue whatever life plan she authentically judges to be valuable.[11] According to Oshana, "an autonomous person's choices must not merely be unobstructed...but, where realistic, these choices must be socially, politically, and economically within his or her reach."[12]

---

[7] See Marina A. L. Oshana, *Personal Autonomy in Society* (Hampshire, UK: Ashgate, 2006). Oshana's important essays on autonomy include Oshana, "Personal Autonomy and Society," *Journal of Social Philosophy* 29 (1998): 81–102; "How Much Should We Value Autonomy?" *Social Philosophy and Policy* 20 (2003): 99–126; "Moral Accountability," *Philosophical Topics* 32 (2004): 255–274; "Autonomy and Self-Identity," in *Autonomy and the Challenges to Liberalism: New Essays*, edited by John Christman and Joel Anderson (Cambridge: Cambridge University Press, 2005), 77–97; "Autonomy and Free Agency," in *Personal Autonomy: New Essays on Personal Autonomy and Its Role in Contemporary Moral Philosophy*, edited by James Stacey Taylor (Cambridge: Cambridge University Press, 2005), 183–204.
[8] Oshana, *Personal Autonomy in Society*, 3.
[9] Oshana, *Personal Autonomy in Society*, 4.
[10] Oshana, "Autonomy and Free Agency," 196.
[11] Oshana, *Personal Autonomy in Society*, 86–87.
[12] Oshana, "How Much Should We Value Autonomy?" 104.

These broad claims about the social and psychological conditions required for personal autonomy are reflected in Oshana's judgments about various case studies in which autonomy may appear to be under threat. Oshana surveys a range of cases in which agents are subject to the domination, rule, or authority of others and, in each case, contends that the agent in such circumstances has been stripped of autonomy, regardless of how the person came to be in that state and independently of the person's reflective appraisals of her situation and its history.[13] For example, by Oshana's lights, the willing, contented slave and the reflectively subservient woman both lack autonomy to a substantial extent. Notwithstanding the alignment between the agent's life and her values or her reflective endorsement of the way she arrived in her circumstances, lives of slavery or subservience compromise self-governance by obstructing the person's powers of self-determination and rendering the person substantively dependent on others who rule major portions of their lives.[14]

In a similar vein, Oshana elsewhere presents the case of courageous Iranian women's advocate and Nobel laureate Shirin Ebadi as an illustration of why, given the subjugation of women in the postrevolution Iranian legal system, even an accomplished jurist, influential writer, and defiant women's advocate like Ebadi fundamentally lacks autonomy.[15] Although Ebadi is a vocal and highly visible proponent for the rights of women in Iranian society, Oshana regards her as being deprived of personal autonomy because the Iranian state stripped her of many of her basic political rights and unfairly deprived her of her economic and professional livelihood as an attorney and judge. Persons in Ebadi's circumstances, on Oshana's analysis, lack the social security "that is forthcoming only when others with whom a person dwells and works and interacts are dispossessed of arbitrary power over the person."[16]

Oshana's appeal to intuitions about the restriction of autonomy in cases such as these clarifies why Oshana regards autonomy as a global feature of persons, as opposed to an episodic, or local, characteristic of an agent's attitudes, values, decisions, or actions.[17] Because she believes that autonomy must guarantee persons a reasonable measure of the social, political, and economic power and authority they need to determine the course of their lives, appraisals of autonomy cannot, in her judgment, be confined narrowly to the local

---

[13] Oshana, *Personal Autonomy in Society*, 52–68. See also her discussion of earlier versions of some of these cases in Oshana, "Personal Autonomy and Society," 86–93.

[14] Oshana, *Personal Autonomy in Society*, 53–60.

[15] Oshana discussed the situation of Ebadi at a workshop on autonomy and social transformation held on March 1–2, 2012, at the University of California, Davis. In a discussion elsewhere of Rosa Parks's protest, Oshana writes, "Any person who lives in an environment she cannot challenge, change, or contribute to without the say-so of others lives in a place where impediments to self-government are present. This person lives in the shadow of others, insecure of what her steps toward self-government might incur from others." See Oshana, *Personal Autonomy in Society*, 175.

[16] Oshana, *Personal Autonomy in Society*, 87.

[17] For instance, see Oshana, *Personal Autonomy in Society*, 2–3.

circumstances of a person's actions. This feature of Oshana's theory can make it seem as if its departure from other, less demanding relational conceptions of autonomy is purely a terminological matter. If, as is the case, many other relational theories attend to the local characteristics of agency while Oshana's conception concerns only certain global features of agency, and if those global features are not reducible solely to local characteristics, then it may appear as if Oshana simply is mapping out a different concept of autonomy than what other relational theorists investigate.

This is not, however, an illuminating explanation of the disagreement about how properly to understand the autonomy of the persons sketched in Oshana's case studies. It is not enough just to say that, on some accounts of local autonomy, the reflectively subservient woman or the committed Iranian women's advocate both count as acting with a significant measure of autonomy in a number of specific circumstances, while, globally, these women suffer radically diminished autonomy because they live under the domination of other persons and practices that deprive them of far-reaching self-determination. For there seems to be a more substantive disagreement at issue, and it is not merely a disagreement about whether a local or a global concept of autonomy is primarily at stake in Oshana's case studies.[18] Rather, the disagreement concerns the role that a conception of personal autonomy should play within a normative social theory that is sufficiently robust to support resistance to women's subordination, along with other liberatory ethical and political stances.

For Oshana, it is the role of a conception of personal autonomy (among other things) to underwrite and explain what is wrong when women are systematically deprived of power and authority in patriarchal societies.[19] Oshana appears to be correct that purely procedural, psychologically constituted conditions of authenticity or reflective endorsement are not entirely sufficient to explain what is wrong when women's social, political, and economic freedoms are obstructed by systems of patriarchal domination. Yet she takes a far more controversial and, in my judgment, unwarranted step in maintaining that it falls among the proper functions of a theory of personal autonomy to afford a comprehensive explanation of such wrongs. This is a matter about which theories of relational autonomy genuinely can disagree, above and beyond the

---

[18] In her review of Oshana's *Personal Autonomy in Society*, Diana Tietjens Meyers, "Review of *Personal Autonomy in Society*," *Hypatia* 23 (2008): 202–206, makes a similar point, contending that such disagreement over Oshana's case studies "isn't merely semantic. What is at stake is the point and purview of autonomy theory.... The underlying issue here is the relation between political desiderata and personal autonomy" (205).

[19] While Oshana's theory of autonomy certainly is not motivated solely by feminist commitments, Oshana's repeated and sustained attention to the psychological and social domination of women makes it clear that explaining the wrongs involved in such domination is one central purpose of her conception of personal autonomy.

question of whether our primary notion of personal autonomy carries global or episodic scope.

I have three basic concerns about Oshana's understanding of the place that personal autonomy should take within broader social theory. First, there are other equally—if not more—attractive and justifiable ways to analyze the wrongs of the social and political domination of women than to say that those wrongs must rest on assaults on women's personal autonomy. Especially in light of the complexity and multidimensional nature of agency under circumstances of oppression, it seems more fitting theoretically not to place the primary burden of explaining what is wrong with such oppression on the concept of autonomy alone. If a conception of autonomy does not need to bear the entire weight of analyzing systems of oppression, then we would not be compelled, as Oshana appears to be, to deny that persons such as Shirin Ebadi exercise a significant degree of autonomy. In any case, Oshana has not presented arguments to establish that this must be the explanatory burden of a conception of autonomy. Her appeals to contestable intuitions about the various case studies she presents do not, by themselves, constitute such arguments.

Moreover, it strikes me as problematic to assume straightaway that appealing to a conception of autonomy is the preferred way to ground an evaluation of women's subordination when feminists themselves have done so much to uncover the suspect masculinist and excessively individualist associations of the notion of autonomy. It is true that Oshana, along with other relational theorists, is proposing that those suspect associations can be supplanted by refiguring autonomy in more socially and relationally constituted terms. But the very fact that feminists have led us to see that healthy suspicion about the place of autonomy within social theory is warranted indicates that Oshana has more work to do if she is to establish that the weight of a liberatory theory of social-relational agency must rest squarely on a conception of personal autonomy.

Third, it is problematic to link autonomy as closely as Oshana does to more just and ideal social circumstances of self-determination, for this has the consequence of making autonomy a far rarer possession or achievement than it actually is. The nature of systemic, institutionalized injustice and unfreedom in human societies is such that a large proportion of humanity will lack a significant measure of autonomy, from Oshana's perspective. I agree with Oshana that autonomy is terribly precious and more fragile than we may like to think. Yet the possibility of significantly autonomous agency is not nearly as rare as Oshana would have it. Even within the restrictions imposed upon persons' lives by unjust systems of domination, most people who lack the full social, political, and economic powers to which Oshana points still possess the resources to take ownership of many of their values, goals, choices, and actions and so exercise authority over their agency. Once more, there is a tendency to regard this type of disagreement about autonomy's normal prevalence and availability as merely terminological. I reject that assessment. It is a matter of much importance to our commitment to the value of autonomy and our prospects for achieving and sustaining autonomous agency whether we regard it as a generally accessible, adult human attainment or whether it is a rarified achievement rendered possible only within relatively idealized social and political circumstances.

2. Autonomy and Internalized Oppression

Like Oshana, Natalie Stoljar also appeals to an intuition about personal autonomy that is rooted in specific feminist social and political commitments to develop her conception of autonomy. As noted earlier, Stoljar explicitly advances the idea that an adequate conception of autonomy must serve substantive feminist convictions about the bearing that gender socialization has upon women's agency. She asserts that an acceptable theory of autonomy must conform to and be able to explain the belief she terms the *feminist intuition*, according to which women whose preferences and decisions are "motivated by oppressive and misguided norms that are internalized as a result of feminine socialization" cannot be autonomous.[20] While most of Stoljar's influential paper, "Autonomy and the Feminist Intuition," is devoted to arguing that only a strong substantive account of autonomy can properly respect the feminist intuition, examining her arguments against procedural, content-neutral conceptions and so-called weak substantive conceptions is not my main interest here.[21] Instead I want to consider whether Stoljar has given us compelling reasons to hold that any satisfactory conception of personal autonomy must sustain the social and political commitments that the feminist intuition reflects. I certainly feel the force of Stoljar's position, as I once held a view much like hers.[22] Yet I do not think that Stoljar succeeds in showing that a suitable conception of autonomy must advance certain feminist convictions in the manner she proposes.

I have two main concerns about Stoljar's understanding of the role of an account of personal autonomy within feminist social theory. First, Stoljar's position fails to afford sufficient room for the legitimate diversity of feminist convictions about how best to understand internalized feminine socialization across a wide range of social, political, economic, historical, and cultural

---

[20] Stoljar, "Autonomy and the Feminist Intuition," 95, 98.

[21] For extended discussion of those arguments, see Paul Benson, "Feminist Intuitions and the Normative Substance of Autonomy," in James Stacey Taylor, *Personal Autonomy: New Essays on Personal Autonomy and Its Role in Contemporary Moral Philosophy* (Cambridge: Cambridge University Press, 2005), 124–142.

[22] See especially Paul Benson, "Freedom and Value," *Journal of Philosophy* 84 (1987): 465–487; Benson, "Autonomy and Oppressive Socialization," *Social Theory and Practice* 17 (1991): 385–408.

circumstances. There can be strong reasons for some women to accept the influence of "stereotypical and incorrect norms of femininity"[23] even as they take genuine ownership of their decisions and actions. Such women's rejection of feminist social ideals need not be taken by those of us with feminist sensibilities as showing that their actions are not meaningfully their own. As Diana Meyers observes, conceptions of autonomy, such as Stoljar's, that embrace strong substantive conditions on what may count as autonomous agency "homogenize authentic selves and autonomous lives. The paradoxical effect of ahistorically, acontextually foreordaining what individuals can and cannot autonomously choose is to *deindividualize* autonomy."[24] Similarly, Marilyn Friedman points out the need for feminist accounts of personal autonomy to "accommodate *another* feminist intuition." Friedman observes that, even within oppressive social conditions that ought to be resisted and overcome, "traditionally subordinate feminine lives nevertheless can and do often nonslavishly embody and express values worth caring about."[25]

Admitting the appropriate diversity of autonomous responses to the influence of internalized lessons of subordination is especially important for feminist conceptions of autonomy because this diversity opens up conceptual space for autonomous criticism of and resistance to oppressive social practices and institutions from within. In other words, such space permits feminists to acknowledge the autonomous agency of those women who come to criticize traditional feminine norms even as they initially accepted the wrongs and injustices to which those norms subjected them.

A second concern about Stoljar's understanding of the role that a conception of autonomy should serve within feminist social theory emerges from the manner in which Stoljar's account seeks to do justice to the lived experience and perspectives of women who have internalized oppressive norms of femininity. On Stoljar's account, the familiar feminist dictum that we should take women's experiences seriously cannot mean that women's sense of their own agential authority must be respected. That is, for Stoljar, women's sense of their own authority should not necessarily be respected on the basis of their autonomy. For the feminist intuition entails that women who regard themselves as competent and worthy to answer for their actions can nevertheless suffer diminished autonomy if their attitudes and decisions are the products of internalized oppressive socialization that they do not see to be misguided. Hence, the social commitments that shape Stoljar's conception of autonomy would lead her to regard the significance of women's experiences as being reflected in the degree to which those experiences evidence their freedom from

---

[23] Stoljar, "Autonomy and the Feminist Intuition," 98.
[24] Diana T. Meyers, "Feminism and Women's Autonomy: The Challenge of Female Genital Cutting," *Metaphilosophy* 31 (2000): 469–491, 480.
[25] Marilyn Friedman, *Autonomy, Gender, Politics* (New York: Oxford University Press, 2003), 25.

compulsory femininity's harmful influences. But there are more natural and straightforward ways to take seriously women's experiences of their agency. We can respect their attitudes toward their status as potential answerers for their actions, even when they have been influenced by their social training to adopt unjustified or harmful attitudes about what they should do or who they should be.[26]

Not only does this way of understanding the value of women's experiences of their agency expand the sphere within which women in patriarchal societies may achieve some autonomy, but it also permits us to distinguish in an appealing way between the self-governance in which autonomous agency consists and the ability to discern the true and the good, which may be termed *orthonomy*.[27] By contrast, Stoljar's normative commitments require her to align autonomy much more closely with the ideal of right rule.[28] Autonomous agency, for Stoljar, is a concept that aims, in part, at capturing the conditions under which persons practically can escape the pervasive influence of false or unjustified social norms. As we have seen, however, this view leads to unpalatable implications, irrespective of how valuable it would be to elude the reach of oppressive socialization.

3. Autonomy and Social Commitments to Inclusion

One may be tempted to think that only proponents of explicitly substantive and constitutively relational conceptions of autonomy, such as Oshana and Stoljar, guide their theories by feminist social or political commitments in ways that give rise to difficulties for their accounts of autonomy. While it tends to be the case that substantive, relational conceptions of autonomy issue more transparently from particular sorts of feminist commitment, it is by no means the case that procedural, or content-neutral, nonrelational conceptions of autonomy emerge independently of efforts to sustain specific kinds of normative commitment. And as we have found to be true of some value-laden theories of personal autonomy, the ways content-neutral theories are informed by feminist social commitments also can suggest grounds for interrogating those theories.

While the theories I discuss in this and the following sections, those constructed by Marilyn Friedman and John Christman, respectively, reject the view that personal autonomy is relational by conceptual necessity, both Friedman and Christman recognize the profound ways social circumstances, practices, roles, and relationships shape persons' autonomous agency. Friedman reminds

---

[26] I return to and expand on this point in Section 5.
[27] Cf. Benson, "Feminist Intuitions and the Normative Substance of Autonomy," 132.
[28] See Stoljar, "Autonomy and the Feminist Intuition," 111n51.

us, for example, that autonomy "cannot emerge except out of social relationships. Although autonomy is individuating in its effects on persons, it never loses its social rootedness."[29] Friedman goes on to say, however, that "what distinguishes an autonomous self from those who are not autonomous but who are equally the products of social context is the degree of individuated distinctness and coherence that an autonomous self achieves by acting in ways that accord with her reaffirmation of certain deeper wants and commitments that characterize her in particular."[30] Christman notes more explicitly the distinction between theories of autonomy according to which social conditions are "contributory factors" and theories in which social relations are "*conceptually* necessary requirements of autonomy."[31] With Friedman, Christman accepts that "social conditions that enable us to develop and maintain the powers of authentic choice and which protect the ongoing interpersonal and social relationships that define ourselves are all part of the *background requirements* for the development of autonomy."[32] Yet he rejects "views that see social conditions as not only supportive of autonomy but [also] *definitive* of it…."[33] It is Friedman's and Christman's rejection of the latter type of position that marks their theories as nonrelational for the sake of the present discussion.

Friedman, like Oshana, initiates her examination of personal autonomy by invoking the notion of being self-determining in one's choices and actions. For Friedman, to choose or act autonomously "the self as a whole, as the particular self she is, must somehow (partly) determine what she chooses and does."[34] Friedman understands the particularity of an agent's selfhood—the agent's "differentiated distinctness"[35]—to reside in her reflective endorsement of certain of her deep and pervasive wants and values. Determination of the person's choices and actions in part by those self-reflectively affirmed attitudes then renders those choices and actions at least minimally autonomous. "Autonomous choices and actions are those that mirror wants or values that an acting person has reflectively reaffirmed and that are important to her."[36] Autonomy is a matter of degree, on Friedman's account, because (among other things) reflective endorsement of one's motives may be more or less probing and extensive. "Practically any self-reflective reaffirmation will do" for minimally autonomous action, Friedman maintains.[37] She also contends that minimal autonomy

---

[29] Friedman, *Autonomy, Gender, Politics*, 17.
[30] Friedman, *Autonomy, Gender, Politics*.
[31] John Christman, *The Politics of Persons: Individual Autonomy and Socio-historical Selves* (Cambridge: Cambridge University Press, 2009), 166.
[32] Christman, *Politics of Persons*, 184.
[33] Christma, *Politics of Persons*, 185.
[34] Friedman, *Autonomy, Gender, Politics*, 4.
[35] Friedman, *Autonomy, Gender, Politics*, 18.
[36] Friedman, *Autonomy, Gender, Politics*, 14.
[37] Friedman, *Autonomy, Gender, Politics*, 7.

requires that one have "significant alternative options"[38] from among which to choose and that one have the competency necessary to act on one's reflectively endorsed wants and values in the face of some obstacles.[39]

Friedman develops two especially important claims about substantive conceptions of autonomy, which she takes to be conceptions that require that autonomous agents choose and act to promote the value of personal autonomy itself in their own lives or, at least, not to undermine or conflict with the value of autonomy.[40] First, Friedman contends that, from the perspective of the content-neutral conception she develops, this sort of substantive autonomy comprises *more* autonomy. That is, even if we understand autonomy to be constituted by conditions of reflective endorsement of one's deep motives and values, independently of the content of those attitudes, a person counts as being more autonomous if she chooses and acts in accordance with the value of autonomy in her life. Hence, Friedman contends that some substantive conceptions of autonomy should be regarded as being continuous with content-neutral conceptions. She writes, "Substantive autonomy involves more autonomy because with it, autonomy seeking becomes a stable and enduring concern of the agent.... She tends to choose intentionally according to that ideal and so helps to secure its ongoing importance as a feature of her character."[41]

While this is a provocative claim, I do not find Friedman's reasoning for it to be sound. It is trivially true that, if one cares about affirming the place of autonomy among one's values and realizing its value through one's conduct, then autonomy has a larger role within one's motives, values, and actions than it would have otherwise. But that does not mean that acting on a central, reflectively affirmed concern for autonomy is itself necessarily more autonomous than acting on a similarly affirmed concern for some other values, including values that may conflict directly with that of personal autonomy. The degree of an agent's autonomy, according to Friedman's own content-neutral criteria, should be independent of the extent of autonomy's importance within the agent's motivational and valuational systems.

More germane to this discussion, however, is a second claim that Friedman makes about substantive conceptions of autonomy in relation to the inclusiveness of the moral and political commitments that substantive, value-laden accounts of autonomy can sustain. Because such accounts advance more restrictive requirements for autonomy, Friedman worries that they could limit

---

[38] Friedman, *Autonomy, Gender, Politics*, 14.
[39] Friedman, *Autonomy, Gender, Politics*, 30.
[40] Friedman, *Autonomy, Gender, Politics*, 19–20. In my judgment, this is an unorthodox way of defining what makes a theory of autonomy substantive. By comparison, see the account in Mackenzie and Stoljar, *Relational Autonomy*, 19–21.
[41] Friedman, *Autonomy, Gender, Politics*, 20.

the practical attainability of autonomy to an advantaged minority and thus be politically untenable in this respect.[42] This concern appropriately reflects feminists' initial skepticism about the value of personal autonomy as a concept that can serve feminist normative commitments. Friedman's concern also mirrors the worries I have raised about the overly restrictive character of both Oshana's and Stoljar's accounts.

But Friedman's concern about the potentially exclusionary implications of substantive accounts of autonomy runs deeper. She maintains that autonomous choices and actions warrant a special form of respect, beyond the fundamental moral respect owed to agents as persons (whether or not they act autonomously). Because substantive conceptions of autonomy are more restrictive, they will entail narrower restrictions on the scope of the special respect due to those who act autonomously. By contrast, content-neutral conceptions will support more permissive grounds for appropriately treating others with such respect since those conceptions set a lower threshold for autonomous action. Thus, if a conception of personal autonomy is to serve a normative commitment to expand the respect owed specially to autonomous agency, then a content-neutral conception, according to Friedman, should be preferred to a substantive theory of autonomy, other things being equal. She maintains that "... an account of autonomy with fewer requirements has, independently of other considerations, the advantage of promoting a more inclusive sense of equal worth."[43]

This argument is noteworthy in part because it demonstrates how a nonrelational, content-neutral account of autonomy can be shaped by practical social commitments to inclusion and to the defeat of unjust advantage, commitments that naturally comport with feminist politics. While Friedman grants that this argument is not grounded in a conceptual analysis of autonomy considered in itself, she indicates that the likely social implications for the ways we identify respect-worthy choices and actions are relevant to the evaluation of a theory of autonomy. "Reducing the requirements for autonomy may minimize the number of persons whose autonomy goes publicly unrecognized because of their social marginalization."[44] Friedman builds on this argument later in her book, contending that personal autonomy is "a necessary condition for being entitled to live free of domination by others," as the disenfranchisement or subordination of those not readily seen to act autonomously is a predictable concomitant of their failure to manifest readily in their agency a claim to the special respect owed to autonomous agents.[45]

---

[42] Friedman, *Autonomy, Gender, Politics*, 23.
[43] Friedman, *Autonomy, Gender, Politics*.
[44] Friedman, *Autonomy, Gender, Politics*.
[45] Friedman, *Autonomy, Gender, Politics*, 68.

I have three kinds of concern about Friedman's claim that the promotion of a more inclusive sense of respect-worthiness for autonomous choices is a warranted social criterion for the acceptability of a conception of autonomous agency. To begin with, the fact that there may well be potential obstacles to the social recognition or appreciation of persons' autonomy, such that the autonomy of socially marginalized persons may regularly be rendered nearly invisible to others, is not necessarily a ground for rejecting a particular conception of what constitutes personal autonomy. In discussing Stoljar's account, I already have noted that conceptions of autonomy that would fuel widespread skepticism about when, if ever, anyone acts autonomously are objectionable for that reason. But Friedman is making a much bolder claim. She is proposing that conceptions of autonomy that have the likely practical consequence that some persons' autonomy may be difficult (though not impossible) for others to recognize can be criticized on that basis. This seems mistaken. For the difficulty of persons' actual autonomy gaining broad social visibility may reflect the regrettable social fact that, owing to differences in social power and privilege, some persons' capabilities for autonomous agency may be less transparent than others' powers of autonomy. I concur with Friedman that this is a very serious social barrier to be identified, resisted, and surmounted. However, it is not, in itself, a reason to reject a particular account of what autonomy consists in. The very fact that one conception of autonomy would make persons' autonomy more readily visible to others than would be the case on another account does not automatically lend weight to the case for the former conception, even if the expansion of the social visibility of and appreciation for autonomy would be a good thing in general.

Second, if this argument of Friedman's against strong substantive theories of autonomy were sound and if such theories could be criticized on the grounds that they set the bar too high for the special respect-worthiness that properly accompanies autonomous action, then it also should be possible that, on social or political grounds, a theory of autonomy could be criticized for setting the bar for respect-worthiness too low. That is, such a theory could be faulted for being unreasonably or excessively inclusive. Friedman's account runs precisely this risk, I believe. Agents who reflectively endorse the deep and pervasive wants and values that motivate their actions and thus who satisfy Friedman's minimal conditions for autonomy nevertheless may lack autonomy if, at the same time, they are afflicted by psychosocial forms of manipulation that assail their fundamental sense of their competence and worthiness to speak for their decisions and actions. I have argued at length for this claim elsewhere and return to it in Section 5.[46]

---

[46] See, e.g., Paul Benson, "Free Agency and Self-Worth," *Journal of Philosophy* 91 (1994): 650–668; Benson, "Taking Ownership: Authority and Voice in Autonomous Agency," in Christman and Anderson, *Autonomy and the Challenges to Liberalism*, 101–126; Benson, "Feminist Intuitions and the Normative Substance of Autonomy."

The political liability for Friedman's position here is that, in virtue of embracing an overly inclusive understanding of autonomy, her account becomes less able to detect politically significant ways social practices and institutions actually do undermine autonomy without disrupting persons' ability to act on their reflectively affirmed or endorsable desires and values. As a consequence, Friedman's view risks making invisible the wrongs that such practices or institutions inflict. If, as Friedman contends, it is politically objectionable for a theory of autonomy to foster the invisibility of certain persons' autonomy, then it should also be politically objectionable for a theory to foster the invisibility of certain kinds of assault on personal autonomy. Friedman's account seems to have just such a consequence.

Finally, I am concerned that Friedman's inclusiveness argument obscures some critically important distinctions. It is important to be able to distinguish, first, between the conditions under which a person *actually* acts autonomously and the conditions under which a person possesses the *capacity* to act autonomously. The former conditions incorporate the latter, but the contrary is not the case. Someone can fail to act autonomously without losing the capacity to have acted autonomously. Typically, the special kinds of respect-worthiness that attach to autonomy do so in relation to the person's capacity for autonomous agency[47] so that failing to act autonomously on a particular occasion does not undermine the special respect or consideration the person deserves as an autonomous agent. For example, a person may fail to act on her deepest, reflectively endorsed wants or values for reasons of temporary akrasia, inattention, or fleeting ambivalence without thereby losing the entitlement to live free of domination or without losing claim to others' respect as an autonomous agent.

Similarly, it is important to distinguish between having the capacity to act autonomously and simply possessing the *potential* to acquire, strengthen, or regain that capacity. As in the former distinction, a transitory undermining of someone's capacity for autonomy does not entirely strip away the grounds to respect the person's autonomous agency if she has the potential to regain that capacity, perhaps as readily as she lost it. In many cases, persons who have suffered diminished capacity for autonomous decision making through illness or disability retain the potential for autonomy. Through modest support from others, they could regain or strengthen their capacity for autonomy sufficiently well to render their decisions worthy of respect. The impairment of the capacity to carry out certain functions required for autonomous action need not entail the destruction of the potential to act autonomously and the respect-worthy status that accompanies it.

---

[47] Friedman seems to acknowledge this, in fact. Cf. Friedman, *Autonomy, Gender, Politics*, 23.

These distinctions, along with others related to them—including the distinction between having the potential for autonomy and simply being a person—illustrate the fact that the bases for various kinds of special respect, consideration, or social recognition are many. In addition, these grounds for respect are realized by degrees; they are hardly all-or-nothing matters. Yet Friedman's account suggests that the conditions for actually acting autonomously are bound in a relatively straightforward manner to the conditions under which agents deserve valuable forms of respect so that accounts that narrow the range of autonomous action necessarily restrict the bases for such respect. This implication need not follow, however, if we bear in mind the distinctions sketched here and others related to them. The bases for valuable forms of respect-worthiness can be realized in many ways even when persons do not act autonomously or suffer limitations in their capacities to do so. Hence, the respect-worthiness of persons' autonomy as agents can be preserved even within conceptions that circumscribe more narrowly than Friedman's account does the conditions under which persons actually act autonomously.

4. Autonomy and Commitments to Democratic Participation

Like Friedman, John Christman also advances a content-neutral, or procedural, conception of personal autonomy that does not hold that any particular sorts of personal or social relation belong constitutively to persons' autonomy as agents. Also like Friedman, Christman defends the content neutrality of his conception and his rejection of constitutively relational elements of autonomy by appealing explicitly to certain social and political values, especially to "the foundation of egalitarian democratic politics,"[48] as he understands it. The particular components of Christman's conception of personal autonomy are generally well known and have been discussed at length elsewhere.[49] These details of his account are not my interest here. Instead, I want to highlight the way he invokes a commitment to social and political inclusiveness in order to defend his understanding of autonomy. I then will note that his position succumbs to one of the serious weaknesses that we have identified in Friedman's account.

Christman's invocation of social and political inclusion as the ground for embracing a purely procedural and nonrelational account of autonomy is not

---

[48] Christman, *Politics of Persons*, 175. Christman does not follow Friedman, however, in thinking that a substantive conception of autonomy can be accepted at the same time, as a matter of being autonomous to a greater degree than the minimal, procedural conditions of autonomy would entail.

[49] For the purposes of the present discussion of relational autonomy, see especially Christman, *Politics of Persons*; John Christman, "Relational Autonomy, Liberal Individualism, and the Social Constitution of Selves," *Philosophical Studies* 117 (2004): 143–164; Christman, "Procedural Autonomy and Liberal Legitimacy," in Taylor, *Personal Autonomy*, 277–298.

equivalent to Friedman's appeal to inclusion, although they are related. As we have seen, Friedman is especially concerned that we construct a conception of the minimal conditions of autonomy so that persons' autonomy has the best chance to be socially visible, irrespective of their various social positions. She wants the autonomous actions of the socially marginalized to have the greatest opportunity, within reason, to be recognized socially so that the special moral and political status that attaches to autonomous agency will not be withheld systematically from socially disadvantaged persons. Christman would not at all be unconcerned with the conditions under which personal autonomy is likely to be recognized and duly esteemed by others. However, his argument for a content-neutral, nonrelational conception of autonomy does not turn on what those conditions might be. Rather, he appeals directly to the conditions for persons' full and equal entitlement to participate in democratic practices and institutions as a primary reason to eschew substantive or relational accounts of autonomy.

According to Christman, persons may have the status of genuine participants in democratic social practices only if they are autonomous agents. Substantive or constitutively relational conceptions of autonomy are unacceptable, he maintains, because they limit the possibility of autonomous agency in ways that conflict directly with the value pluralism and fundamental neutrality among competing, comprehensive conceptions of the good that liberal democracy must sustain. Christman writes, "... An overly restrictive conception of autonomy will fail to recognize the moral status of reflective, self-defining persons whose participation in hierarchical or other kinds of social relations that appear to us (perhaps rightly) as oppressive should not deprive them of the social and political status that autonomy underwrites in democratic practices and institutions."[50]

Christman sees both normatively substantive accounts of autonomy and relational theories of autonomy as failing by this standard of democratic inclusiveness. Both sorts of accounts hold open the possibility that an agent could fail to be autonomous for reasons having to do with the specific values she holds or the particular kinds of relationship she sustains, even when the agent's values, choices, and actions satisfy suitable conditions of authentic and competent reflective acceptance.[51] And that would mean, according to Christman, that the agent should be denied, on the grounds of her lack of autonomy, full participation in democratic practices. Yet a democratic social and political order, properly understood, cannot deny full participant status to persons simply on the basis of the specific values they hold or the particular kinds of

---

[50] Christman, *Politics of Persons*, 173–174.
[51] For Christman's specification of the pertinent authenticity and competence conditions, see Christman, *Politics of Persons*, 142–156, esp. 155–156.

relationship in which they participate. Disagreements about the justifiability of such values or the legitimacy of such kinds of relationship are themselves precisely matters for democratic deliberation, not disagreements to be settled preemptively by way of autonomy's constitution.[52] This is why Christman is especially intent on criticizing conceptions of autonomy that, like those developed by Oshana or Stoljar, are at once value laden and constitutively relational. Such accounts prescriptively infuse certain substantive social or political commitments into the kinds of relationship that they believe are conceptually necessary for autonomous agency. The ways Oshana's and Stoljar's conceptions would narrow the scope of autonomous agency are, for Christman, "tantamount to silencing a voice in the moral landscape that a fully inclusive democracy...should include."[53]

As we found with Friedman's position, however, Christman's argument risks conflating the actual autonomy of an agent's action with the agent's capacity for autonomous agency and further conflates the capacity for autonomy with the conditions requisite for a person to have the status of a full participant in democratic society. Christman couples too tightly the conditions of actually autonomous agency with the grounds of entitlement to democratic participation. As we noted earlier, there are many bases for respect-worthy social and political status; these bases hardly are all-or-nothing matters that align perfectly with the degrees of autonomy realized in our decisions and actions or with the degrees to which we possess the capacity for autonomous choice and action at any particular time. Thus, even if some robust, substantive account of autonomy, such as that reflected in Stoljar's feminist intuition, were to be warranted, it would not follow that persons influenced strongly by false and misguided gender norms would thereby be precluded from legitimate participation in democratic social practices. If actual, episodic autonomy need not be bound tightly to the conditions required for democratic participation, then, pace Christman, it is not the case that the degree of inclusiveness in a conception of autonomy translates directly into the inclusiveness of a genuinely democratic society.[54]

---

[52] Christman recognizes, of course, that certain values and forms of relationship will be necessary for the very realization of democratic procedures. He is concerned about substantive or relational accounts of autonomy that would impose normative constraints on autonomy that are far more restrictive than these basic prerequisites for democratic politics. See, e.g., Christman, *Politics of Persons*, 175n16.

[53] Christman, *Politics of Persons*, 176.

[54] Another worry about Christman's argument from egalitarian democratic inclusion is that his account appears implicitly to adopt substantive and constitutively relational elements of autonomy by way of the broad and incompletely specified competency conditions that he presumes to be necessary for autonomy. See the discussion in Christman, *Politics of Persons*, of the place that interpersonal relations may have within autonomy's competency conditions, 177, 182–183, 184–185. If this is so, then his own account may fail to preserve the value-neutral, nonrelational character that he avows.

5. Agential Voice and Authority in Conceptions of Autonomy

Before proceeding to sketch a more constructive way to conceive the relationship between feminist normative commitments and autonomy, it would be useful to take stock of our examination of Oshana's and Stoljar's relational theories and of Friedman's and Christman's nonrelational theories. We have found that Oshana's and Stoljar's respective ways of situating personal autonomy in relation to feminist social and political ideals are unduly restrictive. Their accounts require that the conditions of autonomous agency be tied directly to certain political ideals—or set directly in opposition to certain forms of systemic social injustice. For Oshana, personal autonomy (characterized globally) must secure agents' power, opportunity, and authority to pursue lives free of unjust domination. Oshana can grant that, within limits, autonomous agents may not choose to act in accordance with fully liberatory and well-justified conceptions of their ends. But if they fail to act in such ways, this will be by their own choice, not due to externally imposed constraints on their power, opportunity, or authority. Stoljar goes still further in the direction of binding autonomy to feminist ethical and political ideals, prohibiting autonomous agents (characterized locally) from adopting values or making choices that depend upon endorsing false, misguided, or unduly oppressive social norms, at least not without possessing the capability to revise and correct their values and judgments in this regard.

Given the pervasively non-ideal social conditions in which we actually live, requirements such as these, according to which personal autonomy necessarily secures fundamental conditions of social justice in the agent's circumstances or precludes certain sorts of ill-justified or misguided normative judgment, carry the implication that personal autonomy is far rarer than we ordinarily would believe.[55] Oshana's and Stoljar's accounts also imply that some illiberal, antifeminist convictions may well defeat a person's autonomy simply in virtue of obstructing the allegedly requisite relationship between the person's values, choices, and actions and the relevant social ideals. Such severe constriction of the domain of personal autonomy stands in need of far more justification than either Oshana or Stoljar provide. Their appeals to worthy social and political ideals for curtailing gender-based subordination cannot, by themselves, afford such justification.

---

[55] Mark Piper suggests that Oshana and Stoljar might respond to this criticism by invoking the scalar character of autonomy. This would allow that many persons could exhibit some degree of autonomy in their actions even if few persons act with full autonomy by Oshana's or Stoljar's lights. To my knowledge, neither Oshana nor Stoljar gives any indication of taking such a stance. Nor do their theories indicate how the minimal conditions for acting with any degree of autonomy at all should be determined. Neither theory adopts Friedman's strategy in this regard.

We have found, as well, that both Friedman and Christman explicitly appeal to ideals of social and political inclusion in ways that extend the scope of personal autonomy too broadly. One reason for the overly permissive character of their theories is that they presume that locally autonomous agency must be coupled tightly to the conditions for basic entitlement to equal respect and democratic participation; autonomy is a condition of a certain respect-worthy social or political status, they believe. I have argued that this approach is mistaken because the conditions for such basic social recognition and political participation are insufficient to ensure that persons act autonomously, or have the capacity to act autonomously, in whatever they choose to do. The conditions for entry into the arena of democratic deliberation are weaker than those demanded by personal autonomy.

This diagnosis of some of the most influential lines of recent argument about whether or not feminist normative commitments favor relational conceptions of autonomy over nonrelational conceptions can be deepened by considering the differences in importance these competing approaches give to the role of autonomous agents' *voices* in their choice making and conduct compared with the importance they assign to persons' agential *authority* over their values, choices, and actions. The more inclusive of these theoretical approaches to autonomy typically assign greater emphasis to the respects in which autonomous agents can give expression, or voice, to what they care about—or at least to what they would find acceptable, or nonalienating, upon reflection. The more restrictive of these approaches typically assign greater emphasis to the ways persons are authorized to embrace values, make choices, and perform actions autonomously, normally with an eye toward identifying some objective constraints on such authority. It is important for present purposes to recognize that this distinction is a matter of emphasis and degree. All reasonable accounts strive, at least implicitly, to acknowledge and understand the roles of both voice and authority in autonomous agency. I will propose that consideration of the ways competing theories of autonomy emphasize these different, though closely intertwined, dimensions of agency reveals how we might constructively improve our understanding of the role that a conception of personal autonomy should serve in relation to feminist social and political commitments.

Notice, to begin with, that nonrelational theories such as Friedman's and Christman's that invoke political arguments as grounds for expanding their inclusiveness do so, in large measure, to protect the voices of individual autonomous agents, or the expressive capacities of their motivation and conduct. For such theories of autonomy, persons who act on authentically formed and sustained—or hypothetically acceptable (or nonalienating) and sustainable— values, wants, and choices are in an appropriate position to give expression, or voice, to what they care about.[56] And what such agents care about may clash

---

[56] For stylistic simplicity I will ignore, for the most part, the particular differences between Friedman's and Christman's respective conditions for personal autonomy. While those differences are

deeply with prevailing social norms or with the substantive constraints implicated in certain interpersonal relationships or social practices in which they participate, however liberatory or oppressive those norms, relationships, or practices may be. For such nonrelational conceptions of autonomy, the imperative of protecting agents' capabilities for voice means being willing to embrace the widest possible range of legitimate social or political disagreement and difference. Any substantive restrictions on the evaluative commitments, relationships, or decisions of autonomous agents could, from this perspective, threaten persons' capability to give voice through their actions to their most important wants or deepest values—or, at least, to what they would accept upon reflection. Theories of autonomy should be as inclusive as they reasonably can be, according to this approach, because this is the best way to ensure that they respect appropriately persons' authentic voices as realized in their decisions and conduct. That is, what is at risk in overly restrictive, insufficiently inclusive conceptions of autonomy is the silencing, or exclusion, of authentic voices, whether this occurs in the context of interpersonal relationships, social practices, or the arena of political life.

By contrast, relational conceptions of autonomy of the sort surveyed thus far typically embrace more restrictive conditions on autonomy as a way of ensuring that autonomous agents are appropriately authorized to govern their effective motives, values, choices, and actions (and the processes by which they arose). On the approaches taken by theorists such as Oshana and Stoljar, authentically formed and sustained motives, values, and actions may arise within social conditions that diminish, circumvent, or undermine agential authority and, in so doing, obstruct the person's autonomy. External social relations and normative practices can be relevant to determination of a person's autonomy, these theorists maintain, because such factors can interfere directly with the person's ability to exercise authority over her choices and actions, however authentically those choices and actions may express what she cares about or wants or would reflectively accept. Thus, whereas nonrelational conceptions of autonomy tend to highlight the dimension of *self* in agential self-governance and therefore emphasize the agent's capacities for voice, relational conceptions tend to highlight the dimension of *governance* in autonomous agents' self-governance and therefore emphasize the conditions of the agent's authority. Most importantly for the present discussion, these divergent emphases are reflected through the ways theorists of autonomy appeal to social and political commitments in the course of defending their preferred theories.

---

considerable, they do not affect the fundamental proposal I am advancing, even though Friedman's account lends itself somewhat more readily to the interpretation offered here than does Christman's account.

The arguments we have presented in the foregoing sections of this paper offer no reason to hold that either of these emphases is uniformly and without exception to be preferred over the other. Both voice and authority are essential facets of autonomous agency.[57] We have encountered good reasons to protect the scope of agents' voices in a conception of autonomy. We also have encountered good reasons for thinking that agential authority requires conditions on autonomy that extend beyond forms of procedural authenticity or reflective self-acceptance alone. Both dimensions of autonomy are vulnerable and subject to threat in social and political circumstances that elicit feminist attention, critique, and advocacy.

What we have found is that inclusive conceptions of autonomy designed to protect voice tend to be excessively inclusive. We have seen, as well, that restrictive conceptions of autonomy designed to secure more robust agential authority also tend to risk excess. Our task, then, is to identify a role for autonomous agency within broadly feminist normative commitments that can incorporate and balance properly both voice and authority. While I cannot develop a full account of autonomy in the space remaining, I will present reasons for maintaining, first, that a certain type of constitutively relational conception of autonomy is favored by the desideratum to balance voice and authority and, second, that this sort of relational conception resonates with feminist social and political commitments in meaningful and promising ways.

It may be misleading to think of "balancing" the dimensions of voice and authority in a conception of autonomy as if these were inherently independent, competing considerations between which we should settle for some trade-off or strike a compromise. In fact, there is a natural way to conjoin these dimensions—even to understand them as being internally related to one another. If the authority that is important for personal autonomy necessarily includes the agent's authority with respect to her voice, then an account of autonomy may be able to protect and promote both agential voice and authority in a manner that meshes with our considered convictions about what it is to act autonomously. More specifically, we can think about the autonomous agent's authority over her choices and actions as consisting in her *authority to speak or answer to others* for her choices and actions. As I have maintained elsewhere, "autonomous agents specially own what they do in that they are properly positioned to give voice to their reasons for acting—to speak or answer for their acts, or to give account of them—should others call for their reasons.... Autonomous agents are authorized to stand at the nodal point defined by the targeting of

---

[57] Cf. Benson, "Taking Ownership," esp. section II, 106–110, for more extended discussion of the normative, social, and discursive aspects of autonomy. That paper approaches the relationship between authority and voice in theories of autonomy rather differently, however, interpreting these concepts against the background of the idea that autonomous agents *take ownership* of their actions in a distinctive way.

potential criticisms and the voicing of reasons in response."[58] Or, to use Andrea Westlund's related terminology, this authority may turn on "the disposition to hold oneself answerable to external critical perspectives"[59] or one's "dispositions for dialogical answerability."[60]

The autonomous agent's voice, on this approach, does not consist simply in her capability to express through her actions what she most cares about or values or would reflectively accept. Instead, the agent's voice is composed of the person's regarding herself as being in an appropriate position to speak for her decisions and actions in response to potential criticisms, irrespective of whether her actions actually issue from her deepest or reflectively acceptable motives or values. And the agent's authority is not a matter of her deciding and acting in social circumstances that are largely free of unjust subordination or of acting on the basis of judgments that have not been influenced inappropriately by misguided or harmful social norms. The agent's authority arises, rather, from her taking up the position of a potential answerer for her actions, from holding herself potentially answerable to others for what she does. Such authority need not depend on the agent's being able to see through misguided gender norms or having the unimpeded social opportunity and power to advance her fundamental aims.

Forging internal connections between agential voice and agential authority in this manner intuitively may seem too weak, as it appeals to self-regarding attitudes that could be wholly unfounded or may result from autonomy-undermining processes. Agents' regard for their own competence and worthiness to answer for their acts can arise under conditions that plainly disrupt their autonomy. Thus, some objective constraints on these attitudes are necessary, including, first, autonomous agents' attitudes toward their own capabilities and worthiness to function as answerers must be formed in a suitably rational way, on the basis of their evidence for such attitudes.[61] Second, autonomous agents must be capable of gaining otherwise socially available information that would be practically germane to the formation of these attitudes and to the making of their decisions. Such capability is impaired, for instance, in societies dominated by Orwellian propaganda. Third, autonomous agents' attitudes must not be modified by processes that circumvent their capacities for rational consideration, as in cases of forcible mind control. Finally, the norms in relation to which agents regard themselves as capable of presenting their reasons must be publicly shareable, in principle.[62]

---

[58] Benson, "Taking Ownership," 108–109. Also see Benson, "Free Agency and Self-Worth."
[59] Andrea C. Westlund, "Rethinking Relational Autonomy," *Hypatia* 24 (2009): 26–49, 28.
[60] Westlund, "Rethinking Relational Autonomy," 35.
[61] John Martin Fischer and Mark Ravizza, *Moral Responsibility and Control* (Cambridge: Cambridge University Press, 1998), 213–214, 235–236, propose a similar condition in their account of taking responsibility for acting from a particular kind of action mechanism.
[62] These four conditions also are presented in Benson, "Taking Ownership," 117–118.

Conceiving in this manner the distinctive forms of voice and authority that characterize personal autonomy should enable the conception of autonomy that results to avoid the respective excesses in inclusiveness and restrictiveness that we identified in the theories surveyed in this chapter. Understanding voice in this way does not restrict substantively the particular values, motives, choices, or actions that autonomous agents can adopt, possess, make, or perform. Agents who take up the position of potential answerers for their actions are not thereby constrained in what they care about, hold to be worthwhile, or aim to do. Simply in virtue of being in a position to speak for their actions, they are not subject in any evident way to direct, substantive constraints on their attitudes or values. Hence, this approach should be capable of realizing to a significant (though not unlimited) extent the inclusiveness that procedural, nonrelational theories typically seek.

At the same time, this approach to conceiving of autonomous agents' authority does not carry unduly restrictive or skeptical implications for the scope of autonomy. While agents will not attain the authority to speak or answer for their actions simply because they meet procedural conditions of authenticity and competence, or the like, the requirements for having such authority do not incorporate the notably idealized social or evaluative conditions that relational theorists like Oshana or Stoljar envisage. Most healthy, socially functional adults are able to sustain the requisite dispositions for dialogical answerability notwithstanding routine social injustices to which they may be subject or the limitations in their apprehension of how best to live their lives or structure human social relations. Hence, this way of relating the dimensions of voice and authority in our understanding of personal autonomy seems neither to be overly restrictive nor excessively inclusive.

Thinking of the distinctive dimensions of authority and voice that comprise autonomy as being internally related in this way, and recognizing that this approach avoids some of the most prominent deficiencies that have surfaced in other influential conceptions of relational and nonrelational autonomy, provides good reasons for holding that personal autonomy is constitutively relational. We cannot make sense of agents' holding themselves to be potential answerers for their choices and actions unless we understand persons to be potential participants in relationships and social interactions in which others can criticize their conduct. We cannot conceive of agents who have the requisite authority and voice to act autonomously apart from a web of relationships and normative domains within which persons are permitted to hold others to expectations and are disposed to present reasons, where appropriate, in response to others' expectations. As we have seen, however, this form of constitutive relationality does not mean that autonomous agents are subject, inherently and directly, to specific, substantive normative constraints on what they want, value, or aim to do. I shall not explore further here how best to understand the normative dimensions of this sort of relational autonomy in the context of distinctions between substantive and content-neutral theories of autonomy.[63]

What does this approach to understanding autonomy's relationality tell us about the role that autonomy should serve in relation to feminist social and political commitments? First, this approach takes seriously women's attitudes toward their own relational position as agents in a natural way and is well suited to detect assaults on women's autonomy that consist in subverting women's sense that they are competent and worthy of speaking for, or giving account of, their own agency. It has long been a defining priority in feminist ethics and politics to take seriously women's experiences, beginning with the ways women interpret and articulate what they experience. When women internalize oppressive social norms and practices, this feminist priority can have the unintended consequence of covering up women's psychological subordination, for the internalization of oppression usually means that women will not interpret their experiences of hurt, limitation, or diminished efficacy as experiences of undue subordination. However, if one key to autonomous agents' requisite self-regard is that they treat themselves as having the authority to speak or answer for their reasons and actions, and if internalized oppression commonly targets women's sense of their own competence and worthiness to answer others' potential criticisms, then this approach is well designed to identify particularly sinister forms of harm characteristically inflicted through the processes by which oppression is internalized.

Indeed, it has been one of the strengths of other relational theories of autonomy that they recognize the threats that internalized oppression poses to autonomy. Because the approach I propose concentrates on autonomous agents' actual, subjective regard for their own answerability, however, it can respond more directly, on a psychological level, to women's own experience of underdeveloped or diminished authority than theories, such as Oshana's and Stoljar's, that appeal entirely to external, more idealized political conditions.

Second, the approach to relational autonomy that has emerged in this discussion characterizes in a more plausible way than other theories the social situation in which autonomous agents frequently find themselves, located in between stark, pervasive injustices that threaten to destroy autonomy, on one

---

[63] For further discussion of whether or not to interpret this approach as weakly, or indirectly, substantive, as I have argued previously, or whether to interpret the approach as yielding only formal, content-neutral conditions on autonomy, see Paul Benson, "Narrative Self-Understanding and Relational Autonomy," *Symposia on Gender, Race, and Philosophy* 7 (2011), http://web.mit.edu/sgrp/2011/no1/Benson0511.pdf; Andrea C. Westlund, "Reply to Benson, Christman, Rocha, and Stoljar," *Symposia on Gender, Race, and Philosophy*, http://web.mit.edu/sgrp/2011/no1/Westlund0511.pdf. Also relevant to this issue is Diana Tietjens Meyers' important contribution to this volume, "The Feminist Debate over Values in Autonomy Theory," in which Meyers argues that the usual ways in which debates between value-laden and value-neutral conceptions of autonomy have been framed conflate two independent axes along which theories of autonomy may incorporate normative substance.

hand, and ideal social and political practices and institutions, on the other, that are only distantly attainable. In contrast with Oshana's theory, my approach makes room for the autonomy of courageous crusaders, like Shirin Ebadi, who plainly assert their authority to speak and answer for their own reasoning and conduct, notwithstanding the grave injustices inflicted upon them. At the same time, my approach allows that, for many other women in postrevolution Iran, crushing restrictions on women's political, professional, and economic rights may have the additional effects of undermining their disposition to hold themselves answerable for what they do, of engendering passivity, and of diminishing their sense of authority to take ownership for their choices. This contrasts with procedural theories that would ask only that autonomous agents act in ways they would reflectively accept, even when their own sense of agential authority has been retarded or destroyed. Any politically useful approach to autonomy must be able to distinguish between the autonomous agency of the defiant resister of oppression (even when her resistance fails to achieve many of its goals) and the damage done to other women's autonomy by that very oppression. It is an appropriate social and political priority that our understanding of women's agency carefully track these differences among individual women's social and psychological locations within the same systems of domination.

Third, the approach proposed here is capable of distinguishing clearly between persons' actual autonomy and their capabilities for autonomous action, on one hand, and their status as full moral and political agents, on the other. For example, women whose autonomy is compromised by profound self-doubt or the pervasive sense that they are socially invisible, and hence are not in a position to speak for their own decisions and actions, are not thereby to be exempted from moral accountability or barred from political participation. It is one thing to be capable of claiming the authority and voice that distinguish autonomous agents; it is quite another to possess the standing of a person with equal moral worth and full rights to political participation, whether or not that standing actually is honored. The latter conditions are necessary for the former, but the converse is not the case. Thus, the view of relational autonomy that emerges in this paper avoids one of the primary difficulties with Friedman's and Christman's nonrelational theories.

6. Conclusion

This chapter opened with the observation that the increasing influence that feminist commitments have had in constructing new theories of personal autonomy has been accompanied by the emergence of increasingly rigid boundaries among feminist accounts of autonomy. Our exploration of the role that a conception of autonomy should have in relation to feminist normative commitments has clarified significant strengths and weaknesses in competing accounts of autonomy that appeal explicitly to feminist perspectives on social and political life. Moreover, our discussion has yielded an approach toward conceiving personal autonomy that points the way toward overcoming some of the fundamental divisions among feminist theorists of autonomy. The favored approach, I have argued, incorporates relational elements as part of the very constitution of personal autonomy. This paper validates, in this respect, the guiding impulse of Mackenzie and Stoljar's volume.

At the same time, the approach favored here conceives of autonomy's relationality in a manner that respects the fundamental notion that autonomous action consists in agential self-governance and thus must be accessible to agents whose wants, values, decisions, and actions vary widely from one person to another. The variability among manners of living that autonomous agents may accept and pursue is sufficiently broad that autonomous agents may reject feminist commitments to resist and overcome women's subordination even as our guiding conception of autonomy is designed to respond to feminist ends. In this regard, feminist refiguration of personal autonomy as relational at once yields valuable theoretical advances in our understanding of self-governing, self-determining action and also confirms some of the limits of autonomous agency in helping us to develop values, decide on courses of action, construct social practices, and achieve lives that are free of hurtful and unjust domination.

Acknowledgments

I am grateful to Mark Piper and Andrea Veltman for their many insightful comments on an earlier version of this chapter.

{6}

The Feminist Debate over Values in Autonomy Theory
Diana Tietjens Meyers

The starting point of this paper is a pair of clashing feminist intuitions about the relationship between values and autonomy. For Natalie Stoljar, desires "influenced by oppressive norms of femininity cannot be autonomous."[1] For Marilyn Friedman, "however oppressive their conditions might be and however much change is morally required, traditionally subordinate feminine lives nevertheless can and do often nonslavishly embody and express values worth caring about."[2] Prioritizing resistance to oppression as an objective for an adequate feminist theory of autonomy, Stoljar calls for a strongly substantive—that is, value-saturated—account. Such an account must deem actions conforming to false conceptions of womanhood nonautonomous regardless of whether the agent has reflected on and endorsed them. In contrast, Friedman prioritizes recognizing and respecting the values and agency of women in patriarchal societies, and her value-neutral view of autonomy allows for the possibility that women's compliance with oppressive feminine norms may be autonomous. Like Stoljar, I think that a feminist account of autonomy must render social critique and oppositional agency intelligible and achievable. However, like Friedman, I doubt that a woman's nonautonomy can be inferred from her compliance with subordinating feminine norms.

Paul Benson and Andrea Westlund have recently taken on the challenge of reconciling the competing intuitions Stoljar and Friedman defend. Eschewing his earlier value-saturated theory of autonomy, Benson's bid to end the Stoljar–Friedman stalemate proposes what he calls a "weak substantive" account of autonomy. I argue, however, that Benson's proposal does not offer a compromise between value-saturated and value-neutral accounts.[3] Instead it adumbrates a previously unnoticed way theories of autonomy incorporate values.

---

[1] Natalie Stoljar, "Autonomy and the Feminist Intuition," in *Relational Autonomy*, edited by Catriona Mackenzie and Natalie Stoljar (New York: Oxford University Press, 2000), 95.

[2] Marilyn Friedman, *Autonomy, Gender, Politics* (New York: Oxford University Press, 2003), 25.

[3] In email correspondence, Benson tells me that he didn't intend to identify a midpoint between value-neutral and value-saturated theories of autonomy. However, I believe that use of the term *substantive* to cover all autonomy theories that incorporate values regardless of how the values are

Westlund advocates an alternative resolution of the two feminist intuitions. Staunchly defending a value-neutral view of autonomy, Westlund argues that her self-answerability theory shows that some forms of subordination are incompatible with autonomy but also that it's a mistake to assume that no traditional feminine life can be autonomous. Although I agree that Westlund avoids the trap of value saturation, I argue that there is a sense in which her position is not value free.

To develop my discussion of Benson and Westlund, I distinguish two ways values may be implicated in autonomy theories: (1) An autonomy theory may prescribe or proscribe certain types of behavior, or (2) an autonomy theory's account of the process of autonomous choice may invoke a set of background values. I use this distinction to demarcate two conceptual axes. The Directivity Axis reveals whether an autonomy theory preempts or honors the judgment of individual agents, whereas the Constitutivity Axis lays bare the normative gears that drive competing accounts of autonomous choice and action. I call the claim that these axes represent philosophically distinct and significant ways autonomy theories deploy values the Double Axis Thesis.

Theories in the value-laden and value-saturated sectors of the Directivity Axis, such as Natalie Stoljar's and Susan Babbitt's, require that autonomous individuals act on emancipatory values or refrain from acting on oppressive disvalues. In contrast, theories on the Constitutivity Axis are value utilizing, for they invoke values other than autonomy to explicate autonomous choice and action. Whereas value-prescriptive theories enunciate a set of action-guiding directives, value-utilizing theories describe modi vivendi for making choices. My own view of autonomy is an example of a value-utilizing account, as is Westlund's, for both adduce subsidiary values to characterize autonomy. Nevertheless, our positions stand at the value-neutral pole of the Directivity Axis, for they do not mandate that autonomous individuals engage in any particular type of behavior other than an autonomy-constituting choice process.

Having established that it is possible for a theory of autonomy to be value-neutral and value-utilizing, I argue that value-neutral positions better serve feminist purposes. As well, I illustrate the philosophical fruitfulness of exposing the values that a theory of autonomy utilizes. This interpretative exercise not only provides a new angle from which to assess the merits of theories, it also helps to clarify how particular autonomy theories connect with different philosophical questions about autonomy.

---

incorporated leads readers to assume that Benson's weakly substantive account is on a continuum between value-neutral (nonsubstantive) theories and strongly substantive theories. As well, I believe that this use of the term *substantive* masks the distinction between the two axes that I present here.

1. Two Value Axes

In this section, I distinguish two axes that represent different ways autonomy theories incorporate and exclude values. Along one axis, autonomy theories vary with respect to their degrees of value prescriptivity. Along the other axis, autonomy theories vary with respect to what I'll call their constitutive value sets. In my view, Benson's conception of a weakly substantive autonomy theory appears to collapse the Constitutivity Axis into the Directivity Axis with confusing results.

The Directivity Axis is scalar, and like a scale for measuring weights its values start at zero and range upward. On the Directivity Axis, theories of autonomy range from value-neutral theories to value-saturated theories with more or less value-laden theories in between. Value-neutral theories place no limits on the values or disvalues that people may autonomously elect to live by. Instead, they assess autonomy on the basis of the motivational structure of the agentic subject and/or on the basis of the procedure behind an individual's choices and actions.[4] Value-saturated theories demand that autonomous individuals repudiate particular disvalues or fulfill particular values. Susan Babbitt's value-saturated position maintains that autonomous individuals must conduct themselves in a manner that satisfies their objective interest in fully flourishing.[5] Falling short of standards of self-respect, dignity, and liberation defeats autonomy, and satisfying these standards forbids compliance with oppressive norms and capitulation to oppressive circumstances.[6] Thus, women cannot autonomously defer to their husbands, and members of marginalized social groups who have the talent to be medical researchers cannot autonomously opt to become pharmacists instead.[7]

It is clear that Natalie Stoljar rejects value neutrality because it fails to support her feminist intuition. However, it is less clear just how prescriptive she thinks an adequate feminist theory of autonomy needs to be, for she offers two versions—one considerably less potent than the other—of her feminist

---

[4] Harry Frankfurt, *The Importance of What We Care About* (Princeton, NJ: Princeton University Press, 1988); Harry Frankfurt, "Reply to Lear," in *The Contours of Agency*, edited by Sarah Buss and Lee Overton (Cambridge, MA: MIT Press, 2002); Friedman, *Autonomy, Gender, Politics*; John Christman, *The Politics of Persons* (Cambridge, UK: Cambridge University Press, 2009); Andrea Westlund, "Selflessness and Responsibility for Self," *Philosophical Review* 112:4 (2003): 483–523; Westlund, "Rethinking Relational Autonomy," *Hypatia* 24:4 (2009): 26–49; Diana Tietjens Meyers, *Self, Society, and Personal Choice* (New York: Columbia University Press, 1989); Meyers, *Gender in the Mirror: Cultural Imagery and Women's Agency* (New York: Oxford University Press, 2002); Meyers, *Being Yourself: Essays on Identity, Action, and Social Life* (Lanham, MD: Rowman and Littlefield, 2004).

[5] Susan Babbitt, "Feminism and Objective Interests: The Role of Transformation Experiences in Rational Deliberation," in *Feminist Epistemologies*, edited by Linda Alcoff and Elizabeth Potter (New York: Routledge, 1993), 246–248.

[6] Babbitt, "Feminism and Objective Interests," 261.

[7] Babbitt, "Feminism and Objective Interests," 249, 251–252.

intuition. Again, Stoljar's feminist intuition is that "preferences influenced by oppressive norms of femininity cannot be autonomous."[8] As I mentioned earlier, this formulation affirms a value-saturated position that rules out autonomous conformity to oppressive feminine norms. Yet Stoljar seems to dilute her intuition a bit when she claims that conduct "*overly* influenced [by] stereotypical and incorrect norms of femininity" cannot be autonomous.[9] It is instructive to explore what she might mean by this qualified claim, for it seems to place her position somewhere in the value-laden sector of the Directivity Axis. Occupying the zone between value saturation and value neutrality, value-laden accounts of autonomy must hold (1) that a person cannot autonomously comply with oppressive norms too much or too often, (2) that a person cannot autonomously comply with the most egregiously oppressive norms but can autonomously comply with norms that are oppressive in relatively minor ways, or (3) both of the preceding.[10]

It is possible to interpret Stoljar's claim that a woman loses autonomy only when oppressive feminine norms carry excessive weight in her life from an objective or a subjective standpoint. An objective reading might hold that extensive gender conformity or compliance with the most damaging feminine norms would entail nonautonomy, but spotty gender conformity or trivial gender conformity would not compromise autonomy. A woman resembling the Stepford fembots might be deemed overly influenced by oppressive feminine norms in virtue of her complete and incessant compliance with those norms.[11] Women who consent to be reinfibulated after giving birth might be deemed overly influenced by oppressive feminine norms in virtue of the grievous harms to their sexuality and the high risk of harm to their health that this procedure involves. Whereas the fembot cousin lacks autonomy because she conforms to gender norms too much, the woman who goes along with female genital mutilation lacks autonomy because of the egregiousness of the feminine norm she adheres to.

A subjective reading of Stoljar's claim that only conduct overly influenced by oppressive feminine norms is nonautonomous would put the issue of motivation in play. Conduct wholly or largely motivated by acquiescence to

---

[8] Stoljar, "Autonomy and the Feminist Intuition," 95.
[9] Stoljar, "Autonomy and the Feminist Intuition," 98. Emphasis added.
[10] My thinking about value-laden theories has been influenced by Jason Stigliano's work in my Spring 2012 Philosophy of Action seminar. It is important to note that in feminist philosophy of action substantive theories of autonomy, which I parse as value-laden and value-saturated theory, were introduced specifically to address the problem of internalized oppression. In this paper, I confine my discussion to feminist autonomy theories. Although Stoljar centers her thinking on the way oppressive gender norms undermine women's autonomy, I formulate my account of value-laden autonomy theories to include compliance with the norms imposed by any type of oppression, for feminist philosophy is centrally concerned with intersections of multiple systems of oppression and privilege.
[11] I take this analogy from the 1975 body-snatcher film *The Stepford Wives*, directed by Bryan Forbes.

oppressive feminine norms cannot be autonomous, whereas conduct motivated in small part and tangentially shaped by oppressive feminine norms may be autonomous. A woman who complies with oppressive feminine norms solely because she desires to fit into a feminine mold cannot be autonomous. However, a woman whose conduct is congruent with oppressive feminine norms but who chooses to act this way mainly for distinctive personal reasons may be autonomous. In other words, a preponderance of individualized motivations in a woman's volitional amalgam would count as insufficiently influenced by oppressive feminine norms to run afoul of Stoljar's feminist intuition. Bearing in mind, though, that the motivational springs of human action are typically multiplex and polyvalent and that distinctive individual concerns normally blend with nods to social convention in human motivational systems, taking motivation into account implies that acting in a way that coincides with oppressive gender norms would raise questions about the agent's autonomy but would not settle them. To settle the question, the fealty to oppressive gender norms built into the agent's motivational system would need to be assessed.

I have generated these interpretations of Stoljar's qualified feminist intuition in order to indicate what sorts of autonomy theories belong in the stretch of the Directivity Axis between value neutrality and value saturation.[12] Value-laden theories, as I call them, do not categorically proscribe all conduct that accords with oppressive norms, nor do they categorically prescribe types of action that betoken repudiation of oppressive norms. Rather, they may curb the extent to which a person can autonomously go along with oppressive norms or the severity of the harm a person can autonomously incur as a result of going along with an oppressive norm, or they may regulate how motivated a person can be to submit to oppressive norms without sacrificing autonomy. Still, they grant autonomy to individuals who occasionally comply with oppressive norms, who don't comply with the most egregiously oppressive norms, or whose conformity to oppressive norms is motivated by considerations other than a desire to model themselves on an oppressive stereotype. In short, value-laden theories are less prescriptive than value-saturated theories and more prescriptive than value-neutral theories.

If this account of the Directivity Axis is right, it calls into question the possibility that Paul Benson's agential ownership account of autonomy lies somewhere between the value-saturated pole and the value-neutral pole of this axis. On the contrary, his agential ownership view of autonomy tentatively sides

---

[12] I won't attempt to determine whether the standards I have sketched are faithful to Stoljar's overall text or whether these standards are more philosophically satisfying than the strong normative competence theory of autonomy that she ultimately endorses at Stoljar, "Autonomy and the Feminist Intuition," 107–108.

with proponents of value neutrality, for it does not affirm that the extent or the gravity of women's compliance with oppressive gender norms is decisive with respect to their autonomy, and it asserts that women can autonomously comply with such norms.[13] If so, Benson's view is not a value-laden position of the sort I have sketched. Nevertheless, he labels his position a *weak substantive* one, which gives the impression that his view is located on the continuum between value-saturated positions that directly impose normative constraints on autonomous choice and latitudinarian value-neutral positions.[14] However, I believe that his explanation of how it is possible for a woman to autonomously comply with an oppressive social norm alerts us to a second axis of analysis for autonomy theories.

At stake in the debate between proponents of value-saturated accounts and proponents of value-neutral accounts is whether it is possible to autonomously conform to oppressive norms. I have suggested that the middle area of the Directivity Axis is occupied by positions that place limits on an autonomous agent's absorption into an oppressive regime but that allow that oppressive norms may have some influence in an autonomous agent's life. According to value-laden theories, autonomy is inversely related to the sway oppressive norms exert over a person's conduct.

In contrast, Benson holds that the autonomy of gender conformists derives from their favorable "attitudes toward their own competence and worth" together with their retention of a "sense of their own authority as reasoning, potentially answerable agents."[15] Those who have these positive reflexive attitudes and take agential ownership are autonomous; those who lack these attitudes and deflect agential ownership are not.[16] If so, autonomy is not devoid of normative content, in Benson's view, yet normative considerations do not enter into his theory in the same way that they enter into value-saturated and value-laden theories. The latter restrict the types of action that an autonomous agent can choose and/or the constellations of motivations that can give rise to autonomous actions. Benson introduces values by another route. For Benson, the psychological values of self-confidence and self-worth are constitutive of autonomous choice and action. Self-confidence is needed to assure you of your ability to explain your actions by citing your reasons, and self-worth is needed to assure you of your entitlement to answer for yourself.[17] Together,

---

[13] Paul Benson, "Feminist Intuitions and the Normative Substance of Autonomy," in *Personal Autonomy*, edited by James Stacey Taylor (Cambridge, UK: Cambridge University Press, 2005), 128–130, 136.

[14] Benson, "Feminist Intuitions," 136, 125.

[15] Benson, "Feminist Intuitions," 136–137.

[16] Benson, "Feminist Intuitions," 128.

[17] Benson, "Feminist Intuitions," 128. Paul Benson, "Taking Ownership: Authority and Voice in Autonomous Agency," in *Autonomy and the Challenges of Liberalism*, edited by John Christman and Joel Anderson (New York: Oxford University Press, 2005), 109, 116.

these capacities endow individuals with the authority to take ownership of their actions, which Benson identifies with autonomy.

In light of the difference between the role that values play in Benson's theory and the role they play in value-prescriptive theories, I do not regard his view as a value-laden theory – a midpoint between value-saturated and value-neutral theories. Instead, I propose classifying his view as a value-utilizing theory. Whereas value-laden theories are sited on the Directivity Axis, value-utilizing theories are sited on a separate axis. On the Constitutivity Axis, autonomy theories do not vary by degrees as gauged by a single measure, such as how many ostensibly oppressive options theories legislate against. Rather, the Constitutivity Axis is composed of an array of qualitatively distinct parcels of values, each of which is implicated in a conception of how to choose and act autonomously. In other words, constitutive value sets are collocations of values that different philosophical accounts of autonomy explicitly or implicitly invoke to explicate the reflective procedure or motivational structure that renders choices and actions autonomous. It is difficult, perhaps impossible, to conceive an account of autonomy that is not value utilizing. Even rational choice theory—a paradigm of value neutrality—rests on a constitutive set of epistemic values including consistency, transitivity, and knowledge of pertinent facts. If so, I would venture that any theory of autonomy can be analyzed both in terms of its place on the Directivity Axis and in terms of the constitutive value set that places it on the Constitutivity Axis.

I have already explored the question of where Stoljar's view of autonomy belongs on the Directivity Axis. I can now add that her view can also be positioned on the Constitutivity Axis, for it invokes a constitutive value set. To accommodate her feminist intuition, Stoljar backs a strong normative competence theory of autonomy. On this view, autonomous individuals must be able to "criticize courses of action competently by relevant normative standards."[18] Two epistemic values—true beliefs about correct norms and reflexive critical acumen—comprise this autonomy theory's constitutive value set. Women who have internalized oppressive feminine norms so thoroughly that their reason detection abilities are riddled with perniciously patterned blind spots are not autonomous because their cognitive capacities lack these epistemic goods. Correlatively, it is arguable that the autonomy of women who have not integrated the most harmful feminine norms into their cognitive capacities or who have also internalized countervailing norms that provide cognitive ballast may achieve some degree of autonomy although they sometimes act in line with oppressive norms.

---

[18] Natalie Stoljar, "Autonomy and the Feminist Intuition," 107, quoting Benson.

Although Benson classifies my view of autonomy as a weakly substantive view, I would resist his suggestion to reposition my view on the Directivity Axis.[19] According to my agentic competency account, autonomous people exercise a repertoire of agentic skills in choosing and acting:

1. Introspection skills that sensitize individuals to their own feelings and desires, that enable them to interpret their subjective experience, and that help them judge how accurate their self-understanding is
2. Communication skills that enable individuals to get the benefit of others' perceptions, background knowledge, insights, advice, and support
3. Memory skills that enable individuals to recall relevant experiences—from their own lives and also those that acquaintances have recounted or that they have encountered in literature or other art forms
4. Imagination skills that enable individuals to envisage feasible options—to audition a range of self-conceptions they might aspire to and to preview a variety of courses of action they might follow
5. Analytical skills and reasoning skills that enable individuals to assess the relative merits of different conceptions of what they could be like and directions they could pursue
6. Self-nurturing skills that enable individuals to secure their physical and psychological equilibrium despite missteps and setbacks— that enable them to appreciate the overall worthiness of their self-understandings and pursuits and to assure themselves of their capacity to carry on when they find themselves wanting or their life directions misguided
7. Volitional skills that enable individuals to resist pressure to capitulate to convention and enable them to maintain their commitment to their values and goals

Embedded in these skills, I discern a panoply of epistemic and psychological values: perspicacity, resourcefulness, creativity, rationality, self-esteem, stability, resilience, tenacity, and corrigibility, to name a few. I grant, then, that my view is value-utilizing, but I do not agree that it is value-laden. Indeed, I contend that the two value axes I have laid out enable me to reaffirm the value neutrality of my view as well as my conviction that value-neutral accounts of autonomy are preferable from a feminist standpoint.

---

[19] Benson, "Feminist Intuitions," 135. Here I repudiate a concession to Benson's argument I made in Diana Tietjens Meyers, "Review of *Personal Autonomy in Society* by Marina Oshana," *Hypatia* 23:2 (2008): 206.

2. Are the Axes Really Distinct and Philosophically Significant?

Judging by Benson's published work, it's unclear whether he would contest my claim that a theory of autonomy that dictates or forbids certain types of behavior as mandatory outcomes of autonomous choice differs in kind from one that requires that autonomous agents exhibit certain values in virtue of the process that is constitutive of autonomous choosing. On the one hand, he might stand by his claim that both his and my views are weakly substantive theories that take a moderate stance compared with value-saturated theories and value-neutral theories. Since value-saturated, value-laden, and what I have termed value-utilizing theories all incorporate norms, he might contend that my distinction between the Directivity Axis and the Constitutivity Axis is nugatory. On the other hand, his defense of his own agential ownership theory seems to belie this criticism of my distinction. To answer the charge that his theory is too voluntaristic, Benson rejects the idea that you must self-consciously adopt the reflexive attitudes he considers constitutive of autonomy – confidence in your ability to answer for yourself and a sense of your worthiness as an agent. In his view, "self-authorization can be entirely attitudinal, implicit, and un-self-conscious in most contexts."[20] If so, the Constitutivity Axis diverges from the Directivity Axis in not requiring that agents embrace justifiable norms or shun unjustifiable norms. I'll argue that the axes are separate and that distinguishing them makes conceptual room for value-neutral autonomy theories without ruling out value-laden and value-saturated theories.

The pictures of developing and practicing autonomy that Benson and I present help to explain the difference between the prescriptions and proscriptions of value-saturated and value-laden autonomy theories, on the one hand, and the constitutive value sets that undergird autonomy theories, on the other. Benson maintains that children consolidate the appropriate reflexive attitudes and learn to self-authorize their conduct as their parents guide them through childhood.[21] Likewise, I maintain that good childrearing includes modeling autonomy competency, offering children opportunities to exercise agentic skills, and prompting them to use these skills frequently.[22] Provided that they've had an autonomy-friendly upbringing, children osmotically acquire the capacities necessary for autonomy and become disposed to avail themselves of those capacities. Having picked up an autonomy-sustaining modus vivendi that cannot be theorized without invoking a set of values, their processes of choosing and acting manifest those values whether or not they explicitly subscribe to them. Just how they choose and act autonomously may be

---

[20] Benson, "Taking Ownership," 114–115.
[21] Benson, "Taking Ownership," 115.
[22] Meyers, *Self, Society, and Personal Choice*, 195–197.

a mystery to them, and the constitutive value set presupposed by their autonomous choices may remain in the background without deleterious effects on their autonomy.[23] They have no more need to theorize their autonomy and commit to exercising the skills that sustain it than they have to comprehend and commit to the physiological processes that enable them to walk around without bumping into things or falling down.

Cheshire Calhoun's distinction between commitments and "deep psychological attractions" is helpful here.[24] Although some philosophers regard motivations that are deep-seated and impervious to change as passive commitments, Calhoun maintains that "all genuine commitments are active in the sense that they are made, not merely discovered as facts about one's psychology."[25] Calhoun allows that decisions can be made with more or less awareness, but she insists that commitments are "authored" both because they arise from decisions for which the agent has reasons and because they require us to make an effort to revive them should they flag and to resist temptations to abrogate them.[26] My claim is that an autonomy theory with a constitutive value set can ascribe autonomy to people who have unwittingly absorbed the relevant cognitive, affective, and volitional dispositions regardless of whether those individuals have decided to deploy those dispositions when they make choices and regardless of whether they have decided to uphold the theory's constitutive value set. Because value-utilizing theories do not require individuals to incorporate the desiderata included in their respective constitutive value sets into their conceptions of the good life, let alone pursue them as instrumental or intrinsic ends, these theories do not require that autonomous individuals be committed to these values.

Now, it goes without saying that people who aren't acquainted with the vocabulary of philosophy of action don't value autonomy under that description. Nevertheless, people commonly do value a solid sense of who they are and what really matters to them, and they value leading a life that is truly their own. Thus, it seems plausible to suppose that many people who have gradually assimilated autonomy capabilities during childhood and who now regularly avail themselves of those capabilities do come to value what philosophers call autonomous choice and action. Moreover, some might form commitments to

---

[23] Westlund echoes this point: "To be self-governing, we don't need to have a clear understanding of what *makes* us self-governing.... We just need to function that way in fact." See Westlund, "Selflessness and Responsibility for Self," 3.

[24] Cheshire Calhoun, "What Good Is Commitment?" *Ethics* 119 (2009): 616–617.

[25] Calhoun, "What Good Is Commitment?" 617.

[26] Calhoun, "What Good Is Commitment?" 617–618. There is of course a familiar logical thesis that you are committed to the presuppositions of your beliefs and to the implications of your belief set. However, transposing this conception of commitment into the realm of practical philosophy would do violence to the subtlety of the distinctions we use to make sense of individuals' normative identities and their conduct. A commitment is not the same as a tentative plan; caring about X is not the same as being committed to X, and so forth.

exercise autonomy capabilities as well as commitments to live by the values that underwrite those capabilities. However, they need not do so to be autonomous. In Calhoun's parlance, their dispositions to exercise autonomy capabilities and thus to go about making choices in ways that coincide with the values implicit in those capabilities can remain deep psychological facts.

Discrete sets of constitutive values underwrite most, probably all, credible theories of autonomy. Consequently, individuals whom a value-utilizing theory judges to be autonomous must manifest the theory's constitutive value set in the way they conduct their lives—their choice processes as well as their ability to carry out their decisions and express their values. According to my view, for example, a person who exercises well-developed, well-coordinated agentic skills will come across as perspicacious, innovative, rational, self-aware, confident of her worth, stable, tenacious, and resilient. Yet nothing prevents a value-utilizing theory from judging people to be autonomous who'd be surprised if someone pointed out to them that they express its constitutive value set in the way they make choices and act on them. This point brings to mind one of Harry Frankfurt's astute observations about autonomy:

> The enjoyment of freedom comes easily to some. Others must struggle to achieve it.[27]

For those who achieve autonomy easily, relying on autonomy skills and expressing an autonomy theory's constitutive values have become second nature. For those who must struggle for autonomy, methodically cultivating autonomous decision-making procedures and resolutely upholding the values that subtend them may sometimes be necessary if they are to sort out their values and stick to their goals.

Taken together, the claims that (1) an autonomous choice process requires exercising a set of capacities, (2) people may regularly exercise these capacities merely as a result of a fortunate upbringing, and (3) these capacities are underwritten by constitutive value sets suggest the need for two axes to characterize autonomy theories. Whereas the Directivity Axis indicates the scope of discretionary choice that an autonomy theory condones, the Constitutivity Axis indicates the values an autonomy theory invokes in specifying the process of autonomous choice.

A strand of Andrea Westlund's thought sheds some light on the idea I'm trying to convey. For Westlund, to be autonomous you must have internalized a disposition to answer for yourself.[28] She emphasizes that self-answerability

---

[27] Harry Frankfurt, *Importance of What We Care About*, 22.
[28] Westlund, "Selflessness and Responsibility," 496; Westlund, "Rethinking Relational Autonomy," 36–37. Please note that Westlund's view is evolving. Although she still holds that her view of autonomy is "formal," she now holds that a disposition to answer for yourself is partly constitutive of the answerability self-relation but not the whole of it. See Andrea Westlund, "Reply to Benson, Christman, Rocha, and Stoljar," *Symposia on Gender, Race, and Philosophy* 7:1 (2011): 2–3, http://web.mit.edu/sgrp; Westlund,

does not depend on favorable beliefs about or attitudes toward yourself, nor does it presuppose that you are symmetrically situated in relation to those who may pose challenges to your commitments or in relation to those with whom you interact most frequently or intimately.[29] It is a "formal relation, constituted by a disposition to respond to normative pressures on one's commitments."[30] Having assimilated this disposition, you take queries about your value commitments from other points of view seriously, and you are prepared to examine your reasons for your commitments.[31] However, satisfying this criterion does not oblige you to engage in hard-knuckle debate with every and any opponent of your beliefs and practices. Challenges sometimes come from left field, and challengers are sometimes out of line.[32] Moreover, telling stories or describing exemplars are acceptable ways to justify your beliefs and actions, and thinking through legitimate challenges privately may suffice.[33] Westlund's answerability criterion cognizes a variety of discursive styles, and it grants individuals a measure of discretion in their encounters with would-be challengers.

Westlund concludes that properly understood, autonomy is relational and value-neutral.[34] In characterizing self-answerability as a formal relationship to potential interlocutors, Westlund sets aside the claim that autonomy requires egalitarian relationships with others or a self-respecting relationship to yourself. Specifically, she is rejecting not only Stoljar's and Babbitt's contention that deference to a subordinate social status is incompatible with autonomy but also Benson's contention that the self-doubt and self-effacement promoted by subordination are incompatible with autonomy.[35] I agree that her theory is value-neutral. Still, I would argue that her account is value-utilizing, for she grounds her conception of answerability in the epistemic value of rational

---

"Autonomy, Authority, and Answerability," *Jurisprudence* 2:1 (2011): 171n25. Here, I quote from her earlier work because she articulates the formality of her position in an especially clear and emphatic way in these papers. In my discussion in Section 4 I'll shift to her modified account of the self-answerability self-relation. I note, though, that it is possible that her contribution to this volume may further amend or jettison parts of the view she has previously published. I won't attempt to take her chapter into account because I haven't had access to it in time to do so. Since my purposes in considering her work are (1) to help me clarify the distinction between the Directivity Axis and the Constitutivity Axis (Section 2) and (2) to illustrate the usefulness of the Constitutivity Axis (Section 4), I don't think my discussion will do any injustice to her work.

[29] Westlund, "Rethinking Relational Autonomy," 27, 39.
[30] Westlund, "Rethinking Relational Autonomy," 37. Also see Westlund, "Selflessness and Responsibility," 520n16.
[31] Westlund, "Selflessness and Responsibility," 497.
[32] Westlund, "Autonomy, Authority, and Answerability," 171.
[33] Westlund, "Rethinking Relational Autonomy," 38–40.
[34] Westlund, "Rethinking Relational Autonomy," 28.
[35] For related discussion, see the valuable distinction in Westlund, "Rethinking Relational Autonomy," 32, between deference and deep deference. As my purpose here is not to assess the strengths and weaknesses of Westlund's account but rather to use her account to illustrate my distinction between the directivity axis and the constitutivity axis, I won't take up the question of whether Westlund's account successfully fends off substantive theories of autonomy.

dialogue and the moral value of interpersonal accountability.³⁶ If so, her claim that answerability is a formal relationship must do double duty. In addition to addressing Stoljar's, Babbitt's, and Benson's reservations about the tenability of value-neutral theories, it must provide a convincing response to the claim that value-utilizing theories don't differ in kind from value-laden or value-saturated theories.

I believe that Westlund underscores the formality of the answerability relationship for the same reason that I refer to autonomy competency as a modus vivendi. Both of us aim to preserve the value neutrality of our views. Westlund's conception of self-answerability as a formal relation and my conception of autonomy competency as a modus vivendi suggest an analogy to the experimental method in science. The experimental method rests on a bundle of epistemic values—for example, accurate data and replicatable results—yet it does not predict what questions scientists will pose or what results their experiments will yield. Likewise, our value-utilizing autonomy theories and the constitutive value sets implicit in them do not predict what autonomous people will choose to do or become other than being autonomous.³⁷ Just as the answerability relationship does not preordain what propositional content your answers will contain, so too autonomy competency does not predetermine the selection of projects and aspirations that you'll decide to organize your life around. Unlike personal life plans or individualized value systems, answerability and autonomy competency are frameworks suitable for anyone to use in conducting a life.

That some sets of constitutive values are amenable to being diverted into the service of a nonautonomous way of life further supports the feasibility of conceiving value-utilizing autonomy theories that are value-neutral. Consider some of the values implicated in the agentic skills I specify. Such attributes as perspicacity, resourcefulness, creativity, rationality, self-esteem, stability, resilience, tenacity, and corrigibility might be directed away from leading a life of your own and dedicated exclusively to raising perfect children or writing great novels. An individual might take up the project of parenting or fiction nonautonomously, and she might assiduously devote her talent and energy to excellent parenting or writing as judged by standards set by others. Living up to

---

[36] Westlund, "Selflessness and Responsibility for Self," 494–495; Westlund, "Rethinking Relational Autonomy," 34–35. Paul Benson, "Commentary on Mackenzie and Poltera (2010) and Westlund (2009)," *Symposia on Gender, Race, and Philosophy* 7:1 (2011): 3 makes a similar point about Westlund's position. And in her response to Benson's commentary, Westlund, "Reply to Benson, Christman, Rocha, and Stoljar," 3, concedes that her view invokes what I am calling a constitutive value set.

[37] This point is on a par with David Velleman's claim about the role of your understanding in autonomous agency. According to Velleman, your understanding is your inalienable point of view in the following sense: You cannot suppress or abandon this capacity without sacrificing your status as an autonomous agent. See J. David Velleman, *The Possibility of Practical Reason* (New York: Oxford University Press, 2000), 137–138.

these external standards might enlist perspicacity, resourcefulness, creativity, rationality, self-esteem, stability, resilience, tenacity, and corrigibility. Yet if she never considers whether her life expresses her distinctive desires, needs, and values—her practical identity as a unique individual—she is not acting autonomously although she may be acting admirably. The same is true of the constitutive value set of Westlund's theory. A physicist could scrupulously adhere to the value of rational dialogue in scientific exchanges and the value of interpersonal accountability in reporting her data, but she might not be in the least disposed to answer for herself in other respects. In other words, the sets of constitutive values that autonomy theories invoke are not equivalent to the practices that the theories specify to explicate autonomy. Only if you make use of the capacities that an autonomy theory sets forth to answer questions about who you are and what matters to you will it judge you to be autonomous. It is not enough to display the values that comprise the autonomy theory's constitutive value set in the pursuit of some project or other.

The sets of constitutive values implicit in Westlund's and my theories do not impeach their value-neutral credentials. However, not all value-utilizing theories are value-neutral. For example, the strong normative competence theory that Stoljar appropriates from Benson's early work is value-utilizing in a way that has prescriptive implications for the choices autonomous agents can make. The epistemic values of true beliefs about correct norms and reflexive critical acumen that are included in the constitutive value set of strong normative competence entail that an autonomous agent cannot forsake genuine norms. Not only must autonomous individuals be able to judge which norms are correct, but also they must be able to discern how those norms apply to their own situations. It seems, then, that Benson is right to charge Stoljar with conflating autonomy with orthonomy.[38]

Value-utilizing theories regard autonomy as a valuable way of life and invoke values to explicate what the process of autonomous choice and action consists in. But whereas value-laden and value-saturated theories proscribe or prescribe the nature of your chosen doings, some value-utilizing theories leave the nature of your chosen doings up to you. Instead of focusing on acceptable outcomes of autonomous choice, value-neutral autonomy theories that are value-utilizing focus on the process of autonomous decision making and decision enactment. Since this is so, pointing out that a theory is value-utilizing really does differ from pointing out that it is value-laden or value-saturated, for value-utilizing theories can secure value neutrality. It is clear, then, that the Constitutivity Axis highlights a relation between autonomy and values that doesn't map onto the Directivity Axis. To advocate distinguishing between these two axes is to advocate what I'll call the Double Axis Thesis.

---

[38] Benson, "Feminist Intuitions," 132.

I close this section as I began it with a reflection on Paul Benson's work on substantive autonomy theory. Near the end of the essay in which he introduces his conception of weakly substantive theories, Benson incisively remarks:

> More interesting is our finding that the distinction between substantive and content-neutral theories, which seemed so sharp and straightforward in earlier phases of contemporary writing on autonomy, should be reconceived as a range of theories that impute *varying kinds of normative substance, through disparate pathways*, to autonomous agency.[39]

Although this passage might be read as affirming a single spectrum of substantive theories, I think that Benson might be receptive to the Double Axis Thesis.[40] After all, he clearly recognizes that different theories incorporate different kinds of norms in different ways, and the purpose of the Double Axis Thesis is to provide a framework for articulating and analyzing this heterogeneity. In the next section, I'll say why as a feminist I advocate the Double Axis Thesis.

3. The Double Axis Thesis and Feminist Autonomy Theory

In Section 1, I probed some well-known feminist autonomy theories to expose the various ways values figure in them. This inquiry led me to distinguish the Directivity Axis from the Constitutivity Axis. Section 2 clarified how the two axes differ and defended the distinction between them. I now urge that the Double Axis Thesis secures two major benefits for feminist philosophy of action. First, by separating the Directivity Axis from the Constitutivity Axis, the Double Axis Thesis avoids foreclosing the category of value-neutral autonomy theories. In my judgment, feminists should prefer a conceptual apparatus that permits assessment of theories that purport to be value-neutral on their merits rather than denying their cogency by fiat. Second, in virtue of recognizing the category of value-neutral autonomy theories, the Double Axis Thesis avoids prejudging how feminist philosophers should theorize the vexed topic of adaptive preferences. I'll offer what I believe to be compelling practical considerations that militate in favor of detaching feminist analyses of adaptive preferences from feminist autonomy theory. To make my case for these claims, I'll rely on the contrast between the Double Axis Thesis, which is conjoined to the conception of the Directivity Axis I laid out in Section 1, and what I'll call the Single Axis Thesis, which holds that all autonomy theories are somehow prescriptive and thus to some degree substantive.[41]

---

[39] Benson, "Feminist Intuitions," 137. Emphasis added.

[40] In email correspondence, Benson has told me that he endorses the Double Axis Thesis as I've laid it out.

[41] Mark Piper explicitly argues for the Single Axis Thesis, though not under that rubric. See Mark Piper, "Autonomous Agency and Normative Implication," *Journal of Value Inquiry* 46:3 (2012): 317–330.

Like most philosophers of action, I take the idea of self-governance through the exercise of practical intelligence to be the core of what we mean by autonomous choice and action. While the theme of self-reflection is pervasive in philosophical accounts of autonomy, different theories accentuate different dimensions of self-governance and subscribe to different accounts of practical intelligence. Some theories prioritize self-expression or self-disclosure. Some stress self-control or self-direction. Some foreground self-ownership or self-responsibility. By no means mutually exclusive, these themes point to nuances that differentiate among approaches to theorizing autonomy. Still, theories of autonomy, including feminist ones, do seem deeply divided between those that see individuality and freedom as the hallmarks of autonomy and those that see responsiveness to reasons as the hallmark of autonomy. The Constitutivity Axis carves constitutive value sets—the values that are implicit in autonomous choice procedures—away from the question of what reasons an agent has to act in the situation she is facing.[42] The Directivity Axis furnishes a tool to conceptualize an important way in which theories that anchor autonomy in responsiveness to reasons differ from those that anchor autonomy in individuality and freedom.

No doubt autonomy theories centered on responsiveness to reasons are heirs to Kant's legacy. The idea that an autonomous person acts on objective reasons discovered through the exercise of reason represents one version of the value-saturated pole of the prescriptivity spectrum. Still, value-saturated theories of autonomy need not valorize reason and marginalize other epistemic faculties. For example, Susan Babbitt's feminist value-saturated theory relies on nonpropositional knowledge and experience of community as resources for detecting genuine reasons.[43] Value-laden theories are less strict about compliance with correct norms. However, they do put a premium on grasping and acting on genuine norms, for you gain autonomy as the influence of oppressive norms wanes in your conduct. In suggesting that people who resist oppressive norms are more autonomous than people who follow them, Marilyn Friedman seems to take up a position in the value-laden sector of the Directivity Axis, her defense of value neutrality notwithstanding.[44] For feminist proponents of value-neutral theory, any other position on the Directivity Axis substitutes moral rectitude—rule by authoritative norms or guarantees of emancipation—for autonomy. Value-neutral theories prize living by your own lights, such as they are. Thus, they carry the banner for the view that leading an autonomous life is principally an exercise in individuality and freedom.

---

[42] However, I note that a constitutive value set that entails a value-saturated position on the Directivity Axis shrinks the gap between the two axes. See my comments on strong normative competence theory in Section 2.

[43] Babbit, "Feminism and Objective Interests," 253–256.

[44] Friedman, *Autonomy, Gender, Politics*, 20–24, 67.

I cannot address the question of the authority for autonomous choice and action in all its complexity here. However, I do want to say a little about why it would be inadvisable for feminists to embrace the Single Axis Thesis. This framework exacts the following trade-off: It downplays the possibility that an individual's distinctive attributes provide the authority for autonomy in order to highlight the fact that all credible autonomy theories incorporate values in some way. Of course, the Single Axis Thesis does not deny that there are stronger and weaker versions of substantive autonomy theories. Some substantive theories issue restrictive commands—for example, an autonomous woman must not risk pregnancy to prove that she's fertile and marriageable.[45] Such strongly substantive theories are far more overbearing than weaker ones that allow women to defer to men's sexual demands and engage in risky reproductive behavior provided that they have distinctive personal motives for doing so.[46] Weakly substantive theories are quite permissive, and they secure greater latitude for agents to express their particular needs, desires, and values.

This being so, it might seem that the Double Axis Thesis sacrifices theoretical parsimony for the sake of a mere label and a misleading label at that. Calling an autonomy theory value-neutral, it might be objected, perpetuates the misconception that it is possible to theorize autonomy without invoking any values apart from autonomy itself. This objection would be sound if I were maintaining an alternative Single Axis Thesis—one that acknowledged only the spectrum ranging from value-saturated theories to value-neutral theories with value-laden theories in between. However, the Double Axis Thesis is designed to perspicuously represent both the possibility that self-expression takes precedence over reason-responsiveness in autonomous action and the insight that all accounts of the process of autonomous choice implicitly or explicitly invoke values. Whereas the array of constitutive value sets on the Constitutivity Axis encodes the latter insight, the value-neutral pole of the Directivity Axis sanctions autonomous expression of individuality.

For feminists, the Double Axis Thesis and its correlative conception of the Directivity Axis are attractive on several counts. One reason to foreground individuality and freedom through value-neutral autonomy theory is to preserve the dynamism of the feminist liberatory agenda. Feminists have repeatedly underscored the personal and societal damage caused by silencing women's voices.[47] Value-neutral autonomy theory guards against suppressing the diversity of women's perspectives and concerns because it does not preemptively

---

[45] Stoljar, "Autonomy and the Feminist Intuition," 99.
[46] For related discussion, see Benson, "Feminist Intuitions," 128–130.
[47] Maria Lugones and Elizabeth V. Spelman, "Have We Got a Theory for You! Feminist Theory, Cultural Imperialism, and the Demand for the Woman's Voice," *Women's Studies International Forum* 6 (1983): 573–581; Maria Lugones, "Playfulness, 'World'-Traveling, and Loving Perception," *Hypatia* 2:2 (1987): 3–19. Meyers, "Gender in the Mirror," 17–22.

deny the autonomy of any woman's beliefs about how she should live. Because its zero point is value neutrality, the Directivity Axis allows for an open-ended view of the scope of autonomous choice. Another advantage of conceiving the Directivity Axis as I propose is that it creates theoretical space for an innovative conception of value-laden theories—theories that take into account the potency or harmfulness of the influence of oppressive norms in individuals' lives. Feminist exploration of this category of theory may prove fruitful, for the value-laden sector of the Directivity Axis invites theorists to develop more refined analyses of how oppression enters into diverse individuals' deliberations and conduct. Finally, the Double Axis Thesis—and specifically the Directivity Axis it posits—clarifies what is at stake in feminist debates regarding adaptive preferences. I turn to that issue now.

In my view, the main appeal of value-laden and value-saturated theories of autonomy stems from feminist concerns about adaptive preferences—preferences that are harmful to the agent, that are formed in response to an oppressive context, and that help to perpetuate oppression. Feminists often affirm that an account of autonomy should have something useful to say about adaptive preferences. But just what an account of autonomy should contribute to discussions of adaptive preferences is controversial.

Value-neutral accounts address the problem of adaptive preferences obliquely. For example, I believe that by and large and in the long run women who have full repertoires of well-developed, well-coordinated agentic skills, who exercise these skills frequently enough to keep them from atrophying, and who mobilize them when they make significant decisions or when they sense trouble in their lives are less likely to submit to oppressive practices and more likely to join with others to overcome oppression.[48] Along similar lines, Westlund adduces relational capacities for self-correction to explain how adaptive preferences can be exposed and shunned. In her view, the process of grappling with "external critical perspectives"—that is, challenges to your beliefs and values that are posed by someone who doesn't share your worldview—can prompt you to reconsider misguided self-subordinating preferences and to modify resulting patterns of behavior.[49] Neither of us believes that any capacity for autonomy provides failsafe protection against the persistence of adaptive preferences, but both of us recognize the potential of exercising agentic capacities for eroding adaptive preferences.

In contrast, value-saturated and value-laden accounts confront the problem of adaptive preferences head-on. To the extent that women enact adaptive

---

[48] Diana Tietjens Meyers, "Feminism and Women's Autonomy: The Challenge of Female Genital Cutting," *Metaphilosophy* 31 (2000): 469–491.

[49] Andrea Westlund, "Autonomy in Relation," in *Out from the Shadows: Analytical Feminist Contributions to Traditional Philosophy*, edited by Sharon Crasnow and Anita Superson (New York; Oxford University Press, 2012), 61, 75–76.

preferences they lack autonomy, and when they shed adaptive preferences they gain autonomy. It is surely tempting to kill two birds with one stone in this way. Yet there is reason to hesitate before adopting this solution.

Babbitt's value-saturated theory espouses conversion experiences that rid you of adaptive preferences as a step toward autonomous agency.[50] Paradoxically, she holds that you can gain autonomy by nonautonomously relinquishing adaptive preferences.[51] Now, few would deny that you can autonomously decide to temporarily suspend autonomous control in order to achieve an autonomously adopted goal—say, undergoing hypnosis to quit smoking. It is clear, though, and Babbitt agrees that involuntarily undergoing a nonautonomous transformation can destroy autonomy.[52] You might end up a mindless acolyte of a crazed cult leader. But because Babbitt's position presupposes that those who induce you to undergo a conversion experience are right about its capacity to augment your autonomy, her position is either incomplete or faulty. Incomplete if it does not furnish criteria for entrusting yourself to convertors or criteria that pick out autonomy-enhancing conversion schemes. Faulty if it leaves autonomy enhancement to luck.

Serene Khader's arguments against analyzing adaptive preferences as autonomy deficits spark related concerns about value-saturated and value-laden theories of autonomy.[53] As Khader observes, building adaptive preferences into a theory of autonomy unwisely presumes that you already know which types of behavior are expressions of adaptive preferences.[54] Khader's more circumspect approach posits a minimal perfectionist account of flourishing—that is, a conception of flourishing that is limited to ensuring basic human needs and that musters broad assent from members of diverse cultural groups.[55] Where women fall short of enjoying this minimal level of flourishing, there are grounds for suspecting that adaptive preferences have taken root, but this suspicion can be vindicated (or quashed) only through a process of deliberative inquiry with the women who lead this form of life.[56] Because people's reasons for acting as they do are not transparent, two individuals may be acting in a seemingly identical way, yet one may be acting on an adaptive preference while the other isn't. If so, adaptive preferences cannot be singled out on the basis of the gendered social meanings feminist theorists ascribe to different types of behavior. It seems, then, that Khader's deliberative approach to identifying adaptive preferences would counsel locating feminist autonomy theories

---

[50] Babbit, "Feminism and Objective Interests," 251.
[51] Babbit, "Feminism and Objective Interests," 254–256.
[52] Babbit, "Feminism and Objective Interests," 251.
[53] Serene J. Khader, *Adaptive Preferences and Women's Empowerment* (Oxford: Oxford University Press, 2011), chap. 2.
[54] Khader, *Adaptive Preferences*, 75, 96–97, 103.
[55] Khader, *Adaptive Preferences*, 21, 138.
[56] Khader, *Adaptive Preferences*, 35–36, 42, 60–73, 138–140.

at the value-neutral end of the Directivity Axis where autonomy depends on the process of choosing rather than on whether the actions that are chosen reinforce oppression or lead to emancipation.

A final worry about identifying more emancipated behavior with more autonomous behavior is that it assigns disproportionate responsibility for social change to individual women. It seems to me that the onus of confronting and overcoming structural injustice should be borne by social movements and persons in politically or economically powerful positions. Yet to avoid having their autonomy downgraded by a value-laden or value-saturated account of autonomy, women facing entrenched patriarchal institutions and repressive practices would be obliged to devise individual workarounds consonant with progressive values. In my estimation, then, such theories load too much of the work of fighting injustice onto vulnerable individuals. Of course nothing is likely to change for the better unless the victims of oppression band together and take collective action. Still, theories of autonomy that make assessments of autonomy contingent on social activism or on individual defiance of unjust norms are in a kind of double jeopardy. Such theories risk condemning autonomous commitments to practices that feminists currently abhor, and they also risk celebrating the autonomy of individuals who are nonautonomously enacting values that feminists currently approve. Both types of jeopardy bespeak a failure to keep in mind that feminist values and goals are always subject to contestation and have undergone striking changes over time.

For all of the preceding reasons, I believe that value-neutral autonomy theory best serves feminist aims. Consequently, I urge feminists to embrace the Double Axis Thesis, which fields a conception of the Directivity Axis that renders value-neutral theory intelligible. Still, this conclusion hardly settles the question of which value-neutral theory—that is, which account of the process of autonomous choice and action—is most in tune with feminist aims. The Constitutivity Axis, I'll argue, provides a novel diagnostic tool for assessing the merits of competing value-neutral theories of autonomy.

4. The Constitutivity Axis as Philosophical Tool

It is a truism that autonomy is a cluster concept, for *autonomy* is a term of art, and different theories of autonomy are designed for different philosophical purposes. Examples of philosophical problems that theories of autonomy may seek to solve or contribute to include:

1. When are individuals responsible for what they do?
2. How can action be guided by reasons?
3. Who is entitled to give or withhold consent to government?
4. When is paternalistic intervention justified or unjustified?

5. What conditions secure social freedom or emancipation?
6. How is it possible to lead a life of your own?
7. What sorts of choices and actions promote personal fulfillment or self-realization?

Because these problems are interrelated, philosophers often undertake to solve more than one of them with a single theory of autonomy. Some examples: David Velleman aims to provide an account of acting for reasons that accords with our conventions of assigning responsibility for action; John Christman aims to provide an account of leading a life of your own that ensures that the vast majority of adult humans qualify as citizens whose consent confers legitimacy on governments; Marina Oshana aims to provide an account that binds leading a life of your own to social freedom and opportunity.[57] I cannot explore the full range of autonomy theories here. However, it is incumbent on me to indicate how philosophers can profitably use the leverage of the Constitutivity Axis. In my view, positioning autonomy theories on the Constitutivity Axis by teasing out their constitutive value sets exposes the inner workings of divergent autonomy theories and thereby connects each theory to a subset of philosophical problems regarding autonomy.

Since I have argued that feminists are well-advised to adopt a value-neutral position on the Directivity Axis, I will examine Westlund's value-neutral, value-utilizing theory of autonomy to clarify the philosophical promise of the Constitutivity Axis. Because Westlund's self-answerability theory aims to account both for leading a life of your own and for placing moral limits on paternalism, it needs to supply an account of autonomy as well as an account of nonautonomy. However, I'll urge that her account of autonomy presupposes one constitutive value set, whereas her account of nonautonomy presupposes another. Thus, focusing on the Constitutivity Axis suggests that Westlund overreaches in attempting to address both the problem of self-direction and the problem of justified paternalism in one fell swoop. Nevertheless, I'll argue that her view is particularly helpful for judging when paternalistic interventions are appropriate in real-world medical and social service settings.

Recall that for Westlund self-answerability—that is, the self-relation in which the agent "holds herself to the *expectation* or *demand* that she respond appropriately to legitimate criticism, experiencing herself as owing a suitable response, at least under certain conditions"—is a necessary condition for autonomy.[58] Westlund is surely correct that we are likely to regard people who address earnest queries about their practical commitments in a forthright

---

[57] Velleman, *Possibility of Practical Reason*; Christman, *Politics of Persons*; Marina Oshana, *Personal Autonomy in Society* (Aldershot, UK: Ashgate, 2006).

[58] Westlund, "Autonomy, Authority, and Answerability," 171; Westlund, "Selflessness and Responsibility for Self," 500, 503; Westlund, "Rethinking Relational Autonomy," 28.

fashion as autonomous and therefore immune to paternalistic interference.[59] Conversely, in some circumstances we become skeptical about someone's autonomy when she mouths someone else's words or reasons in a tight little circle, always sidestepping what an interlocutor who is not like-minded is pressing her to consider.[60] When the stakes are high and time is short, such resistance to rational exchange lowers the barriers against paternalistic intervention. In these respects, Westlund's view is clearly in sync with our interpersonal practices of autonomy attribution and our closely related practices with respect to treating others paternalistically.

Still, Westlund's ambition is not confined to depicting how we judge whether someone is autonomous and whether we should defer to her decisions about her life. In her view, the psychological state of readiness to respond to external challenges to your action-guiding commitments together with your sense that it is imperative to do so is "a crucial part of what *constitutes* [you] as self-governing."[61] How can the Constitutivity Axis help us to think through this claim?

As I pointed out earlier, Westlund's avowed constitutive value set is composed of the epistemic value of rational dialogue and the moral value of interpersonal accountability. This pair of values brings the question of the relation between the stance of self-answerability and the practice of answering for yourself to the fore. The appeal of the epistemic value of rational dialogue is that it introduces an independent check on your thought processes, and the appeal of the moral value of interpersonal accountability is that it rules out sinking into solitary complacency. As a participant in ongoing rational dialogue with different-minded conversation partners who hold you accountable for the cogency of your answers, you can be confident that you really do value what you profess to value and that you really do want to lead the life you're living. Yet Westlund's comments about the practice of answering for yourself do not comport with this robustly relational interpretation of her position.

According to Westlund, autonomous agents must maintain attitudes of humility and open-mindedness toward their values and goals—that is, they must acknowledge their fallibility and be prepared to recognize the possibility that they've been mistaken about what's truly worthwhile.[62] However, she regards comparatively attenuated forms of dialogical engagement and accountability as compatible with humility and open-mindedness. I have already mentioned that she countenances less formal discursive styles than rational debate, such as telling pertinent stories or describing admirable persons and their conduct. As well, she leaves it to individuals whose values and desires

---

[59] Westlund, "Selflessness and Responsibility," 498.
[60] Westlund, "Rethinking Relational Autonomy," 32–33.
[61] Westlund, "Selflessness and Responsibility," 503.
[62] Westlund, "Selflessness and Responsibility," 508; Westlund, "Reply to Benson," 4.

are being challenged to judge whether an interlocutor's objections to her values and desires deserve a response. Here I stress that satisfying Westlund's self-answerability criterion does not always require individuals to address critical challenges posed by an actual interlocutor, nor does it always require them to answer such challenges in an actual conversation. Instead, you may think up arguments against your values and desires from a point of view opposed to your own and formulate responses in your mind's eye.[63] Indeed, Westlund has recently severed self-answerability from actually answering for yourself: You can be self-answerable if you would respond to self- or other-generated challenges should they ever arise.[64]

This steadily thinning view of what counts as answering for yourself raises questions about the tie between the self-answerability criterion Westlund defends and the constitutive value set she articulates. Since she holds that rational dialogue can take place internally, she cannot also hold that there must be an independent check on the pointedness of the objections you raise and the adequacy of your replies. Since she holds that interpersonal accountability need not be instantiated in conversations with actual interlocutors, she cannot also hold that discursive isolation is necessarily inimical to autonomy. Insofar as your desires and values have never been called into question, you need not answer for them at all. Neither dialogue with others nor internal dialogue is needed to certify that they are your own. On all of these counts, the constitutive relationality of Westlund's theory is compromised.[65]

A more fitting constitutive value set for Westlund's fully developed view would conjoin reflexive insightfulness with accountability to yourself.[66] Conceptualizing answerability according to this constitutive value set would reflect the allowances Westlund rightly makes for self-questioning as a form

---

[63] Westlund, "Selflessness and Responsibility," 506, 507, 510; Westlund, "Rethinking Relational Autonomy," 37–41; Westlund, "Reply to Benson," 4.

[64] Westlund, "Reply to Benson," 5.

[65] Westlund can't resolve this problem by affirming that generating internal dialogues and being accountable to yourself for your actions presuppose that you've internalized the answerability mode of relating to others, for this move would reduce answerability to a causally relational, as opposed to a constitutively relational, theory of autonomy. Nor does her claim in Westlund, "Relational Autonomy," 35, that "the internal psychological condition of the autonomous agent...point[s] beyond itself, to the position the agent occupies as one reflective, responsible self among many" resolve this problem. If this internal psychological condition is never activated by external challenges to your important values and desires, an autonomous person will be indistinguishable from a nonautonomous person. For related discussion, see Westlund, "Autonomy, Authority, and Answerability," 175; also see Westlund, "Reply to Benson," 5.

[66] This pair of values brings out the kinship between Westlund's thought and the suggestion in Thomas Nagel, *The View from Nowhere* (New York: Oxford University Press, 1986), 127, that the "best we can do is to try to live in a way that wouldn't have to be revised in light of anything more that could be known about us." In email correspondence, Westlund speculates that it may be possible to theorize reflexive insightfulness and accountability to yourself relationally. So she may seek to salvage the constitutive relationality of her view by offering such an account in future work.

of answerability. Moreover, because authorizing people to meet the answerability condition intrapersonally doesn't rule out making use of interpersonal strategies to deepen your self-knowledge and to strengthen your resolve, it preserves a benign form of relational autonomy. Not only do the quality of your internal dialogue and your determination to uphold certain standards seem more germane to Westlund's avowed project—namely, theorizing what it takes for choices and actions to be genuinely your own—but also these values tally better with the linkage Westlund affirms between self-responsibility, possessing a self, and answerability.[67] Unfortunately, if Westlund were to adopt the constitutive value set I've proposed, she would be committed to a constitutive value set that is out of alignment with a major argument that she offers in support of her view.

Westlund takes up feminist concerns about the deleterious impact that internalized oppression and adaptive preferences have on autonomy when she urges that a virtue of her answerability account is that it clarifies what it is to lack reasons of your own for avowing the values you avow or for wanting what you want.[68] Her characterizations of nonautonomy as being "tightly gripped" by a value system or by a practical reasoning procedure and being "utterly impervious" to objections suggest that nonautonomous agents suffer from an intellectual form of locked-in syndrome. If this metaphor is apt, staging internal dialogues and accounting for yourself to yourself are bound to perpetuate your agentic malady rather than release you from it. It seems, then, that either Westlund must embrace a requirement for autonomy that she herself regards as implausibly strong—communicating your responses to critical challenges lodged by other people in face-to-face encounters—or she must jettison her claim that her view makes sense of lacking autonomy because you are in the grip of a dubious value system or a defective reasoning policy.

It's hardly surprising that the constitutive value set that shores up Westlund's full account of self-answerability is at odds with the constitutive value set that shores up her account of being tightly gripped. The elastic constitutive value set I've associated with her account of autonomy—reflexive insightfulness together with accountability to yourself—makes needed conceptual room for degrees of autonomy and pockets of autonomy. Someone might be fully answerable—introspectively attuned to her needs and lucid about her reasons—with respect to making medical decisions about her health but marginally

---

[67] Westlund, "Selflessness and Responsibility," 495–500; Westlund, "Rethinking Relational Autonomy," 28–30, 37–38; Westlund, "Autonomy in Relation," 70–76. Although Westlund asserts that "we have good reason to treat pressures toward self-answerability...as the very form that the pressures toward the self-governance of practical reasoning take," I note that urging someone to "think for herself" is no less salient a form that pressures toward self-governance take, and this advice comports with the modified constitutive value set I've proposed. Westlund, "Selflessness and Responsibility," 501.

[68] Westlund, "Selflessness and Responsibility," 500–505; Westlund, "Rethinking Relational Autonomy," 28–30, 32–33; Westlund, "Autonomy in Relation," 74–76.

answerable—a bit muddled about her needs and hesitant about her reasons—with respect to her dealings with a domineering husband. If Westlund's theory is to capture the complexity of women's autonomous agency, it must be able to discriminate fine-grained gradations of degree as well as the qualities of relationships that are more and less conducive to answering for yourself. Perhaps the woman who finds herself tongue-tied when answering to her domineering husband is able to be sharply self-critical and articulate in answering criticisms in a quiet moment alone. The constitutive value set I've ascribed to Westlund's nuanced answerability theory accommodates this possibility.

However, because being tightly gripped is an absolute state of nonautonomy, a commensurately exacting constitutive value set is needed to underwrite it. Whereas a modulated theory that accommodates internal reflection as a basis for autonomy would confer autonomy on deeply deferential and blindly fanatical individuals, a theory of autonomy premised on the constitutive value set of rational dialogue and interpersonal accountability would not. If Westlund's (and my) intuition that these individuals aren't autonomous is correct, the less stringent constitutive value set I've attributed to Westlund's fully developed position effectively abandons them to their nonautonomy.

This split between the version of Westlund's view that is needed to account for autonomy and the version that is needed to account for nonautonomy deprives her of a key argument for her answerability requirement. Once the two constitutive value sets are in view, it is evident that her fully developed theory of autonomy is too permissive to explain nonautonomy. Although it is an open question whether a single theory might be able to explicate autonomous choice and action as well as nonautonomy resulting from adaptive preferences, so far as I can see Westlund does not provide a theory that accomplishes both aims.[69]

At this point, however, I would like to set aside these difficulties and consider a notable strength of Westlund's position. Here, too, it is helpful to examine its underlying constitutive value set. In the course of presenting and defending her view, Westlund describes a number of plausible scenarios in which someone's autonomy comes under scrutiny, and these discussions demonstrate the tremendous practical appeal of her position. Social workers and medical practitioners are often called on to judge whether a client or patient has the cognitive wherewithal to competently direct her own affairs. A theory committed to the constitutive value set of dialogical rationality and interpersonal accountability suggests a sensible strategy for arriving at assessments of autonomy in these social service and medical settings.

---

[69] As I mentioned in Section 3, Serene Khader warns against theorizing adaptive preferences as autonomy deficits.

There's no simple protocol for interviewing a person in a way that elicits reliable evidence of her self-answerability. Drawing out a stranger, attentively tracking her idiosyncratic thought processes, and probing them gently and sympathetically is no easy matter.[70] Moreover, conclusions about a person's autonomy based on her testimony must be regarded as controvertible judgments. But detecting self-answerability is decidedly less abstruse than deciding whether someone is identified with the desire she intends to act on or whether she would be alienated from the desire if she were to reflect on it in light of the history of its development.[71] Similarly, it demands a decidedly less tricky evaluation than trying to gauge the extent, depth, and frequency of someone's self-reflection, the intensity and certainty of her affirmation of a desire, the depth or pervasiveness of her affirmed desire, the variety and efficacy of her agentic capacities, and so forth or trying to gauge someone's overall proficiency with respect to autonomy competency and whether she is successfully exercising these skills.[72] In practical settings where momentous decisions must sometimes be made quickly, these four accounts seem fanciful if not downright comical.

Self-answerability anchored in the constitutive value set of rational dialogue and interpersonal accountability may be the best available criterion of agentic competency in time-sensitive, high-stakes decision contexts. Given the gravity of the affront to personal dignity that unwarranted paternalism inflicts together with the superordinate importance of protecting nonautonomous individuals from irremediable harm, self-answerability arguably strikes a feasible and principled balance for assessments of agentic competence. Indeed, my own multidimensional theory of autonomy complements Westlund's by supplying a rationale for regarding self-answerability as a sufficient condition for autonomy in social service and clinical settings. Surely it is reasonable to suppose that people who command the agentic skills that make up autonomy competency and who are able to deploy those skills in coping with their current situations will be able to produce sensible answers to questions about their medical treatment or public assistance options thereby satisfying professionals charged with both respecting their autonomy and promoting their interests that they meet Westlund's answerability requirement. Although I have reservations about whether a conception of answerability premised on the constitutive value set of dialogical rationality and interpersonal accountability is a necessary condition for autonomy, I am inclined to accept this conception as

---

[70] As Westlund, "Rethinking Relational Autonomy," 40, rightly observes, "Part of the burden for facilitating justificatory dialogue thus falls on the shoulders of the would-be critic, who must position herself appropriately with respect to the agent in question."

[71] Frankfurt, *Importance of What We Care About*, 58–68; Christman, *Politics of Persons*, 145.

[72] Friedman, *Autonomy, Gender, Politics*, 7–20; Meyers, *Self, Society, and Personal Choice*; Meyers, *Gender in the Mirror*; Meyers, *Being Yourself*.

a sufficient condition for acknowledging the autonomy of a person who is a candidate for paternalistic intervention.

5. Summary of the Benefits of the Double Axis Thesis

My aim in the forgoing discussions of Khader's theory of adaptive preferences and Westlund's self-answerability theory was not to reach a definitive judgment as to the merits of their positions but rather to illustrate the philosophical payoffs of the Double Axis Thesis. Here I review the benefits of distinguishing the Constitutivity Axis from the Directivity Axis. First, a theory's location on the Directivity Axis signals its understanding of the authority for autonomous agency—objective reasons or your distinctive self. Second, the Double Axis Thesis shows that coherent theories of autonomy can be both value-neutral and value-utilizing. Third, putting theories under the microscope of the Constitutivity Axis can reveal sources of strain and strength in their normative underpinnings. In other words, by exhibiting the implicit value investments of theories of autonomy, the Constitutivity Axis highlights ways in which autonomy theories tally (or fail to tally) with paradigmatic cases of autonomy. Finally, because analyzing a theory's constitutive value set discloses value commitments that might otherwise go unnoticed, the Constitutivity Axis clarifies how and why theories of autonomy converge and diverge, and it facilitates connecting theories to different philosophical problems concerning autonomy. As a result, the Constitutivity Axis helps philosophers of action avoid talking at cross-purposes.

I recognize that these are modest claims. Nevertheless, if I have succeeded in providing a better map of the terrain of feminist work on autonomy and in ending some faux controversies among feminist philosophers, I'll be satisfied with those achievements.

Acknowledgments

Thanks to Andrea Veltman, Mark Piper, Andrea Westlund, Paul Benson, and the participants in the Relational Autonomy: Ten Years On conference for their invaluable comments on an earlier version of this paper.

A Commitment to Autonomy Is a Commitment to Feminism
Marina Oshana

1. The Problem

It is generally believed that autonomy consists, at least in part, of the ability to choose and to act according to the direction of one's will, values, and preferences. Most of us in Western, liberal societies highly prize autonomy, to such an extent that a legal right to autonomy is ensconced in constitutional principles as well as in the tradition of common law. In what follows, I argue that if a moral and legal right to autonomy is to be respected then we must be committed to feminism as a moral and a political ideal. In addition, if we are committed to feminism as a moral and a political ideal then we must also be committed to autonomy as a condition to which people are morally and legally entitled.

To do this, I will use one type of life as a case in point as well as two personal histories. The type of life I will discuss is that of a low-wage laborer in the United States. One of the two personal histories is the self-reported life story of political activist Ayaan Hirsi Ali.[1] The second example was recently reported in the *New York Times* and recounts the ordeal of a young Afghani girl.[2] There are, of course, limitations to the conclusions one can draw about feminism and autonomy from either story or from my remarks about low-wage labor. I do not wish to generalize the cases, but I believe they are instructive. They all lead me to wonder just how feminists construe autonomy and just how far defenders of autonomy want to carry the banner of feminist causes. And they make me wonder why the term *feminist* irks people or strikes the ear as an outmoded moniker.

---

[1] Ayaan Hirsi Ali, *Infidel* (New York: Free Press, 2007).
[2] Alissa J. Rubin, "For Punishment of Elder's Misdeeds, Afghan Girl Pays the Price," *New York Times*, February 16, 2012, http://www.nytimes.com/2012/02/17/world/asia/in-baad-afghan-girls-are-penalized-for-elders-crimes.html?_r=1&ref=todayspaper.

Let me begin by explaining what I mean by *autonomy* and by explaining how I understand the concept of feminism. Autonomy literally means "self-rule" or "self-governance." A person is autonomous when she is self-governing. She is self-governing when she has a kind of authority over oneself as well as the power to act on that authority. As I have argued elsewhere, the kind of authority involved must be of a form and extent sufficient for a person to influence and to oversee those of her choices, actions, and relationships that are definitive of successful practical agency of a fairly comprehensive variety.[3] This means that the presence of social roles and relations that afford a person this influence and authority are decisive if the person is to count as genuinely self-determining, *whatever* her choices are for and however laudable they appear to be. I characterize autonomy in this way because I take seriously the idea that people are complex beings and because I am concerned with issues having to do with self-governance under a broad spectrum of social conditions. I also take seriously the idea that autonomy offers one dimension for evaluating human development.[4] Being autonomous implies that certain capabilities are available to the agent, some of which are social and political in nature.

I will define feminism, as others have, as "an intellectual commitment and a political movement that seeks justice for women and the end of sexism in all forms.... Feminism is a belief in and advocacy of equal rights for women based on the idea of the equality of the sexes."[5] Feminist ethics and politics are concerned with issues pertinent to women's autonomy, including "ending the oppression, subordination, abuse, and exploitation of women and girls, wherever these may arise."[6] To some, the label feminist has an antiquated ring. It conjures up images of bra burners, Gloria Steinem aviator frames, and an era—allegedly past—when women's rights were in need of political support. Others find the label distasteful, seeing it as evoking opposition to men (or to what men allegedly represent) or to traditional values and social practices such as marriage and a desire to raise a family. These are crude caricatures, of

---

[3] See Marina Oshana, *Personal Autonomy in Society* (Aldershot, UK: Ashgate, 2006), 64–67. Psychological autonomy (in the realm of the "inner citadel") is incapable of empowering a person in many areas of life that are crucial to successful agency where conditions of this sort are present or probable. Moreover, neither a legal right of authority over one's affairs nor a moral right of authority shall suffice for autonomy.

[4] What I will say on this point echoes some remarks made by Martha C. Nussbaum, *Women and Human Development: The Capabilities Approach* (The Seeley Lectures), (New York: Cambridge University Press, 2000); Nussbaum, "The Future of Feminist Liberalism," reprinted in Cheshire Calhoun, ed., *Setting the Moral Compass: Essays by Women Philosophers* (New York: Oxford University Press, 2004), pp. 72–88; and Nussbaum, *Creating Capabilities: The Human Development Approach* (Cambridge: Belknap Press, 2011).

[5] In formulating this definition, I relied on Sally Haslanger and Nancy Tuana, "Topics in Feminism," 2004, http://plato.stanford.edu/entries/feminism-topics/ (original publication February 7, 2003).

[6] Marilyn Friedman, "Feminism in Ethics: Conceptions of Autonomy," in *The Cambridge Companion to Feminism in Philosophy,* edited by Miranda Fricker and Jennifer Hornsby (Cambridge: Cambridge University Press, 2000), 205.

course, but in the past twenty years they have been affirmed to a surprising degree, especially among younger adults. Keeping these definitions of autonomy and of feminism in mind, let us turn to the cases I mentioned: the low-wage laborer; Ayaan Hirsi Ali; and a young Afghani girl.

2. Autonomy and Wage Labor

Autonomy-undermining social conditions that fall heavily on women are to be found in the secular world of Western free enterprise. Certain areas of wage-labor are illustrative of this phenomenon. Consider the circumstances of the hotel maid, the housecleaner, the waitress, the nursing home aide, and the Wal-Mart salesperson depicted in Barbara Ehrenreich's excellent book *Nickel and Dimed*.[7] These workers are disproportionately female.[8] Their situations are not uncommon. They perform work that is back-breaking, poorly remunerated, lacking in benefits, and without security of employment. Each is emblematic of labor that is consistently exploitative and autonomy depriving.

I say this because it is a well-supported fact that persons require a minimum level of economic self-sufficiency to minimize the likelihood that "others

---

[7] Barbara Ehrenreich, *Nickel and Dimed: On (Not) Getting By in America* (New York: Metropolitan Books, 2001).

[8] Sarah Jane Glynn and Audrey Powers, See *The Top 10 Facts About the Wage Gap: Women Are Still Earning Less than Men across the Board,* Center for American Progress, April 16, 2012, http://www.americanprogress.org/issues/labor/news/2012/04/16/11391/the-top-10-facts-about-the-wage-gap/, report that "more than one-quarter of the wage gap is due to the different jobs that men and women hold." Notably, "women are more likely to work in low-wage, 'pink-collar' jobs such as teaching, child care, nursing, cleaning, and waitressing. The top ten jobs held by women include secretaries and administrative assistants (number one); elementary and middle school teachers (number four); cashiers and retail salespeople (number six); maids and housekeepers (number ten), and waitresses. These jobs typically pay less than male-dominated jobs and are fueling the gender wage gap." In addition, Glynn, "The Wage Gap for Women: The Consequences of Workplace Pay Inequity for Women in America," August 16, 2012, http://www.americanprogress.org/issues/labor/news/2012/08/16/12029/fact-sheet-the-wage-gap-for-women/, cites the familiar statistic that "women who work full time year round continue to earn only about 77 percent of what men earn. The gap between the median wage for a man and that of a woman in 2010 was a whopping $10,784 per year. That is enough money for the average woman to fund a year of higher education and a full year of health care costs, while still having more than $2,400 to contribute toward her retirement." The U.S. Department of Labor, Bureau of Labor Statistics, "Characteristics of Minimum Wage Workers: 2011," March 2, 2012, http://www.bls.gov/cps/minwage2011.htm, reports that "in 2011, 73.9 million American workers age 16 and over were paid at hourly rates, representing 59.1 percent of all wage and salary workers. Among those paid by the hour, 1.7 million earned exactly the prevailing Federal minimum wage of $7.25 per hour. About 2.2 million had wages below the minimum.... About 6 percent of women paid hourly rates had wages at or below the prevailing Federal minimum, compared with about 4 percent of men." The Department of Labor, "Labor Force Statistics from the Current Population Survey," February 16, 2011, notes, "Women who worked full time in wage and salary jobs had median weekly earnings of $657 in 2009. This represented 80 percent of men's median weekly earnings ($819)." To learn more, see Women in the Labor Force: A Databook (2010 Edition), BLS Report 1026, December 2010, http://www.bls.gov/cps/demographics.htm#women.

might gain control over them through their needs."[9] Persons who rely on day labor or low-income unskilled labor for their livelihood generally live in economically precarious conditions. Often their physical and psychological states are fragile as well. The same can be said of someone who is one paycheck away from homelessness. Most occupy a state of vulnerability that, fortunately, is not a feature of the actual situation of persons such as myself. Most persons in my position—well-educated, successful academics who enjoy the security of a tenured job and its benefits—are autonomous. We who enjoy this kind of security have genuine control over affairs of importance to us in large part because we are *not* living hand to mouth.

Of course, we must accept that some degree of insecurity and dependency is present even in the lives of well-situated adults. Obviously, not all of instances of insecurity and dependency compromise self-government in a serious way. How are we to distinguish genuine threats to autonomy from more benign and commonplace lapses of practical control and authority? I suggest we employ a three-step assessment.[10] To determine whether a person's situation in life undermines the practical control demanded of autonomy, we must ask, first, what is the insecurity a person encounters? Are significant areas of a person's life at risk? Significant areas will encompass those in which a person has a fundamental interest. For instance, such areas include the interest one has in choosing one's partner, in making choices about whether to start a family, and in one's pursuit of a career. In addition, most humans have a deep-seated investment in the quality of their future lives, and what they can plan, hope for, and expect depends in no small part on their current state of autonomy. Notably, too, self-governance in these areas signals one's success as a human agent. Being a successful agent means being capable of more than simple intentional action. It means being able to *own* one's action. Next, we must ask what is required to challenge the insecurity. How demanding is the type and level of exertion a person must expend to confront the conditions of insecurity and dependence that may undermine her autonomy? Finally, what effect does this have on the person? What does it cost a person when struggle and indefatigability are the price one must pay to have ownership over significant domains of one's life?

If an individual is financially insecure and this insecurity means she cannot challenge potential encroachments on the part of those who have power over her, then her autonomy will be diminished and of less practical value.

---

[9] Diana Meyers, *Self, Society, and Personal Choice* (New York: Columbia University Press, 1989) 12. As Meyers observes, "If one can take care of oneself, one is beholden to no one—neither to the state nor to any other individual" (12).

[10] The three-step assessment is developed in greater detail in my paper, Marina Oshana, "Is Social-Relational Autonomy a Plausible Ideal?" in *Personal Autonomy and Social Oppression: Philosophical Perspectives*, edited by Oshana (London: Routledge, forthcoming).

Successful agency—the cornerstone of autonomy—calls for an absence of exploitation, of which financial exploitation is one variety. If those who are more powerful are in a position to exploit the less powerful, to "forcibly extract labor from those who are economically or otherwise disadvantaged," the result is an assault on autonomy.[11] Extraction of labor is, plausibly, "forcible" if one's circumstances leave one with little alternative but to acquiesce. As Marilyn Friedman notes, "Having to let the needs and desires of another person determine the course of one's behavior in order to survive is a tragically heteronomous mode of existence."[12] In contrast, the person who has the benefit of financial security is less susceptible to these encroachments.

Control and authority can be undermined in different ways, one of which is by the prevalence of psychological, material, and social impediments. Archetypal examples are the conditions that black and mixed-raced persons confronted in South Africa under the official governmental policies of apartheid and life for persons of color in the era of Jim Crow segregation laws in the United States. But an impediment need not rise to the level of the systemic oppression of apartheid or Jim Crow: dependency on some forms of low-wage labor can be fairly characterized as an impediment of this sort.

Practical control and authority can also be undermined when they serve a person only in activities that are of little import to human life. Again, none of us has control and authority over every component our lives, at all times. But we do not require "muscle" of such an all-encompassing variety to be self-governing. In general, while the range of control a person requires will reflect the unique interests and ends of the person, the fact of control will be invariant. For example, while an autonomous academic will require the presence of a unique set of practical conditions that support the variety of tasks essential to her profession and an autonomous day-wage laborer will require that similarly distinctive conditions be in place, neither will count as autonomous unless both can determine the trajectory of their lives without undue cost.

The aim of this section has been to offer a general conception of autonomy and to shed light in a broad way on the variety of autonomy-constraining circumstances persons confront. One variety of life that illustrates the threat to autonomy distinctively borne by women is that of low-wage and pink-collar labor. I have suggested criteria for delineating circumstances that jeopardize autonomy from more mundane conditions that are less problematic in this regard. In Section 3, we will consider the cases of Ayaan Hirsi Ali and of a young Afghani girl. Both highlight the threat to autonomy faced by females from certain aspects of conservative patriarchy of a sort found in predominantly

---

[11] Tommie Shelby, *We Who Are Dark: The Philosophical Foundations of Black Solidarity* (Cambridge, MA: Belknap Press, 2005), 193. For a development of this claim, see Oshana, "Is Social-Relational Autonomy a Plausible Ideal?"

[12] Friedman, "Feminism in Ethics: Conceptions of Autonomy," 219.

Islamic cultures (as well as in very conservative strains of Christianity and some ultra-orthodox sects of Judaism).

3. Cultural and Religious Patriarchy

AYAAN HIRSI ALI

Even while the details of her autobiographical narrative have been challenged, facts about Ayaan Hirsi Ali's life attest to a remarkable set of experiences. Hirsi Ali spent her youth in a seminomadic Somali Muslim family, mainly in Kenya. Her mother was a devout adherent of Wahhabi Islam, a particularly conservative, politicized, and patriarchal variety practiced largely in Saudi Arabia. In her own words, Hirsi Ali lived "by the Book, for the Book."[13] But after witnessing the frustration and experiencing firsthand the misplaced anger of her mother, Hirsi Ali came to believe that she had to escape Somali culture. Failing to do so, she feared she would suffer her mother's fate. In Hirsi Ali's estimation, her mother had sublimated her independent spirit to prevailing patriarchal and religious expectations, with the result that she became "a devoted, well-trained work-animal."[14] Had she remained, Ali remarks, "I could never become an adult. I would always be a minor, my decisions made for me. But I wanted to become an individual, with a life of my own."[15]

Thus, it came about that in 1992 at the age of twenty-two Hirsi Ali fled to the Netherlands, claiming political asylum under the pretense that she was escaping a forced marriage. (This claim was later admitted to be false.) In the aftermath of September 11, 2001, she denounced Islam and converted to atheism. By 2002, she was elected to the Dutch parliament "on a wave of anti-immigrant sentiment."

Hirsi Ali has made it her mission to criticize Islamic customs. In particular she has taken to task emigrant Muslim communities in Europe and the United States for what she regards as their failure to embrace the secular political customs of their adopted nations. In 2004, Hirsi Ali wrote the screenplay and provided the voice-over for filmmaker Theo van Gogh's made-for-television piece *Submission*. The subject of the film was the treatment of women in Islamic culture. This was recounted by way of the tale of a Muslim woman coerced into a violent marriage, raped by an uncle, and then viciously punished for adultery.[16]

---

[13] Hirsi Ali, "To Submit to the Book Is to Exist in Their Hell," *Sydney Morning Herald*, June 4, 2007, http://www.smh.com.au/news/opinion/to-submit-to-the-book-is-to-exist-in-their-hell/2007/06/03/1180809336515.html.

[14] Johann Hari, "My Life under a Fatwa," *Independent*, November 27, 2007, http://www.independent.co.uk/news/people/profiles/ayaan-hirsi-ali-my-life-under-a-fatwa-760666.html.

[15] Hari, "My Life under a Fatwa."

[16] "Juxtaposed with passages from the Qur'an were scenes of actresses portraying Muslim women suffering abuse. The film also features an actress dressed in a semi-transparent burqa who has texts

The film, which aired on Dutch television in August 2004, infuriated members of the Dutch-Muslim community who viewed it as insensitive, profoundly sacrilegious, and untruthful. On November 2, 2004, van Gogh was assassinated by Mohammed Bouyeri, an Islamic radical and member of the Hofstad Group.[17] Impaled upon the knife stabbed into van Gogh's body was a five-page letter condemning Hirsi Ali to death as an apostate. After a fatwa—a decree of death—was delivered against her in 2004, Hirsi Ali lived under armed guard. In 2006, she moved to the United States, following uproar over the lies she had told to obtain asylum, which grew to include a false name and birthdate. She now holds a fellowship at the conservative American Enterprise Institute in Washington, D.C.

Depending on your point of view, Hirsi Ali is "a radical individual freedom fighter," someone who has "put her life on the line to defend women against radical Islam,"[18]—Islam of a sort that presses for the institution of Islamic law in government and civic life—or she is "a chameleon of a woman" with a "talent for reinvention"[19] whose motives are to be regarded with some skepticism. Notably, her refusal to distinguish mainstream Islam of a sort practiced by roughly three million people in the United States from its politicized and radicalized variants is empirically misguided and deeply troubling, not least of all to feminist Muslim women.[20] For instance, she charges that all of Islam is "full of misogyny."[21] But whatever you think about Hirsi Ali—and let me be upfront about the fact that I am not a fan of hers—she presents an absorbing

---

from the Qur'an written on her skin. The texts are among those often interpreted as justifying the subjugation of women." Toby Sterling, "Dutch Filmmaker Theo Van Gogh Murdered," *Chicago Tribune*, November 2, 2004, http://metromix.chicagotribune.com; "Gunman Kills Dutch Film Director," BBC News, November 2, 2004, http://news.bbc.co.uk/2/hi/europe/3974179.stm.

[17] This was an Islamic militant group of men of Dutch and Moroccan descent who met in The Hague and who had been tried in Dutch appellate court on charges of fomenting terrorism. BBC News, "Dutch Jail 'Terror Group' Muslims," March 10, 2006, http://news.bbc.co.uk/2/hi/europe/4793546.stm. For an update in the case, see "Court Orders Retrial of Dutch Terror Group," Radio Netherlands Worldwide, February 2, 2010, http://www.rnw.nl/english/article/court-orders-retrial-dutch-terror-group; Wendy Zeldin, "Netherlands: Retrial of Hofstad Group," Library of Congress, February 22, 2010, http://www.loc.gov/lawweb/servlet/lloc_news?disp3_l205401830_text.

[18] Patt Morrison, "Feminism's Freedom Fighter," *Los Angeles Times*, October 17, 2009, http://articles.latimes.com/2009/oct/17/opinion/oe-morrison17.

[19] *Economist*, "A Critic of Islam," February 8, 2007, http://www.economist.com/node/8663231.

[20] Iranian American author Firoozeh Dumas is one such critic. http://firoozehdumas.com/ The estimated number of Muslims really is rough. Statistical citations range from two to five billion. See http://www.religioustolerance.org/isl_numb.htm, http://www.adherents.com/largecom/com_islam_usa.html, and http://www.islam101.com/history/population2_usa.html.

[21] In Bob Drogin, "Book Review: *Nomad* by Ayaan Hirsi Ali," *Los Angeles Times*, June 7, 2010, http://articles.latimes.com/2010/jun/07/entertainment/la-et-book-20100607, writes: "Fired with the zeal of a convert, Hirsi Ali insists Islam and the West are locked in "a clash of civilizations"…The "dysfunctional Muslim family constitutes a real threat to the very fabric of Western life," and the "Muslim mind" is "in the grip of jihad."

picture of one woman's determination to assert her autonomy against the most resistant of forces.

Moreover, Hirsi Ali's call for heightened scrutiny of political Islam does not reflect simple paranoia or alarmism. In 1991, Sharia law, which is based on the Qur'an, became authorized for use in arbitration over civil matters such as property rights, divorce, and child custody in Ontario, Canada, ostensibly as a way to lessen the load borne by the civil courts. Margaret Wente of the *Globe and Mail* wrote of the decision:

> The arbitrators can be imams, Muslim elders or lawyers. In theory, their decisions aren't supposed to conflict with Canadian civil law. But because there is no third-party oversight, and no duty to report decisions, no outsider will ever know if they do. These decisions can be appealed to the regular courts. But for Muslim women, the pressures to abide by the precepts of sharia are overwhelming. To reject sharia is, quite simply, to be a bad Muslim.... Opponents of the new tribunals argue that the government's imprimatur will give sharia law even greater legitimacy.... What is called sharia varies widely (in Nigeria, for example, it has been invoked to justify death by stoning). The one common denominator is that it is strongly patriarchal.[22]

The decision to authorize sharia law has been hotly contested. Some of the most vocal opponents are Muslim women who emigrated to Canada and whose children are Canadian by birth. Two of these women are Alia Hogben, who headed the pro-faith Canadian Council of Muslim Women, and Homa Arjomand.[23] Arjomand recounts the following story in support of her concern:

> "I have a client from Pakistan who works for a bank," Ms. Arjomand tells [Wendt]. "She's educated. She used to give all her money to her husband. She had to beg him for money to buy a cup of coffee. Then she decided to keep $50 a month for herself, but he said no." They took the matter to an uncle, who decreed that because the wife had not been obedient, her husband could stop sleeping with her. (This is a traditional penalty for disobedient wives.) He could also acquire a temporary wife to take care of his sexual needs, which he proceeded to do. Now the woman wants a separation. She's fighting for custody of the children, which, according to sharia, belong to the father."[24]

---

[22] Margaret Wente, "Life under Sharia, in Canada?" *Globe and Mail*, May 29, 2004, http://www.theglobeandmail.com/news/national/life-under-sharia-in-canada/article743980/.
[23] http://www.nosharia.com/.
[24] Wendt, "Life under Sharia?"

SHAKILA'S STORY

We move now to the third case, which was reported in February 2012 in the *New York Times*. In 2010, Shakila, an Afghani Pashtun girl from rural Kunar Province was abducted and enslaved for a year under a traditional Afghan method of justice known as *baad*.[25] Shakila was eight years old at the time. *Baad* uses girls as compensation for moral and cultural transgressions perpetrated by their relatives and tribal elders. In Shakila's case, the violation occurred when one of her uncles ran off with the wife of a regional leader. During the course of the year, Shakila was beaten, deprived of food, and confined for most of the day. She managed, miraculously, to escape, but her ordeal is hardly over. Fearing retribution, her family has fled their home, and they now eke out a precarious living some distance from their village.

The objective of *baad* is to appease the anger of an injured family and to partially reimburse them for whatever loss they suffered. In addition, by forcing a girl into slavery, feuding families are integrated, thus minimizing the prospect of sustained hostility. While *baad* is technically illegal, it is widely accepted in rural Pashtun regions as a form of justice emanating from a Jirga, the judicial court of tribal elders. Shakila's father's response to her abduction makes plain that he had no quarrel with the practice of *baad*. Rather, his objection was that Shakila had been promised in infancy in marriage to someone else; she was thus someone else's property, not his to dispose of. His view is commonplace even among members of the legislature. Fraidoon Mohmand, a member of Parliament from Nangarhar Province, assesses the practice from a pragmatic, utilitarian standpoint. He states that "giving baad has good and bad aspects. The bad aspect is that you punish an innocent human for someone else's wrongdoings, and the good aspect is that you rescue two families, two clans, from more bloodshed, death and misery." Like most men in this culture, Mohmand believes the good outweighs the bad; the girl given away may suffer "for a year or two, but when she brings one or two babies into the world, everything will be forgotten and she will live as a normal member of the family." His rosy assessment was challenged by the Afghan women interviewed for the piece. One woman, Nasima Shafiqzada, who oversees women's matters for Kunar Province states that "the woman [or girl] given to a family in baad will always be the miserable one." The girl not only represents the enemy but also at a tender age "is completely unprepared both for the brutality she will encounter because of it and for the sexual relations often demanded of her."

---

[25] Alissa J. Rubin, "For Punishment of Elder's Misdeeds, Afghan Girl Pays the Price," *New York Times*, February 16, 2012, http://www.nytimes.com/2012/02/17/world/asia/in-baad-afghan-girls-are-penalized-for-elders-crimes.html?_r=1&ref=todayspaper. Baad is not an Islamic practice. The *Times* reports that it predates Islam and can be traced to an era "when nomadic tribes traveled Afghanistan's mountains and deserts."

The cases of Hirsi Ali and of Shakila discuss examples from Muslim culture. The reader might well criticize them as being cheaply purchased by exploiting Western liberal bias and of being bluntly inattentive to widely (and rightly) discredited cultural imperialism. And indeed, one need exert only mild effort to find cognate examples within certain cultural enclaves in Western societies where non-Muslim culture does not predominate. Although low-wage labor of the sort discussed in Section 2 is not a social practice rooted in patriarchy or religion, it is widespread in the West and destabilizes autonomy disproportionately for women. It would seem obvious that feminists would take up the campaign of low-wage laborers on the grounds that their economic vulnerability makes equal opportunities for self-governance (for women and men) a struggle. It would seem obvious that feminists would take up the banner of females in patriarchal societies on the grounds that they endure customs that violate autonomy. Just as Hirsi Ali's life in Kenya meant subjugation and a loss of autonomy, Shakila's tale illustrates a socially entrenched practice that unquestionably fails to respect the dignity and the autonomy of females. It seems equally apparent, to my mind at any rate, that champions of autonomy would decry the blatantly sexist (and thus arbitrary) basis on which female low-wage workers are financially exploited. Similarly, I would expect proponents of autonomy to denounce the manner in which girls in Shakila's situation are deprived of their rights of self-governance. Neither, however, is true. Not all feminists have embraced the value of autonomy as readily as one might suppose, nor have some proponents of autonomy unequivocally taken up the banner of feminism. Let us explore why this is the case. Having done so, we will be in a better position to see why both would be better off as allies.

4. Autonomy

Those of us in Western, liberal societies tend to construe autonomy, at a minimum, as the desirable condition of being free to choose and to act according to the direction of values and preferences that are one's own. At the same time, most of us are drawn to the idea that autonomy can, in theory at least, be realized through myriad ways of life and are wary of the idea that only certain social arrangements befit self-governance. Some even go so far as to claim (as does Andrea Westlund) that "there is no contradiction between self-responsibility and self-subordination."[26] It is enough, Westlund argues, that a person has freely accepted her situation and can answer for her commitments in the face of critical challenges to these. The person who can do this will count as self-responsible and so autonomous, even if these commitments are

---

[26] Andrea Westlund, "Rethinking Relational Autonomy," *Hypatia* 24:4 (2009): 32.

self-subordinating and even if they manifest a lack of self-respect, assuming the person has not internalized whatever social expectations might force this commitment. Westlund's position is developed in an effort to accommodate the belief that to respect autonomy is to permit persons to fashion and pursue their own conceptions of the good.

Though critical of Western feminism, the feminist philosopher Uma Narayan argues for autonomy in a similar vein.[27] Narayan contends that Western feminists stereotype the lives of many Third World women, regarding them either as "prisoners of patriarchy," forced to accept oppressive lives, or as "compliant dupes of patriarchy," so dominated by the prevailing culture that they have lost any capacity for critical, reflective, independent judgment. As a result, Narayan advocates a fairly thin construction of autonomy along the lines offered by Westlund.

Now, it would be easy to argue that the feminist commitments to women's empowerment and to analyzing and resisting the circumstances of women's subordination draw on *some* conception of autonomy as part of what such commitments entail. I confront a more difficult task—or, rather, two tasks. One task is that of establishing the claim that a feminist society must respect autonomy as I have characterized it. That is, I need to establish that a commitment to "thick" autonomy is necessary to achieve feminist goals. My view is that such a commitment is in fact embraced far more readily than many feminists and theorists of autonomy have allowed. I hope to persuade the reader that even those scholars who see themselves as advocating thin conceptions of autonomy in fact advocate conceptions of autonomy that are thick, even while they may not realize the thickness of their conceptions. In addition, I need to show is that respecting autonomy means supporting feminist concerns. One cannot claim to be a champion of autonomy at the same time one resists in a general way feminist projects and concerns. The relation between autonomy and feminism is one of mutual entailment.

The truth of neither assertion—that a commitment to feminism entails a commitment to (thick) autonomy and that a commitment to autonomy entails a commitment to feminism—is obvious. Indeed, some have questioned whether there is in fact a genuine disagreement between myself and feminists who do not think autonomy entails feminism, and who do not even invoke autonomy in articulating feminist concerns.[28] One explanation for the putative lack of disagreement is that the account of autonomy I invoke and the conception as it is deployed by feminist scholars are different conceptions. Perhaps feminists work with so narrow an interpretation of autonomy that the thesis

---

[27] Uma Narayan, "Minds of Their Own: Choices, Autonomy, Cultural Practices, and Other Women," in *A Mind of One's Own: Feminist Essays on Reason and Objectivity*, 2nd ed., edited by Louise M. Antony and Charlotte E. Witt (Boulder, CO: Westview Press, 2002), 418–432.

[28] I thank Wilson Mendonça for pressing this point.

that autonomy is related (in some way) to feminism will be utterly without controversy. By contrast, the account of autonomy I advance is quite broad. My position is that a person is autonomous when she has (1) the ability to superintend those of her decisions, activities, and personal associations that are central to human agency, (2) the warrant to do so, and (3) the power to act on that ability. Together, these imply the presence of social roles and relations of a particularly autonomy-friendly variety. Many might not interpret autonomy as I have done; they may accuse my conception of being an interpretation of autonomy that includes ideas of agency, self-sufficiency, individuality, empowerment, and human dignity. They might protest that autonomy as I have defined it imports narrowly Western values or values that peremptorily designate the good for any person, regardless of what the person professes her conception of the good to be. In a nutshell, some would argue that we must attend to the distinction between thin autonomy of a sort that may well be comfortable with feminism and a thick or substantive species of autonomy of a sort that some feminists dispute. Even if I am correct that feminists must value the broader conception of autonomy, feminists need not agree that this is what autonomy *is*. It is certainly true, for example, that Westlund supports feminism, even if she does not do so on the basis of a thin construction of autonomy alone.

But I think there is more agreement than there is disagreement regarding the proper interpretation of autonomy for feminist concerns. Most feminists do not advocate just a commitment to a legal or moral right to self-governance but also a commitment to self-governance as an actual state of life. The appearance of disagreement might be traced to the belief that the conception of autonomy I advance is normatively substantive in the sense proposed by Natalie Stoljar and by Paul Benson. But in fact I am not claiming, as Stoljar and Benson have claimed, that the autonomous agent cannot internalize oppressive norms or that she cannot value subordinate roles, although as a matter of empirical fact doing so may be correlated with or give rise to diminished autonomy.[29] What I am claiming—and here I suspect most feminists at any rate agree—is that the practical control autonomy demands draws both from sources internal to the agent and from external authority of a variety that mandates the absence of domination. And I am claiming, further, that autonomy is a matter of living in this way regardless of a person's preferences and subjective interests. If there is convergence of opinion on this point, then there is less daylight between the thicker, more socially demanding notion of autonomy I advance and whatever account of autonomy is congenial to feminists.

For this reason, I think there is something perplexing about the view of autonomy taken by Westlund and the view of feminism taken by Narayan. It is

---

[29] My account is minimally substantive in that the autonomous agent cannot internalize oppressive norms to such an extent that doing so critically undermines the possibility of effective practical control.

true that not everyone will include an autonomous life among the objectives he or she esteems. It is also obvious (and I would say regrettable) that not everyone will embrace the concerns of feminism. But although neither Westlund's construal of autonomy nor Narayan's views about western feminism call for legal rights to nondomination, and while both would grant that someone could freely choose to be dominated, I suspect neither Westlund nor Narayan would claim autonomy was a feature of life for persons such as Shakila (or for Hirsi Ali before she fled to the Netherlands). And I think they could deny that Shakila and Hirsi Ali lacked autonomy because respect for feminism, along with the practical resources feminism requires of society, was missing from their lives.[30] If we take seriously the goals of feminism—namely, advocating for the equal rights of women and ending the oppression and exploitation of women and girls—then we cannot rest content with a thin variety of autonomy premised on a person's free acceptance of and willingness to defend her circumstances. It really would not make any practical difference to Hirsi Ali if she had accepted her life in Kenya or if Shakila had been a bit older and had agreed to be used in *baad. Baad* violates autonomy owing to the patently chauvinist foundation on which girls are divested of the power of self-governance, creating a situation in which some persons are in no way capable of freely choosing their way of life. What this signals to my mind is that scholars such as Narayan and Westlund may in fact construe autonomy rather thickly as a de facto or actual state of life. Any situation where people live in common and where some have power over others will only be congruent with feminist concerns if thick autonomy is respected. It is one thing to acknowledge a variety of social arrangements that comport with individual ideals and quite another to assert that each of these arrangements will provide a life of autonomy. The three-step assessment for autonomy serves as a filter for the satisfaction of feminist criteria as gauged by the details provided by the assessment: (1) what areas of life are insecure, (2) what is called for to diffuse the insecurity, and (3) what effect does this have on the lives of the parties?

5. Autonomy and Human Development

The previous discussion suggests that a commitment to feminism involves a commitment to thick autonomy. In this section, I would like to explore the other side of the equation, namely, the idea that one who is committed to autonomy must also be committed to feminist goals such as the empowerment of women and girls. Let us begin by noting that respecting the autonomy of

---

[30] The same could be said of some low-wage pink-collar workers whose employment conditions are precarious.

women requires that we take seriously the centrality they accord interpersonal relations in their lives. A classic feminist insight into the nature of women's moral experience is that women are more likely than are men to value relational interdependency; the moral perspective of women reflects this. Women (it is argued) have a relational conception of moral ideals and appear less inclined than do men to dismiss the emotions as a legitimate and essential component of moral judgment. This does not mean that women care less about their own powers of self-governance than do men or that the concept of autonomy must demand less of the social and relational conditions women encounter for their autonomy to be valued. What it means is that taking seriously any woman's autonomy involves honoring her interdependent, social personality.

What does this require? The capabilities approach to human and moral development articulated by Martha Nussbaum and Amartya Sen offers an answer to this question. The approach is congenial to the account of autonomy I advance and offers a reason to treat thick autonomy as an essential element of women's development.[31] Let me say a bit more about why I think this is so. The cornerstones of classical liberalism and, more specifically, of the idea of liberal justice are the concepts of individual choice and liberty. Any liberal ideology will begin with these two cornerstones and from these describe the public and institutional arrangements best tailored to guarantee their presence in human life. Nussbaum argues, however, that we need to recast liberal theory in a way that preserves these cornerstones while also capturing what it means to be a flesh and blood human functioning in the real world. To this end, liberalism would do well to begin with a conception of persons as immersed in relationships of caring and dependency. These relationships reflect the diverse intellectual, emotional, and bodily abilities persons possess. What we must do, counsels Nussbaum, is start with a conception of the person that corresponds to this human experience—the person "as both capable and needy"—as opposed to a conception of persons as the impartial moral deliberators or self-interested contractors that populate the philosophical imaginations of Kant, or Rawls, or contractarian theory.[32] Having done so, we will see that assessing who qualifies as well-off according to liberal justice calls for a measurement that includes, among primary goods, the ability of persons to take part in an extensive range of human endeavors. With "a suitable list of the central capabilities as primary goods, we can begin designing institutions by asking what it would take to get citizens up to an acceptable level on all these capabilities."[33]

---

[31] I thank Maria Silvia Possas for suggesting the connection between my conception of autonomy and the liberal capabilities view of Nussbaum and Sen.

[32] Nussbaum, "Future of Feminist Liberalism," 79.

[33] Nussbaum, "Future of Feminist Liberalism," 79.

Nussbaum is not prepared to say just what that level would involve, but she does offer hints. With Sen, she defines capabilities as "substantial freedoms" of the sort that include combinations of opportunities to function in various ways. Importantly, capabilities "are not just abilities residing inside a person but also the [totality of] freedoms or opportunities created by a combination of personal abilities and the political, social, and economic environment."[34] For instance, she would include among the basic goods the need for care—which is something that all of us, given our "animality," will require at some point.

The Nussbaum–Sen approach suggests that autonomy as I have characterized it is a capability, located among the list of primary goods "founded in the dignity of human need itself,"[35] such that any measurement of liberal justice calls for a measurement that includes autonomy. The principal questions posed by Nussbaum and Sen for the more comprehensive assessment of justice they advocate are, "What are people capable of doing?" and "How are people able to live?" Both Nussbaum and Sen note that what people seek is meaningful lives for themselves; what I would add is that being self-governing is an element of a meaningful life and, more generally, that people are most capable of accomplishing this if they are self-governing in a robust way.[36] To put the point somewhat differently, autonomy is, borrowing from terminology employed by Jonathan Wolff and Avner de-Shalit, a particularly "fertile" capability, that is, a capability that is essential to removing "corrosive disadvantages" of the sort that undermine other dimensions of a person's experience that spell out how the person is able to live—dimensions such as health, well-being, social respect.[37] Autonomy lends security to these other capabilities, promising that one can bank on their presence in the future. And this type of security "is an objective matter...for each capability we must ask how far it has been protected from the whims of the market or from power politics."[38]

If my appropriation of elements of the capabilities approach in defense of robust autonomy survives inspection, then the strain of liberalism behind which some feminists and autonomy theorists seek the protective shelter of neutrality is not nearly as neutral as might be hoped with respect to the social

---

[34] Nussbaum, *Creating Capabilities*, 20.

[35] Paraphrased from Nussbaum, "Future of Feminist Liberalism," 79.

[36] Some people might quarrel with the idea that a life bereft of autonomy is a meaningless life. Let me be clear that I am not claiming that meaning can only be found in lives that are rich with autonomy. In other work, I have taken pains to show that autonomy is not the sole good and that there are other measures of a meaningful life, such as flourishing or satisfaction. Oshana, *Personal Autonomy in Society*. Nonetheless, I think ample evidence can be marshaled in support of the claim that where people do lead meaningless lives, the reason for the meaninglessness can be "a lack of opportunities for growth, development and relationship, which can be due to oppressive social relations" (Andrea Veltman in editorial commentary). A robustly autonomous person avoids these circumstances.

[37] Jonathan Wolff and Avner de-Shalit, *Disadvantage* (New York: Oxford University Press, June 2007). Their work is discussed in Nussbaum, *Creating Capabilities*, 44.

[38] Nussbaum, *Creating Capabilities*, 43.

goods and capabilities all persons are assumed to need. Autonomy is in some measure constitutive of a meaningful life for persons. And, in truth, other philosophers whose scholarship often addresses explicitly feminist concerns but who publically have challenged (indeed, disavowed) portions of the account I defend nonetheless speak of the conditions needed to realize a feminist society in terms that echo the capabilities approach. Marilyn Friedman, for instance, argues that "in order to challenge the formidable structures of male domination that remain in this world, it is crucial for feminism to insist that mature women are as capable as men of being full moral agents in their own rights and *should no more be dominated or controlled over the course of their lives* than men are."[39] Being as capable as men entails having a commensurate array of opportunities and a network of support at the ready, as championed by the capabilities approach.

We might press this point from a different direction. A right of autonomy is found in the moral idea that persons have an inherent dignity in virtue of which they are entitled to a certain standing that constrains both how persons are to be treated and what they are permitted to do and expected to do vis à vis one another. I think it is clear that if many of the rights that we indisputably have are to be respected, then autonomy must be respected as well. And for autonomy to be respected, the social institutions that permeate our affairs—and this includes institutions of law, whether they are found in the United States or in Afghanistan—must afford us de facto and de jure power to counter attempts to intrude capriciously in our lives. This requirement is especially pressing in cases such as Shakila's, where attempts to deprive a person of her rights are rampant. No person who is in a society, and particularly those who are most vulnerable, can determine how she shall live unless she is part of enduring social relations and shared traditions that afford her authority over the most fundamental areas of her life, in law and in practice, and without undue cost. If we are committed to something more than the legal promise of autonomy and if we are committed to more than a moral right of self-governance—if, that is, we are committed to an idea of autonomy as a practical condition in which a person is empowered to choose what to do by means of her own authority—then it seems straightforward that a commitment to autonomy entails a commitment to feminism as a moral and a political ideal. This is certainly a conclusion to which we are led if we follow Nussbaum and Sen in drawing on a richer variety of social goods deemed essential to the promises of liberal justice.

---

[39] Friedman, "Feminism in Ethics," 216. Emphasis added.

6. Some Objections

Let us turn to some objections that my account might face. To begin, what would be the consequences for my account if a commitment to autonomy entailed a commitment to a social structure that is de facto supportive of women's equality and equal rights while lagging in a moral commitment to the equality of women? A number of modern affluent societies might meet this description, including, perhaps, the United States. Indeed, this possibility is reminiscent of the criticism some feminists have registered against classical liberalism as an adequate political philosophy, one attentive to the status of women.[40] Mark Piper worries that this would be "enough to undermine the notion that a commitment to thick autonomy entails a commitment to the moral aspects of feminism dealing with a commitment to the equal value of women."[41] I am not sure I share Piper's worry. It may be that such societies are only committed to autonomy of a thinner variety. In the United States there is certainly ample lip service to the moral dimensions of feminism; it is in the lack of a tangible commitment to the institutional and practical dimensions of feminism—where this would call for a commitment to thick autonomy—that the true nature of this commitment is revealed. Such societies do not really support feminist goals in a functional way—if they did, the United States would have passed an equal pay for equal work amendment long ago. The failure to do so belies not just a commitment to the moral claim that men and women have equal value but also a commitment to thick autonomy. It may also be the case that a commitment to thick autonomy is incumbent on a commitment to de facto support of equality but less so to the moral dimensions of equality. Perhaps the moral commitment is less urgent than is the commitment to practical equality. I myself think that de facto support is unlikely absent an attendant moral commitment and that a commitment to moral equality in itself is cold comfort for one whose autonomy is elusive or denied altogether in fact.

A second worry for the account I defend was raised by John Christman in conversation. Christman suggested that it is an implication of my position that only feminists can be autonomous. It would certainly seem a stretch to deny that nonfeminists can be autonomous, and if the view I was defending yielded this result the account would be less plausible. Fortunately, this is not an implication of my account. That a person manages to live according to ideals and allegiances that are recognizable as her own, without troublesome interference, is a real possibility even for people who repudiate any

---

[40] See, e.g., Susan Moller Okin, *Justice, Gender, and the Family* (New York: Basic Books, 1989); Catherine Mackinnon, "Reflections on Sex Equality under the Law," *Yale Law Journal* 100:5 (March 1991): 1281–1328; Mackinnon, *Feminism Unmodified: Discourses on Life and Law* (Cambridge, MA: Harvard University Press, 1987).

[41] In private commentary.

allegiance to feminist ideology. The "would-be surrendered woman" whose desire to give herself over to the direction of her husband is frustrated given the plainly self-governed life she leads is a case in point. In such cases, the repudiation of feminism is accompanied by a repudiation of robust autonomy as a desirable condition of life. But rejecting an idea will not amount to rejecting the state that the idea captures or to divesting oneself of that state. I can reject the ideals of feminism even while (and perhaps because) I am autonomous.

A third complaint may be pressed by feminists who urge a more communitarian than classical liberal political ideology and who allege that personal autonomy is less desirable than I have portrayed it, certainly less desirable than Western liberalism would have us believe. They argue that autonomy is a value opposed to "social" virtues such as caring, empathy, loyalty, regard for and commitment to others and as antithetical to cooperative projects.[42] These social virtues characterize the lives of women. By contrast, autonomous agents are said to be excessively self-absorbed, self-created individuals, dependent on none but themselves, bound by no limitations other than those they levy on themselves. But this style of life is drawn from the experience of men and neglects what is of importance to women from a woman's perspective.

This is not, however, a sensible depiction of autonomy. The problem with this picture does not reside in the idea that an autonomous individual is, loosely speaking, sovereign over her decisions and actions. The worrisome aspect of this story is that it caricatures autonomy, presenting it as a value that commends a form of individualism that is hostile to social goods and relationships. To portray persons as radically independent individuals ignores the social dimension of our lives and discounts the importance of interpersonal relationships. But we all know that a theory of autonomy demanding radical independence of this variety would be implausible and undesirable. None of us is self-created; each of us is shaped by his environment, just as each of us—if we are lucky, at any rate—is supported by interpersonal relations. (Oddly, I suspect it is this confused caricature of autonomy that springs to the minds of some persons when they recoil from the label *feminist*. They equate *autonomy independence* with *denigration of traditional ties*. The irony is that the caricature is one that has gained some traction among some feminist critics of autonomy.) In any case, feminists who interpret autonomy in this fashion commit a mistake, as do antifeminists whose rejection of feminism arises from this misleading interpretation of autonomy.

---

[42] The discussion that follows is from Marina Oshana, "The Autonomy Bogeyman," *Journal of Value Inquiry* 35:2 (June 2001): 209–226.

7. Conclusion

If we accept what I have said about autonomy, then I think we can expect feminism of at least a modest variety. The point is not that in some cases the concerns of feminism and of autonomy go hand-in-hand. The point is that respecting autonomy means respecting feminist concerns and vice versa. Proponents of autonomy must unequivocally uphold feminism. And being committed to feminist concerns leads one more closely to a robust relational account of autonomy than might initially seem the case. Recall my initial definition of feminism as "a belief in and advocacy of equal rights for women based on the idea of the equality of the sexes." People who are autonomous have a characteristic type of social standing. This is the social standing people have "when they live in the presence of other people and when, by virtue of social design, none of those other dominates them."[43] This characterization is consistent with the initial definition I offered, namely, that a person is autonomous when she makes decisions and engages in actions by means of her own authority. I would also suggest that it is a definition of autonomy that ought to be accepted by feminists, even those who worry about an excessively individualistic conception of that state.

To avoid misunderstanding, let me state clearly that the point I wish to make is that one cannot be *committed* to autonomy unless one is *also committed* to feminism and, conversely, that one cannot be *committed* to feminism unless one is *also committed* to autonomy. This does not mean that any society in which autonomy happens to be realized by its members will be a society committed to feminism. A society may be inconsistent in upholding those goals to which it professes commitment or may fail to give sufficient weight to these goals. What I have attempted to do in this paper is show why, to the extent that autonomy is prized, feminism ought to be prized as well and vice versa. Thus, despite criticisms of certain interpretations of autonomy from feminists and despite the idea that under certain conditions autonomy and oppression may be compatible, I have uncovered no discussion in the philosophical literature or in feminist commentary that would cast serious doubt on the idea that a commitment to autonomy is a commitment to feminism and vice versa. Despite the interminable debate over thick and thin conceptions of autonomy, my position is that most theorists of autonomy are not as thin as they think.

---

[43] Philip Pettit, *Republicanism: A Theory of Freedom and Government* (New York: Oxford University Press, 1997), 122.

Acknowledgments

Earlier versions of this paper were presented at a workshop on Relational Autonomy organized by the Department of Philosophy at McGill University in Montréal, September 2012, at the Federal University of Rio de Janeiro, June 2012, and at the Center for Practical and Professional Ethics, California State University, Sacramento, February 2012. I thank the members of the workshop and the audience on these occasions for their helpful remarks.

{ PART III }

Autonomy, Reasons, and Care

{ 8 }

Emotions, Reasons, and Autonomy
Christine Tappolet

As Alison Jaggar notes in her paper "Love and Knowledge: Emotion in Feminist Epistemology," "not only has reason been contrasted with emotion, but it has also been associated with the mental, the cultural, the universal, the public and the male, whereas emotions have been associated with the irrational, the physical, the natural, the particular, and of course, the female."[1] If we add the quite common thought that autonomy and reason are closely associated, the question can arise whether women are even capable of autonomy.

This train of thought can be expressed in the form of what is likely to seem a rather ludicrous line of thought.

The Ludicrous Argument:
1. Women are emotional.
2. Emotional agents cannot be autonomous.

Therefore, women cannot be autonomous.

Even though there is surely no lack of proponents of this view in the history of ideas, it is clear that few contemporary thinkers would be inclined to embrace such an argument, which is likely to strike most of us as both "repugnant and factually unsubstantiated."[2]

One notable complication comes from feminist criticisms, according to which autonomy is a dubious masculinist ideal. Lorraine Code writes: "Autonomous man is—and should be—self-sufficient, independent, and self-reliant, a self-realizing individual who directs his effort towards maximizing his personal gains.... In short, there has been a gradual alignment of autonomy with individualism."[3] On such a view, which equates autonomy with

---

[1] Alison Jaggar, "Love and Knowledge: Emotion in Feminist Epistemology," *Inquiry* 32 (1989): 166.
[2] Diana Tietjens Meyers, "Personal Autonomy and the Paradox of Feminine Socialization," *Journal of Philosophy* 84 (1987): 621.
[3] Lorraine Code, "Second Persons," in *What Can She Know? Feminist Theory and the Construction of Knowledge*, edited by Lorraine Code (Ithaca, NY: Cornell University Press, 1991), 78.

self-centered individualism, that autonomy might not be an option for women and other beings who undergo emotions should appear welcome.

However, as many feminists have convincingly argued, autonomy need not be conceived in terms of such a dubious ideal. Autonomy can, and indeed has been, reconceptualised from a feminist perspective.[4] What lies at the heart of the feminist reconfiguration of the concept of autonomy is the undeniable fact that agents are socially embedded. This is the thought that the label *relational autonomy* aims at capturing. Whatever the details this new conception of autonomy is taken to have, it holds the promise of an attractive ideal, which few would want to forsake. This reconfigured conception of autonomy thus gives good reasons to resist the *Ludicrous Argument*.

The question that arises is how exactly the Ludicrous Argument should be resisted. One route is to argue that even though there is a grain of truth in the hackneyed association of emotions with women, it would be a mistake to infer that women cannot be autonomous. Another route is to claim that there are no important gender differences at the affective level in the sense that all normal human beings undergo emotions, while denying that there is any incompatibility between being emotional and being autonomous. Whichever route is preferred, the crucial question is that of the relation between emotions and autonomy.[5] This is the question I want to focus on in this paper, thereby leaving aside the complex empirical issue of gender differences regarding emotions.[6]

It will be useful to begin by saying a few words about the concept of autonomy. In the sense of this term at stake here, to be autonomous is for an agent to steer her own course through life rather than being the mere plaything of winds and currents. The thought is that an agent is autonomous when she governs herself. Thus, what can be considered her authentic self and not some foreign force, be it external (such as an abusive husband or degrading socialization) or internal (such as a compulsive desire), directs her thoughts and actions. One prominent idea is that personal autonomy requires critical

---

[4] See Jennifer Nedelsky, "Reconceiving Autonomy: Sources, Thoughts and Possibilities," *Yale Journal of Law and Feminism* 1 (1989): 7–36; Marilyn Friedman, "Autonomy and the Social Relationships: Rethinking the Feminist Critique," in *Feminists Rethink the Self*, edited by Diana Tietjens Meyers (Boulder, CO: Westview Press, 1997); Catriona Mackenzie and Natalie Stoljar, *Relational Autonomy: Feminist Perspectives on Autonomy, Agency, and the Social Self* (New York: Oxford University Press, 2000); Marina Oshana, *Personal Autonomy in Society* (Aldershot, UK: Ashgate, 2006).

[5] Interestingly, this is a question that has been on the agenda of relational autonomy theorists. See Mackenzie and Stoljar, "Introduction, Autonomy Refigured," in Mackenzie and Stoljar, *Relational Autonomy*, 21–22.

[6] One difficulty comes from the fact that there could be gender differences concerning (1) the kinds of emotions that tend to be felt, (2) what tends to trigger emotions of the same kind, (3) the different aspects of emotions, such as expression and motivation, and (4) the regulation of emotions. Another difficulty is that generalisation of this kind are in danger of downplaying individual as well as sociocultural differences.

reflection. It is insofar as the agent subjects her motivations and action-guiding principles to critical reflection that she can be taken to be autonomous.[7]

This notion of autonomy is thought by many to be closely related to that of agency, or at least to the kind of agency, sometimes called *full-fledged* or *full-blooded*, which is often considered to be characteristic of human beings.[8] In the introduction to his collected papers, Gary Watson asks: "What makes us agents—that is, individuals whose lives are attributable to them as something they (in part) conduct, not just something that occurs?"[9] To answer this question, Watson appeals to the notion of a "capacity for critical evaluation." As he puts it, "we are agents because (and insofar as) we shape our lives by the exercise of normative intelligence," which according to him involves a capacity to respond relevantly to reasons.[10] On the assumption that autonomy can be spelled out in terms of a capacity for critical evaluation that involves reason-responsiveness, the question of the relation between emotions and autonomy becomes, at least partly, that of the relation between emotions and the capacity to respond to reasons.

Reason-responsiveness accounts of autonomy, which can be considered broadly Platonic, are not the only accounts of autonomy on the market. Drawing on the Humean tradition, some accounts emphasize the importance of the motivational cum affective in autonomy. The foremost example of this kind of accounts is Harry Frankfurt's hierarchical model of free will and autonomy, which is exclusively framed in terms of conative states of different orders.[11] Building on Frankfurt's model, David Shoemaker proposes an account that takes emotions to be essential to autonomy. According to Shoemaker, autonomy involves acting on one's cares, understood not as motivational states but as emotional dispositions. What he claims, thus, is that "the emotions we have make us the agents we are."[12] The idea is that the emotions we feel are intimately related to who we are, for they reveal what we deeply care for. Emotions, rather than potentially distorting reflection, would be essential to authenticity and thus also to autonomy. By contrast with reason-responsiveness accounts,

---

[7] See, e.g., Marilyn Friedman, "Autonomy and the Split-Level Self," *Southern Journal of Philosophy* 24 (1986): 19–35.

[8] For the term *full-blooded*, see J. David Velleman, "What Happens When Someone Acts?" *Mind* 101 (1992): 462.

[9] Gary Watson, "Introduction," in *Agency and Answerability: Selected Essays* (New York: Oxford University Press, 2004), 1.

[10] Watson, "Introduction," 2.

[11] See, e.g., Harry Frankfurt, "Freedom of the Will and the Concept of a Person," *Journal of Philosophy* 68 (1971): 5–20. Note that insofar as Frankfurt suggests that reflection is the source of higher-order volitions, the contrast is less stark. See, e.g., Frankfurt, "Freedom of the Will and the Concept of a Person," 7.

[12] David Shoemaker, "Caring, Identification, and Agency," *Ethics* 114 (2003): 94; see Tappolet, "Autonomy and the Emotions," *European Journal of Analytic Philosophy: Special Issue on Emotions and Rationality in Moral Philosophy* 2 (2006): 45–59.

an account in terms of care might appear to be more congenial to a feminist rejection of the Ludicrous Argument. However, I shall argue that it would be wrong to believe that the two accounts are fundamentally opposed.

My plan is the following. In the first section, I present an account of emotions according to which emotions are a kind of perceptual experience and suggest that emotions can grant us a privileged access to values and reasons. In the second section, I turn to the relation between emotions and reason-responsiveness. In particular, I focus on cases of akrasia in which emotions conflict with the agent's better judgment and argue that even in such cases we are able not only to track reasons but also to be reason-responsive when we act on our emotions. Put simply, what I propose is that reason-responsiveness requires the exercise of agential virtues. In the last section, I examine the implications of this account of emotions for both reason-responsiveness and care-based accounts of autonomy. The first point I spell out is that emotions and autonomy need not be at odds. The second point is that a better understanding of emotions reveals that the two approaches are not as opposed as they might at first appear.

1. Emotions and the Perception of Values

Emotions make for a complicated field of inquiry. A first source of complication is that emotional, and more generally affective, phenomena are highly variegated. It is thus common to distinguish between actual episodes of emotions, such as the fear you feel when you realize that someone is following you on your way home, and the disposition to undergo a range of emotional experiences, such as arachnophobia. A second source of complication is that emotions are naturally taken to be divided into different kinds. We distinguish not only among fear, disgust, and anger but also among pride, joy and hope, to name only but a few. Finally, a third source of complication is that emotions are complex phenomena. A typical episode of fear at someone who is following you involves a number of different elements. You hear someone following you, you appraise the situation as a threat, you undergo physiological changes such as an increased heart rate, your face will adopt a typical expression; in addition, you will feel a specific pang. Your attention will focus on the supposed threat, your mind will be filled with thoughts related to the situation and how to escape it, and you will be motivated to take up a specific course of action, if only to walk as fast as you can. Such complexity makes it difficult to develop a satisfactory theory of emotions. A central question any theory of emotion has to address is which elements, if any, are essential to emotions.[13]

---

[13] The best introduction to emotions theory I am aware of is Julien Deonna and Fabrice Teroni, *The Emotions: A Philosophical Introduction* (New York: Routledge, 2012).

To introduce the account I find most plausible, let me consider an example offered by Marilyn Friedman of a woman who has been socialized to believe that a woman's place is in the home and who has thus embraced principles that prevent her from critically questioning her way of life but who experiences emotions that conflict with her overall assessment of her life. As Friedman notes, her "frustration, grief, and depression...may be her only reliable guides" to a more autonomous path.[14] More generally, Friedman suggests that emotions or more generally affective states constitute "touchstones of a sort for the assessment of the adequacy of one's principles."[15] The claim that affective states in general and emotions in particular constitute what can be considered to be epistemic touchstones in the assessment of our normative judgments is grounded in a conception of emotions, according to which emotions have two key characteristics: (1) emotions have cognitive content; and (2) emotions can conflict with conceptually articulated states, such as beliefs and judgments.

As recent debates in emotion theory make clear, these two features are central to an account of emotions according to which emotions are, in essence, a kind of perceptual experience.[16] What is specific to these perceptual experiences is that they represent their object in evaluative terms.[17] When appropriate, fear would thus consist in the perception of something as fearsome, and the same would hold for disgust and the disgusting, admiration and the admirable, and so forth. On what I take to be the most plausible version of such an account, emotions have representational, albeit not conceptually articulated, content. Emotions represent their object as having specific evaluative

---

[14] Friedman, "Autonomy and the Split-Level Self," 30–31. Cf. Alison Jaggar, "Love and Knowledge: Emotion in Feminist Epistemology"; Karen Jones, "Emotion, Weakness of Will, and the Normative Conception of Agency," in *Philosophy and the Emotions*, edited by Anthony Hatzimoyis (Cambridge: Cambridge University Press, 2003).

[15] Friedman, "Autonomy and the Split-Level Self," 30–31.

[16] See Alexius Meinong, "Ueber Emotionale Präsentation," *Kaiserliche Akademie der Wissenschaft in Wien* 183, Part 2, *On Emotional Presentation*, translated with an introduction by Marie-Luise Schubert Kalsi (Evanston, IL: Northwestern University Press, 1917), 1–181; Ronald de Sousa, *The Rationality of Emotion* (Cambridge, MA: MIT Press, 1987); de Sousa, "Emotional Truth," *Proceedings of the Aristotelian Society* 76 (2002): 247–263; Christine Tappolet, "Les émotions et les concepts axiologiques," in *La Couleur des pensées, Raisons Pratiques*, edited by Patricia Paperman and Ruwen Ogien, (Ville: Édition, 1995), 237–257; Tappolet, *Émotions et Valeurs* (Paris: Presses Universitaires de France, 2000); Tappolet, "Emotions, Perceptions, and Emotional Illusions," in *Perceptual Illusions: Philosophical and Psychological Essays* (Palgrave-Macmillan, 2012); Sabine Döring, "Explaining Action by Emotion," *Philosophical Quarterly* 53 (2003): 214–230; Döring, "Seeing What to Do: Affective Perception and Rational Motivation," *Dialectica* 61 (2007): 361–394; Jesse Prinz, *Gut Reactions: A Perceptual Theory of Emotion* (New York: Oxford University Press, 2004); Prinz, "Is Emotion a Form of Perception?" *The Modularity of Emotions, Canadian Journal of Philosophy* 32 (2008): 137–160; Julien Deonna, "Emotion, Perception and Perspective," *Dialectica* 60 (2006): 29–46.

[17] The account is often presented in terms of perceptions instead of perceptual experiences, but because emotions can misfire, the perceptual account claims only that emotions are the perception of evaluative properties unless defeated. By contrast with perceptions, perceptual experiences are not factive. If you perceive that the cat is black, then it is black, but you can of course have the perceptual experience of a gray cat as black.

properties, as fearsome or disgusting, even though the agent who undergoes the emotion need not possess the relevant evaluative concepts (e.g., fearsome, disgusting).[18] Thus, an emotion of fear with respect to a dog will be appropriate just in case the dog is really fearsome.

What makes what can be called the Perceptual Theory of Emotions attractive is that it steers a middle course between two opposed accounts of emotions, each of which has some plausibility but both of which are ultimately unsatisfactory. At one end of the spectrum, there is the so-called Feeling Theory, according to which emotions consist in states, such as bodily sensations, that are characterized by the way they feel but that have no representational content.[19] At the other end of the spectrum lies the Judgmental Theory, according to which emotions are or necessarily involve conceptually articulated judgments so that to fear something would amount to judge that the thing in question is fearsome.[20] The main objections to the Feeling Theory are that it cannot take into account that emotions have intentional objects (e.g., we are afraid of a dog, angry at someone) and that it fails to make room for the fact that we assess emotions in terms of how they fit their object, such as when we say that it is inappropriate to feel fear at an innocuous spider. Apart from the fact that it does a poor job at accounting for the fact that emotions are felt states, what plagues the Judgmental Theory is that it is incompatible with the observation that one can undergo an emotion without possessing the relevant concepts—one can be afraid of something without possessing the concept of fearsomeness, for instance.[21]

By contrast, the Perceptual Theory can readily acknowledge that emotions are felt states, in the sense that there is something it is like to undergo an emotion of fear or of admiration. But the Perceptual Theory is in a better position than the Feeling Theory in that it can make room for the fact that emotions have intentional objects and allows for cognitive assessment in terms of how well emotions fit their object. At the same time, since the content of emotions is not taken to be conceptually articulated, the Perceptual Theory is not committed to the claim that emotions require concept possession.

---

[18] For concepts and nonconceptual contents, see, inter alia, Gareth Evans, *Varieties of References* (Oxford: Clarendon, 1982); Christopher Peacocke, *A Study of Concept* (Cambridge, MA: MIT Press, 1992).

[19] See William James, "What Is an Emotion?" *Mind* 9 (1884): 188–204; Carl G. Lange, *Om Sindsbevaegelser: Et Psyki-fysiologisk Studie* (Kjbenhavn: Jacob Lunds, 1885), translated in *The Emotions*, edited by C. G. Lange and William James (Baltimore: Williams and Wilkins, 1922).

[20] See Robert C. Solomon, *The Passions* (Indianapolis: Hackett Publishing Company, 1976); Martha Nussbaum, *Upheavals of Thought: The Intelligence of Emotions* (Cambridge: Cambridge University Press, 2001).

[21] The same problem arises for so-called Judgmental Theories, according to which the cognitive states are taken to be thoughts (Patricia S. Greenspan, *Emotions and Reasons* (New York: Routledge and Kegan Paul, 1988)) or construals (Robert C. Roberts, *Emotions: An Essay in Aid of Moral Psychology* (Cambridge: Cambridge University Press, 2003)).

The main argument for the perceptual account is an argument by analogy. It is based on the observation that emotions and sensory perceptions, such as visual or tactile experiences, share a number of important features.[22] Like sensory perceptions, emotions appear to have a characteristic phenomenology; both emotions and sensory perceptions are in general caused by things in our environment; both fail to be directly subject to the will; both appear to have correctness conditions, in the sense that they can be assessed in terms of how they fit the world; and finally both can conflict with judgment. As is made clear in the Müller-Lyer illusion, we can see two lines as being of different lengths while judging they are of the same length, and we can feel fear at something that we judge to be harmless.[23] As will be clear, these last two features are the ones that are central in an explanation of the role of emotions as epistemic touchstones spelled out by Friedman.

Of course, there are also a number of differences between emotions and sensory perceptual experiences.[24] For instance, there are no sensory organs underlying emotions, and unlike sensory perceptions emotions themselves rely on what are often called cognitive bases—you need to see or hear, or else remember something, to be afraid of it. Even though there is no space to argue for this claim here, I believe that taking these points into account makes for a more nuanced picture of emotions than the analogies with sensory perceptions initially suggest, but they do not impugn the core of the perceptual account.[25]

To better to understand what the Perceptual Theory entails with respect to the epistemic role of emotions, consider again an episode of fear. If it is true that fear is, for example, the perception of a dog as fearsome, it will also be true that fear will inform an agent about what she has normative reasons to do.[26] For hardly anyone would deny that something's being fearsome is a pro tanto reason to do or refrain from doing certain things. This

---

[22] See Meinong, *On Emotional Presentation*; Tappolet, *Émotions et Valeurs*, chap. 6; Prinz, *Gut Reactions. A Perceptual Theory of Emotion*, chap. 10; Prinz, "Is Emotion a Form of Perception?"; Deonna and Teroni, *Emotions*, chap. 6; Michael S. Brady, "Emotions, Perception and Understanding," in *Morality and the Emotions*, edited by Carla Bagnoli (New York: Oxford University Press, 2001), chap. 2.

[23] See, inter alia, Tappolet, "Emotions, Perceptions, and Emotional Illusions," in *Perceptual Illusions: Philosophical and Psychological Essays*, edited by Clotilde Calabi (Houndsmill, UK: Palgrave-Macmillan, 2012).

[24] See de Sousa, *Rationality of Emotion*; Bennett Helm, *Emotional Reason: Deliberation, Motivation, and the Nature of Value* (Cambridge: Cambridge University Press, 2001); Mikko Salmela Salmela, "Can Emotions e be Modelled on Perceptions?" *Dialectica* 65 (2011): 1–29; Deonna and Teroni, *Emotions*; Jérôme Dokic and Stéphane Lemaire, "Are Emotions Perceptions of Values," *Canadian Journal of Philosophy* 43 (2013): 227–247; Brady, "Emotions, Perception and Understanding."

[25] See Tappolet, "Emotions, Perceptions, and Emotional Illusions"; Tappolet, *Emotions, Values, and Agency* (Oxford: Oxford University Press, forthcoming).

[26] I understand normative reasons to be considerations that speak in favor of beliefs or actions. See Thomas Scanlon, *What We Owe to Each Other* (Cambridge, MA: Harvard University Press, 1998).

is particularly difficult to deny if one assumes, as appears plausible, that fearsomeness supervenes on dangerousness.[27] That the dog is fearsome and thus dangerous is plausibly seen to be a consideration that speaks in favor of doing something to avoid the threat, at least under the assumption that the agent desires to avoid physical harm. What is important to emphasize is that the emotion informs the agent of the fearsomeness and danger that threatens her independently of what she judges. Thus, she might mistakenly judge that the dog is a harmless puppy. There would thus be a conflict between what she feels and what she judges. What is noteworthy is that in such a case, by contrast to the cases that first come to mind, it is the judgment and not the fear that gets things wrong. As a result, acting on the emotion would be more advisable than acting on the judgment. It would amount to acting on correct information about the reason the agent has for acting in a certain way.

As this example makes clear, what follows from the Perceptual Theory is that insofar as emotions are perceptions of evaluative properties, and thus of the practical reasons that depend on evaluative properties, emotions provide privileged epistemic access to practical reasons. To use Karen Jones's apt phrase, emotions can key us to real and important considerations that speak in favor of acting in certain ways, without always presenting that information to us in a way susceptible of conscious articulation.[28] That emotions have this role explains why they can constitute touchstones against which to test our action-guiding principles. There might be a debate about how to understand the nature of deliberation, but whatever the details it follows from the account of emotions proposed here that they may have a crucial role to play in the assessment of our normative judgments.[29]

Let us accept, then, that emotions can afford us a privileged access to evaluative properties and practical reasons. As such, this makes emotions indispensable in an account of agency. This is not a small feat, but at the same time one might wonder whether this claim does full justice to emotions and their role in agency. An important question is whether being moved to action by an emotion, be it fear or compassion, for example, amounts to acting *for* a reason, or *in the light* of a reason. In other words, the issue is how emotions relate to reason-responsiveness.

---

[27] For the claim that the fearsome supervenes on the dangerous, see de Sousa, *Rationality of Emotion*.

[28] See Jones, "Emotion, Weakness of Will," 181.

[29] The main options are a coherentist model according to which emotions and normative principles have to be brought into reflective equilibrium (see Friedman, "Autonomy and the Split-Level Self") and a foundationalist conception, which grant emotions a defeasible but foundational justificatory power (see Tappolet, *Émotions et Valeurs*).

2. Emotions and Reason-Responsiveness

In terms of Jones's useful distinction between *reason-tracking* and *reason-responding*, the question is whether emotions merely allow us to track reasons—to register reasons so that the agent can behave in accordance with them—or whether acting on the basis of an emotion may involve responding to a reason. Jones summarizes what is required to be a reason-responder, which she characterizes as someone who responds to reasons as reasons. Jones explains, "To be able to respond to reasons as reasons, an agent requires critical reflective ability, dispositions to bring that ability to bear when needed, and dispositions to have the results of such reflection control [her] behaviour."[30] As we saw in the introduction, the ability to respond to reasons is often considered to be essential to full-fledged agency and hence of autonomy. Accordingly, the important question is whether emotions merely allow for the tracking of reasons or whether we can be genuine agents who are guided by reasons when we are moved by our emotions.

The majority view is that our emotions do not, as such, allow us to respond to reasons.[31] When we undergo an emotion, we, or maybe more accurately some mechanism in us, might at best be tracking reasons, but we do not respond to reasons in virtue of our emotions. What is taken to be necessary for responding to reasons is deliberation (i.e., reflection about practical reasons), and this, it is thought, requires judgments about the agent's practical reasons. Such reflective responsiveness is explicitly related to full-fledged agency. Thus, Jay Wallace writes:

> The motivation and actions of rational agents are guided by and responsive to their deliberative reflection about what they have reason to do. Unless this guidance condition (as we may call it) can be satisfied, we will not be able to make sense of the idea that persons are genuine agents, capable of determining what they shall do through the process of deliberation.[32]

On a natural understanding of what rational guidance involves, it is only insofar as an agent acts in accordance with her judgment as to what she has most reason to do that she can be said to respond to reasons.

However, as Jones argues, there is an alternative account of what is required for reason-responsiveness that is more favorable to emotions. According to Jones, acting on the basis of emotions can involve genuine agency, provided

---

[30] Jones, "Emotion, Weakness of Will," 190.
[31] See Velleman, "What Happens When Someone Acts?"; Christine M. Korsgaard, "The Normativity of Instrumental Reason," in *Ethics and Practical Reason*, edited by Garrett Cullity and Berys Gaut (Oxford: Clarendon Press, 1997); R. Jay Wallace, "Three Conceptions of Rational Agency," *Ethical Theory and Moral Practice* 2 (1999): 219; Kieran Setiya, *Reasons without Rationalism* (Princeton, NJ: Princeton University Press, 2007).
[32] Wallace, "Three Conceptions of Rational Agency," 219.

that the action expresses the agent's commitment to what she calls *regulative guidance*. Regulative guidance involves "the on-going cultivation and exercise of habits of reflective self-monitoring of our practical and epistemic agency."[33] An action caused by emotions, or for that matter by any other reason-tracking subsystem, thus manifests genuine agency "just in case the agent's dispositions to reflective self-monitoring are such that she would not rely on that first order sub-system were it reasonable for her to believe that it failed to reason-track."[34] Thus, an agent who acts on, say, her anger might be responding to reasons even if she acts against her judgment concerning what to do. The angry agent is responding to reason if she has well-tuned self-monitoring habits, such that she would not have relied on her anger if there had been reason for her to believe that her anger was misleading her. In other words, what is required for reason-responsiveness is nothing but the exercise of well-tuned epistemic and practical habits, that is, of what can be described as agential virtues.

This *Agential Virtue Account*, as I shall call it, is highly attractive. In the remainder of this section I will provide what can be considered as a partial defense of the account. More precisely, I will argue that it is not threatened by a number of worries that have been or might be raised. The first volley of worries is due to Sabine Döring. Döring explicitly criticizes Jones's account, and it is instructive to start with her arguments. According to Döring, the "main problem of Jones's analysis is that it remains obscure how, in the case of conflict between two reason-tracking sub-systems, the agent may decide which sub-system is to be given preference."[35] What Döring has in mind, just as Jones, are cases of akrasia, that is, cases in which there is a conflict between the conclusion of the practical reasoning of an agent—her better judgment—on one hand and her motivation and intentional action on the other hand. More specifically, she is thinking of cases of akrasia in which the practical conclusion of an agent and what she feels conflict, and it is the feeling that appears to better fit the agent's reasons.[36] The classic example is that of Huckleberry Finn, who is torn between his judgment that he ought to denounce Jim to the slave hunters and his feelings for Jim. Döring asks: "If Huck is mistaken in the example, how could he have avoided the mistake? ... What Huck needs to know is whether he should here and now follow his sympathy or had better stick to his judgment."[37] Now, it clearly would have been useful for Huck to know whether to follow his judgment or his feelings. The question, however,

---

[33] Jones, "Emotion, Weakness of Will," 194.
[34] Jones, "Emotions, Weakness of Will," 195.
[35] Sabine Döring, "Why be Emotional?" in the *Oxford Handbook of Philosophy of Emotion*, edited by Peter Goldie (Oxford: Oxford University Press, 2010), 290.
[36] See Alison McIntyre, "Is Akratic Action Always Irrational?" in *Identity, Character and Morality*, edited by Owen Flanagan and Amélie Rorty (Cambridge, MA: MIT Press, 1993); Nomi Arpaly and Tim Schroeder, "Praise, Blame and the Whole Self," *Philosophical Studies* 93 (1999): 161–188.
[37] Döring, "Why be Emotional?" 290.

is whether a general account of agency should be expected to help Huck in that matter. What the Agential Virtue Account says, simply, is that insofar as Huck's self-monitoring habits are well tuned, he can be considered to be reason-responsive. This might appear disappointing as advice to Huck, but what has to be underlined is that no general account of agency can ensure that people in Huck's position arrive at the correct answer. It might be useful make a comparison to the moral case: what has to be distinguished in the moral case is the advice to an agent who has to take moral decision, on one hand, and a general account of right action, on the other hand. The former pertains to the theory of deliberation and decision making, whereas the latter requires a substantive moral theory.

According to Döring, the problem that she sees in Jones's account has a deeper source. It emerges from the fact that Jones fails properly to distinguish between *objective* and *subjective* reasons, a distinction she takes from Niko Kolodny.[38] Objective reasons are defined as reasons that depend on objective features of the agent's situation, while subjective reasons are claimed to be what the agent justifiably sees as reasons, given the content of her mental states. In essence, subjective reasons are the agent's take on her objective reasons, somewhat idealized by the justification condition. According to Döring, the "guidance condition implies that an account of practical rationality ... must be given in terms of subjective reasons: an agent is rational to the extent to which he is guided by his subjective reasons."[39] Given this claim, it does not come as a surprise that she disagrees with the Agential Virtue Account. Rational guidance requires that the agent be guided by what she explicitly takes to be her reasons, that is, by her practical judgments.

Let us look at the specific form the objection against Jones's account takes. Spelling out Jones's proposal in terms of objective and subjective reasons, Döring claims that it is objective reasons that we track while it is subjective reasons to which we respond. She spells out the problem as a conscious and explicit conflict between two objective reason-tracking systems and claims that in such a case of conflict it is it unclear what subjective reasons the agent has.[40] Given this way of construing the conflict, Döring claims that there is only one option, namely, appealing to the agent's higher-order reflective and self-monitoring capacities: "In the end, it will come down to a *judgment* about what one ought to do in the given situation."[41] It is on these grounds that Döring infers that acting on one's feelings instead of following one's judgment is irrational.

---

[38] See Niko Kolodny, "Why Be Rational?" *Mind* 114: 181–200.
[39] Döring, "Why be Emotional?" 287.
[40] Döring, "Why be Emotional?" 290.
[41] Döring, "Why be Emotional?" 291.

A first, merely terminological, difficulty is that, as far as I can see, talk of objective versus subjective reasons is misleading in that it gives the false impression that there are two kinds of reasons.[42] Introducing subjective reasons is like introducing subjective cats and poppies next to cats and poppies. It seems far simpler to replace talk of objective versus subjective reasons with the distinction between reasons on one hand and the agent's (idealized) take on reasons on the other hand. On this distinction, both tracking and responding concern the same thing, namely, reasons. But while tracking need not involve judgments, responding typically does—typically, but not necessarily, because responding can involve emotions and other subsystems, provided that they are well tuned.

Yet the real problem with Döring's suggestion is that we need to follow our practical judgment to be reason-responsive. It might be correct that from the point of view of the agent the only thing that she can envisage in the event of a conflict between the verdicts of two subsystems is to appeal to a judgment about what do to. But this is a far cry from showing that acting on that judgment is what an agent ought to do. This is so because as is made clear in the case of Huck there might be a gap between the agent's take on her reasons and her actual practical reasons.[43] Given this, it is only prima facie that an agent ought to follow her better judgment.

This is good news for the Agential Virtues Account. However, there are other worries that one might have with respect to the suggestion that acting according to an emotion in the face of one's judgment might consist in responding to a reason. One important question is whether or not the akratic action can really be attributed to the agent. One might think that it is not Huck who is in charge when he fails to denounce Jim against his better judgment. This is exactly what David Velleman suggests regarding the case of someone who loses his temper when meeting with an old friend for the purpose of resolving a minor conflict.[44] What Velleman suggests is that in such a case it is not the agent who is in charge. He writes, "It was my resentment speaking, not I."[45] This is clearly something we might be tempted to say, would it be only to avoid blame. However, we may also doubt whether a person who argues on these lines is necessarily right to say that she was not in charge. According to the Agential Virtue Account, whether or not it is the agent who is in charge does not depend on the agent's take but on whether the dispositions to reflective

---

[42] To be fair, it has to be noted that Döring explicitly states that "subjective reasons are derivative of objective reasons, and that they do not constitute a second class of normative reasons beyond objective reasons." Döring, "Why be Emotional?" 287.

[43] As McIntyre, "Is Akratic Action Always Irrational?" argues that this point can be made without postulating external reasons, for an agent can be wrong about his own motivational set.

[44] See Velleman, "What Happens When Someone Acts," 464–465.

[45] Velleman, "What Happens When Someone Acts," 465. Cf. Wallace, "Three Conceptions of Rational Agency," 222, for a similar point.

self-monitoring that constitute agential virtues are in place. What the account tells is that if the conditions that it spells out are satisfied, then the agent is in charge, despite his being reluctant to admit it. This is, I believe, an attractive feature of the Agential Virtue Account.

Finally, let me consider a last worry. On the story proposed here, emotions can inform us about our practical reasons, depending on how reliable these emotions are. Moreover, undergoing an emotion and acting on its basis can constitute responding to a reason, and it does constitute responding to a reason when the relevant emotional disposition or dispositions—the subsystem—are well tuned. Accordingly, acting on the basis of an emotion can amount to acting in light of one's reasons. But how could this be the case, one might ask, if the agent is not *aware* of the reasons she has? And how could the agent be aware of her reasons otherwise than by having beliefs or judgments regarding those reasons? Another way to express the same worry is to claim that reasons need to be transparent to the agent: to be motivated by a reason, that is, to act for a reason, an agent needs to be aware of that reason, where awareness is understood to require belief or judgment.[46]

In reply, one may be tempted to deny that awareness requires judgment and appeal to the fact that emotions are conscious experiences. One could thus claim that emotions allow us to be aware of values and hence of the corresponding reasons. After all, nobody would deny that there are both judgmental and perceptual ways to be aware of poppies and their shapes and colors. So why not say that when fearing something we are aware of that thing's fearsomeness? One worry here is that emotional experiences appear to lack the phenomenal transparency that characterizes sensory perceptions. The best way to describe my experience of red poppies is to talk about red poppies. But it seems that this is not so with emotions. Arguably, the best way to describe what it is like to undergo fear or anger or regret is not to refer to the objects of these emotions and their properties. This suggests that when undergoing an emotion we are not stricto sensu aware of the relevant evaluative properties.

There is some leeway here, for in fact we quite often find ourselves describing what our emotions are about to describe what it felt to experience them. Thus, we describe what were afraid of—the huge hairy spider that suddenly fell from the tree, for instance—to explain what we felt.[47] Moreover, it should be noted that the worry in question is mitigated by the fact that we commonly

---

[46] See Melissa Barry, "Realism, Rational Action, and the Humean Theory of Motivation," *Ethical Theory and Moral Practice* 10 (2007): 231–242, 323; Maria Alvarez, *Kinds of Reasons: An Essay in the Philosophy of Action* (Oxford: Oxford University Press, 2010), 25; Setiya, *Reasons without Rationalism*, 40. Setiya takes it as obvious that whenever we act for a reason, we not only believe but we also know that we are acting for that reason: "The second insight is that we know without observation not only what we are doing, but why" (40).

[47] Thanks to Mark Nelson for suggesting this point.

form evaluative judgments on the basis of the emotions we feel. For instance, when angry at someone because of some remark, we tend to judge that this person's remark was offensive. Thus, emotions typically come with a disposition to make corresponding evaluative judgments. Finally, the claim that the putative phenomenal transparency of emotions indicates that there is no awareness of evaluative properties appears committed to the assumption that the awareness of something needs to be explicitly articulated in terms of concepts; it would only be when we form judgments about things that we can be said to be aware of them.

Be that as it may, the very claim that an agent needs to be aware of a reason—whether that entails judgment or another kind of awareness—to be motivated by that reason already appears too strong to be plausible. Switching to a case that does not involve emotions, habitual actions can certainly be motivated by reasons even though we are not aware of the reasons for which we perform these actions when we perform them. Indeed, the whole point of the Agential Virtue Account is to make room for actions that are not explicitly guided by articulated reasons but nonetheless appear to exhibit full-fledged agency.

It might be replied that cases of habitual actions are quite different from emotional actions.[48] In the case of habitual actions, agents can readily reconstruct the reasons behind what they are doing. Consider my habit of having an espresso at ten o'clock. It is easy for me to see that having an espresso at ten o'clock is not only pleasant but also useful in terms of productivity. By contrast, we often are at loss when we try to reconstruct the reasons behind actions motivated by emotions. This, it can be argued, is particularly striking in Huck's case. From his point of view, it is bound to appear utterly unjustified not to have denounced Jim.

It is important to recognise the difference between habitual and emotional action. However, the contrast should not be exaggerated. A first point is that there are cases of habitual actions in which it is less easy to reconstruct the reasons behind what we are doing. We are all aware of some strange habits we have, in favor of which we find nothing to say even on reflection. Indeed, in some cases, acting out of habit can be in conflict with our better judgment. This is a natural way to understand Davidson's famous teeth-brushing case.[49] You are lying in your bed when you realize that you have forgotten to brush your teeth. On reflection you conclude that you should just stay in bed and do nothing about it—there is no harm in not brushing your teeth just this one time, and getting up would spoil your calm. But off you go and brush your

---

[48] Thanks to Karen Jones for raising this question.
[49] See Donald Davidson, "How is Weakness of the Will Possible?" in Davidson, *Essays on Actions and Events* (Oxford: Oxford University Press, 1980; original publication 1969).

teeth. It is to be expected that in such a case you will find it hard to reconstruct the reasons behind your action.

The second point to make is that in fact we are often in a position to reconstruct the reasons behind emotional action. Consider again Velleman's case of the person who loses his temper when meeting with his friend.[50] In the case Velleman imagines, later reflection leads the protagonist to realize that accumulated grievances had crystalized in his mind into a resolution to end the friendship. Thus, the reasons for the burst of anger are in fact accessible to the agent. According to Velleman, the fact that the reasons are accessible to the agent is not sufficient to make it the case that the action is done for a reason. In fact, the anger case is his main example of an action that is less than full-blooded.

The Agential Virtue Account has a very different, and I believe more plausible, take on cases like this. The third and most important point, thus, is that according to the Agential Virtue Account what counts is not so much the possibility of reason reconstruction as the exercise of agential virtues. The point to emphasize is that the description of the case leaves open whether or not the dispositions of reflective self-monitoring were in place. It is true that in the absence of any reason to believe that the agent in question has such dispositions, Velleman appears right when claiming that the action failed to involve reason-responsiveness. However, we might easily imagine a case in which being moved by anger expresses well-tuned dispositions, such that the agent would not have relied on her anger if there would have been reason for her to believe that her anger was inappropriate.

More would have to be to be said to spell out and fully defend the Agential Virtue Account.[51] Questions arise regarding the nature and functioning of the dispositions of reflective self-monitoring. What exactly are these epistemic and practical habits—what I have called *agential virtues*—and how do they relate to epistemic and practical norms and goals? Also, one might wonder how much room there is for an agent to cultivate and exercise such dispositions, assuming that basic aptitudes and socialization are bound to be decisive factors. In particular, one might wonder whether the counterfactual description in terms of what would the agent would have done had there been reasons for her to believe something makes for a problematically circular account of reason-responsiveness in that it explicitly refers to reasons. There are important and difficult questions, but for now I will leave them aside and turn to what the proposed account entails for autonomy theories.

---

[50] See Velleman, "What Happens When Someone Acts," 464–465.
[51] In this appeal to virtues, the account proposed is similar to Setiya's suggestion that good practical reasoning can be specified only in terms of ethical virtues. See Setiya, *Reasons without Rationalism*.

3. Emotions and Autonomy Theories

As I noted in the introduction, it is often taken for granted that emotions and autonomy are at odds. Giving voice to this intuition, Laura Ekstrom writes:

> We do not act autonomously in acting on passions, whims, and impulses because these overtake us; we are generally passive with respect to them, they do not engage our understanding or capacity for reflective evaluation. We make our lives more our own by examining such impulses and by acting in accordance with our evaluations.[52]

If the picture I have sketched is on the right lines this negative conception of emotions is not warranted. It can surely be acknowledged that in some cases the undergoing of an emotion is a barrier to autonomy. Our emotions sometimes get things wrong and thus fail to track reasons. And acting on an emotion might fail to consist in responding to reasons because agential virtues are not in place. Quite generally, given their influence on action and thought, the effect of emotions can be particularly pernicious. However, the wholesale rejection of emotions is not warranted. Insofar as emotions are perceptual experiences of evaluative properties, they can, and sometimes do, inform us about our practical reasons and hence play a crucial role in the assessment of our normative principles. So it is deeply mistaken to suggest that critical reflection is something that is independent of the emotions we feel and incompatible with the fact that an emotion is felt.

Furthermore, the wholesale rejection of emotions is misguided because acting on an emotion can be acting in light of reasons we do have. Thus, to the extent that reason-responsiveness is a central aspect of autonomy, emotions are far from being at odds with autonomy. Autonomy accounts that place reason-responsiveness at the core of autonomous agency have to accept emotions as a potential source of autonomous actions. There might be some disagreement as to what other ingredients autonomy requires—such as psychological integration or a sense of our status as agents. But whatever the details of one's full account of autonomous action, it has to be conceded that insofar as emotions and reason-responsiveness are not at odds emotions and autonomy need not be either.

Another implication of the account of emotions proposed here is that care accounts of autonomy, or at least the version of such accounts according to which emotions are essential to autonomy, should not be taken to be antithetical to reason-responsiveness accounts.[53] This is because on this version cares

---

[52] Laura W. Ekstrom, "Autonomy and Personal Integration," in *Personal Autonomy*, edited by J. S. Taylor (Cambridge: Cambridge University Press, 2005), 160.

[53] In his later work, Frankfurt suggests that love is an essential feature of the self, but it is far from clear that what he calls "love" involves emotions. See Harry Frankfurt, *Necessity, Volition and Love* (Cambridge: Cambridge University Press, 1998).

are complex emotional dispositions. As Shoemaker puts it, "Talk of caring is simply a way of referring to the range of emotional reactions one is expected to have with respect to the fortunes of the cared-for object."[54] To care for someone or for something consists in being disposed to undergo a number of emotions, depending on the good or bad fortune of whom or what (e.g., persons, ideals) one cares for. We feel sadness when things go bad for the object of our care, joy when things go well, hope that things will go well, fear that things will go badly, and so forth. Now, according to Shoemaker, freedom and thus autonomy depend on acting on our strongest cares.[55] Shoemaker expresses this thought in the following manner:

> If we attach free agency to willing action, then, and willing action consists in the action I genuinely want to do, and what I genuinely want to do depends on what I care most about in any particular situation, then free agency is grounded in care. To the extent that what I do does not ultimately depend on my strongest care(s) at the time of action, I am unfree.[56]

The question is what kind of states the emotions that constitute our cares are. On the Perceptual Theory I have sketched, cares are dispositions to undergo states that are perceptual experiences of evaluative properties. Thus, they are dispositions to undergo states that can, when things go well, inform us about the practical reasons we have. To the extent that our emotions fit their objects, they happen to inform us correctly about the reasons we have. Thus, in such favorable cases, our dispositions to feel these emotions are dispositions to be keyed to practical reasons. In such cases, acting on our cares consists in acting in ways that reflect the reasons we have. Given this, it has to be acknowledged that our cares can be essential to reason-responsiveness. According to the Agential Virtue Model, this will be the case when the agent displays well-tuned epistemic and practical dispositions.

Consider what happens when you care for a friend. To care for a friend is to be disposed to be happy if she thrives, unhappy if she is not well, and fearful when something threatens her. Thus, on the account of emotions proposed here, caring involves being disposed to perceive the friend's happiness as good and her unhappiness as bad. And a friend's happiness being good surely is a reason you have to do a number of things, such as helping her when she needs and asks for it. Thus, if you help your friend, what you do corresponds to the reasons you have that are tracked by the emotions that constitute your caring for your friend. Moreover, in the light of the Agential Virtue Account, it must be allowed that acting on the basis of your cares can well consist in responding

---

[54] David Shoemaker, "Caring, Identification, and Agency," *Ethics* 114 (2003): 94.
[55] Shoemaker, "Caring, Identification, and Agency," 103–104.
[56] Shoemaker, "Caring, Identification, and Agency."

to reasons. Thus, if your dispositions are well tuned, your acting on the basis of your cares consists in responding to reasons.

The lesson, then, is that insofar as emotions are central to care accounts of autonomy based on care can make room for the intuition that reason-responsiveness is central to autonomy. Even though there is likely to be disagreement about other putative ingredients of autonomy, the two kinds of accounts need not be in disagreement as to the importance of reason-responsiveness in autonomy.

4. Conclusion

To conclude, let me return to what I referred to as the Ludicrous Argument. In a nutshell, what is wrong with the argument is the idea that being liable to undergo emotions and, in particular, that experiencing an emotion, is incompatible with autonomous agency. Emotions have traditionally been taken to be dubious and unreliable elements in our psychology, which have to be submitted to some taming process, such as critical scrutiny and reflective endorsement. There has recently been a general tendency to see emotions in a more positive light, something that echoes feminist concerns. Following that tendency, what I have tried to show in this paper is that the negative conception of emotions as they relate to autonomous agency is severely misguided. Even though emotions do not involve conceptually articulated contents, there are reasons to consider them to be perceptual experiences of a kind, in that they have intentional objects and representational content. This is why to be properly reason-responsive and autonomous we should listen to our emotions.

Acknowledgments

Earlier drafts of this chapter have been presented at the round-table on the rationality of emotions, Pacific APA, Seattle, 2012, organized by Marina Oshana; at the conference on relational autonomy, organized by Catriona Mackenzie and Natalie Stoljar, McGill, September 2012; at the Philosophy Institute, Stockholm University; at the Department of Philosophy, York University; at the Centre Interfacultaire en Sciences Affectives, University of Geneva; and the Congress of the CPA, Victoria, 2013. For discussions and comments, I am grateful to Rachel Barney, Åsa Carlsson, John Christman, Julien Deonna, Vincent Duhamel, Marilyn Friedman, Bruno Guindon, Nancy Hirshmann, Louis-Philippe Hodgson, Karen Jones, Catriona Mackenzie, Colin MacLeod, Diana Meyers, Mark Nelson, Graham Oddie, Jonas Olson, Marina Oshana, Antoine Panaioti, Gopal Sreenivasan, Natalie Stoljar, Sarah Stroud, Jennifer Szende, Fabrice Teroni, Joey van Weelden, and especially to the editors of the volume, Andrea Veltman and Mark Piper.

{ 9 }

Autonomy and Self-Care
Andrea C. Westlund

For more than two decades, feminist philosophers have been developing important new conceptions of autonomy that take the sociality of human agency appropriately seriously. Interestingly, this relational turn has at the same time ushered in a new debate about the nature of autonomous agents' attitudes toward themselves as individual agents. Some relational theorists have argued, for example, that a sense of individual self-worth[1] or self-trust[2] may be necessary for autonomy. One important question this debate has raised is whether or not the resulting conception of autonomy will be normatively neutral.[3] For purposes of this paper I will bracket that question and focus instead on the relationship between autonomy and self-regarding attitudes themselves. What has begun to emerge in the feminist literature is a conception of autonomy in which the autonomous agent must stand in a special kind of relation to herself.[4] I think there is something deeply right about this idea. In this paper I try to flesh out one kind of self-relation that is required for autonomy and to explain what it has to do with relationality of the more familiar, interpersonal variety.

---

[1] See Paul Benson, "Feeling Crazy: Self-Worth and the Social Character of Responsibility," in *Relational Autonomy: Feminist Perspectives on Autonomy, Agency, and the Social Self*, edited by Catriona Mackenzie and Natalie Stoljar (New York: Oxford University Press, 2000), 72–93.

[2] See Carolyn McLeod and Susan Sherwin, "Relational Autonomy, Self-Trust, and Health Care for Patients Who Are Oppressed," in Mackenzie and Stoljar, *Relational Autonomy*, 259–279.

[3] See Paul Benson, "Taking Ownership: Authority and Voice in Autonomous Agency," in *Autonomy and the Challenges to Liberalism: New Essays*, edited by J. Christman and J. Anderson (Cambridge: Cambridge University Press, 2005), 101–126; Benson, "Feminist Intuitions and the Normative Substance of Autonomy," in *Personal Autonomy*, edited by James Stacy Taylor (Cambridge: Cambridge University Press, 2005), 124–42; John Christman, "Relational Autonomy, Liberal Individualism, and the Social Constitution of Selves," *Philosophical Studies* 117:1–2 (2004): 143–164; Christman, "Procedural Autonomy and Liberal Legitimacy," in Taylor, *Personal Autonomy*, 277–298; Andrea C. Westlund, "Rethinking Relational Autonomy," *Hypatia* 24:4 (2009): 26–49.

[4] Of course, self-governance is itself a kind of self-relation. The idea I pursue in this paper is that the autonomous agent is self-governing at least in part in virtue of standing in another, conceptually distinct sort of relationship to herself, namely, a relation of self-care.

The self-relation I have in mind is not exactly one of self-trust or self-worth (at least as these are usually understood), since it does not involve any kind of positive self-assessment. But I argue in this paper that we have reason to consider it a form of self-care. In the first section of the paper, I set out three related conceptions of care, developed by Harry Frankfurt, Agnieszka Jaworska, and Jeffrey Seidman. In the second section, I raise some worries about the way these conceptions have figured in an authenticity-based approach to autonomy and begin to sketch out an alternative, answerability-based approach. In the third section, I put Jaworska's and Seidman's conceptions of care to new use and develop an account of *self*-care that emphasizes care for one's reasons. Finally, in the fourth section I elucidate the two-sided relationality of this kind of self-care. I argue that caring about one's reasons implies caring about intersubjective assessments thereof and that the relation of self-care therefore implies openness to the reasons of others.

1. Care

The recent literature on care has grown along two almost entirely separate lines. One line focuses primarily on the place of care in morality and tends to concern itself almost exclusively with care as an attitude toward other persons. This strand has developed out of pioneering work in feminist ethics by Carol Gilligan, Nel Noddings, Sarah Ruddick, and others and by now includes much interesting work on dependency and disability as well.[5] For the most part, this body of work does not bear directly on issues of autonomy, though the strand of Gilligan's argument I develop later in this paper is an important (and generally overlooked) exception.

The other line of work is more immediately relevant to my project, focusing as it does on the role of care in human agency or autonomy. This literature tends to range more widely over care as an attitude toward objects, places, ideals, and so forth in addition to persons. It has been inspired at least in part by Harry Frankfurt's groundbreaking work on personhood and freedom of the will, particularly in its later manifestations.[6] In addition to Frankfurt himself,

---

[5] See Carol Gilligan, *In a Different Voice* (Cambridge, MA: Harvard University Press, 1982); Nel Noddings, *Caring: A Feminine Approach to Ethics and Moral Education* (Berkeley: University of California Press, 2003); Sara Ruddick, *Maternal Thinking: Toward a Politics of Peace* (Boston: Beacon Press, 1995). On dependency and disability, see Eva Feder Kittay, *Love's Labor* (New York: Routledge, 1999). I would place Stephen Darwall's care-based analysis of welfare in this category as well. See Darwall, *Welfare and Rational Care* (Princeton, NJ: Princeton University Press, 2002). Though it does not directly address feminist issues, Darwall himself describes his work on welfare and care as inspired partly by Noddings and other feminist theorists.

[6] Harry Frankfurt, "On Caring," in *Necessity, Volition, and Love* (Cambridge: Cambridge University Press, 1999), 155–180.

Agnieszka Jaworska and Jeffrey Seidman have made important contributions on this front.[7] In this section I trace out the account of care that emerges from their work. It is a compelling account, and I will ultimately argue that care (thus understood) does play an important role in self-government—just not exactly the same role that Frankfurt, Jaworska, and Seidman have assigned it.

Frankfurt, Jaworska, and Seidman all frame questions about autonomy in terms of the distinction between what is internal and what is external to the agent's will. In doing so, all three focus on what many philosophers now refer to as *authenticity* conditions of autonomy. These conditions specify what it is that makes an attitude, motive, or desire truly one's own or, as Frankfurt and Jaworska put it, internal to the self. On authenticity-based views, self-governance is quite literally a matter of governance *by* the self. We need to be able to distinguish between what belongs to the self and what does not to know if an agent is self-governing with respect to any particular choice or action. We must, as it is often put, be able to identify the agent's "standpoint" or those attitudes that have the authority to "speak for" the agent.

In its earlier versions, Frankfurt's hierarchical account of internality focused on a thin notion of reflective endorsement, involving higher-order desires to be moved by particular first-order desires. Over time, however, a species of care has come to play an increased role in his account. To care about something, for Frankfurt, is to have and identify with a higher-order desire in favor of the persistence of a lower-order desire for that thing. The persistence of the desire in question cannot be a matter of mere volitional inertia; to count as an instance of caring, it must be actively willed by the agent. This means that the agent must not merely endorse but actually be "disposed to support and sustain his desire [to φ] even after he has decided that he prefers to satisfy another desire instead."[8] Caring, on this view, is not primarily (or merely) a matter of having certain feelings or beliefs but rather of having a certain configuration of the will. Caring about something is a matter of being *committed* to one's first-order desire for that thing, where being committed entails having the structure of aforementioned higher-order desires and dispositions.[9]

So what role does caring, thus understood, play in autonomy? For Frankfurt, individuals govern themselves "to the extent that the commands that they obey, whether based upon rules or not, are their own commands."[10] Frankfurt's

---

[7] See Agnieszka Jaworska, "Caring and Internality," *Philosophy and Phenomenological Research* 74:3 (2007): 529–568; Jaworska, "Caring, Minimal Autonomy, and the Limits of Liberalism," in *Naturalized Bioethics: Toward Responsible Knowing and Practice*, edited by H. Lindemann, M. Verkerk, and M. U. Walker (Cambridge: Cambridge University Press, 2009), 80–105; Jeffrey Seidman, "Valuing and Caring," *Theoria* 75 (2009): 272–303. Though I do not examine it in this paper, David Shoemaker develops a similar, care-based account in Shoemaker, "Caring, Identification, and Agency," *Ethics* 114:1 (2003): 88–118.
[8] Frankfurt, "On Caring," 160.
[9] Frankfurt, "On Caring," 161.
[10] Frankfurt, "On Caring," 131.

most distinctive move, in his later work, has been to argue that the commands of love are at least as authoritative for us as the commands of duty or reason. Indeed, since Frankfurt takes love to define our essential nature as persons and to settle our final ends, it is reasonable to read his account as one on which autonomy is ultimately grounded in love *rather* than in reason. On his view, what we love has a distinctive claim to mark out our standpoint as persons or at least what is most central to that standpoint. Since love is a species of caring, the result is a view that links autonomy very clearly to care, via the internality of cares to the self.[11]

In "Caring and Internality," Jaworska accepts that an attitude is truly one's own if it is internal to the will and also that our cares are invariably internal. But she departs from Frankfurt by insisting that care is first and foremost an emotional attitude and not just a commitment of the will. Jaworska argues that Frankfurt's volitional treatment of care and internality is too reflective: in requiring agents to have a structure of attitudes about attitudes, Frankfurt's view (and other similarly hierarchical views) puts care beyond the reach of agents who are not yet, or are no longer, cognitively sophisticated enough to have such higher-order attitudes but who seem obviously to care about things and to have, in that sense, a standpoint of their own. Young children and other marginal agents (e.g., those in early stages of dementia) seem to be capable of care, and their cares (like anyone else's) seem invariably to be internal to them.

Jaworska draws on Michael Bratman for a revised Frankfurtian conception of internality and on Bennett Helm for a more congenial account of care. From Bratman she adopts the idea that an attitude is internal if it has as part of its function "to support the psychological continuities and connections that constitute the agent's identity and cohesion over time."[12] Where she differs from Bratman is in the range of attitudes that she thinks may perform this function. While Bratman focuses on plans, policies, and other distinctively *reflective* attitudes, Jaworska argues that *any* attitude, reflective or not, that plays the relevant role should count as internal. At least some emotions, she argues, fit the bill.

To understand her point, we must distinguish between primary and secondary emotions. Primary emotions, Jaworska explains, "involve more or less fixed patterns of emotional responses to specific, immediately sensed features of one's environment," such as stereotypical reactions of fear, disgust, rage, or surprise.[13] These do not, in her view, play any special role in unifying our

---

[11] What we love is a subset of what we *cannot help* caring about, in the aforementioned sense of caring. When we love something, Frankfurt claims, we have a disinterested desire for its flourishing. This desire, since we cannot help but have it, and cannot help but want to have it, sets boundaries on our will that we willingly embrace. It determines what we can and cannot bring ourselves to choose and do and in this way defines the contours of our will and our essential natures as persons.

[12] Jaworska, "Caring and Internality," 552.

[13] Jaworska, "Caring and Internality," 555.

agency over time. A secondary emotion, by contrast, is a response to one's conscious, deliberate understanding of a situation. She cites gratitude, envy, jealousy, guilt, hope, and grief (among others) as examples of emotions of this sort, which "presuppose...high-level processing of the situation."[14] There is good evidence, elaborated by Antonio Damasio, that brain injuries that compromise secondary emotionality also cause severe deficits in agents' abilities to plan and coordinate their activities over time. As Jaworska puts it, "secondary emotions support entire networks of psychological continuities and connections" and appear to be "a necessary substratum of the planning- and intention-based continuities and connections" on which Bratman has focused.[15] While it is easy to imagine feeling a primary emotion as an alien or overwhelming force, Jaworska claims, such secondary emotions as joy, grief, or gratitude strike us as invariably internal.

Jaworska argues that care, too, is properly understood as a secondary emotion that supports a network of psychological continuities and connections. She defines care as a structured compound of emotions, emotional predispositions, and desires that all construe the same object as "a source of importance commanding emotional vulnerability."[16] The object of care is, in Bennett Helm's terms, the unifying *focus* of this compound of attitudes; it is what the complex emotion is *about*. In addition to their joint connection to a single object, Jaworska notes, Helm has shown that the attitudes involved in caring are subject to two distinct patterns of rational requirement. On one hand, "tonal commitments" require agents to respond with positive or negative emotions (joy or satisfaction versus sadness or grief) as the focus of their care fares well or badly; on the other, "transitional commitments" require agents to feel forward- or backward-looking emotions (fear or hope versus relief or frustration) depending on the agents' temporal perspective on the fate of the object. Jaworska points out that these networks of continuities and connections not only directly contribute to the support of an agent's identity over time but also imbue objects with importance in a way that can and typically does support the development of other, higher-order unifying attitudes, such as the intentions, plans, and policies on which Bratman focuses.

In "Valuing and Caring," Seidman largely accepts the Jaworska–Helm conception of care but argues that it does not succeed in explaining what ties together the various elements of caring (emotions, emotional dispositions, and desires) such that they jointly constitute a single attitude. To fill this

---

[14] Jaworska, "Caring and Internality," 555.
[15] Jaworska, "Caring and Internality," 556.
[16] Jaworska, "Caring and Internality," 560. *Object* is to be understood broadly, as including not only material objects and particular individuals but also states of affairs, sequences of events, places, ideals, relationships, and more.

explanatory gap, he argues, we must recognize that caring includes not just emotional dispositions but also cognitive ones.

The various components of caring are, of course, linked in that they are focused on a single object. But a caring agent might have a range of other attitudes toward that same object without those attitudes being part of his or her caring. Nor, Seidman argues, do the tonal and transitional commitments identified by Helm suffice to pick out all and only the right attitudes, either. Seidman points out that a son's irritation at his father's humming may be robustly interconnected, both tonally and transitionally, with other attitudes toward the father yet have nothing to do with the fact that he cares for him.

According to Seidman, what does help unify the attitudinal patterns that constitute care is the agent's perception of the focal object as *important*. More precisely, the fact that an agent perceives an object as important stands in an explanatory relation to the attitudes that are constituents of her concern for that object. To see an object as important (to oneself), Seidman argues, is to see it as a source of practical reasons (for oneself).[17] Seeing some object X as a source of practical reasons does not entail actually believing it to be a source of practical reasons. Sometimes our perceptions and judgments come apart. But Seidman argues that seeing something in a certain way does, in "normal circumstances, where no countervailing beliefs defeat this disposition" *dispose* one to believe it is that way.[18] Seeing some object X as important—seeing X as a source of practical reasons—disposes the agent to believe that X *is* a source of practical reasons.

The fact that an agent sees X as a source of practical reasons, and is thus disposed to believe that she has the reasons in question, explains certain of her emotions, emotional dispositions, and desires as well as the rational patterns among those emotions, and those emotions (the ones linked together by their common explanation in perceptions of importance) are the ones that constitute concern for the object in question. Other emotions (such as irritation at one's father's humming) are not explained by one's perception of the father as important and thus are not part of caring for him. Seidman's point, in short, is that we cannot identify the emotions, emotional dispositions, and desires that constitute caring without appeal to perceptions of importance and the cognitive disposition (to believe one has reasons) that these perceptions involve.

Thus amended, Seidman agrees with Jaworska that our cares are invariably internal to us and have a legitimate claim to constitute the agent's "standpoint."

---

[17] Jaworska seems to agree with at least this part of Seidman's claim, since she argues in "Caring, Minimal Autonomy, and the Limits of Liberalism" that in acting on one's cares one acts on the perception of a reason. But as far as I understand her position, she would resist the further idea that perceiving something as a reason also disposes one to *believe* it is a reason. This disposition would be beyond the cognitive capacities of some of the marginal but still (on her view) caring agents that she considers minimally autonomous.

[18] Seidman, "Valuing and Caring," 286.

Indeed, Seidman argues that the emotional and cognitive dispositions involved in caring establish a more robust form of diachronic unity than the policies and plans on which Bratman focuses. In addition to unifying agency across time, Seidman argues that our concerns generate a diachronically unified *subjectivity*, or, as he also puts it, "a temporally extended subject...with a cognitive and emotional 'take' on the world."[19] This is important, Seidman thinks, because when we ask what attitudes speak for the agent we really have more in mind than just "a locus of deliberation and action."[20] Our concerns may conflict with one another and with our self-governing policies—but action motivated by our concerns will nonetheless always be expressive of "who we are" as subjects.[21]

2. Mental Freedom

There is much that seems promising about this view, as a view of what I've been calling authenticity. It gives a neat explanation of what unifies raw psychic materials into a well-defined (even if complex or conflicted) subject, with a "take" of its own, that endures across time. If autonomous choice or action is fundamentally choice or action that expresses "who the agent is," this care-based account seems like a strong contender for telling us how to identify a "who" in the first place. But there is a significant worry about this whole approach to the concept of self-governance: such views do not explain how being just exactly who we are can sometimes constitute a failure of autonomy.

Within the framework of a purely authenticity-based account of autonomy, this objection will not sound like a sensible one, for there is no conceptual space between authenticity and autonomy on such views. But I think we must *make* space if we are to do justice to pretheoretical intuitions about an important set of cases.[22] The cases I have in mind are ones in which agents identify so thoroughly with their concerns that they are unable to entertain the possibility that they might be mistaken or that their concerns might require defense. Highly dogmatic agents are sometimes like this, and I've argued that deeply deferential agents share a version of the same agential pathology.[23] Such agents are impervious to ordinary forms of critical dialogue that most of us

---

[19] Seidman, "Valuing and Caring," 296. *Concern* is Seidman's term for "the mental state we ascribe to an agent when we say that she *cares* about something." See Seidman, "Valuing and Caring," 282.

[20] Seidman, "Valuing and Caring," 296.

[21] Seidman, "Valuing and Caring," 296.

[22] Andrea C. Westlund, "Reply to Benson, Christman, Rocha, and Stoljar," *Symposia on Race, Gender, and Philosophy* 7:1 (2011): 1–6, http://web.mit.edu/sgrp.

[23] Andrea C. Westlund, "Selflessness and Responsibility for Self: Is Deference Compatible with Autonomy?" *Philosophical Review* 112:4 (2003): 483–523; Westlund, "Rethinking Relational Autonomy," 26–49.

take for granted. We might aptly describe them as being "in the grip" of their concerns, or perhaps as "under the influence" of their concerns. Acting under the influence of a concern for which one does not hold oneself answerable is intuitively incompatible with self-governance, even if it is consistent with the demands of authenticity. In other words, autonomy and authenticity (at least as the latter is usually conceived) may sometimes come apart.[24]

Jaworska seems to share this intuition, since she begins, in subsequent work, to move away from a purely authenticity-based view.[25] The autonomous agent, she argues, guides her action in light of the reasons she sees (in virtue of caring about certain things) to pursue or promote relevant ends. But something more is required: "Our theory," she writes, "must stave off the possibility that seeing a reason would simply amount to being in the grip of the reason."[26] Jaworska argues that autonomy requires what she calls "mental freedom," and that mental freedom is incompatible with being "rigidly stuck" in some "inflexible" emotional view or assessment of facts or reasons.[27]

I would agree with Jaworska that being mentally "unfree" is intuitively incompatible with autonomy and that being rigidly stuck in one's identity-constituting concerns is incompatible with mental freedom. To be stuck in a certain view of one's reasons (either for action or for emotion) implies not just a benign stability or absence of change but also a problematic inability to change. An agent unable effectively to revise or change her concerns under any conditions seems intuitively unable to govern herself, even if her choices and actions are determined by those very concerns. Perhaps she *has* a self, but she does not seem to be doing much in the way of governing.

Of course, an inability to change one's view of one's reasons could be explained in a variety of ways. One might lack certain critical reasoning or other straightforwardly cognitive skills, and this would, plausibly, undermine autonomy. Such skills are surely amongst what many philosophers now refer to as *competence* conditions for autonomy. But straightforwardly cognitive skills do not seem to be all that Jaworska has in mind. She claims, for example, that the agent must be "capable of imaginatively entertaining alternatives"[28] and that she must be open to the possibility that further reflection would change her view of what reasons she has. By reflection, Jaworska clarifies, she does not

---

[24] Westlund, "Reply to Benson, Christman, Rocha, and Stoljar." Later in the paper I consider a different conception of authenticity, proposed by Marina Oshana, which would be more closely aligned with autonomy as I understand it.

[25] Jaworska, "Caring, Minimal Autonomy, and the Limits of Liberalism."

[26] Jaworska, "Caring, Minimal Autonomy, and the Limits of Liberalism," 95.

[27] Jaworska, "Caring, Minimal Autonomy, and the Limits of Liberalism," 97.

[28] Jaworska, "Caring, Minimal Autonomy, and the Limits of Liberalism." The ability to imagine oneself or one's views as other than they are is a competence condition on autonomy that has been convincingly defended by Catriona Mackenzie, "Imagining Oneself Otherwise," in Mackenzie and Stoljar, *Relational Autonomy*; Diana Meyers, *Self, Society, and Personal Choice* (New York: Columbia University Press, 1989), 259–279.

mean Frankfurtian, higher-order reflection on lower-order motivational states but direct reflection on considerations relevant to the choice of a particular course of action. To have mental freedom, the agent must not only be capable of such reflection but must also be open to the possibility that engaging (or re-engaging) in it would change what she sees as a reason.

What does it mean to be open to this possibility? Merely acknowledging that reflection could, in principle, lead one to embrace an alternative perspective is not enough. For one might be unshakably indifferent to that possibility or even adamantly (perhaps unconsciously) determined *not* to engage in reflection, precisely because it could lead to some uncomfortable change. True openness of the sort Jaworska has in mind seems to include some readiness to engage (under at least some conditions) in reflection that is understood, by the agent, to be potentially transformative. One intuitively relevant—and common—condition calling for engagement is that in which one finds one's concerns, or the actions they motivate, challenged (either directly or indirectly) by the points of view of others. One is frequently called upon to *answer* for oneself, or to account for one's motivating concerns, in response to the concerns of others.

Thus understood, the attitude that Jaworska takes to be required for mental freedom is very close to what I refer to as an attitude of responsibility for self or self-answerability, an attitude that I take to be required for autonomy.[29] But I think the inclusion of this condition represents a significant departure from the authenticity-based model that Jaworska otherwise seems to embrace and that it points to a further disposition—beyond the emotional and cognitive dispositions that she and Seidman identify—that is characteristic of autonomous agency. To be appropriately open-minded, it seems to me, one must have a disposition to answer for one's concerns when called upon to do so, unless there are defeating conditions that render the call itself, or an effort to answer it, inappropriate in the circumstances.[30] Caring is partly constituted by a disposition to believe one has reasons to feel and act in certain ways, but autonomy (insofar as it requires mental freedom) requires that we also be disposed to suspend such beliefs, or at least hold them at arm's length—in dialogically appropriate contexts.

Of course, a too easy surrender of the beliefs one is disposed to hold is not intuitively compatible with autonomy, either. A social chameleon who abandons and replaces her identity-constituting concerns anytime she comes under pressure from without hardly seems to exercise enough control over her concerns to count as self-governing. Mental freedom may be incompatible

---

[29] Westlund, "Selflessness and Responsibility for Self"; Westlund, "Rethinking Relational Autonomy."

[30] I discuss some defeating conditions in Westlund, "Rethinking Relational Autonomy."

with being rigidly stuck, but it seems equally incompatible with a complete lack of stability in one's concerns.

Fortunately, readiness to engage in potentially transformative reflection does not imply readiness to capitulate at the least provocation. Our attempts to answer for our concerns often, at least at first, take the form of self-defense or self-advocacy. When faced with a challenge, we tend to want to communicate the value of what we take to be important, and the appropriateness of giving it the place we do in our deliberative life. Though it is relatively easy to veer into excessive defensiveness, there is a principled reason for self-advocacy as a default strategy: we cannot be willing to give up our cares at the drop of a hat, for this is incompatible with truly caring about the things we think we care about. This imperative reflects an important kernel of truth in Frankfurt's thesis that care is a commitment of the will: in its desiderative dimension, care requires more than simply having a desire (even a very strong one) and more also than wholeheartedly endorsing that desire. It also means wanting to *continue* to have the desire, even when one decides that it would be better, all things considered, not to act on it. The impulse to self-advocacy reflects this stabilizing dimension of care.

At the same time, though, for the agent genuinely to be mentally free, the impulse to advocate for oneself must be moderated by an appropriate attitude of humility. One must recognize that it is sometimes appropriate for self-advocacy to give way to self-scrutiny and be prepared to let self-scrutiny take its potentially transformative course when warranted. If one is not prepared to do this, one is (once again) rigidly stuck in a way that cannot amount to self-governance. It might help to think of the autonomous agent as possessed of certain characteristic virtues, in a broadly Aristotelian sense: she must avoid both an excess and a defect of answerability and openness and must know how to be open and answerable to the right degree and in the right circumstances.

3. Self-care

In this section, I develop a conception of mental freedom as entailing an attitude of *self*-care. The conception of self-care I defend is inspired in part by Carol Gilligan's vision of moral maturity, as laid out in her classic work *In a Different Voice*, and in part by Michel Foucault's notion of "care of the self," as developed in some of his later writings. This might seem like an unlikely pair of influences for a view of autonomy. It is not clear that either Gilligan or Foucault even accepts autonomy as a concept in good standing, nor do they have much theoretically in common with one another. But the view I defend is only loosely derived from certain of their ideas, which are (admittedly) taken out of the context of their wider bodies of work. Ultimately, I argue that self-care is a higher-order attitude of care (a compound of emotions, desires, and dispositions) focused on the first-order cares that Jaworska and Seidman take to make up the agent's standpoint or self.

Gilligan is best known for her path-breaking and controversial views about gender and moral development. But the aspect of her work that is most relevant to my argument has been much less widely discussed: it is the picture she paints of moral *maturity* and, in particular, of the morally mature agent's relationship to her own choices. Many of the troubled girls and women she interviews, particularly in her chapter on abortion decisions, seem at first to speak from a position of compromised autonomy. They feel helplessly constrained by their understanding of what others want from them and often describe themselves as "having no choice" about what to do when faced with a moral dilemma.[31] Gilligan points out that, while the feeling of powerlessness is very real for these women, it stems in large part from a confused abdication of responsibility for their own responses to their situations. Instead of seeing themselves as agents with a decision to make, they feel pushed and pulled by the demands of others and can assert themselves in only relatively inchoate ways. They do not see themselves as *choosing* what to do.

But a number of Gilligan's interviewees' have transitioned out of this stage of moral development, and what they say about the experience of coming to terms with their agency is very interesting. Several of her subjects, for example, dwell on the importance of taking care (or, as we sometimes say, taking pains) with their decisions. One subject, for example, claims that when deciding what to do one must take a critical view and be as "conscious" or "awake" as possible, "to consider all that's involved."[32] Another stresses the importance of being conscious of one's power or influence as a chooser and taking responsibility for the consequences of one's choices, both for oneself and for others.[33] A third emphasizes coming to terms with the fact that not all conflicts have a tidy or obviously right resolution and that one must exercise judgment to the best of one's ability and accept responsibility for the consequences of doing so.[34] In these and other similar passages, a common theme begins to emerge: moral maturity requires recognition of one's power to influence outcomes by exercising choice, acceptance of what we might (in Rawlsian terms) call the burdens of judgment, and willingness to take responsibility for exercising judgment in

---

[31] For these women, any course of action other than the self-sacrificing one feels unthinkable and the "chosen" course of action feels not so much chosen as inevitable. Notice, however, that the passivity they experience does not seem to be an instance of Frankfurtian alienation from their motives. Though Gilligan's subjects are distressed by their situations, many of them do seem to identify with their selflessness, understood in terms of an overriding imperative to maintain relationships and serve others' needs. The problem, as I go on to emphasize, is that they do not see themselves as *choosing* what to do, even when they act in accordance with this imperative.

[32] Gilligan, *In a Different Voice*, 99.

[33] Gilligan, *In a Different Voice*, 139.

[34] Gilligan, *In a Different Voice*, 118.

such conditions. "The essence of moral decision," Gilligan concludes, "is the exercise of choice and the willingness to accept responsibility for that choice."[35]

I want to argue that taking care with one's decisions, and accepting responsibility for one's judgments, is in fact a form of self-care. This might sound like an odd claim. But think of the way Foucault uses the phrase *care of the self* in his later writings about ancient Greco-Roman culture.[36] He does not, by this phrase, mean concern for one's material or bodily well-being or one's own interests or desires, at least not in any straightforward sense. The care he describes is targeted instead at the "soul"—meaning, as Foucault emphasizes, the *activity* of the soul, and not the "soul-as-substance."[37] Foucault shows how the ancients exhibited care of the self-as-soul through various activities of self-examination, self-articulation, and self-management. Of particular interest to Foucault is their engagement in various forms of self-writing, in which they both recorded their own thoughts and actions and drew on publicly accepted discourses to monitor and shape their principles of choice and action. Greco-Roman self-writers took notes on themselves, compiled fragments of advice and wisdom from public sources (sometimes to be shared), narrated their activities in correspondences with friends, and, in some cases, produced quasi-confessional journals that were private but explicitly intended to encourage the kind of self-examination and self-correction that is otherwise prompted by the critical gaze of others.

Foucault's discussion of these practices brings into focus a notion of self-care that bears a clear connection to answerability and responsibility for self. Foucault, tellingly, uses not only the phrase "care of the self" but also "*government* of oneself" to describe the practices to which these self-writing activities contributed.[38] Like some of Gilligan's subjects, Foucault's self-writers manifest strong concern for their own agency. In reflecting on and monitoring their principles of choice and action, they "take pains" over the practical perspectives or standpoints that define them as subjects. They care, in a practical or volitional sense, about who they are, and this care clearly involves a sense of responsibility, or answerability, for their deliberative activities.

Care of the self in the practical or volitional sense is clearly just one thing that we might have in mind when we speak of "self-care," and I do not mean it to subsume or replace all other uses of the phrase. Concern for one's material or bodily well-being, or for one's own interests or welfare, are also forms of self-care (arguably more familiar forms), and there is nothing inherently suspect or problematic about these attitudes. Gilligan, in fact, argues that the morally mature agent *must* treat herself as a proper object of care, in what I take to

---

[35] Gilligan, *In a Different Voice*, 67.
[36] Michel Foucault, *Ethics: Subjectivity and Truth* (New York: New Press, 1994).
[37] Foucault, *Ethics*, 231.
[38] Foucault, *Ethics*, 207.

be one of these alternative senses. She argues that to achieve moral adulthood a woman must shift from a perspective of selfless goodness to one that emphasizes truth—by which she seems to mean honesty about one's own needs and desires, along with recognition of oneself as a proper object of caring attitudes. The morally mature agent cares for herself (among other things) in the sense that she treats her own interests as worthy of consideration, and she will seek to minimize hurt to *all* involved, not just to others at the expense of herself.

But notice that the agent who cares for herself in this sense—treating her own interests as worthy of consideration—will still face the challenge of integrating her various concerns with one another and exercising judgment with respect to their apparent claims. Even if one thinks one's own interests and needs matter and must be taken into account, one can easily imagine being paralyzed in cases of conflict or being "rigidly stuck" in some particular conception of how competing claims should be handled. (Consider a well-known example from Gilligan's own research. When asked how to resolve a conflict between self and other, eleven-year-old Jake doesn't miss a beat: "You go about one-fourth to the others and three-fourths to yourself.")[39] Gilligan's most thoughtful interviewees, and Foucault's self-writers, recognize and thematize the need to exercise judgment and to take responsibility for doing so. Their attitudes, I suggest, point to a distinctive kind of self-care that is focused on the self in its deliberative or practical mode.

What is it, then, to care for oneself in the practical sense? If we accept something like the Jaworska–Seidman conception of care, then care of the self, like care of anything else, will be constituted by a complex of emotions, desires, and cognitive and emotional dispositions that are bound together by a perception of their focal object as a source of practical reasons. In this case, instead of being focused on other persons, objects, or ideals, the attitudes involved in self-care will be focused on elements of the caring agent's own deliberative perspective or standpoint and will be bound together by a perception of that standpoint itself as a source of reasons (for the agent). Suppose we also accept that one's standpoint is constituted by one's first-order cares (though not, to be clear, the further idea that having one's choices determined by such a standpoint suffices for autonomy). Self-care, then, would turn out to be a higher-order attitude of care focused on the first-order attitudes of care that make up one's subjective practical perspective. Caring about oneself would mean, in a manner of speaking, caring about one's cares.

One might object that while *everyone* cares about what she cares about (this is a mere tautology), not everyone cares about herself. So the definition of self-care I've just offered must be wrong. But my claim is *not* that the self-caring person, call her S, cares about herself simply *in virtue of* caring about X, Y, and

---

[39] Gilligan, *In a Different Voice*, 35.

Z, things that (by hypothesis) she happens to care about anyhow. It is instead that S cares about herself (in the sense at issue) if and only if she cares about her *caring attitudes*: she has certain higher-order attitudes toward, and dispositions concerning, the clusters of emotions, desires, and dispositions that constitute her first-order concerns for X, Y, and Z.

Even this claim could be interpreted in more than one way. The relevant question might, for example, just seem to be whether one's emotions are apt and well-proportioned, *given* that one sees X as important, or whether one actually has the dispositions and desires that one who cares about X should have. These questions take for granted the focus of the care and address the *quality* of one's attitudes toward that object, targeting the possible discrepancy between what one thinks one cares about and what one really does care about. It opens up a space for assessing someone's care as defective on its own terms, and it makes possible the judgment that, if someone's attitudes are defective enough, they might not qualify as "care" at all.

This might be part of what's involved in care of the self, in the loosely Foucaultian sense I've been putting forth. But this interpretation of what it is to care about caring doesn't yet address Jaworska's concern about mental freedom. For even if someone cares about X badly rather than well—even if she cares *so* badly that we are tempted to conclude that she doesn't truly care about X at all—it is possible for that person to be rigidly stuck in her view of X as a (purported) source of reasons. But one cannot be rigidly stuck in such a view of X if one is also concerned about that very way of viewing it, and this is surely part of what it is to care about one's cares. Caring about one's first-order concerns includes caring not just about the fit between one's emotions and dispositions and what one sees as important but also about the question of what one sees as important itself. More simply put, the agent who cares about herself, in the sense I want to isolate, cares about her reasons.

So what is it to care about one's reasons? I take it that a practical reason is a consideration that favors some particular course of action or emotional response on the part of the agent to whom it applies and that to see something as a reason is likewise to see it as favoring some action or emotion. Favoring, of course, is not an ideally perspicuous notion, but I think that a reason can be (slightly) more precisely characterized as a consideration that may enter into a viable defense or justification of a course of action or response. One who cares about her reasons, then, is subject to a constellation of emotions, desires, and dispositions focused on considerations she sees in this light, attitudes that are jointly explained (following Seidman) by her perception of those considerations as important. One who cares about her care for X, and thus about her X-based reasons, sees her care for X as important and as the source of a distinctive set of reasons.

When an agent cares about her care for X, she will want to protect that care from being too easily eroded. She will not, however, want to maintain her perception of X's importance (and her related sense of reasons) at any cost. As Seidman points out, the kind of reasons one takes oneself to have, in virtue of an object's perceived importance, will depend on the kind of thing that object is. A practical reason, I've claimed, is a consideration that can enter into a viable defense or justification of a particular action or emotional response. I propose that one who cares about her reasons must be attuned to the suitability of her apparent reasons for playing this justificatory role. More intuitively speaking, part of what it is to care about our concerns is to be concerned for their aptness. Think of it this way: only someone who doesn't care *what* she cares about could be untroubled by a charge that a given care has been misplaced. Caring about one's concerns counterbalances, to some degree, the cognitive disposition to take appearances of reasons at face value. Perhaps more accurately, it defines some of the conditions under which that disposition may be defeated.

One who does care what she cares about will be heartened by evidence that supports her perception of X as important and troubled by signs that this perception may instead be misleading. In the face of challenges to her X-based reasons, she will be disposed either to advocate on their behalf or to revise or reject them, depending on the perceived merit of the challenge. One who cares about her reasons will desire that she see as reasons only things that are well suited to playing their intended justificatory role, will have positive and negative emotions in response to evidence that this is or is not the case, and—perhaps most importantly, for our purposes—will be disposed to be rationally responsive to critical perspectives on her (purported) reasons. In this way, she takes responsibility for her reasons. Let us call this self-relation one of practical self-care.

4. Self-care and Relational Autonomy

Thus far I have followed Jaworska in treating *mental freedom* as a condition of autonomy and have argued, further, that mental freedom requires practical self-care. Does this picture have any bearing on the feminist point that autonomy must be understood as relational? Self-care is clearly a *self*-relation. But standing in some sort of relation to oneself is not, at least at first glance, the kind of relationality that relational theorists of autonomy have in mind. Relational conceptions of autonomy are meant, first and foremost, to establish the role played by *social* relations in autonomous agency.

Some assign to social relations a purely *causal* role in the development of autonomy competencies. Others regard social relations as, in one way or another, partly *constitutive* of autonomy. I fall into the latter camp, having argued elsewhere that responsibility for self is a dialogical disposition that requires seeing oneself always as potentially part of a deliberative dyad.[40] The self-responsible

---

[40] Westlund, "Rethinking Relational Autonomy."

agent holds herself to an expectation or demand that she respond appropriately to legitimate requests for justification, experiencing herself as *owing* a suitable response, at least under certain conditions. Answerability for oneself is, on my view, a special kind of (normative) competence condition on autonomy, resembling what Stephen Darwall calls "second-personal" competence.[41]

Here I've been arguing that the autonomous agent must care about her reasons and that caring about one's reasons opens one up to potentially transformative deliberative engagement with others. That autonomy should be so closely associated with openness to change—and particularly with change that is instigated by others—may sound counterintuitive, since we have become so accustomed to associating autonomy with authenticity, and authenticity with the idea of being true to oneself. But Marina Oshana argues convincingly that the form of authenticity most relevant to autonomy might involve something more like *honesty* with oneself.[42] (Gilligan might be pursuing a similar intuition when she describes the transition to moral maturity in terms of a commitment to truth.) Being honest with oneself about one's reasons is a way of being honest about who one is, but not one that will always leave the self unchanged. Whereas changing who one is in response to brute physical or psychological force, browbeating, or emotional manipulation would obviously be incompatible with autonomy, adjusting one's practical perspective or agential standpoint in response to reasons given by others is another matter. Self-government does not intuitively require insulation from *this* kind of external influence; even pretheoretically, self-government would seem likely to require honesty about one's reasons, and honesty about one's reasons would in turn seem to require sensitivity and appropriate responsiveness to critical perspectives.

One might object that it is not *always* incumbent upon us to care what others think of our commitments and, moreover, that sometimes we positively *should not* care what others think. A devoted parent, for example, need not be open to abandoning or substantially modifying his commitment to his child, and he appears lacking neither in self-care nor in autonomy when he refuses to entertain doubts about the aptness of his care. I do not dispute this claim, at least at the level of abstraction at which it is here posed. Most of us would, if pressed, have at least something to say in defense of caring for our children, but a challenger to whom we actually had to articulate such a defense would strike us as obtuse to the point of irrelevance. It is hard to imagine a challenge to parental care (as opposed, say, to a criticism of a particular way of

---

[41] See Darwall, *Second Person Standpoint*. I have more to say about the relationship between self-answerability and second-personal competence in Andrea C. Westlund, "Autonomy, Authority, and Answerability," *Jurisprudence* 2:1 (2011): 161–179.

[42] Marina Oshana, "Autonomy and the Question of Authenticity," *Social Theory and Practice* 33:3 (2007): 411–429. Oshana calls this an "epistemic conception" of authenticity. See Oshana, "Autonomy and the Question of Authenticity," 412.

interpreting or enacting parental care) that would, in ordinary circumstances, warrant sustained attention and scrutiny. Not every challenge is a serious challenge, and the agent who is *appropriately* responsive to critical perspectives will recognize this fact. Of course, our assessments of seriousness are themselves fallible, and one can no more avoid the burdens of judgment in this domain than in any other.

It is worth emphasizing that, even where one takes a challenge to be serious, self-care does not *always* lead to self-transformation. I maintained earlier that answering for oneself does not always mean acceding to the claims of others and that the autonomous agent knows when to advocate for as well as when to scrutinize and revise her commitments (or at least she exercises good judgment with respect to such matters and takes responsibility for doing so). The relation of self-care, as I've described it, embodies this complexity. There is a kind of built-in stability in the attitude of caring for one's reasons, since caring about one's reasons means responding to them *as important* and not simply to be trifled with. But stability is not rigidity, and what saves it from rigidity is a degree of flexibility.

If I am right, this flexibility is a product of our (appropriately moderated) openness to the perspectives of others. The disposition to answer for oneself is perhaps best characterized as a disposition to be engaged by other practical reasoners, with their own take on what matters, in a kind of shared deliberation regarding what one has reason to do or feel. Though it would take further argument to make this case, I suspect that the relational core of Gilligan's view might usefully be cashed out in terms of an orientation toward such shared deliberation. The idea is meant to resonate with the social dimension of Foucault's notion of care of the self as well. For Foucault, "care of the self... implies a relationship with the other insofar as proper care of the self requires listening to the lessons of a master. One needs a guide, a counselor, a friend, someone who will be truthful with you."[43] Even the more private forms of self-writing seem, in Foucault's rendering, to depend on a model of interpersonal engagement and responsiveness.[44]

So, I contend, there is at least one important respect in which autonomy is relational in an interpersonal (and not purely intrapersonal) sense. Indeed, on the view I've been defending in this paper, the relationality of autonomy and the self-regarding attitudes on which it depends are nonaccidentally bound up with one another. Self-care and self-responsibility are two facets of the same self-relation, involving the same normative and dialogical competence to answer for oneself.

---

[43] Foucault, *Ethics*, 287.
[44] Foucault, *Ethics*, 219–221.

Acknowledgments

I would like to thank Andrea Veltman and Mark Piper for their very helpful comments on earlier drafts of this paper. I am also grateful for valuable feedback from participants in the Relational Autonomy Workshop at McGill University in the fall of 2012, as well as participants in the 2013 Summer Retreat on Love and Human Agency at Lake Tahoe. I also benefitted a great deal from discussion with audiences at my Brady Lectures at Northwestern University in the spring of 2013, and I thank the Brady Program in Ethics and Civic Life at Northwestern University for its support during the time in which I did much of my work on this paper.

{ PART IV }

Autonomy, Oppression, and Adaptive Preferences

{ 10 }

Coping or Oppression: Autonomy and Adaptation to Circumstance

John Christman

Feminists have been rightly concerned with questions surrounding the agency status of people who appear to adapt to oppressive circumstances by altering their character in ways that seem to internalize that oppression. Much fruitful discussion has taken place about those people, women in particular, who seem to accept (or even claim to value) life situations that appear to the critical observer to be stultifying and dominating and in that way incompatible with autonomous agency.[1] This vexing problem focuses our attention on the seeming conflict in feminist sensibilities between, on the one hand, respecting the choices of actual women as well as being open to difference, and on the other hand, decrying the oppressive social conditions that bear down on women in this way.

Interestingly, however, far less attention has been given to the ways that people routinely reshape themselves in response to unforeseen and uncontrollable circumstance in ways that sometimes undercut autonomy but at other times do not. We have accidents, take risks that turn out badly in ways we are unprepared for, undertake radically indeterminate projects such as having a child or entering a relationship, and often fall victim to the decisions of others, the operation of impersonal institutions, and simple natural events that determine the available course of our lives. Changes in life options can give rise to changes in character, for example, learning to be accommodating to a partner's

---

[1] See, e.g., Paul Benson, "Autonomy and Oppressive Socialization" *Social Theory and Practice* 17 (1991): 38–408; Diana T. Meyers, "Feminism and Women's Autonomy," in *Gender in the Mirror: Cultural Integrity and Women's Agency* (New York: Oxford University Press, 2002), chap. 1; Marina Oshana, *Personal Autonomy in Society* (Aldershot, UK: Ashgate, 2006); Marilyn Friedman, *Autonomy, Gender, Politics* (New York: Oxford University Press, 2003); Anita Superson, "Deformed Desires and Informed Desire Tests," *Hypatia* 20:4 (2005): 109–126; Uma Narayama, "Minds of Their Own: Choices, Autonomy, Cultural Practices, and Other Women," in *A Mind of One's Own: Feminist Essays on Reason and Objectivity,* edited by Louise M. Antony and Charlotte E. Witt (Boulder, CO: Westview Press, 2001); Andrea Westlund, "Selflessness and Responsibility for Self: Is Deference Compatible with Autonomy?" *Philosophical Review* 112:4 (October 2003): 483–523.

unexpected habits or training ourselves to like children's games to play with our children.

Among these benign cases of adjustment to life's challenges are instances where the process of adaptation is more extreme: for example, a person has a severe accident or has a special needs child or an unplanned pregnancy, which completely alters her life trajectory. These are cases where relatively dramatic adjustments to a person's life ambitions and even sense of herself must take place, yet in at least some such cases the person retains or regains her autonomy. The interesting question, then, is what exactly marks off the cases of agency-undermining adaptation from those where self-government is maintained.[2]

Consider, for example, two cases. The first involves Abby.

Abby was always an athletically active girl and young woman. She was a runner and even trained for marathons on more than one occasion. One of her dreams was to run in the Boston marathon because she grew up near there. She apparently displayed the characteristics typical of a self-governed life. At the age of twenty-five, however, she was in a very serious car accident that left her permanently paralyzed from the waist down. As a result she was to be wheelchair-bound for the rest of her life. While completely despondent for a time, eventually Abby came to accept her condition. She continued to exercise, though she became less interested in outdoor activity. Instead, she picked a long-abandoned interest in writing and came to devote herself to fiction. After a time she became an accomplished short story writer and poet.

The second case is that of Kaew, a modest and demure Thai woman who at the age of twenty-two realized that to be a good provider for her family she had to look for employment where she could find it. As a result, she agreed to go to Japan to work at what she thought was a factory. When she arrived she was told she had to work at a "snack bar" (a bar and brothel) and that she had to pay off an exorbitant debt for the transport from Thailand. She worked at the bar and repaid the debt after four years, serving "clients" daily without a break and under constant threat of violence if she ever thought of attempting to leave. However, when her debt was paid off, she stayed on at the bar and continued to work as a prostitute, sending money back to her family. Eventually, she became one of the managers of the bar and facilitated the trafficking and sex work of other young women.[3]

In both cases the person changes radically over time in response to severely altered (and constrained) circumstance. Both individuals abandon earlier

---

[2] A classic discussion of this issue is in Jon Elster, *Sour Grapes* (Cambridge: Cambridge University Press, 1983).

[3] In both these cases I discuss only the subject herself, but of course the broader social and interpersonal network within which these events and processes take place is crucial to our understanding of the case. I mention such factors in the upcoming discussion. Also, all of the cases described in this paper are distillations of actual stories.

ideals about how their lives would go; in both cases, they rearranged their (presumably self-directed) projects and plans, indeed their senses of themselves, in response to changes in life options that they did not choose and would not have chosen. While of course there are numerous important differences between the cases, it is striking that we may have no hesitation in responding to the first with admiration and the second with pity and perhaps disdain. More to the point, we would not think that anything about the story of Abby (as told here) indicates a lack of autonomy after her adjustment, but we may well see Kaew as a straightforward case of the loss of autonomy or at least as problematic. What account of autonomy can be given that picks out the key differences between these cases?

I will say more about these and related cases as we proceed. My plan here is to examine a variety of approaches to diagnosing when alterations in character and values mark a loss of autonomy and when such alterations count merely as a healthy adaptation to constrained circumstances. After critically considering these approaches I will try to defend a broadly procedural approach to self-government that, I will suggest, can account for processes of adaptation of the sort being considered. However, my point is not to fully defend such an account of autonomy but merely to refine this approach to include a condition that I will call *reflexive self-affirmation*, a notion akin to what some other theorists have insisted on under the guise of self-worth and self-trust, though not exactly in the form they have done so.

One more important preliminary: the cases I describe are roughly drawn to be sure, but more importantly judgments about these cases will perforce be made from the equally underdescribed vantage point of detached philosophical analysis. This way of proceeding, it must be emphasized, leaves out two important factors in actual determinations of people's self-government (or lack thereof): one is their *own voices* in reporting their condition (and their judgments about it); and another is a specification of the *contexts* in which attributions of autonomy are in fact made, including the effect that those attributions might have on the autonomy of the agent in question. Indeed, in this latter category we should include reference to the dynamic interaction between those ascribing autonomy (as a classification) and the persons whose autonomy is at issue. The contexts where such judgments are made, expressed, and perhaps filed in official documents may have a direct effect on the state of the person herself relative to her self-government. In my conclusion I will return to these neglected aspects of such cases and discuss how attributions of autonomy involve dynamic exchanges between observers and observed (or, e.g., aid workers and clients, officials, and victim/survivors).[4]

---

[4] It is also manifestly true that the picture of a person like Abby (and others—see following) woefully underdescribes the conditions of disability. See, e.g., Carolyn Ells, "Lessons about Autonomy from the Experience of Disability," *Social Theory and Practice* 27:4 (October 2001): 599–615.

1. The Range of Cases and Asymmetries of Judgment

The contrasts between Abby and Kaew are numerous, but my point was not to draw any quick conclusions from our reactions to them. However, if we lay out a certain array of types of cases of this sort, I think we will see a certain asymmetry in our reaction that will prove instructive in refining our theoretical accounts of self-government.

Consider two variations on the previous cases:

Bernice was also an active, athletic person who relished physical activity and had aspirations similar to Abby's. She also had an accident that left her permanently disabled. But unlike Abby, she never adjusted to her life in a wheelchair; she turned to alcohol and never gave up the intense pain medication she was prescribed. She was also bitter and resentful at losing out on the life she had always imagined. At age forty she has now isolated herself from friends and support networks that would have attempted to steer her into a lifestyle commensurate with her capacities. She is, in a word, consumed by resentment.

Parallel to this is the case of Irina, who like Kaew was forced into prostitution and debt bondage. Like Kaew she was forced to remain in this life for an extended period. Irina, however, never stopped resisting her condition. She always held a fierce, though necessarily concealed, hatred of her captives and her life. She looked for any means of escape, making complex and elaborate plans to hide money away, venture out from the bar, and hopefully befriend a sympathetic and resourceful friend who could help her escape. Alas, however, during the time we are considering here, she never found one.

All of these cases are, again, terribly underdescribed.[5] And because of their brevity these descriptions cannot support very confident intuitive judgments about how to classify these individuals in terms of their status as self-governing agents. But my aim is to point out a general asymmetry that can be noticed, I think, in our reactions to them that will motivate our theoretical discussion: in the case of the two accident victims, it appears that acceptance, adjustment, and adaptation in the case of Abby points *toward* seeing her as a case of recovery of self-government, while Bernice's resistance and refusal to adjust points *away* from that judgment.[6] But in the cases of Irina and Kaew the direction of classification seems to be reversed. At first glance, at least, it seems that that Irina retains a modicum of self-government *just because* she resists

---

[5] One assumption about all four cases that should be mentioned is that all these individuals are relatively autonomous when the events in the stories begin to unfold.

[6] Again, I am not saying with any confidence that we would agree that Bernice lacks autonomy—much more needs to be known about her to say—but clearly her resentment and resistance to her condition make her *less* self-governing than Abby.

and resents her constraining condition, while Kaew might be seen as losing her autonomy just because she has adapted to her condition and altered her identity in response to it.

The array of cases of this sort is variegated in innumerable ways. However, I want to point to two dimensions of contrast that suggest dividing them up into four categories. First, there is adaptation or not. That is, Abby and Kaew adapted to their circumstance in the sense that at least some aspects of their identity and value scheme changed as a result of their constraining circumstances.[7] On the other hand, Bernice and Irina did not adapt to their condition; they remained resentful and resistant, or so I am describing them.

Second, the sources of constraint are radically different in the two sets of cases. In one, I am stipulating that the events that gave rise to the constraint are normatively neutral: the accidents that caused Abby and Bernice's disabilities were not anyone's fault, nor can they be described as "unjust" in any straightforward sense. In contrast, the conditions of Kaew and Irina are manifestly unjust, and "oppressive" as I use the term.

What is interesting, and what I take now as the pivot point for the remainder of this discussion, is that our reaction to whether the person's self-government is retained vis-à-vis her adaptation (or not) shifts depending on whether the source of the constraining condition is unjust (or not). Or to put things the other way around, our judgment about whether she is self-governing vis-à-vis oppressive circumstances shifts depending on whether she adapts or not. What I will argue, however, is that it is not the oppressive nature of the circumstances itself that determines this asymmetrical reaction; rather, it is the particular ways that radically constrained life options operate on the capacity for self-government and self-affirming practical identity of the agent herself.

Before discussing various approaches to these issues, it might be helpful to set the stage with a brief discussion of the model of agency and practical reason I am relying on here and, by extension, what we mean by adaptation. Autonomy involves basic skills and competences related to choice, deliberation, action, and interaction. Several accounts of such skills have been given, and clearly a broad range of competences is necessary for deliberate choice and action to take place.[8] Indeed, some theorists claim that autonomy requires only competency skills, ones involving introspection, communication, memory, imagination, analytical reasoning, self-nurturing, and resistance to pressures

---

[7] I label Abby's circumstance constraining for illustrative purposes. When adaptation is complete, and especially when the physical and social environment is sufficiently accommodating, the word *constraining* may not be an apt descriptor for her life situation.

[8] See, e.g., Diana Meyers, *Self, Society and Personal Choice* (New York: Columbia University Press, 1989); Paul Benson, "Feminist Intuitions and the Normative Substance of Autonomy," in *Personal Autonomy: New Essays on Personal Autonomy and Its Role in Contemporary Moral Philosophy*, edited by James Stacey Taylor (Cambridge: Cambridge University Press, 2005), 124–142.

to conform.[9] Others, however, have insisted that more is needed, in particular to distinguish autonomous agency from mere practical rationality. Specifically, it is claimed that autonomy requires the authenticity of the values and motives involved in action.[10]

Moreover, it can be claimed that self-governing agents choose on the basis of a value orientation that both justifies those choices and orients their understanding of the options they face and the relative importance of the considerations bearing on action. The most basic set of commitments and values that structure deliberation and choice in this way can be called our practical identity, following Christine Korsgaard.[11] Such identities guide choice but, as I said, also orient our perception of the options before us. Practical identities function over time to organize both an ongoing life narrative and memories of past decisions and experiences. We always think *as* a certain kind of person, even if that identity is necessarily inchoate, subject to alteration and renegotiation, and perhaps never fully transparent to our introspective reflection. Even for trivial and quotidian choices, the way we perceive and evaluate the options open to us reflects our practical orientation to the world, and this perspective, in turn, reflects our social identities to some degree (though of course the extent of the salience and functional force of such identities varies significantly).

This way of understanding practical reason in general, and autonomy in particular, is certainly not uncontroversial. But here I merely want to identify components of self-governing choice to fix ideas of interest. For in the cases we are imagining here, what we are calling *adaptation* involves fundamental shifts in key aspects of persons' practical identities, where they are forced by circumstance to renegotiate their sense of themselves, their value priorities, and their plans and projects. Over sufficient time, some of the most basic (even self-defining) values of the persons we are considering have faded into the background, hardly functioning to motivate thought or orient reflection. Abby no longer much thinks about marathons, daily morning jogs, or exercises in aerobic endurance of the sort that so preoccupied her in the past. Of course in moments of nostalgic musing she thinks of the life she lost and perhaps wistfully recalls wanting to train for her beloved Boston marathon. But this is similar to the way we all reflect on lives we once wished for but that no longer guide our choices. After a time, Abbey's pangs of longing have faded and such imaginings don't figure at all in her motivational complex; she is

---

[9] See, e.g., Meyers, *Gender in the Mirror* (New York: Oxford University Press, 2002), 20–21.

[10] For an argument to this effect, see John Christman, *The Politics of Persons: Individual Autonomy and Socio-historical Selves* (Cambridge: Cambridge University Press, 2009), chap. 7.

[11] Korsgaard, *The Sources of Normativity* (Cambridge: Cambridge University Press, 1996). Marilyn Friedman also sees autonomy as relative to our basic values. See Friedman, *Autonomy, Gender, Politics*, chap. 1.

now completely overtaken by her writing routine, her public readings, literary discussions, and various other of her new life's passions.[12]

But I focus here, somewhat myopically perhaps, on the changes in these persons' practical identity as a mode of mental functioning, orienting perception and deliberation and grounding evaluative reflection, in the hopes that a fuller picture that includes bodily components would be consistent with this level of description. When the circumstances radically changed for people like Abby and Kaew, a process began that resulted in a reordering of their values and priorities, culminating in a new way of looking at and experiencing the world.

2. Adaptation and Autonomy

What we have before us is an initial puzzle, namely, that adaptation of one's practical identity to new constraints suggests, in one case, that autonomy is maintained (Abby) but that the very same adaptation in another case marks a move toward heteronomy (Kaew). Moreover, resistance to adaptation suggests the dilution of self-government in one case (Bernice) but not in another (Irina). What approach to autonomy best helps us account for these asymmetries?

I divide responses to such cases into two categories: structural and procedural.[13] Structural accounts make central reference to aspects of the social circumstance of the agent, independent of her perspectival take on those elements. Procedural accounts view autonomy with reference only to the skills and reflective dispositions of the agent herself from her perspective (perhaps making reference to the processes by which such skills and reflections came to be exercised). These are rough categories, but I will give particular examples presently. The key idea is that procedural accounts refer exclusively to the capacities and perspective of the agent and mention structural aspects of their condition or the content of their values only derivatively, as a means of filling out the procedural conditions themselves.

---

[12] It must be noted here, as many other theorists have emphasized, that the scenario I am sketching also involves radical changes in forms of embodiment and that, insofar as intelligence, memory, and identity are in large part constituted by somatic elements, Abby's bodily change has changed herself in quite literal ways (though I am not claiming in metaphysical ways necessarily—she is still the same person in that sense). As many feminists have claimed, our bodies and their capabilities and habits form who we are and help form our values and modes of reflection and action. See, e.g., Diana Meyers, "Decentralizing Autonomy: Five Faces of Selfhood," in Meyers, *Being Yourself: Essays on Identity, Action, and Social Life* (Lanham, MD: Rowman and Littlefield, 2004); Catriona Mackenzie, "On Bodily Autonomy," in *Handbook of Phenomenology and Medicine*, edited by S. K. Tombs (The Netherlands: Kluwer, 2001), 417–439.

[13] These classifications echo, though do not precisely mirror, distinctions in the literature between externalist and internalist accounts. For discussion, see, e.g., Marina Oshana, "Personal Autonomy and Society," *Canadian Journal of Philosophy* 29:1 (Spring 1998): 81–102.

Some relational accounts of autonomy count as "structural" in my sense. Marina Oshana, for example, requires not only procedural requirements for autonomy but also external, sociorelational conditions. On her account, the conditions of autonomy include various internalist requirements of the sort procedural accounts feature, such as epistemic competence, rationality, and procedural independence as well as certain normatively substantive conditions such as self-respect. The specifically sociorelational conditions Oshana lists include the following: the person enjoys social and psychological security (others cannot deprive the person of de facto or de jure power and authority "characteristic of global autonomy"); the person can pursue goals different from the goals of those who have influence and authority over her; the person is not required to take responsibility for another's needs unless reasonably expected in light of her particular function; the person enjoys financial self-sufficiency adequate to maintain independence from others; and the person is not deceived.[14]

I have discussed this view elsewhere,[15] but I am not concerned to be critical of it here as a plausible account of a kind of autonomy. It is an ideal of an independent life that, in some contexts, could well serve as a component of the requirements of social justice. I mention it, however, because the purely structural (sociorelational) elements Oshana mentions will not suffice to make the distinctions in judgment we began with, in particular the contrasting reactions to Abby and Bernice, on one hand, and to Kaew and Irina on the other. For both pairs of individuals exist in similar sociorelational settings. Yet we view their mode of adaptation to those settings as different in crucial ways. This suggests that insofar as the structural, external conditions of the cases don't explain the contrasts correctly, then these contrasts will best be drawn by the procedural components of the account, a point to which I will return.

Other theorists insist on structural (nonprocedural) elements for autonomy that refer to the interpersonal and social dynamics of agency but focus the effect of such relations on the agency of the person, especially in regard to vulnerabilities she may experience in exercising that agency. Consider, for example, several views that all require that interpersonal recognition or acknowledgment of the person's normative authority (or self-worth, or answerability) is necessary for autonomy to obtain.[16] Catriona Mackenzie is typical of these

---

[14] Oshana, "Personal Autonomy and Society," 86.

[15] Christman, *Politics of Persons*, chap. 8.

[16] These different accounts I have in mind are from Catriona Mackenzie, "Relational Autonomy, Normative Authority and Perfectionism," *Journal of Social Philosophy* 39:4 (Winter): 512–533; Paul Benson, "Taking Ownership: Authority and Voice in Autonomous Agency," in *Autonomy and the Challenges to Liberalism: New Essays*, edited by J. Christman and J. Anderson (Cambridge: Cambridge University Press, 2005), 101–126; Andrea Westlund, "Selflessness and Responsibility for Self: Is Deference Compatible with Autonomy?" *Philosophical Review* 112:4 (October 2003): 483–523; Joel Anderson and Axel Honneth, "Autonomy, Vulnerability, Recognition, and Justice," in *Autonomy and the Challenges*

views in insisting that autonomy requires more than merely the individual enjoyment of a sense of normative authority, more also than granting *oneself* that authority; it also requires external recognition by others of that authority, in addition to being competent and reflective. Mackenzie claims that "an agent's sense of herself as having a rightful claim to normative authority...[is] based on intersubjective recognition" by others. In this way, an agent's status as having normative authority over her values and decisions (what others have called self-trust) has both "first-personal" and "relational" aspects.[17] For views like this one, the question of whether adaptation involves a failure of autonomy in a structural sense is more nebulous.

Let us consider, then, how adding such an interpersonal recognition requirement may help us in our differential responses to the cases we have been considering. Specifically, let us focus on cases of what we can call resistant slaves. What I mean are people like Irina who never cave in to the oppressiveness of their conditions either by losing their oppression-independent self-understanding or by losing their will to resist, even though no (nonsuicidal) opportunities to express that resistance afford themselves. There are any number of variations on such cases and variations along several dimensions. For instance, slave narratives from the American South describe people who never lose their desire to be free, but within the seemingly permanent circumstances of servitude they make elaborate plans and develop projects they can truly call their own, for example, their efforts to avoid being sold away from their children and spouses.[18] As just one example, consider a description by one Charity Bowery, a slave in North Carolina, of her plans to save money to buy her children from her owner:

> From the time my first baby was born, I always set my heart upon buying freedom for some of my children. I thought it was more consequence to them than to me; for I was old and used to being a slave. But mistress McKinley wouldn't let me have my children. One after another—one after another—she sold 'em away from me. Oh, how many times that woman broke my heart![19]

Such stories include descriptions of elaborate and complex struggles to achieve such important goals, and they abound in accounts of slave life, a life that surely fails to meet the structural desiderata of views like Oshana's as well as the interpersonal requirements of some relational accounts.

---

to *Liberalism: New Essays*, edited by John Christman and Joel Anderson (Cambridge: Cambridge University Press), 127–49.

[17] Mackenzie, "Relational Autonomy," 514.

[18] Most slaves had no ultimate power over these processes. But many had some, and even if they had no ultimate sway over whether their wishes were carried out the fact that they maintained them throughout their captivity is what is relevant here. See, e.g., John Blassingame, ed., *Slave Testimony: Two Centuries of Letters, Speeches, Interviews, and Autobiographies* (Baton Rouge: Louisiana State University Press, 1977).

[19] Blassingame, *Slave Testimony*, 262.

In all such cases, two important factors remain in play. First, these agents maintain a practical identity that is continuous with their pre- or nonoppression selves. Their value priorities and senses of themselves are not crushed by their captivity, even if they are prevented from acting on them. Second, such persons are without most if not all of the social conditions that many relational theorists require for autonomy. I am not claiming that such people are in any way fully autonomous, and externalist relational theories, such as Oshana's and relational views like Mackenzie's, may explain why not. But I do think there is another sense of minimal autonomy that they *do* maintain, one that importantly distinguishes them from those who *are* crushed by circumstance into either internalizing the oppressive values structuring their domination or losing completely any effective power to act on their own at all. My point so far is merely that models of autonomy that stress structural injustice and those that feature interpersonal recognition have not quite located that difference.

This last point may be too hasty, however, for we must ask further whether and in what sense resistant slaves might experience the recognitional acknowledgment that theorists such as Mackenzie and others say is necessary for autonomy. This is a difficult question for many reasons. One reason is that it may be difficult to discern what modes of recognition and respect are being shown such people or what level of such respect they are recognizing, even in cases where we may know a great deal about their situation and psychology. Moreover, their situation picks up on an ambiguity in some recognitional accounts, namely, whether acknowledgment of the normative authority of these agents (for example) must be *public* or if it can be simply a kind of internal voice that the persons in question can listen to and gain strength from. And if it must be outwardly displayed, if signs and behaviors must *show* such recognition, who must show it? The powerful people that have the most influence over the person and her social environment? Or can it be similarly oppressed compatriots? If the latter, or if (as some writers claim) the recognition can be a purely imaginative one involving internalized voices by the agent herself, one wonders if such recognition is too weak, in that even young children can experience a recognitional acknowledgment from their dolls and invisible playmates in developing a sense of themselves. And in other cases, recognition of deliberative capacities is not yet *deserved*, no matter how much people claim it for themselves. A precocious eleven-year-old, for example, may claim full powers of independent judgment for herself and even insist on being recognized as such, but others may nevertheless recognize that such confidence is not quite merited as yet.[20]

Now many structural theorists have made it clear that internalized recognition, where a postulated community of compatriots that one engages with in

---

[20] Paul Benson mentions this last point as a possible objection. See Benson, "Taking Ownership," n. 63. Also, both Benson and other theorists in this literature have discussed the ambiguities I mention

imaginative dialogue can provide the kind of recognition of normative authority being described.[21] Charles Taylor states forthrightly that it can, in saying that even the isolated artist who speaks a language that is not understood or acknowledged by her age still engages in dialogic interaction with the voices of other internalized listeners that gives her a sense of agency and effectance.[22] But notice that the requirement that such internalized recognition is necessary for self-government is that it is *effective*: it gives the agent the sense of identity and self-worth needed to give force to her plans and endeavors. This implies that what matters, in the end, is the individual's power of agency and that whatever form or mode of social interaction that is necessary to maintain such a power is required as a causal condition for it.

The idea of the resistant victim of oppression raises issues for other accounts as well. For example, in the context of a discussion of informed desire accounts of the good, Anita Superson analyzes the phenomenon of "deformed desires."[23] On her view, having a sense of "equal self-worth" is required for us to be able to say of a person that her desires are not deformed—desires, say, to conform to oppressively patriarchal norms. In this discussion, she considers the account offered by Uma Narayan concerning the way that women (for example) reflect a kind of authentic agency in negotiating their place in a (to an observer) stultifying and oppressive environment. Narayan believes that "bargaining" with patriarchy makes a woman's deformed desires her own. She understands Muslim women's choice to wear a veil as a " 'bundle of elements,' some of which they want [for example, ones reflecting their commitments to various aspects of their own religious, social, and communal identities] and some of which they do not want, and where they lack the power to 'undo the bundle' so as to choose only those elements they want."[24]

This scenario parallels the picture of the strategizing and resistant slave: one who lives within crushing and unjust constraints yet shows genuine signs of agency and self-directedness. What Superson says about Narayan, however, indicates that she would resist such a classification. In considering the case of veiling by Muslim women, she writes:

> It seems to me that the woman who chooses veiling after bargaining over her conflicting desires, in part because she believes that she needs to send

---

here. See, e.g., Benson, "Taking Ownership"; Andrea Westlund, "Replies," *Symposia on Race, Gender, Race, and Philosophy* 7:1 (Winter 2011), http://sgrp.typepad.com/sgrp/winter-2011-symposium-mackenzie-poltera-and-westlund-on-autonomy.html.

[21] See, e.g., Mackenzie, "Relational Autonomy"; Andrea Westlund, "Selflessness and Responsibility for Self." See also Andrea Westlund, "Rethinking Relational Autonomy," *Hypatia* 24:4: 26–49.

[22] Charles Taylor, *The Ethics of Authenticity* (Cambridge, MA: Harvard University Press, 1991), 32–33.

[23] Superson, "Deformed Desires and Informed Desire Tests."

[24] Narayan, "A Mind of One's Own."

a message to men about modesty and propriety, lacks sufficient belief in her self-worth to insist that men be the ones to change their attitudes toward women who do not veil.... A person who exhibits full agency and self-direction cannot choose to have desires that are coercive, ones making her act in ways she otherwise would not. She cannot freely make these desires her own, and if she has them, she cannot be fully self-directing.[25]

The word *coercive* in the second to last sentence is ambiguous, since calling desires coercive may already assume a categorization that we are trying to discern. More to the point, however, I conclude from Superson's observation here that she simply doesn't *believe* that a woman can maintain a sense of self-worth in negotiating conditions of this sort, which she (Superson) takes to be so dehumanizing. She may well be right. But this shows that her criticism turns on skepticism that the women actually *have* a sense of self-worth, not that they cannot be called self-governing agents in such conditions even if they did so. I won't comment on women who wear traditional dress, but my reading of many first-person reports of survivors of slavery and oppression leave me little doubt that the women and men in many cases maintained a strong sense of self-worth while struggling against such horrific constraints. Similar judgments are made by other observers and participants concerning decisions to adapt to traditional and arguably oppressive conditions, by making them in some way part of one's identity.[26] This is not to say that these observations are obviously correct in the end, only that the possibility that they are correct shows that neither relations of equal status nor overt recognition of one's status (worth) by surrounding others is always required for authentic agency, which is the crucial conceptual point.

One of the most detailed recent accounts of the phenomenon of adaptive preferences has been undertaken by Serene Khader who is also highly critical of procedural (and in general, autonomy-based) attempts to define what she calls *inappropriately adaptive preferences* (IAPs).[27] Khader considers several versions of procedural autonomy and argues in each case that they fail to adequately identify IAPs. The version that comes closest to what I will defend here is what she calls the capacity to live according to a life plan.[28] She claims, however, that those with IAPs do not uniquely fail to live according to an identifiable life plan, if indeed one could be articulated (which is doubtful). At least

---

[25] Superson, "Deformed Desires," 423.

[26] See, e.g., Saba Mahmoud, *The Politics of Piety* (Princeton, NJ: Princeton University Press, 2005).

[27] Serene Khader, *Adaptive Preferences and Women's Empowerment* (New York: Oxford University Press, 2011). For her criticism of proceduralist views, see Khader, "Adaptive Preferences and Procedural Autonomy," *Journal of Human Development and Capabilities* 10:2 (July 2009): 169–187.

[28] Khader, "Adaptive Preferences and Procedural Autonomy," 177ff. See also Khader, *Adaptive Preferences and Women's Empowerment*, chap. 2. Khader cites Diana Meyers, "Personal Autonomy and the Paradox of Feminine Socialization," *Journal of Philosophy* 84:11 (1987): 619–628, as the source of the view she discusses.

they do not fail to do this in any way different from how those with nonadaptive preferences might. Moreover, there is no single life story that uniquely picks out the personal history against which reflective judgments about current desires are to be made, both in the normal case and for those with IAPs.[29]

First, however, it is not clear that life stories framed by practical identities are as inaccessible as Khader suggests, as most people can readily express the kind of person they are, their basic values, and the way they've developed in light of these values. Giving reasons for our actions demands as much. More importantly, however, Khader argues against using a notion of autonomy that relies on maintaining a sense of self-esteem. She argues that many who adapt their preferences to conform to oppressive circumstances do not lack global self-esteem in any sense. "It is implausible," she writes, "that most persons with APs think they are unworthy human beings who cannot make claims on others."[30]

However, in the view developed herein, where I argue that being unable to be guided by a practical identity that one can affirm the value of through one's actions and reflections indicates IAPs, does not rest on the assumption that *global* self-esteem is the marker of nonadaptation. I accept that a person's identity is segmented into overlapping practical self-conceptions (e.g., being a father, a survivor, a caring person, a professional). What is required, however, is that one must be guided by a self-understanding that reflectively expresses a way of being one can accept without alienation. Khader's criticisms of procedural views do not undercut that approach.[31]

What I have tried to show here, then, is that structural accounts that require just social relations or expressions of recognition do not adequately capture the difference between autonomy and adaptation we are seeking, however powerful they may be for other purposes. Before moving on to a positive view, however, let us consider one final discussion of autonomy that may shed light on such judgments. Sarah Buss has recently argued that accounts of autonomy that require self-reflection and internal control over first-order desires all fail to fully account for what makes such desires one's own.[32] She takes to task accounts of autonomy (which can serve to confer accountability of the right sort) that see it as an idealized form of agency control. Such views all fail to capture what is distinctive about autonomous agency because we can be authentic

---

[29] Khader, "Adaptive Preferences and Procedural Autonomy," 178.
[30] Khader, "Adaptive Preferences and Procedural Autonomy," 181.
[31] Khader's arguments are quite thorough, and my discussion may well not adequately reflect their nuance so the comments in the text must be taken as a summary judgment rather than a painstaking argument. Also, she goes on to develop a view of IAPs based on the idea of *flourishing* which deserves more discussion. Khader, *Adaptive Preferences and Women's Empowerment*. For reasons laid on the rest of this paper, however, it will be clear why I would reject such a perfectionist approach.
[32] Sarah Buss, "Autonomous Action: Self-Determination in the Passive Mode," *Ethics* 122:4 (July 2012): 647–691.

relative to habitual, unreflective, automatic, and other actions over which we exhibit no real agentic control, she argues.[33] Moreover, those views that require higher-order reflective endorsement all fall prey to what has been labeled elsewhere as the regress problem: that is, no noncircular account of what gives those higher-order reflections special status can be given without postulating ever higher levels of reflection. Referring to procedural independence simply gives a name to what needs to be explained and pointing to examples such as brainwashing and manipulation do not explain exactly why and how these things undermine agency.[34]

These criticisms of procedural accounts are well taken, and in the final section I will try to address them in part. However, Buss also urges us to take a different tack in thinking about autonomy, to forget about seeing self-government as a kind of supped-up agency, where we have the greatest reflective control over ourselves. Rather, she thinks that crucial aspects of agency—mental, emotional, and other states—causally produce our actions so we are essentially passive in regards to them. As she says, "Nothing active can sustain its [the agent's] activity without passively relying on everything that makes this activity possible."[35] A person's character causes her action, and this is why we can attribute those actions to her; however, she is essentially passive regarding her character in important respects.

In explicating this view, Buss also looks at a certain asymmetry of judgment concerning actions and their causes, noting that factors we regard as positive that drive a person to act are thought of as commensurate with agency while negative factors are thought to undermine it. To explain this asymmetry, she posits the view that factors incommensurate with human flourishing undermine agency but that those supportive of such flourishing do not. She says little to illuminate what she means by *flourishing* and how we are to delineate the factors she has in mind, but hers is generally a structural account in the nomenclature I used earlier. An external, objective appraisal of the agent's environment determines the quality of her agency and not an account of the internal workings of her reflection and judgment.

I will comment on the usefulness of this account to explain the different asymmetry that we are considering in a moment, but I want to note first that an alternative explanation for the different reactions we have toward positive and negative factors she describes is available to us. Namely, we can easily say that positive compulsions are not out of synch with the normative frame or schema that structures one's identity—unless of course they are: imagine the

---

[33] Buss, "Autonomous Action."

[34] Buss, "Autonomous Action." The views she is referring to most directly are those of Harry Frankfurt and Gerald Dworkin. For Dworkin's views on procedural independence, see Dworkin, *The Theory and Practice of Autonomy* (Cambridge: Cambridge University Press, 1990), chap. 1.

[35] Buss, "Autonomous Action," 658.

person in the manic phase of what used to be called manic depression (bipolar disorder). When a person is so overtaken with an overflow of powerful positive emotion that she appears not to be herself it is because that level of positive intensity is seen to be (and let's imagine in the case it is) a force out of synch with the normative frame definitive of the person's identity. When your manic sister wants to hug you too much, too often, going on about how wonderful you are, it can (sadly) become clear that she is in the grips of an episode. Consider also a person on the drug ecstasy: he is intensely explaining to you how awesome you are. None of these are counterflourishing actions or emotions per se. What makes them suspicious is that they run counter to what the person would normally do. They reveal the workings of psychic forces that are out of synch with the person's identity.

More pointedly, however, the distinction between agency sustaining and agency undermining causal factors, for Buss—a distinction she describes as turning on whether such factors contribute to basic human flourishing—won't help to explain our different reactions to people like Abby and the others. For clearly the factors that caused both Abby and Bernice to readjust their aspirations were *harmful*—a terrible accident—but the difference in their reactions was, I would insist, a result of the methods they used to come to understand and process those factors. Similarly, both Kaew and Irina are reacting to negative (counterflourishing) environmental factors, but they differ in their reaction to them, a difference that marks their different status as autonomous agents, I would suggest.

So although Buss may be right in what she says about a certain notion of agency—there may well be multiple takes on agency available to us depending on the purpose of assigning that label to people—it won't help in our present task. However, in the final section, where I make a general suggestion that distinguishes the cases in question along the lines of a procedural account of autonomy, it will be necessary to again take into consideration the challenges Buss raises for similar such accounts in the literature.

3. Procedural Autonomy and Self-affirmation

Throughout this discussion I have been trying to shed some light on the daunting problem of internalized oppression by focusing on more commonplace cases of adaptation and adjustment, even when that involves significant shifts in one's value commitments and practical identity. In what follows I want to discuss a procedural approach to autonomy that, with some amendments, helps us focus on the aspect of those adjustments that allow self-government to maintain or reestablish itself, in contrast with cases where it is undermined. What I propose is to take onboard the claim many have made in similar theoretical contexts—namely, that autonomy must involve the (weakly substantive) requirement of a sense of self-worth—but motivate that requirement in a slightly new way.

The point is to defend an approach to autonomy that helps distinguish these different modes of adaptation and to explain why some of them allow agents to retain self-government while others do not. I have briefly argued in the previous section that structural accounts of this difference are not likely to be successful, though of course my discussion was far from exhaustive. But my rough conclusion is that it is not merely the injustice of the circumstances under which adaptation takes place that classifies that process as autonomy undermining. Something more must be said. To say more, let me develop an argument for including self-worth—or what I will call reflexive self-affirmation—as a condition of autonomy.

Proceduralist accounts of autonomy are those that attempt to explicate the notion of self-government without essential reference to the evaluative content of the desires, values, and character traits of the autonomous person but rather to specify the competences and processes of the formation of those desires and values that mark them out as autonomous. Now it has been claimed that proceduralist accounts that claim value neutrality are actually driven to what are called *weakly substantive* views. This can be said to maintain the spirit of neutrality and sensitivity to difference that motivates proceduralism in this context but more adequately capture the way some value commitments will be, by their psychological function, required for self-government. The commitment most often mentioned is some variation on self-trust.[36]

I am sympathetic with this move, as long as it is described in the proper way, namely, that certain value commitments are required for autonomy because the core conditions of autonomy (e.g., reflective, competent, self-acceptance) cannot be achieved without those commitments but not because such commitments are inherently valid or justified.[37] I will return to this point in a moment.

---

[36] The argument concerning weakly substantive views of autonomy can be found in Sigurour Kistinsson, "The Limits of Neutrality: Toward A Weakly Substantive Account of Autonomy," *Canadian Journal of Philosophy* 30:2 (2000): 257–286. For discussion of self-trust as a requirement of autonomy, see, e.g., Benson, "Autonomy and Self-Worth," *Journal of Philosophy* 91:12 (1994): 650–668; Carolyn McLeod, *Self-Trust and Reproductive Autonomy* (Cambridge, MA: MIT Press, 2002); Trudy Govier, "Self-Trust, Autonomy and Self-Esteem" *Hypatia* 8:1 (1993): 99–119.

[37] That is, we do not go from the assumption that certain values are objectively valid to the conclusion that failure to grasp these values is a mark of a lack of competence, as some theorists do. See, e.g., Susan Babbitt, "Feminism and Objective Interests: The Role of Transformation Experiences in Rational Deliberation," in *Feminist Epistemologies*, edited by Linda Alcoff and Elizabeth Potter (New York: Routledge, 1993), 24–64. See also Natalie Stoljar, "Autonomy and the Feminist Intuition," in *Relational Autonomy*, edited by Catriona Mackenzie and Natalie Stoljar (New York: Oxford University Press, 2000), 94–111.

The historical approach to autonomy that I and others utilize emphasizes the diachronic nature of the agent and the procedures that mark self-government.[38] My attempt to defend an historical account utilized the condition of reflective acceptance of one's motives (without alienation) in light of one's history and in relation to one's diachronically structured practical identity.[39] The problem Buss and others raise with this account is that acts of reflection, even the hypothetical reflection I require, can themselves be manipulated and no account of "adequate" reflection can be given that doesn't assume that we already know what self-government *is*.

I now see that the account of self-acceptance upon reflection is in crucial ways undertheorized. On one hand it, from the critical self-reflection views from which it arises, it may inherit the challenge of a regress and the specter of voluntarism (despite attempts to avoid it). That is, either the acts of self-reflection are themselves in need of self-ratification, or we must assume a self-evaluation of its own attitudes without a basis. In addition to weakening the attitude that confers agential status on lower-order motivations to alienation (rather than endorsement), I also insisted that the reflection need only be hypothetical. Moreover, I also claimed that the reflection need not be "deep" in the sense of considering a world where one did not have the attitude (since that may be psychologically impossible for many autonomous agents) but only generally evaluative, where one considers the importance of the attitude, its implications for oneself and others, and its connections to other aspects of the self.

These moves add up to a picture that is really not a hierarchical view at all, I now see, at least not in the sense of postulating levels of mental activity that are ordered in terms of their centrality to the self. Rather, saying that the autonomous person acts from motives that she would reflectively accept as part of her practical identity is not to imply that the reflective self is more central somehow to our agency but rather that acting from motives that can be self-reflectively endorsed in light of one's practical identity themselves have a special status (vis-à-vis authenticity). That is, in acting deliberately, one *reflexively* (not necessarily *reflectively*) affirms the value of the practical identity that motivates and justifies that act. In a manner akin to a recursive function, when one acts intentionally one engages a practical identity that affords value to that choice and in so doing reflexively reinforces the value of having that practical identity.[40] I act *as* a certain type of person when I act, and in so doing I repeatedly reinforce the value of being such a person—at least when things are going well.

Reflection does play a role in this process because we are often called on to reconsider our actions in light of our basic values. In particular, because of the

---

[38] Other historical accounts include Al Mele, *Autonomous Agents* (New York: Oxford University Press, 1991); John Martin Fischer and Mark Ravizza, *Responsibility and Control: A Theory of Moral Responsibility* (New York: Cambridge University Press, 1998).

[39] This is a highly truncated summary of the position. Christman, *Politics of Persons,* chap. 7.

[40] Cf. Keith Lehrer, *Self-Trust: A Study of Reason, Knowledge and Autonomy* (New York: Oxford, 1997).

socially embedded nature of actions, we must coordinate our acts and reasons with others, either by being called on to account for our actions and values in ways that force us to reflect on them or by listening to the reflections of others in acting with them or in response to them.[41]

But deliberate action for the self-governing agent may well be passionate, committed, unflinching, and hence nonreflective in any given instance. This does not mean, however, that such action is unthinking or not underwritten by one's basic values (often quite the contrary). But it does mean that in acting one engages the value orienting function of one's practical identity and in so doing reaffirms that identity as worth having and acting upon. In this way I agree with Buss when she underscores the ways we are often passive in relation to the elements of our character that motivate and justify our autonomous actions.

The model of intentional action I utilize here relies a great deal on Korsgaard's "self-constitution" account of agency.[42] On her view, when one acts intentionally one is guided by a standard of success or failure, which is given both by the teleological structure of action (one chooses an action with a purpose in mind) and by the evaluative organization of the practical identity that grounds the choice. In this picture, acting is always value conferring in two directions. When our actions are guided by our practical identities, we both project value onto those actions and, reflexively, inherit their value in being their source. Now Korsgaard's picture of action and identity is much more detailed than this and is embedded in a Kantian framework that I don't want to commit to here (necessarily). I want merely to extract the central element of her view of action, namely, that we constitute ourselves in action and reflexively affirm the value of the identities that underwrite those actions when we choose them.

There are, as has been suggested, important interpersonal and social elements to this process. I agree, but in a particular way that should be clarified to retain the procedural status of the view. The nomenclature of practical identities, the terms in which value orientation expresses itself, involves a rich language of roles, social categories, and standards of behavior. We see ourselves and act *as* a certain kind of person, such as being a mother or a teacher or a Muslim or a woman, and those self-descriptors carry with them socially structured expectations and motivations. These terms do not merely refer to a set of values or propositionally structured commitments that one can say one *believes in* (though those surely figure in our identities). Rather, these categories orient our way of seeing the world and prioritizing values and options to

---

[41] These observations can be read as a partial response to some critics of my view. See, e.g. Diana T. Meyers, "Review of *The Politics of Persons*," *Hypatia* 27:1 (March 2011): 227–230.

[42] Christine Korsgaard, *Self-Constitution: Agency, Identity, and Integrity* (Oxford: Oxford University Press, 2009).

act.⁴³ The core of the postulate of self-worth, I suggest, is that those descriptors can be understood as naming a life worthy of pursuit from one's own perspective. They are often self-validating in practical reflection because they stand in for a host of interconnected values that, in turn, justify action. One need only think, "As a mother, I put my children's needs above my own" and not feel the need to further reflect (in the normal case) on whether it is a good thing to be a mother of this sort.⁴⁴

I say in the normal case because I am describing here cases of nonalienated self-affirmation. Alienation occurs when these feedback mechanisms break down or cease to function, when affective concomitants to acting from one's practical identity are in conflict or misaligned, when one feels shame or embarrassment, or when feelings of inner conflict undercut the usual motivational function of acting on "your" values. When these motivational feedback effects do not line up this is a signal that the values are not yours in the proper sense, that you are hiding something from yourself or feeling resistance to an imposed or artificial (to you) set of values. But when alienation is not an issue, acting from one's settled identity requires no overt reflective endorsement from a detached viewpoint.

This is important because it encapsulates the way that social recognition functions in the reflexive operation of self-affirmation. Intentional action is motivated in part by a self-understanding under an evaluative identity category; such a category is recognized in some publicly manifested way, as self-validating, as worthy of pursuit. There need be no actual spokesperson, as it were, for that value, but it must be publicly available in some way. This is because a purely private category reduces to simply a set of desires, a nexus of motives that are merely how one is but are not reflexively self-justifying in this way. Of course these publicly available categories of affirmation need not be instantiated in actual relations among people—this is the aspect of the structural accounts from which we are departing. Rather they must be available to the agent to use to understand herself and to feel motivated to continue acting in the way she understands herself to be. No one needed to actually tell Emily Dickenson that she was a wonderful poet, but the idea of "successful poet" was available to her to evaluate her commitment to her way of life and to help her affirm it.

In the present context, it is important to note also some of those identity categories might include things like *rebel, outcast, prisoner, pariah,* and *slave.*

---

⁴³ Cf. David Velleman, "Identification and Identity" and "The Centered Self" in *Self to Self* (Cambridge: Cambridge University Press, 2007), 253–283.
⁴⁴ This is akin to what Stephen Darwall, "Two Kinds of Respect," *Ethics* 88:1 (October 1977): 246–261, labels "recognition self-respect." Also, I do not take up the details of these similarities or the complexities of self-respect itself. For discussion see Robin Dillon, "Self-Respect: Moral, Emotional, Political," *Ethics* 107:2 (January 1997): 226–249.

Under these descriptors, the person is guided by an evaluative identity that precisely rejects or is rejected by her social context, yet by the very nature of such a social location this fact fails to undercut the motivational power of that identity. Testimonials from slaves and imprisoned persons suggest how such persons seem to be able to continue their struggle for meaning despite a complete lack of affirming feedback from surrounding others, in particular those who directly exercised power or whose perspective so influenced the dominant symbolic structure of their dominated lives.[45]

The actual expression of social recognition of an agent by others often utilizes a social category that captures the object of that recognition, the type of person one is, but it is often quite contentious both what category of identification is appropriate in a given instance and what such categorizations mean. In cases of adaptation to change, one could well abandon a social identity that one had been recognized under in the past—Abby was known as an outdoors person, a runner, an athlete but now would not use those terms to describe herself. But one may use terms that make sense of that very change: I am a *survivor*, a teacher with disabilities, a resilient person able to change in response to challenges. These descriptors carry with them a sense of self-affirmation that other terms might not allow. Bernice, for example, may see herself as a (crippled) runner and hence unable to pursue a self-affirming life. The dynamics of recognition, if they are manifested in actual interpersonal exchanges, may distort the value frames that allow, in some cases, the capacity for self-governing agency.[46]

Now it might be thought that I have taken a needlessly serpentine route to a very familiar destination, namely, that attitudes of self-regard are required for autonomy. I accept that the destination is familiar, and I am happy to join company with many insightful theorists of autonomy and agency here; however, I also want to draw some minor contrasts.

As an example we can look at Paul Benson's subtle account of the requirement of self-authorization for autonomy, authorization that requires that autonomous agents must be accountable to others, to be able to respond to "potential challenges which, from [the person's] *own* point of view, others might appropriately bring to his view."[47] For Benson, this need not be a reflective act: we may exhibit the attitudes in question by way of our activities

---

[45] Again, cf. Velleman, "Centered Self," when he says, one must be able to intend to act in way one is understood by others. The view I take here resembles the approach in Benson, "Taking Ownership," in claiming that autonomy involves being in a position to answer for oneself"—see "Taking Ownership," 101–126. A parallel similarity can be seen with Andrea Westlund's account.

[46] Relevant here is the discussion in Susan Brison, *Aftermath* (Princeton, NJ: Princeton University Press, 2002), chap. 3, of how survivors of trauma must recreate self-narratives that include the trauma itself.

[47] Benson, "Taking Ownership." For a similar account, see Westlund, "Rethinking Relational Autonomy."

that effectively place ourselves in a position to answer for our actions. Benson contrasts this with identity-based accounts of autonomy claiming that authenticity of actions is secured when they relate to my identity as a caring, reflectively willing creature. Benson argues that such theories are either too weak (when reflective self-endorsement is merely apathetic or undeveloped) or too strong (since many trivial or habitual actions would not pass the test but they are clearly autonomous).

I will not reply to the criticisms Benson wields against my own view in this context,[48] but I want to point out how the procedural account I defend here can take onboard the requirement of reflexive self-acceptance that Benson insists upon. Recall that the question we are trying to ask, in effect, is when a person's responses to the constraints of her circumstances, whether caused by oppression or accident, are such as to undercut the self-affirmation (e.g., answerability, self-ascribed normative authority) that is inherent in autonomous action. I am not sure how Benson's condition does that since it will depend greatly on what we take to be the "appropriate" modes of answerability. If Bernice's attitude toward herself can be expressed as, "Sure I desire to get into this sodding wheelchair each day, but that is only because of that damned accident; it's a situation I deeply hate," then it seems clear that she fails to value her normative position adequately, and she does so because of the origins of that position. But we do not want to demand complete acceptance of the constraints that circumscribe one's motivational structure, for then none of us would pass the test for autonomy: we all can say that we would aspire to different things if there were no (or fewer) barriers in front of us. The question is: when does the weight of the constraints on our existence effectively undercut the authenticity of our self-endorsements; when are we simply slaves of our condition?

This question points to the mysterious core of many accounts of self-governing action: the phenomenon of *owning* the motivational and evaluative structure that issues in action, of seeing it as one's own. One element of this phenomenon is clear enough, namely, that one sees one's motives as *worth having*, but another is left obscure, namely, seeing them as *mine*. But what is this "my having" that is operating here?

Benson's claim is that being answerable is an active process. However, despite his guidance on what should be meant by this, it merely may end up restating this mystery, I think, for he admits that the activity in question need not involve reflective choice (though it must be purposeful).[49] Reflecting on the condition of Bernice forces us to ask where the point is when the fact that

---

[48] See also Paul Benson, "Autonomy and Oppressive Socialization," *Social Theory and Practice* 17 (1991): 385–408. For a version of my view that attempts to avoid these criticisms, see Christman, *Politics of Persons*, chap. 7.
[49] Benson, "Taking Ownership," 113.

one's motivational set is so structured by the contingencies of one's condition (as all our motives are to some degree) that one can no longer see it as one's own but simply as the result of (in this case) an accident that "happened to me."

What I have to offer here is the following: an agent lacks this kind of ownership—is alienated in my sense—when the feedback mechanism I have been describing between deliberating from within a practical identity and conferring (recursively) value back to that identity does not function. Bernice acts out of an identity of a disabled person but cannot accept the reflexive self-affirmation that might come from so doing. She lacks a key component of self-respect, namely, a self-understanding as a being with dignity whose deliberative perspective is worth having as one's own.

Irina maintains this loop but in a different way, for she understands herself under the label of *survivor*, one who does what is required of her circumstance even when she begrudgingly acts from within an externally imposed identity of *prostitute*, which she rejects even when acting as one. The feedback mechanism of reflexive self-affirmation operates for her under the description of *survivor* so her effective self-worth is intact. This explains our willingness to see her as at least minimally autonomous in her struggles.

So the condition of alienation can be stated this way: one is alienated when one's practical identity fails to provide motivations that carry with them reflexive self-affirmation of a sort that issue in further solidification of that identity and subsequent decisions of the same sort. I tried to get at this idea in earlier work but expressed it in terms of reflection: adequate reflection is what would issue in similar self-acceptance over a variety of conditions. Here I am using the language of reflexive self-affirmation: the nonalienated agent acts in a way that sheds positive light on her identity as a person acting that way, giving her further motivation to continue to do so.

Now despite these observations I do not want to exaggerate my differences from theorists who insist on social recognition in their relational accounts of autonomy, and I readily accept that the points I am making here are highly resonant with points made by others in the literature. But even if this is what was meant all along by these thinkers, I hope to have provided even further argument for its necessity, at least as described in the narrow and qualified way I do here.

Moreover, I hope to have shown that such a postulate aids in distinguishing modes of adaptation that maintain autonomy from those that do not. To see this, let us now return to the cases of Abby et al. Our intuitive judgment is that Abby, who alters her values in response to her accident, and Irina, who refuses to adapt to her circumstance, retain a kind of autonomy that the other people I described seemed not to. The reason I am suggesting here for why this obtains is that in these cases the person was able to maintain a diachronic practical identity under which her life was one she could regard as worthy of pursuit. They were able to retain a sense of reflexive self-affirmation despite needing to negotiate through stultifying constraints. Notice that the language of self-affirmation is not one of celebration, and often thinkers who tread similar paths exaggerate the degree to which we must value the lives we lead to be self-governing in leading them.[50] But lives so often involve deep ambivalence and profound compromise in merely negotiating through the perilous challenges of a modern existence. What must be the case is that one affirms one's identity to a degree that allows the motives stemming from that identity to be reason giving. But in so doing valuing oneself must merely be seen as self-*acceptance* but not valuing one's life all things considered.

The threshold of what I elsewhere called nonalienation (from oneself) is being able to reflexively confer value on actions guided by one's identity (under the relevant category term), actions which by that token reflect value back on that very identity. Bernice, the person who resists change after her accident and leads a life of bitterness and regret, has lost her autonomy (to some significant degree) insofar as she can no longer see her decisions as arising from a self-affirming understanding of herself. She decides to use her wheelchair *begrudgingly*, and she fights through the psychological pain of her existence with resignation and bitterness. Since she cannot reflexively affirm her outlook on her options, the choices she makes do not reflect a self-governing mode of existence. At least, insofar as we think self-government is lost or severely diluted here, it is this inability to reflexively affirm her identity that explains it. It is not, I argue, the fact that external circumstances have altered her option set, for that is true of others who did not lose their autonomy.

Of course, much could be said to explain differences in these cases along different lines. For example, living through a severe accident and being forced into sex work are deeply traumatic, and surviving trauma requires its own process of reestablishing a functional self-narrative.[51] Moreover, there is every reason to think that those who internalize oppressive value schemes such as Kaew also lose many basic competences that are central to autonomy: they may suffer from drug addiction or lose emotional and psychological capacities required for self-directed choice, empathy, and imagination. Surely in most such cases this is the way to understand the loss of autonomy. But I merely want to add that in those perhaps rare cases where at least basic competences are established or restored but where persons adapt their values to the requirements of their constrained circumstances, a necessary condition of their retaining autonomy is that they are able to reflexively affirm the practical identity (under

---

[50] Korsgaard, for example, says that a practical identity is a normative conception of the self containing one's guiding principles: it is "a description under which you value yourself." Christine Korsgaard, *Sources of Normativity* (Cambridge: Cambridge University Press, 1996), 101. This is ambiguous between self-acceptance and self-celebration I think.

[51] For a rich account of such a process, see Brison, *Aftermath*.

a relevant description) that provides reasons for actions, plans, and ongoing projects.

In cases of internalized oppression, the actual diagnosis of the retention of autonomy may be difficult or impossible to make, but that may be due to the indeterminacy of what practical identity category is operative for the person. Is a person like Kaew, for example, best seen as one who embraces the identity of a *resilient survivor* and who engages in prostitution because her life options limit her to such choices as a method of, say, providing for her family? If so, then if other conditions of autonomy are met we should not withhold that label to her. However, if we are suspicious, as Superson is in the case of veiling, that acceptance of the identity category that requires such behavior could not but be the result of a self-abnegating identity, then we can label the person heteronomous. But this is not due to anything inherently degrading or undignified about that behavior itself, independent of its effect on the person's sense of self-worth.

4. Conclusion: The Dynamics of Autonomy Attribution

To sum up, to help sort out whether those who adapt to their circumstances by seemingly internalizing oppressive conditions in which they live are autonomous or not, I asked us to consider contrasting cases among those who have and have not made such self-alterations. Those contrasts, I claimed, suggested an asymmetry in our judgments about whether adapting to constraining circumstances indicates a loss of autonomy or its reestablishment. I argued that the structural character of those conditions alone—whether the source of the constraint was unjust actions or conditions or merely an accident—was not the crucial determinant of whether autonomy is preserved. Though I did acknowledge that relational and interpersonal dynamics of the situation are relevant to that determination; I merely insist that this necessity is contingent upon the contribution to the full functioning of the procedural requirements of autonomy.

I claimed, however, that a procedural account of autonomy could help explain these asymmetries by including a requirement of reflexive self-affirmation along the lines that other relational theorists in the literature have suggested, but I claimed that such a view is not constitutively relational except in the indirect manner in which value categories (in terms of which a person develops a self-affirming practical identity) are acknowledged somehow in the social landscape as marking a life worthy of pursuit. I argued that this social element is required not because of the intrinsic value of those relations or those pursuits but because of the social-psychological effect that such public acceptance has on the ability of a person to be reflexively self-affirming. But it is this latter condition that marks autonomy, and it admits of great variability in the dynamic of public affirmation, as the cases of the rebel and resistant slave indicate.[52]

I want to close here by emphasizing the way accounts of autonomy should include reference to the need for persons *themselves* to participate in the very determination of their autonomy status. That is, the sites where the attribution of autonomy operates often exhibit power dynamics that make not only the expression of a person's practical identity (for example) but also its very determination difficult. A person may be unclear what value category best describes the struggles she is engaged in, and whether or not she is autonomous may turn on whether she can make that determination and secure a sense of self-worth that comes with it.[53]

This is more than an epistemological issue. It is not merely that our theoretical account of autonomy is complete, and we merely must be careful when attempting to discover if its conditions are met in a given case. Rather, the dynamics of interaction at the site where autonomy determinations are most crucial are noninstrumentally relevant to whether or not the person is in fact autonomous. This is because people often need helpful interlocutors (e.g., carers, therapists, aid workers, friends) to help establish the practical orientation that organizes their reflective practices. In this way, autonomy is also relational.[54]

How theoretically described conditions must be established by actual social practice is a complex topic that I want merely to gesture at here.[55] However, I want to close this discussion with an insistence that models of self-government include desiderata that rely on persons' actual participation and self-expression to determine the presence of those desiderata. In this way,

---

[52] This last point echoes views developed by Diana Meyers in a different context, when she argues that what she calls value-saturated accounts of autonomy fail to accommodate cases where people in oppressive circumstances can sometimes exercise autonomy in strategically negotiating their lives within those circumstances. Moreover, she argues that such views must be sensitive to the ways that the *voice* with which a person may try to express her reaction to her condition is not heard or understood by the listening public or surrounding others, making a condition of external recognition of the person's value orientation a problematic requirement. See Diana T. Meyers, "Feminism and Women's Autonomy: The Challenge of Female Genital Cutting," *Metaphilosophy* 31:5 (2000): 469–491.

[53] For a sensitive account of this dynamic, see Catriona Mackenzie, Christopher McDowell, and Eileen Pittaway, "Beyond 'Do No Harm': The Challenge of Constructing Ethical Relationships in Refugee Research," *Journal of Refugee Studies* 20:2 (May 2007): 299–319.

[54] In this way I agree with Elizabeth Ben-Ishai when she argues that ascribing autonomy to persons affords them a status that is required for self-government, even in cases where their capacity for self-government is apparently lacking or marginal. I disagree, however, that such ascription is *constitutive* of autonomy (rather than causally contributory to it) for reasons similar to my departure from the aforementioned relational accounts. See Ben-Ishai, "Sexual Politics and Ascriptive Autonomy," *Politics and Gender* 6:4 (2010): 573–600.

[55] For one attempt to elaborate on this point, see John Christman, "Relational Autonomy and the Social Dynamics of Paternalism," *Ethical Theory and Moral Practice* (Special Issue, forthcoming).

the person's voice, aided by a cooperative social context that elicits that voice in effective ways, is central to the determination of her autonomy.

Acknowledgments

The author is grateful to the participants and organizers of the workshop "Relational Autonomy 10 Years On," where an earlier version of this chapter was read. Special thanks is also due to Mark Piper and Andrea Veltman for comments on an earlier draft of this chapter.

{ 11 }

Autonomy and Adaptive Preference Formation
Natalie Stoljar

At a Sunday Bible-study group I attended for teenage girls, the mother who was teaching had the girls hold hands, march in a circle and say: "My husband will treat me like the princess that I am. He will be the head of my household." But the girls' own ambitions seemed at odds with that vision. One girl earlier confessed that her biggest earthly temptation during her college years was likely to be "pursuing too many higher degrees." Another was known to her friends in the group as the "future president." I got the sense that relying on a man was not what they considered their best option.[1]

Many philosophers think that the inculcation of gendered norms is harmful to *autonomy*: for instance, gendered socialization may damage the skills and competencies required for autonomy; oppressive stereotypes may block the ability to imagine alternatives thereby limiting and constraining life plans; hostile and sexist responses to women's aspirations may impair ambition and damage self-esteem so that even if nonsexist options are institutionally available girls do not pursue them.[2] It is encouraging that some of the young girls described at the outset of this paper articulate ambitions for themselves that do not require deference to men, but it remains to be seen whether any of them find the resources to resist their socialization and put these ambitions into effect.

In this chapter, I focus on an argument claiming that the inculcation of oppressive norms damages autonomy in a particularly insidious way. Agents who are oppressed come to internalize their oppression: they come to believe in the ideology of oppression and to make choices, and form preferences and desires,

---

[1] Hanna Rosen, "Who Wears the Pants in This Economy?" *New York Times Magazine*, August 30, 2012.

[2] See, e.g., Diana T. Meyers, *Self, Society and Personal Choice* (New York: Columbia University Press, 1989); Paul Benson, "Free Agency and Self-Worth," *Journal of Philosophy* 91 (1994): 650–668; Catriona Mackenzie, "Imagining Oneself Otherwise," in *Relational Autonomy: Feminist Perspectives on Autonomy, Agency and the Social Self*, edited by C. Mackenzie and N. Stoljar (New York: Oxford University Press, 2000), 124–150 (and in general all articles therein).

in the light of that ideology. Ann Cudd says that oppression creates *deformed desires*, "in which the oppressed come to desire that which is oppressive to them... [and] one's desires turn away from goods and even needs that, absent those conditions, they would want."[3]

Sandra Lee Bartky describes an example of this process in her analysis of the phenomenology of oppression. Through what she calls the "interiorization of the fashion–beauty complex," agents come to believe oppressive norms that tie appearance to self-worth.[4] Bartky says that "repressive satisfactions"—that is, deformed desires—"fasten us to the established order of domination, [to] the same system... produces false needs" and that false needs are produced by the "denial of autonomy."[5] These remarks suggest that desires that reinforce one's own oppression are morally problematic because they are formed by agents with impoverished autonomy. The oppressive conditions are responsible for the desires, not the agent herself.[6]

Theorists of oppression propose that oppression is distinctive because it a group harm. Oppression occurs when a group suffers systematic injustice due to institutional structures or background social practices.[7] Paradigm examples of oppression are systematic injustices suffered by groups whose members share social identities, for instance those of class, gender, race, sexuality, or disability. Although oppression employs the notion of group disadvantage, agents who are members of oppressed groups are also harmed as individuals. Cudd identifies both material and psychological harms of oppression.[8] For instance, racial segregation in the United States is a material and economic injustice that

---

[3] Ann E. Cudd, *Analyzing Oppression* (New York: Oxford University Press, 2006), 181.

[4] Sandra L. Bartky, *Femininity and Domination: Studies in the Phenomenology of Oppression* (New York: Routledge, 1990), 39.

[5] Bartky, *Femininity and Domination*, 42.

[6] Anita Superson, "Deformed Desires and Informed Desire Tests," *Hypatia* 20 (2005): 109–126; Superson, "Feminist Moral Psychology," *The Stanford Encyclopedia of Philosophy*, (Fall 2012 Edition); <http://plato.stanford.edu/archives/fall2012/entries/feminism-moralpsych/>.

[7] I follow authors such as Iris M. Young, "Five Faces of Oppression," reprinted in *Rethinking Power*, edited by T. Wartenberg (New York: State University New York Press, 1992), 174–95; Sally Haslanger, "Oppressions: Racial and Other," in *Racism in Mind*, edited by M. P. Levine and T. Pataki (Ithaca, NY: Cornell University Press, 2004), 97–123; Cudd, *Analyzing Oppression*. These authors give accounts of oppression that focus on systematic harm to groups; on these accounts, individuals who suffer harms of oppression are harmed in virtue of their group membership. Haslanger points out that oppression can be perpetrated by agents, or it can be *structural*; that is, systematic disadvantage to a group can occur as a result of social practices even in the absence of agents or legal institutions that intentionally perpetrate the oppression. Although here I take systematic harm to a group and concomitant harm to individuals in virtue of their group membership as sufficient for oppression, I wish to leave open the possibility that single agents or nongroups could suffer oppression. Hence, I leave open the question of whether systematic harm to a group is necessary for oppression. I also do not employ the notion of autonomy in the definition of oppression. Cf. Daniel Silvermint's position on which he claims that oppression obtains when "an individual's autonomy or overall life prospects are systematically and wrongfully burdened." Silvermint, "Oppression without Group Relations," unpublished manuscript, Montréal, Canada, 5.

[8] Cudd, *Analyzing Oppression*.

victimizes a group. Black Americans suffer systematic disadvantage through residential, job, and school segregation. Individual agents who are black are harmed in virtue of their group membership; they are prevented from attending better schools, doing better jobs, and living in the more affluent areas. Similarly, the unjust stereotyping of a social group can cause members of the group to suffer psychological harms such as humiliation and shame.

In addition to direct material and psychological harm, Cudd describes *indirect* psychological harms that originate within the psychology of the oppressed themselves and hence are often responsible for the self-perpetuating and entrenched nature of oppression. On her account, deformed desires are indirect harms that can be mistaken for "legitimate expressions of individual differences in taste" when in reality they are "formed by processes that are coercive: indoctrination, manipulation and adaptation to unfair social circumstances."[9] If Cudd is right, we have a neat argument for the conclusion that oppression undermines autonomy: gender oppression leads to deformed desires and deformed desires constitute autonomy impairments.

One version of the argument is that desires for one's own oppression are ipso facto deformed due to their contents. For example, Anita Superson claims that deformed desires fail a properly fleshed-out "informed desire test." They are irrational and impair autonomy because desiring one's own oppression is inconsistent with the agent having an appropriate sense of her own moral worth.[10] For the purposes of this paper, I set aside Superson's position and focus on a second possible argument that deformed desires are autonomy impairments, namely, deformed desires are *adaptive preferences* and for that reason "paradigmatically nonautonomous."[11] In Jon Elster's canonical example of sour grapes, a fox, after finding that he can't reach some grapes, decides

---

[9] Cudd, *Analyzing Oppression*, 183.

[10] Superson, "Deformed Desires and Informed Desire Tests." Superson claims that choosing or preferring one's own oppression is analogous to choosing slavery; it is making a special kind of moral mistake. Although Superson characterizes her position using a Kantian interpretation of an informed desire test, her argument suggests that she is committed to a "strong substantive" account of autonomy in which "the contents of the preferences or values that agents can form or act on autonomously are subject to direct normative constraints." Paul Benson, "Feminist Intuitions and the Normative Substance of Autonomy," in *Personal Autonomy: New Essays on Personal Autonomy and Its Role in Contemporary Moral Philosophy*, edited by James Taylor (Cambridge: Cambridge University Press, 2005), 133. As Benson points out, in Natalie Stoljar, "Autonomy and the Feminist Intuition," in Mackenzie and Stoljar, *Relational Autonomy*, I conflated this strong substantive account with a strong normative competence condition of autonomy. Although deformed desires would be counted as nonautonomous due to their contents on strong substantive accounts, it is less clear whether agents who have deformed desires would fail a normative competence condition. For a fuller explanation of different versions of substantive account, see Natalie Stoljar, "Feminist Perspectives on Autonomy," *The Stanford Encyclopedia of Philosophy*, (Summer 2013 Edition); http://plato.stanford.edu/archives/sum2013/entries/feminism-autonomy/.

[11] James S. Taylor, *Practical Autonomy and Bioethics* (New York: Routledge, 2009), 71. Indeed, Cudd says that *adaptive preference* is another term for deformed desire. Cudd, *Analyzing Oppression*, 180–181.

that he doesn't want the grapes after all. Elster takes this to be an unconscious and nonautonomous process that he calls "adaptive preference formation."[12] The unconscious accommodation of desires to feasible options often occurs in conditions of oppression. For example, a girl raised in a patriarchal household may come to prefer domestic chores because other nontraditional options are not feasible for her.[13]

Scholars of development ethics also employ the notion of adaptive preference formation.[14] Martha Nussbaum and Amartya Sen focus on agents' habituation to conditions of severe deprivation.[15] On the face of it, deprivation and oppression are not the same injustice. Oppression occurs in affluent societies in which people are not typically victims of severe economic deprivation. The young girls described in the opening quote are members of a group that is subject the patriarchal oppression but they live in conditions of relative affluence.[16] It is plausible, however, that agents in conditions of severe deprivation in the developing world are members of a group that is subject to economic oppression. In their own cultural context, they may also suffer oppression as women or as members of particular ethnic minorities. As we will see, there are sufficient similarities among the two sets of examples to treat them together for purposes of an analysis of autonomy.

There are two main challenges to the position that preferences that are adapted to the circumstances of oppression are deformed and constitute autonomy impairments. The first, articulated recently by Serene Khader, claims that even if desires for oppressive conditions are morally problematic in some sense, this is *not* because they are "autonomy deficits."[17] Khader identifies a category of "inappropriately adaptive preferences" that are morally problematic mainly because they are inconsistent with the flourishing of the agent who forms the preference.[18] However she argues that adaptive preferences are not autonomy deficits on either "procedural" or "substantive" accounts of

---

[12] Jon Elster, "Sour Grapes—Utilitarianism and the Genesis of Wants," in *Utilitarianism and Beyond*, edited by A. Sen and B. Williams (Cambridge: Cambridge University Press, 1992), 219–238; Elster, *Sour Grapes: Studies in the Subversion of Rationality* (Cambridge: Cambridge University Press, 1983).

[13] Donald Bruckner, "In Defence of Adaptive Preferences," *Philosophical Studies* 142 (2009): 307–324, 309.

[14] Serene J. Khader, *Adaptive Preferences and Women's Empowerment* (New York: Oxford University Press, 2011), 10.

[15] See, e.g., Amartya Sen, "Gender Inequality and Theories of Justice," in *Women, Culture, and Development: A Study of Human Capabilities*, edited by M. Nussbaum and J. Glover (Oxford: Clarendon Press, 1995), 259–273; Martha Nussbaum, *Women and Human Development: The Capabilities Approach* (Cambridge: Cambridge University Press, 2000); Nussbaum, "Adaptive Preferences and Women's Options," *Economics and Philosophy* 17 (2001): 67–88. Note that the phenomenon of adaptive preference formation was invoked by Elster, Sen, and Nussbaum to critique preference utilitarianism.

[16] I am grateful to Daniel Silvermint for discussion of this point and to Daniel Silvermint and Daniel Weinstock for helpful conversations about Khader's book.

[17] Khader, *Adaptive Preferences and Women's Empowerment*.

[18] Khader, *Adaptive Preferences and Women's Empowerment*, 51.

autonomy. Procedural theories claim that critical reflection is sufficient for autonomy: agents are autonomous when they critically reflect on their motivations, beliefs, and values in the right way. Procedural approaches seek to define autonomy using morally neutral conditions such as reflective endorsement or nonalienation.[19] Substantive theories build in normative conditions, for instance moral attitudes to oneself or background moral conditions.[20] Khader considers examples of adaptive preferences including women's preferences to malnourish themselves to feed their male relatives or their endorsement of harmful practices like genital cutting. She argues that neither the tests employing critical reflection required by procedural accounts nor the tests employing moral conditions required by substantive accounts show these adaptive preferences to be autonomy impairments.

A second challenge claims that preferences that are adapted to the circumstances of oppression are not deformed; rather, they are a rational response to difficult and distressing circumstances in which options are curtailed. These preferences have been described as the products of a rational process of "bargaining with patriarchy"[21] or one in which they reflect a rational compromise because they correspond to the second best alternative that is available to the agent under the circumstances.[22] The challenges are united by various common underlying concerns, for instance that treating oppressed and deprived people as lacking autonomy in effect extinguishes or disrespects their agency, their choices of values and conceptions of the good; that it amounts to an empirically inaccurate generalization about their psychologies; or that it potentially licenses coercive government intervention in their lives.

My goal in this paper is to argue against both these challenges and to dispel some of the worries underlying them. I agree with Khader that adaptive

---

[19] For reflective endorsement see Marilyn Friedman, *Autonomy, Gender, Politics* (New York: Oxford University Press, 2003). For nonalienation see John Christman, *The Politics of Persons: Individual Autonomy and Socio-historical Selves* (Cambridge: Cambridge University Press, 2009).

[20] For a detailed explanation of this distinction, see Catriona Mackenzie and Natalie Stoljar, "Introduction: Refiguring Autonomy," in Mackenzie and Stoljar, *Relational Autonomy*, 3–34; Stoljar, "Feminist Perspectives on Autonomy." There are additional ways of dividing up theories of autonomy. For example, procedural theories may be either *internalist*, requiring only internal psychological conditions to spell out autonomy, or *externalist*, requiring additional historical conditions that are external to agents' present internal psychological states. Alfred Mele, *Autonomous Agents: From Self-Control to Autonomy* (New York: Oxford University Press, 1995). Other externalist theories are not procedural and employ, for instance, the notion of adequate options (Joseph Raz, *The Morality of Freedom* (Oxford: Oxford University Press, 1988)) or socio-relational conditions (Marina Oshana, *Personal Autonomy in Society* (Aldershot, UK: Ashgate, 2006)). The latter externalist positions may also require a background moral theory to spell out precisely the external conditions that are incompatible with autonomy. Thus, externalist theories are often substantive as well. I leave these complexities aside here.

[21] Uma Narayan, "Minds of Their Own: Choices, Autonomy, Cultural Practices and Other Women," in *A Mind of One's Own. Feminist Essays on Reason and Objectivity*, second edition, edited by L. Antony and C. Witt (Boulder, CO: Westview, 2002), 418–432.

[22] H. E. Baber, "Adaptive Preference," *Social Theory and Practice* 33 (2007): 105–126.

preferences should not be *defined* using the notion of autonomy. They are formed through psychological processes and should be defined using psychological criteria. Nevertheless, I argue that on several prominent theories of autonomy, both procedural and substantive, the adaptive preferences of concern to feminist theorists (deformed desires) will count as impairments of autonomy.[23] I distinguish two models of adaptive preferences, both of which originate in Elster's work. The first, the *psychological processes model*, proposes that adaptive preferences are produced by a distinctive causal and psychological process. On this model, it is the flawed process that is responsible for the autonomy impairment. The second, the *freedom to do otherwise model*, characterizes adaptive preferences as adjustments that occur when options that agents would choose under other or better conditions are excluded from their feasible set. On this model, it is the limitation of free agency or freedom to do otherwise that is responsible for the autonomy impairment.

Sections 1 and 2 address the claim that adaptive preferences are not autonomy impairments. I first consider adaptive preferences construed on the psychological processes model and argue that historical, procedural theories of autonomy have the prima facie resources to count deformed desires as autonomy impairments through the device of *procedural independence*.[24] However, I claim that procedural independence cannot fully explicate why deformed desires are autonomy impairments without importing a background moral theory into the procedural account. Thus, deformed desires are counterexamples to procedural accounts of autonomy that employ a morally neutral test. Section 2 addresses the second model that claims that deformed desires are adaptive in a problematic sense because they fail a freedom to do otherwise test. I argue that this test is a moral one and moreover that agents whose preferences fail this test are precisely those agents who count as having impaired autonomy on well-known substantive accounts of autonomy.

---

[23] Khader seems to have recently modified the objection saying that adaptive preferences "sometimes reveal—though need not reveal—compromised autonomy." Serene Khader, "Must Theorising about Adaptive Preferences Deny Women's Agency?" *Journal of Applied Philosophy* 29 (2012): 302–317, 312.

[24] I leave aside structural and internalist forms of procedural theory, such as that offered by Harry Frankfurt, *The Importance of What We Care About* (New York: Cambridge University Press, 1988). For Frankfurt, a sufficient condition of local autonomy is (appropriately understood) endorsement or wholehearted identification at a time with a preference or desire. There are objections to this kind of theory. See, e.g., Stoljar, "Feminist Perspectives on Autonomy." Moreover, as David Zimmerman, "Making Do: Troubling Stoic Tendencies in an Otherwise Compelling Theory of Autonomy," *Canadian Journal of Philosophy* 30 (2000): 25–53, 25, points out, Frankfurt's position risks being committed to an unpalatable consequence, namely, that "acting freely is a matter of 'making do,' that is of bringing oneself to be motivated to act in accordance with the feasible, so that personal liberation can be achieved by resigning and adapting oneself to necessity." Zimmerman's interesting point needs further examination, but it does suggest that Frankfurt's theory is the wrong place to look for an explanation of the nonautonomy of adaptive preferences.

I conclude therefore that Khader is wrong to claim that the adaptive preferences of concern to feminists are not autonomy deficits.

Sections 3 and 4 turn to the second challenge claiming that what are called *deformed desires* are not deformed but instead are rational accommodations to bad options. I argue in Section 3 that, even if many adaptive preferences are the products of a rational cost–benefit analysis that is endorsed by the agent, this does not settle the question of whether the decision is autonomous. Autonomy theorists often distinguish between the competency and the authenticity dimensions of autonomy[25] or the mental capacities required for autonomy and additional conditions such as adequate significant options.[26] The ability to engage in a cost–benefit analysis may be sufficient to establish some version of rational competency, but it does not follow that the product of this process satisfies the further criteria necessary for autonomy.[27] Section 4 attempts to dispel the worries underlying arguments against classifying adaptive preferences as autonomy impairments.

1. The Psychological Processes Model

As Elster points out, "sour grapes" is a common psychological phenomenon: "people tend to adjust their aspirations to their possibilities."[28] For example, a wage laborer may initially resist a move from agricultural work in the country to factory work in the city but may come to prefer city life as a result of the experience of factory work. Although the outcome of this process is an adjustment of the laborer's preferences to his current feasible options (those offered by city life), Elster claims that if the preference for city life is a stable and irreversible preference due to a process of learning and experience it should be distinguished from the problematic phenomenon of adaptive preference formation that is reversible and probably involves "habituation and resignation."[29] Similarly, adaptive preference formation is to be distinguished from the *deliberate* adjustment of desires to possibilities in character planning:

> Adaptive preference formation differs from deliberate character planning. It is a causal process that takes place "behind my back" not the deliberate shaping of desires... The psychological state of wanting to do a great many things that you cannot possibly achieve is very hard to live with. If the escape

---

[25] See, e.g., Christman, *Politics of Persons*.
[26] See, e.g., Raz, *Morality of Freedom*.
[27] I argued for this position in Stoljar, "Autonomy and the Feminist Intuition."
[28] Elster, "Sour Grapes," 219. See also David Zimmerman, "Sour Grapes, Self-Abnegation and Character Building," *Monist* 86 (2003): 220–241; Bruckner, "In Defence of Adaptive Preferences"; Ben Colburn, "Autonomy and Adaptive Preferences," *Utilitas* 23 (2011): 52–71, for explications of this idea.
[29] Elster, "Sour Grapes," 221.

from this tension takes places through some causal mechanism, such as Festinger's "reduction of cognitive dissonance," we may speak of adaptive preference change. The process then is regulated by something like a drive, not by a conscious want or desire.[30]

On this model, adaptive preferences are formed by a distinctive psychological process. The agent unconsciously turns away from a preference that they would otherwise have had to avoid the unpleasant sense of frustration or cognitive dissonance that accompanies having preferences for inaccessible options.[31] The process can occur both in cases of preference *change*, such as that of the fox, and preference *formation*, such as girls in patriarchal households who unconsciously turn away from inaccessible nontraditional options. The model does not employ the concept of autonomy in the definition of adaptive preference formation. Rather, adaptive preferences are thought to be nonautonomous because a "blind" and "unconscious" causal mechanism appears to be incompatible with autonomy; it is not intentional or under the agent's control.[32] The psychological processes model also does not justify the claim that feminists often seem to endorse, namely that desires for oppressive conditions *automatically* count as deformed and nonautonomous. If a girl who is raised in a patriarchal household comes to prefer domestic roles over other options, her preference could be the result of learning and experience (autonomous) or the result of adaptive preference formation (nonautonomous): "one cannot tell from the preferences alone whether they have been shaped by adaptation."[33] The question therefore is whether the process of formation of the preferences corresponds to an autonomy-undermining process.

Critics of Elster point out that it is implausible that blind and unconscious processes of preference formation are always incompatible with autonomy. Donald Bruckner considers an agent whose spouse dies. After a period of mourning, she gradually relinquishes the preference to have significant experiences with the spouse and acquires a preference to have these experiences with a new spouse.[34] It seems that, preferences that are the products of unconscious causal mechanisms are not necessarily nonautonomous despite the fact that they are formed behind the agent's back. Further, Bruckner employs empirical evidence to argue that adaptive preferences can help to promote a valuable life because adapting to one's circumstances can be conducive to

---

[30] Elster, "Sour Grapes," 224.
[31] Zimmerman, "Sour Grapes," 221–222, notes that the process could be "sub-personal" rather than unconscious. I note this possibility but do not consider it here.
[32] If it is not intentional action, it seems that it cannot be autonomous because even if intentional action is not sufficient for autonomous action, it is necessary.
[33] Elster, "Sour Grapes—Utilitarianism and the Genesis of Wants," 225.
[34] Bruckner, "In Defence of Adaptive Preferences"; see also Colburn, "Autonomy and Adaptive Preferences," 57.

subjective well-being, which itself is partially constitutive of a valuable life.[35] He concludes that preferences that are formed through a process of unconscious accommodation to feasible options should be considered presumptively rational and autonomous. The presumption will be defeated if the agent on examination fails to endorse (repudiates) the preference or, if she did not examine it, would fail to endorse it had she examined it.[36] Bruckner thinks that the causal mechanism of formation of a preference is irrelevant to its autonomy (or nonautonomy); rather, the key is the way a preference is retained.[37]

John Christman's notion of the socio-historical self also suggests that unconscious processes of preference-formation are compatible with autonomy.[38] There are many aspects of the self that are not the product of voluntary choice or deliberation. Consider a passage from Shane Phelan: "I was a lesbian. I experienced that moment partially as discovery: so this was the difference I had always felt but never had a name for."[39] For Christman, preferences or desires will be nonautonomous only if they fail either a competency condition or a "hypothetical reflection" condition. Competency corresponds to the capacity of the agent to form effective intentions relative to a desire as well as to reflect critically about the desire. The hypothetical reflection condition employs the notion of nonalienation to characterize authenticity and hence autonomy.[40] Alienation is a "combination of judgment and affective reaction. To be alienated is to feel negative affect, to feel repudiation and resistance…"[41] On Christman's account, if one is (or would be) alienated from a desire but does not succeed in repudiating it, one is inauthentic and heteronomous with respect to the desire. In Phelan's case, her unconsciously formed preferences about her sexual identity are autonomous because she is not (or would not be) alienated from them.

Neither the test suggested by Bruckner nor Christman's hypothetical reflection condition would classify deformed desires as nonautonomous. Consider agents whose preferences for traditional feminine roles are deeply ingrained through oppressive socialization. Due to the effects of the oppressive ideology, the agent treats false stereotypes as natural and formulates desires and plans based on the stereotype. Such agents are unlikely to experience alienation from either the norms that they have internalized or the preferences formed on the basis of those norms. In the absence of actual alienation, is it plausible to conclude that alienation would obtain were the agent to reflect on how her

---

[35] Bruckner, "In Defence of Adaptive Preferences," 314–315.
[36] Bruckner, "In Defence of Adaptive Preferences," 318–319.
[37] Bruckner, "In Defence of Adaptive Preferences," 319.
[38] Christman, *Politics of Persons*.
[39] Christman, *Politics of Persons*, 124–125. Christman quotes from Shane Phelan, *Getting Specific: Postmodern Lesbian Politics* (Minneapolis: University of Minneapolis Press, 1996), 52–53.
[40] Christman, *Politics of Persons*, 155–156.
[41] Christman, *Politics of Persons*, 144.

preferences were formed? No doubt young women who adopt traditional female roles would think it entirely appropriate that they were taught to do so by their mothers. As Paul Benson argues, in cases in which oppressive norms are very deeply ingrained it is not plausible to think that the agent would repudiate or feel alienated from desires based on the norms even after reflecting on their process of formation.[42]

Moreover, on Christman's account, forming a different preference in a situation of reduced options to avoid or eradicate actual (or counterfactual) cognitive dissonance may well be a paradigm case of autonomous preference formation. By hypothesis, the fox's desire for the grapes, combined with their unavailability, led to alienation. Hence, in resolving the cognitive dissonance by repudiating the desire for the grapes, the fox eradicates his alienation and seems to achieve autonomy on Christman's account. Similarly, the adaptive preference of girls for traditional female roles (by hypothesis) is the result of the inaccessibility of nontraditional options in the patriarchal context. Girls turn away from inaccessible nontraditional options in part to avoid the frustration of desiring the inaccessible. Hence, alienation would accompany the inaccessible, rejected preference, not the one the agent actually adopts. On Christman's view, the preference for the traditional, feasible, option is the autonomous one.

One option for Christman would be to bite the bullet: since alienation is not or would not be experienced by agents whose preferences are unconsciously adapted to oppressive conditions, these preferences are not autonomy impairments. However, there may be further resources available on his historical and procedural account that will help to demarcate autonomous adaptive preferences from nonautonomous ones.[43] The hypothetical reflection condition, although it purports to offer a historical condition of autonomy, actually requires only that the agent reflect in the present about the historical formation of her desires. Procedural theorists have noticed that critical reflection in the present is not sufficient for autonomy and claimed that present reflection must not be the product of a distorted causal mechanism leading to its formation.[44] As Khader herself points out, an "independence of mind" or "procedural independence" condition has been considered a necessary condition of autonomy on standard procedural accounts.[45] For instance, Gerald Dworkin argues that

---

[42] Paul Benson, "Autonomy and Oppressive Socialization," *Social Theory and Practice* 17 (1991): 385–408.

[43] I am grateful to Mark Piper for suggesting this possibility.

[44] Gerald Dworkin, *The Theory and Practice of Autonomy* (Cambridge: Cambridge University Press, 1988); Mele, *Autonomous Agents*.

[45] Khader, *Adaptive Preferences and Women's Empowerment*, 74. Khader goes on to ask whether various conditions mentioned in procedural theories of autonomy would count adaptive preferences as nonautonomous, but she does not explore procedural independence. She does discuss Elster's idea that adaptive preference formation is an unconscious process that operates behind the agent's back under the heading "life-planning as personal history" (85). However, her objection to this possibility seems

certain influences—such as hypnotic suggestion, manipulation, and coercive persuasion—can subvert agents' critical faculties and undermine their procedural independence.[46] Christman himself mentions that hypothetical critical reflection must not be constrained by "reflection-distorting" factors such as "constriction, pathology, or manipulation" or "being denied minimal education and exposure to alternatives."[47] Indeed, in early work, Christman compares "happy slave" cases in which the slave has "expunged her desires for freedom only as a result of the oppressive presence of the restraints she faces" with slaves who continue to resist their circumstances and desire their freedom.[48] He claims that if preference formation "resulted from the very presence of a...restraint, bearing down on the agent and forcefully causing a change in the desire," it is implausible that the desire change is an increase in freedom.[49] In other words, the accommodation of a happy slave to her circumstances does not make her autonomous; rather, the presence of coercive, external restraints that inhibit the free formation of her preferences constitutes an autonomy impairment.[50]

Thus, if we understand adaptive preferences using the psychological processes model, the test of procedural independence could be used to identify adaptive preferences that are also nonautonomous. The question then becomes whether the causal and psychological mechanisms that produce deformed desires render them autonomy impairments. Khader considers several examples of the adjustment of options to possibilities that have been labeled "deformed" in development ethics. One is that of intrahousehold food distribution.[51] Some women in South Asia starve or malnourish themselves to feed their husband and male children. Khader points out that such preferences are related in complex ways to religious and gender norms that link self-deprivation and self-discipline. She describes the case of an "elderly Javanese woman [who] recalled being told as a child that women needed to discipline themselves, because they were superior to men who could not control themselves."[52] Khader

---

off the mark. She writes, "Thinking of [adaptive preferences] this way commits us to a dubious metaphysical position...that there is one authoritative narrative about why a person forms a preference at the moment that it happens" (85). I do not believe that Elster is presupposing this metaphysical commitment. He is claiming that there is a psychological and theoretical difference between unconscious (adaptive) causal mechanisms and deliberate, conscious and planned ones.

[46] Dworkin, *Theory and Practice of Autonomy*, 18.
[47] Christman, *Politics of Persons*, 147, 155.
[48] John Christman, "Liberalism and Individual Positive Freedom," *Ethics* 101 (1991): 343–359, 354.
[49] Christman, "Liberalism and Individual Positive Freedom," 353.
[50] A recent discussion of adaptive preference formation explicitly adopts the position that adaptive preference formation is an unconscious process that violates procedural independence. Ben Colburn, "Autonomy and Adaptive Preferences," argues that an independence test fails when the formation of a preference is subjected to *covert influence*. Like subliminal influence, covert influence is a mechanism that produces desires in agents through a process in which the agent is not aware of the causal explanation of her preferences.
[51] Khader, *Adaptive Preferences and Women's Empowerment*, 78.
[52] Khader, *Adaptive Preferences and Women's Empowerment*, 81.

notes that this woman seems committed to her values and reflective about the ways her values inform her decision to malnourish herself. Hence, Khader thinks there is no autonomy deficit on procedural accounts that employ a critical reflection condition. However, on the account I am now considering, being reflective in the present is not sufficient for autonomy. The question is whether the preference to deprive oneself of food due to the internalization of misogynistic norms is procedurally independent—that is, whether the influence on the formation of the preference constituted coercive persuasion or was reflection-distorting due to insufficient exposure to alternative possibilities or some other factor.

Whether or not a preference fails a test of procedural independence is in principle a case-by-case question. However, if theorists of oppression are correct, we can make some general claims about the desires of members of oppressed groups: they are often "formed by processes that are coercive: indoctrination, manipulation and adaptation to unfair social circumstances."[53] Thus, prima facie, the desires of members of oppressed groups for their own oppression fail a test of procedural independence such as that of coercive persuasion.

Procedural accounts of autonomy therefore potentially employ conditions that would classify adaptive preferences as autonomy impairments. The problem for such accounts is whether the processes that violate procedural independence, like coercive persuasion, can be spelled out in a satisfactory way without importing background moral conditions. Cudd argues that a purely empirical account of coercion is unsatisfactory because it cannot distinguish between a hard choice and a forced choice.[54] Similarly, to flesh out the reflection-distorting influences that correspond to lack of minimal education or inadequate exposure to alternatives, we need some normative account of what counts as minimally satisfactory education or adequate alternatives. Therefore, although procedural theorists can explain how desires for oppressive conditions are nonautonomous, the explanation comes at the expense of maintaining the moral neutrality of their own theory.

2. The Freedom to do Otherwise Model

In the last section we considered a psychological processes model of adaptive preference formation that was derived from Elster's distinction between adaptive preference formation and the similar processes of learning and deliberate

---

[53] Cudd, *Analyzing Oppression*, 183.
[54] Cudd, *Analyzing Oppression*, 126–129. I am therefore in broad agreement with Khader when she says that procedural theories need to be "[supplemented] with a theory of the good." Khader, *Adaptive Preferences and Women's Empowerment*, 95.

Autonomy and Adaptive Preference Formation 239

character planning. On that model, adaptive preferences are accommodations to feasible options that lack autonomy due to a distorted underlying causal mechanism. Elster also offers an analysis of adaptive preferences that employs the notion of freedom to do otherwise:

> We can exclude operationally one kind of non-autonomous wants, viz adaptive preferences, by requiring freedom to do otherwise. If I want to do x, and am free to do x, and free not to do x, then my want cannot be shaped by necessity.[55]

On this second model, preferences are adaptive and nonautonomous because they fail the freedom to do otherwise condition and are shaped by necessity. The Javanese woman forms a desire to malnourish herself only because she is not free to flout the cultural and religious norms that lead to the desire. The girl raised in a household in which she is always expected to help her mother with the traditional chores comes to prefer these chores only because other options are not available to her.

Nussbaum applies the freedom to do otherwise model in her analysis of the preferences of poor working women in India. One of her examples is that of Vasanti who chooses to remain in an abusive marriage because she thinks that although the abuse "was painful and bad, but, still, a part of women's lot in life, just something women have to put up with as part of being a woman dependent on men, and entailed by having left her own family to move into a husband's home."[56] Nussbaum thinks that Vasanti's preference is adaptive; it is accommodated to her feasible options and lacks the condition of freedom to do otherwise.[57] Nussbaum points out, however, that there will be many examples of the accommodation of preferences to feasible options that fail the test of freedom to do otherwise yet are reasonable and conducive to the agent's well-being. Being a basketball player is not a feasible option for a short person, and being an opera singer is not a feasible option for someone with a weak singing voice. Adjusting one's expectations to accommodate the feasible options in these cases seems perfectly reasonable and a good thing to do.

In Vasanti's case, the desire to remain in an abusive relationship is by hypothesis not a good thing for her. Her choice is the result of her freedom being constrained in a morally problematic way. Thus, Nussbaum claims that Elster's morally neutral account of adaptive preferences is inadequate. To distinguish the basketball player and the opera singer from Vasanti and to explain why agents like Vasanti have adaptive preferences that lack autonomy, we need a "substantive theory of justice and central goods": "People's liberty can indeed be measured, not by the sheer number of unrealizable wants they have, but by

---

[55] Elster, "Sour Grapes," 228.
[56] Nussbaum, "Adaptive Preferences and Women's Options," 68–69.
[57] Nussbaum, "Adaptive Preferences and Women's Options," 68–69.

the extent to which they want what human beings have a right to have."⁵⁸ The freedom to do otherwise condition must therefore be understood as a moral condition. If agents' preferences are accommodated to external options only because the options are limited by unjust social circumstances, their preferences are shaped by necessity in a way that restricts their freedom.

For Nussbaum, adaptive preferences are morally problematic in situations in which agents face a morally inadequate set of options. In such circumstances, when preferences are accommodated to the options, and agents do not desire what they have a right to have, their autonomy is impaired. Thus, for Nussbaum, adaptive preferences are morally problematic precisely because they are (substantive) autonomy deficits. In response to this kind of position, Khader proposes a perfectionist definition of adaptive preferences. A preference is inappropriately adaptive when it is inconsistent with a person's basic flourishing, formed under conditions non-conducive to basic flourishing, and would not have been formed under conditions conducive to basic flourishing.⁵⁹ Agents like Vasanti satisfy the definition and have inappropriately adaptive preferences. But Khader claims that such preferences do not correspond to autonomy impairments even on substantive accounts of autonomy.⁶⁰

Let me address Khader's argument by focusing on her discussion of Joseph Raz's substantive theory.⁶¹ Raz proposes that autonomy requires adequate external options in addition to mental ability and independence from coercion and manipulation by other agents.⁶² For example, he describes a "hounded woman"—a woman on a desert island who is hounded by a wild animal and has to spend all her time and energy planning for survival. The woman has a variety of options in addition to the mental abilities necessary for planning, but the options she has are inadequate. For one thing, they are "dominated by her one overpowering need and desire to escape being devoured by the beast."⁶³ For another, having adequate options is understood by Raz as a moral

---

⁵⁸ Nussbaum, "Adaptive Preferences and Women's Options," 79.
⁵⁹ Khader, *Adaptive Preferences and Women's Empowerment*, 51.
⁶⁰ Khader, *Adaptive Preferences and Women's Empowerment*, 95–106.
⁶¹ Khader, *Adaptive Preferences and Women's Empowerment*, 99–102, also discusses other possible substantive approaches to spelling out the notion of autonomy such as "substantive autonomy as being motivated by good norms." This label is misleading because *being motivated by good norms* does not name a conception or theory of autonomy but rather a piece of evidence that a theory of autonomy will have to explain. For example, Stoljar, "Autonomy and the Feminist Intuition," claims that many feminists think that, when agents are motivated by false and oppressive norms, the agent's autonomy is called into question. I go on to make a conditional claim: *if* we accept this intuition, *then* a strong substantive theory of autonomy will need to be invoked to explain it. As mentioned already, my discussion at the time did not properly distinguish between two possible substantive theories: a strong substantive account that is content based; and a (strong) normative competence account. As I argue here, I still think that a substantive account of autonomy is needed to explain why desires for one's own oppression seem to be autonomy impairments. But I do not now think this has to be a strong substantive account that is content based.
⁶² Raz, *Morality of Freedom*, 369.
⁶³ Raz, *Morality of Freedom*, 374–376.

requirement: "autonomy requires that many morally acceptable options be available to a person."[64]

Khader interprets Raz's test as follows: "autonomous preferences are preferences that reflect an agent's own preferences and are *consistent with her flourishing.*"[65] She considers the case of a person who chooses to be a bullfighter and argues that, since this a dangerous sport, it is not compatible with the agent's flourishing. Khader suggests that choosing bullfighting would count as an autonomy impairment on Raz's account and further that, since choosing bullfighting is not intuitively an adaptive preference, the category of adaptive preferences cannot coincide with the category of autonomy impairments delivered by Raz's account.

This argument is too quick. Choosing bullfighting may be dangerous and incompatible with flourishing (in some sense), but if the agent has a variety of morally adequate options in addition to bullfighting the agent and her choice to pursue bullfighting are nevertheless autonomous on Raz's account. The agent must have the capacity to choose the good, that is, a choice among morally adequate options, but there is no requirement that particular choices are consistent with flourishing. Suppose we assume that bullfighting constitutes a morally bad option because it is dangerous and undermines the agent's well-being. (Note that this is not a very plausible assumption because not all dangerous life choices are morally impermissible.) Even this assumption does not negate the agent's autonomy but only the value of the exercise of autonomy in the particular case. Raz argues that "autonomy is valuable only if it directed at the good.... Autonomy is consistent with the presence of bad options, [but] they contribute nothing to its value."[66] Choosing a bad option in a situation in which the agent has a variety of morally acceptable ones is an autonomous choice, though not a valuable one.[67] Conversely, agents like Vasanti who are living in conditions of severe deprivation lack morally acceptable options and hence are obvious cases of nonautonomous agents on Raz's theory. Coming to

---

[64] Raz, *Morality of Freedom*, 378.
[65] Khader, *Adaptive Preferences and Women's Empowerment*, 102. Emphasis added.
[66] Raz, *Morality of Freedom*, 411.
[67] I have based my discussion on one possible reconstruction of Khader's argument. Her remarks are very brief, so I may have misunderstood what she has in mind. Here is another possible reconstruction: she seems to take Raz's position as equivalent to a strong substantive view that employs normative constraints on the content of preferences. She claims that adaptive preferences cannot be defined using contents alone. (This is correct; a preference for bullfighting may be or may not be adaptive and non-autonomous.) Hence she may be saying that adaptive preferences do not correspond to the category of nonautonomous preferences on Raz's account because the latter is a content-based account. I think however that the analysis of Raz as offering a content-based account is mistaken. As we saw, he thinks that autonomous agents can have preferences with bad or immoral content. Hence his account is substantive in a different sense from strong substantive accounts. The moral constraints are derived from the notion of adequate options, not from the immorality of the content of agent's preferences.

prefer one's severely limited options (i.e., adapting one's preferences to one's feasible option set) corresponds to exercising impaired autonomy.

In general, adaptive preferences as Khader defines them would count as autonomy deficits on Raz's adequate options test. On her account, basic flourishing or well-being is defined using a "minimal, vague and cross-culturally acceptable conception" of the good.[68] It is clear that, if an agent lacks the options required for minimal flourishing, she would also be deprived of morally adequate options. Thus, a preference that is formed only because better options are inaccessible to the agent—that is, a preference that would be classified as adaptive on Khader's definition—also would be classified as nonautonomous on Raz's approach to autonomy.

Khader acknowledges that adaptive preferences on her model are likely to be ruled nonautonomous on Raz's account because they are shaped by inadequate options. But she claims that "calling [adaptive preferences] autonomy deficits and incorporating a conception of the good into autonomy leads us to policies that are decidedly illiberal."[69] She worries that if we characterize adaptive preferences in response to oppression, poverty, and deprivation as lacking autonomy, this will license coercive governmental policies that will override the voluntary choices of such agents, thereby compounding their oppression and deprivation. Thus, Khader's main objection to characterizing adaptive preferences as autonomy deficits is a moral one.[70] I postpone discussion of moral objections to Section 4.

Up to now, the discussion has focused on the intersection of Raz's account of autonomy and the adaptive preferences of agents in conditions of severe deprivation. It may be more difficult to invoke Raz's theory to account for the deformed desires of agents in affluent societies. Notice first, however, that while oppressed people in Western countries often live in conditions in which minimal flourishing is possible, it does not follow that the conditions required for minimal well-being rise to the level of adequate options. Second, as Raz and others point out, autonomy comes in degrees. The options of members of oppressed groups—for education, housing, social services, medical care, employment—are often compromised by comparison with the options of members of groups that are not oppressed.

Consider a phenomenon that Cudd describes as "oppression by choice."[71] Cudd observes that in a labor market in which the average wage for women is significantly less than it is for men, it might be rational for a mother rather than

---

[68] Khader, *Adaptive Preferences and Women's Empowerment*, 103.

[69] Khader, *Adaptive Preferences and Women's Empowerment*, 103.

[70] Cf. Ann Cudd, "Review of Khader's *Adaptive Preferences and Women's Empowerment*," *Notre Dame Philosophical Reviews*, 2012, http://ndpr.nd.edu/news/27280-adaptive-preferences-and-women-s-empowerment/.

[71] Cudd, *Analyzing Oppression*, 146–153.

a father to choose to be the primary caregiver of children, that is, to choose either to work part-time work or not to work at all. At the individual level, it is a rational choice because overall the family will be financially better off. But Cudd points out that when the choice is made by many individuals it leads to a vicious cycle in which structural inequalities are reinforced. By choosing to stay home and become the primary caregiver of children, the mother will become a domestic specialist—a specialist in work that is unpaid and undervalued as a contribution to society—whereas the father will acquire experience and seniority in whatever area of paid employment he takes on. When many women make the same individual rational choice, this in turn will reinforce social perceptions that women are primarily unpaid domestic workers rather than potential wage earners. The cycle is oppressive because as a result of the individual women's choices, "employment opportunities are continually degraded both for the individuals and for women as a group."[72]

Cudd argues that although women in affluent Western societies are thought to have occupational free choice, in fact their options are morally constrained (relative to those of men); moreover, their options become progressively more constrained as a result of the choices that are initially made *rationally* in response to the structural inequalities. The argument suggests that women—and members of oppressed groups in general—have fewer morally adequate options and hence less autonomy than comparable members of nonoppressed groups. The phenomenon of oppression by choice is not equivalent to adaptive preference formation because the former involves deliberate planning whereas the latter does not. Nevertheless, in both cases agents' freedom to do otherwise is compromised relative to that of members of groups who are not oppressed.

3. Choosing among Bad Options

I argued in sections 1 and 2 that prominent theories of autonomy, both procedural and substantive, have the resources to classify many adaptive preferences as autonomy impairments. In this section I turn to a differently framed challenge to deformed desires, namely, the position that preferences adapted to the circumstances of oppression are *not* deformed. It is claimed that, rather, they are a rational (and therefore autonomous) response to circumstances in which agents have limited options. For example, Uma Narayan argues that they are the outcomes of a rational process of "bargaining with patriarchy,"[73] and Harriet Baber proposes that deformed desires correspond to the second

---

[72] Cudd, *Analyzing Oppression*, 150.
[73] Narayan, "Minds of Their Own."

best alternative that is available to the agent under the circumstances. When the best alternative is inaccessible, it is rational to choose second best.[74]

The different versions of the challenge diverge in an important respect. Baber, whose focus is to provide a defense of preference utilitarianism against Nussbaum's critique, argues that many preferences that are called "adaptive" are not in fact genuine preferences at all. Choices in response to what she calls a "raw deal" may not be what agents really prefer. On the other hand, feminist critics like Narayan (and Khader), whose focus is to defend women's agency, claim that preferences for sexist norms or bad circumstances are genuine preferences. In many cases these preferences are reinforced by other goals that the agent takes to be valuable. Khader discusses women who opt for genital cutting or clitoridectomy. She points out that often women are motivated by the wish for community belonging and social recognition, in particular by the goal to promote the marriageability of their daughters.[75] Similarly, the aforementioned preference for malnourishment of the Javanese woman is reinforced by religious conviction. Women's preferences seem genuine when considered in conjunction with these other factors.

Narayan and Baber do, however, offer parallel arguments for the rationality of putative deformed desires. Agents living under oppression or deprived conditions are capable of utility maximization; they are capable of engaging in cost–benefit analyses that weigh up the options available and of making a choice among options on the basis of this analysis. In particular, they note that most agents rank *bundles* of options, not options in isolation. Consider Narayan's example of a community of women in India, the Sufi Pirzadi, who "live in relative purdah (seclusion) within the home and are expected to veil when they are in public."[76] These women acknowledge that purdah severely limits their education and mobility and has the effect of making them dependent on male members of the community. But they also explicitly recognize benefits, for instance, that veiling signifies "womanly modesty and propriety" and their "superior standing vis-à-vis other Muslim women."[77] She argues that due to their cultural and religious context these women cannot separate out preferences that limit their movement and promote their dependence from those that promote the piety and modesty that they value: the options come as a bundle.

Baber makes the same point in her analysis of Vasanti. She points out that Vasanti may prefer a bundle of options including abuse and having a roof over her head over a bundle that contains no abuse and being on the street. It is not irrational to choose the former bundle but rather an example of rational

---

[74] Baber, "Adaptive Preference."
[75] Khader, *Adaptive Preferences and Women's Empowerment*, 100–101.
[76] Narayan, "Minds of Their Own," 420.
[77] Narayan, "Minds of Their Own," 420–421.

calculation under oppressive conditions in which the agent gets some advantages and forgoes others:

> We might with equal justification understand Vasanti's decision as the result of a utility calculation given a reasonable assessment of her options and the probabilities of various outcomes. Vasanti recognizes that given her circumstances, staying in an abusive marriage is her best bet if she wants to have a home and basic necessities: even if she would rather avoid getting beaten, she is prepared to take on that cost in order to avoid her least preferred outcome: homelessness and destitution.[78]

Thus, for both Baber and Narayan, putative deformed preferences are not deformed but rather instances of the exercise of rational agency in which agents rank bundles of options under difficult circumstances.

Baber offers a second argument as well: although Vasanti and other agents may appear to have preferences for oppressive conditions, in fact we cannot infer that they prefer what they choose: "making the best of a raw deal when no other alternatives are available is not the same as preferring it."[79] Consider the fox. According to Baber, the fox's preferences have not changed; he is only pretending to himself that he does not value or want the grapes. If a bunch of grapes suddenly became accessible to him, he would "jump" at them, and hence, his preference for the grapes persists.[80] The fox engages in a rational process of settling for second best. The fox's possible options are (1) grapes and no felt frustration, (2) no grapes and no felt frustration, and (3) no grapes and felt frustration.[81] Although the fox cannot have the best option (1), he "prefers serenity over felt frustration" and thus eradicates the felt frustration that comes with continuing to want the grapes. Similarly, Vasanti does not really prefer domestic abuse. She would jump at a better situation were it accessible to her. But staying under her husband's roof and putting up with the abuse is a rational choice because it is better than the alternative, namely, no abuse and homelessness.[82]

These arguments contain two basic ideas. The first denies that the desires of agents who endorse apparently harmful practices such as clitoridectomy or practices in which their rights are curtailed such as purdah are deformed. On the contrary, these agents are rational choosers with complex motivations who are making the best of the circumstances in which they find themselves. The second idea is that there is a difference between what the agent chooses and

---

[78] Baber, "Adaptive Preference," 113–114.
[79] Baber, "Adaptive Preference," 114.
[80] Preferences are understood as behavioral dispositions, not occurrent feelings. Baber, "Adaptive Preference," 312.
[81] Baber, "Adaptive Preference," 111.
[82] Baber, "Adaptive Preference," 114.

seems to prefer, and what they really prefer. Since many agents like Vasanti, if offered better options, would jump at them, what they choose is not what they really prefer. It is a compromise in the face of a terrible situation in which what they really prefer is inaccessible to them.

One can agree with both of these ideas. Yet neither establishes that agents like the Sufi Pirzadi, Vasanti, or for that matter women in Western contexts who appear to adapt to oppressive conditions are autonomous. Engaging in a cost–benefit analysis may be sufficient for formal rationality yet insufficient for autonomy.[83] As we have seen, theories of autonomy typically distinguish between competency conditions and additional conditions such as authenticity or availability of adequate options. Thus, it is possible that the agents under consideration satisfy competency and formal rationality conditions yet nevertheless fail to be autonomous. For the same reasons, Baber's argument that agents like Vasanti make rational choices that might enhance their subjective well-being given their options is also not incompatible with attributing lack of autonomy to Vasanti and agents like her. The ability to improve one's well-being under conditions in which one's options are curtailed is not equivalent to exercising autonomy.

Indeed, not only is Baber's analysis not incompatible with attributing an autonomy impairment, it also provides an implicit argument that the choices of agents like Vasanti are not autonomous. In effect, Baber is distinguishing between apparent and true preferences.[84] She thinks that reversible adaptive "preferences" are not true preferences and that the true preferences are revealed by the behavioral dispositions to jump at alternative better options. Hence, the fox and Vasanti are deceiving themselves about what they truly prefer. Many theories of autonomy, however, would consider self-deception and autonomy incompatible. For instance, Diana Meyers argues that one of the skills required for agents to be autonomous is that of self-discovery; agents who are blind to their own true preferences are not exercising this skill and are not autonomous.[85] The reversibility of a preference therefore would be evidence that it is not autonomous because reversibility suggests that it is merely apparent not real. (Indeed, this may be the intuition behind Elster's original classification of adaptive preferences as reversible and nonautonomous and hence unlike the irreversible—and autonomous—preferences that come about through learning.)

Other theories suggest that apparent self-deception is compatible with autonomy, but only if self-deception occurs in the service of right reasons. For example, Henry Richardson argues that an agent is autonomous if she

---

[83] Stoljar, "Autonomy and the Feminist Intuition."

[84] Nussbaum, "Adaptive Preferences and Women's Options," 73, discusses this line of thought while referencing John Harsanyi's distinction between *manifest* and *true* preferences.

[85] See, e.g., Meyers, *Self, Society and Personal Choice*, 47.

acts on a conception of objective moral reasons.[86] He compares the fox's reasoning with that of the character Bully Stryver in Charles Dickens's novel *A Tale of Two Cities*. Mr. Stryver selects "the beautiful and kind Lucie Manette" as his future wife. When she refuses, he persuades himself and others that he never loved her or wished to marry her. In other words, he adopts the fox's strategy of self-deception. He denies that he ever wanted to marry Lucie; he "shields himself from significant loss" and eliminates the frustration and embarrassment at being refused. Richardson claims that nevertheless Mr. Stryver's adaptive preference formation in this case is autonomy preserving because it promotes self-respect and thereby corresponds to acting on a conception of (actual) moral reasons.[87] Richardson's analysis could be applied to Khader's examples of adaptive preference formation, such as that of the Javanese woman who undernourishes herself in part because she thinks it promotes spiritual enlightenment. Given the cultural context, the preference may be an instance of acting on actual moral reasons such as self-respect. But in other cases, including perhaps that of Vasanti, if agents' preferences are not consistent with acting out of self-respect they would count as autonomy impairments.

Baber's discussion raises a further issue. It is not typical that preferences for oppressive conditions can be shown to be unstable and hence for that reason to be merely apparent. It is not the case that women, if given the opportunity, would always jump at the chance of alternative nonsexist roles. For example, there is evidence that the norm that only men are appropriate heads of households is remarkably resistant to shifts of context. A recent article in the *New York Times Magazine* discusses the situation of families in a small town in the United States in which due to a factory closure many men who had been employed and relatively affluent lost their jobs.[88] In several of these families, the wives, although they had not previously worked, had become successful primary breadwinners for the family. At the same time, the men struggled with adjustment to being financial dependent on their wives, and both husbands and wives clung to traditional roles including the designation of the husband as head of household. Hence there is evidence that cases in which agents adopt oppressive norms (or social roles that are formed by oppressive conditions)[89] are instances

---

[86] Henry Richardson, "Autonomy's Many Normative Presuppositions," *American Philosophical Quarterly* 38 (2001): 287–303.

[87] Richardson, "Autonomy's Many Normative Presuppositions," 292. One could interpret Richardson as claiming that agents who act in the service of right reasons are not *really* self-deceived because acting on right reasons is doing what rational agents *really* want to do. Sarah Buss, "Autonomous Action: Self-Determination in the Passive Mode," *Ethics* 122 (2012): 647–691, 666, captures the gist of this kind of analysis of autonomy when she writes: "Every rational agent wants to do what she (really) has reason to do; so, insofar as her action is not (adequately) responsive to (the real) reasons for and against acting this way, it does not (adequately) express her defining desire; so there is an important respect in which this action is not attributable to her [i.e., not autonomous]."

[88] Rosen, "Who Wears the Pants in This Economy?"

[89] Cudd, *Analyzing Oppression*, 181, points out that there is a difference between desires to subject oneself to oppression and desires for social roles that are the effects of oppression: "It is not that [the

of stable preferences in which agents have adapted to patriarchal social structures. Baber considers an analogous case of a Cambodian prostitute, Srey Mom, whose freedom was bought from the brothel owner by a *New York Times* journalist.[90] Although subject to appalling conditions in the brothel, Srey Mom had come to prefer some if its material advantages such as jewelry and a cell phone. When given the opportunity to return to her village, she does so, but after a while she returns to prostitution. Baber proposes that the preference for a life of prostitution is a stable and genuine adaptive preference; moreover, given the other options available to Srey Mom, it is too quick to conclude that returning to prostitution is not in her interests or that it fails to promote her well-being.[91]

These examples reinforce the point that although the reversibility of a preference may be evidence that it is merely apparent, it does not follow that stable and irreversible preferences are always autonomous.[92] As we saw sections 1 and 2, even stable and irreversible preferences might fail the tests of procedural independence or adequate options. Similarly, even if a choice promotes an agent's subjective well-being because it is the best of the bad options available (as in the case of Srey Mom), this does not imply that the choice is autonomous.

4. The Possibility of Coercion and Other Worries

Many of the objections to treating deformed desires as autonomy impairments are not conceptual but moral, pragmatic, and empirical. Khader often claims that characterizing agents with adaptive preferences as nonautonomous would license coercive policies. For example, she writes that "if people whose preferences do not manifest a value for their own independence are not autonomous, public institutions may reasonably coerce those people into changing their preferences."[93] She also thinks that the characterizations of agents' desires as deformed and nonautonomous are problematic empirically because it tends to overlook the complexity of their motivations and that this may result in policies with an "ineffective focus."[94] Baber emphasizes the point that oversimplified accounts of the motivation of agents in deprived circumstances can

---

oppressed] will prefer oppression to justice or subordination to equality, rather they will prefer the kinds of social roles that tend to subordinate them."

[90] The Srey Mom example is taken from Nicholas D. Kristof, "Bargaining for Freedom," *New York Times*, January 21, 2004.

[91] Khader, *Adaptive Preferences and Women's Empowerment*, 130, argues that preferences such as that for malnourishment could enhance the interests or well-being of the agent, for example, "self-depriving behavior often elicits actual rewards."

[92] Cf. Elster, "Sour Grapes," 221.

[93] Khader, *Adaptive Preferences and Women's Empowerment*, 98.

[94] Khader, *Adaptive Preferences and Women's Empowerment*, 100.

be empirically inaccurate and morally problematic. For example, she criticizes Nussbaum's reference to Vasanti being in a "slumberous state" before being exposed to programs in which she came to be aware of her rights.[95] Indeed, many theorists are concerned that denying that women's adaptive preferences are autonomous is equivalent to denying their agency. In this section, I attempt briefly to dispel these worries.

I do not believe that denying autonomy is tantamount to denying agency. *Autonomy* and *agency* are not equivalent concepts. As we have seen, agents that are judged to have autonomy impairments often retain the full gamut of complex mental capacities. They retain the mental abilities required for planning and weighing up competing options. They retain abilities that are closely related to autonomy such as forms of rationality and the capacity for self-control.[96] Khader articulates a notion of adaptive preference that does not rely on the notion of autonomy. Yet she acknowledges that various aspects of agency may be damaged in agents who have adaptive preferences and that noncoercive interventions may be justifiable to attempt to improve agents' deliberative capacities.[97] Her argument itself suggests that agency and autonomy are distinct ideas.

The wish to defend a robust conception of women's agency under conditions of oppression is underwritten by a very legitimate concern. Focusing on deficiencies in agents' psychologies may end up "psychologizing the structural"—that is, putting causal responsibility for oppression inappropriately on the agent rather than appropriately on the unjust social conditions.[98] Remarks such as that women's agency is "pulverized" by patriarchy or that Vasanti was in "slumberous state" or even that desires for one's own oppression are "deformed" are rhetorical forms of words that potentially reinforce the problem.[99] I agree that these labels are misleading and better avoided.

The negative labels also obscure the subtleties of the autonomy analysis of adaptive preferences. For instance, theories of autonomy distinguish between local and global autonomy. When theorists of autonomy claim that a preference or desire is nonautonomous, this usually means that the conditions for local autonomy—namely, what is required for particular choices, preferences, or desires at particular times to count as autonomous—do not obtain. Vasanti's decision to stay in an abusive marriage may well be locally nonautonomous. If it is, her degree of overall autonomy is reduced, but her agency is relatively unaffected. Global autonomy corresponds to an agent's ability to lead

---

[95] Nussbaum, "Adaptive Preferences and Women's Options," 74; Baber, "Adaptive Preference," 114, 126.
[96] Mele, *Autonomous Agents*.
[97] See, e.g., Khader, *Adaptive Preferences and Women's Empowerment*, 33.
[98] Khader, *Adaptive Preferences and Women's Empowerment*, 11.
[99] Narayan, "Minds of Their Own," 422, refers to a remark of Catherine MacKinnon that women's agency is "pulverized."

an autonomous life. Global autonomy theorists typically introduce external conditions such as inadequate moral options or socio-relational conditions.[100] For instance, Marina Oshana argues that autonomy is a temporally extended, global condition of agents in which they have "de facto power and authority over choices and actions significant to the direction of [their lives]."[101] Severely constraining external conditions remove the de facto power required for autonomy. Hence, global theories do not usually focus on agents' psychological capacities at all; they do not impugn agency or psychologize the structural. Indeed, on global theories, it is precisely the structural conditions that impair autonomy.

Let us now turn to the question of coercion. Khader notes that for liberal political theory, "autonomy [is] the capacity that exempts people from being subject to coercion."[102] She claims that, once agents are judged to be lacking autonomy, liberals do not have the resources in their theory to block policies that override agents' voluntary choices. Let us suppose it is true that for liberals respect for agent autonomy is the most important moral reason for treating coercive interference with agents as illegitimate. This does not entail that coercive policies are always morally permissible in cases of nonautonomy or lack of autonomy: it does not entail that "public institutions may reasonably coerce...people into changing their preferences." Indeed, coercive policies aimed at changing people's preferences may well be self-defeating if they harm or damage agents' autonomy further under the guise of promoting it.

Khader imagines a policy that denies poor women health care unless they stop the practice of malnourishing themselves to feed their male relatives.[103] Putting aside the fact that denying malnourished people health care would be criticizable on the grounds that it would exacerbate the physical harm they are already suffering, such a policy would be self-defeating. Autonomy is a matter of degree and there are different dimensions of autonomy. It would be self-defeating for a policy whose aim is to augment autonomy to further undermine what little autonomy agents have or to undermine one dimension of autonomy while promoting another. On Raz's account, for instance, a policy that subjected people to direct coercion would inhibit an important dimension of autonomy.

The default position for liberals, in part due to respect for the value of autonomy itself, is that coercive policies are not justified unless the goal is to prevent harm.[104] In the West, this issue can arise for example in cases of mental

---

[100] For inadequate moral options, see Raz, *Morality of Freedom*. For socio-relational conditions, see Marina Oshana, *Personal Autonomy in Society*.
[101] Oshana, *Personal Autonomy in Society*, 2.
[102] Khader, *Adaptive Preferences and Women's Empowerment*, 103.
[103] Khader, *Adaptive Preferences and Women's Empowerment*, 104.
[104] See, e.g., Raz, *Morality of Freedom*.

illness or religious values. Suppose a person with a mental illness lacks the competencies required for full autonomy. From a liberal perspective, there is no justification for subjecting this person to any sort of coercive policy unless she is likely to harm herself or others. Similarly, preferences against certain forms of life-saving medical intervention can be based on religious beliefs. Jehovah's Witnesses think that blood transfusions are contrary to biblical injunctions. Even if a theory of autonomy judges this religious conviction to be the result of indoctrination and hence (for instance) to be incompatible with the requirement of procedural independence, there is no justification for subjecting Jehovah's Witnesses to coercive policies to change their convictions. Coercive intervention such as enforced blood transfusions may be justifiable, but only as a last resort to prevent harm.

Khader seems to accept that the harm principle potentially could provide a justification of a coercive policy. She writes that "we should focus on changing 'cultural practices' only when they cause some sort of [serious] harm or wrong to individuals."[105] In the case of genital cutting, for example, there is wide variation among physical practices as well as among social benefits that ensue. The practice does not always constitute serious harm.[106] Khader is right to say that the mere fact that an agent's endorsement of the practice of genital cutting is driven by a cultural belief that is false and misogynistic does not provide a justification for coercive intervention. But there is stronger position running through Khader's critique: namely, that noncoercive policies, if their aim is to change people's cultural beliefs or conceptions of the good, are never permissible because cultural beliefs and conceptions of the good are delivered by autonomous agency.[107]

This position is implausible. Although liberals (especially proponents of procedural theories of autonomy) put a lot of weight on respecting individual agents' conceptions of the good, nevertheless they endorse the value of autonomy and some version of the harm principle. Since some conceptions of the good are harmful or inconsistent with agents' own autonomy, not all conceptions of the good are equally valuable. As Catriona Mackenzie argues, "ruling out coercive political means for promoting autonomy ... does not entail ruling out other political means for encouraging citizens to pursue valuable goals— for example, incentive and reward schemes ...; health promotion campaigns; funding subsidies for the arts, and so on."[108] Indeed, since autonomy is a value

---

[105] Khader, *Adaptive Preferences and Women's Empowerment*, 101.
[106] Khader, *Adaptive Preferences and Women's Empowerment*, 101.
[107] Khader seems to thinks that noncoercive interventions are permissible to promote, for example, deliberative aspects of agency, but these would fall short of policies whose aim is to change conceptions of the good.
[108] Catriona Mackenize, "Relational Autonomy, Normative Authority and Perfectionism," *Journal of Social Philosophy* 39 (2008): 529.

liberals endorse, noncoercive policies that attempt to promote the value of autonomy may be a requirement of justice on liberal political theories.[109]

Conclusion

In this chapter, I set out to examine the consequences for autonomy of the phenomenon of adaptive preference formation in which the oppressed come to "desire that which is oppressive to them."[110] Feminists often seem to suggest that internalized oppression ipso facto impairs autonomy and that the notion of adaptive preference offers support for that conclusion. The preceding discussion has shown that the situation is more complicated. Adaptive preferences are not autonomy deficits by definition, and neither is it the case that all unconscious accommodations to feasible options count as autonomy impairments. On the other hand, many of the adaptive preferences of concern to feminists are autonomy impairments. I argued that even if adaptive preferences are not deformed but rather rational and reasonable decisions in the face of oppression, this does not show that they are autonomous. Preferences adapted to oppressive conditions fail the tests introduced by both procedural and substantive theories of autonomy. The key reason that they fail these tests—whether it is a test of procedural independence or an adequate options test—is that the moral constraints faced by members of oppressed groups due to their oppression reduce their psychological freedom.

Acknowledgments

For helpful discussion and comments, I am indebted to Mark Piper, Andrea Veltman, my fellow contributors to this volume, and the other participants in the workshop "Relational Autonomy: 10 Years On," held at McGill University in September 2012. I am also grateful to the Social Sciences and Humanities Research Council of Canada for a grant that supports my research on autonomy and oppression, and for a second grant that made the workshop possible.

---

[109] I am grateful to Catriona Mackenzie for many discussions that have helped me think through these ideas.

[110] Cudd, *Analyzing Oppression*, 181.

{ PART V }

Autonomy in Social Contexts

{ 12 }

Raising Daughters: Autonomy, Feminism, and Gender Socialization

Mark Piper

> Hence it is no small matter whether one habit or another is inculcated in us from early childhood; on the contrary, it makes a considerable difference, or, rather, all the difference.
> —ARISTOTLE

In August 2011, my wife gave birth to our first child, our daughter, Helena. We soon found that we had little time or energy to reflect on much beyond the question of how best to manage the learning curve—often joyful, just as often overwhelming—forced upon new parents. But when we could reflect, our thoughts revolved frequently around the central question of how best to meet the immense responsibility, not just of raising a child, but also specifically of raising a daughter in a society still saturated with gender-based inequalities of many powerful kinds. Although not under any illusions that parental instruction alone, however enlightened, is sufficient to counteract the widespread and entrenched institutional obstacles to gender equality, we were (and remain) convinced that proper parental instruction can go a long way toward putting girls on the best footing for their future struggle for personal development and social equality. But how best to go about this? How best to raise our daughter in a manner that encourages her future autonomy but at the same time informs her understanding of her gender in a way that is supportive of the wider aims of feminism itself? As preparations for this volume proceeded, these concerns gradually came to the fore of my reflections and prompted me to write on precisely these topics. My goal in this paper is to argue for a form of gender socialization for daughters, mediated by parental instruction, that is best suited to achieving the twin goals of enhancing daughters' future autonomy and instilling in them a view of what it means to be a woman in such a way that they will grow to be strong advocates of the social cause of gender equality. In the remainder of these introductory comments, I wish to set out the problems discussed in this paper more carefully. I will then proceed to canvass and consider three strategies for a feminist theory of female gender socialization and argue for the form of female gender socialization that I believe holds out the best promise of meeting the vital goals mentioned above.

Traditional female socialization processes tend to be autonomy subverting for women.[1] Women are often taught to be subordinate to men, to focus on "feeling" rather than thinking, and to confine their attentions to the home. Girls are presented with stories and images in entertainment and the media that support the notion that women should be largely focused on gaining acknowledgment from men and should identify their "true" selves with their outward appearance. These factors, and many more like them, combine to tend to make women more submissive, less confident in themselves, and faced with diminished opportunities for self-development and self-expression. The result of these factors is the creation of an inequality between the autonomy prospects for men and women that is disadvantageous for women. Let us call this the *autonomy gender inequality problem*. Overcoming this problem requires initiatives at several levels.[2] Among these initiatives, one central challenge for feminists is to outline a strategy for parentally guided gender socialization that will attenuate the autonomy gender inequality problem. Girls should be gender socialized in a way that supports and enhances their future autonomy rather than hinders it.[3]

It is clear that a solution to the autonomy gender inequality problem should be part of a feminist theory of gender socialization (henceforth GS). But it is also the case that a theory of GS that is autonomy supporting does not constitute a complete feminist theory of GS. A feminist theory of GS also requires an account of how girls should be raised to view being female in a manner that is supportive of feminism. In short, it is not evident that raising a girl in an autonomy-enhancing manner will, by itself, lead her to view her *femaleness* in a feminism-supporting way. Hence, in addition to containing a solution to the autonomy gender inequality problem, a feminist theory of GS must also include resources for teaching girls to be supportive of the values contained in feminism in a manner that advances feminist aims in society. Assuming that both of these aspects are necessary for a feminist theory of GS, however,

---

[1] Simone de Beauvoir, *The Second Sex*, translated and edited H. M. Parshley (London: Lowe and Bridone, 1953); Janet Shibley Hyde and Nicole Else-Quest, *Half the Human Experience: The Psychology of Women*, eighth edition (Belmont, CA: Wadsworth, 2013); Diana Meyers, *Self, Society, and Personal Choice* (New York: Columbia University Press, 1989); C. Renzetti and D. Curran, "Sex-Role Socialization," in *Feminist Philosophies*, edited by J. Kourany, J. Sterba, and R. Tong (Upper Saddle River, NJ: Prentice Hall, 1992).

[2] Beauvoir, *Second Sex*, 680–682.

[3] It should be noted that many theorists who have dealt with what I am calling the autonomy gender inequality problem have not described it as a problem of autonomy per se. Often the presence or absence of other qualities will be pointed out: qualities such as subordination, oppression, and reduced opportunities. But all of these negatively affect the future autonomy of women and are included as part of the autonomy gender inequality problem in the present work.

it remains unclear (1) whether a feminist theory of GS can combine these two aspects at all, and, if they can be combined, (2) what the resulting theory would look like.

In this paper I first argue that there is no inherent contradiction in a feminist theory of GS that is both autonomy enhancing and supportive of feminism. I then argue for a particular feminist theory of GS that best satisfies the demands of promoting autonomy and the normative demands of feminism itself.

1. Definitions and Assumptions

By *autonomy* I understand personal autonomy, or self-determination: a complex psychological property composed of a constellation of enabling properties whose possession enables agents to reflect critically on their natures, preferences, and values; to locate and endorse their most authentic commitments; and to live consistently in accordance with these.[4] As many theorists have noted, the internal capacities associated with autonomy possession can be organized into two categories: authenticity conditions and competency conditions. Authenticity conditions refer to the cluster of agential capacities that allow for accurate introspection of one's authentic self. Competency conditions refer to the cluster of capacities that make it possible to live out one's authentic self-conception consistently in the face of potential interference by recalcitrant inner urges and external resistance of various kinds. Autonomy is thus *self-determination* in the sense that an autonomous agent determines her life in accordance with her (authentic) self.[5] Authenticity conditions provide access to the authentic self, and competency conditions allow for the maintenance and promotion of one's authentic self-conception as one goes through life. Agents have the capacity for autonomy to the degree that they possess these kinds of supporting capacities and are actually autonomous to the degree that these capacities are employed to bring about autonomous living within external circumstances (relations to family and friends, economic conditions, or sociopolitical arrangements) that are autonomy supporting.[6] Those who do

---

[4] Gerald Dworkin, *The Theory and Practice of Autonomy* (Cambridge: Cambridge University Press, 1988); Meyers, *Self, Society, and Personal Choice*; Marilyn Friedman, *Autonomy, Gender, Politics* (New York: Oxford University Press, 2003).

[5] For discussion of the question of whether autonomy possession requires normative commitments, see, e.g., Friedman, *Autonomy, Gender, Politics*; Marina Oshana, *Personal Autonomy in Society* (Aldershot, UK: Ashgate Publishing, 2006); John Christman, *The Politics of Persons: Individual Autonomy and Socio-historical Selves* (Cambridge: Cambridge University Press, 2009).

[6] See Joel Anderson and Axel Honneth, "Autonomy, Vulnerability, Recognition, and Justice," in *Autonomy and the Challenges to Liberalism: New Essays*, edited by John Christman and Joel Anderson (Cambridge: Cambridge University Press, 2005), 127–149; Oshana, *Personal Autonomy in Society*.

not possess autonomy are heteronomous; these persons lack the aforementioned capacities and as a result generally live according to determinations that do not stem from their authentic selves. Such persons include those who are blindly conforming, brainwashed, or easily manipulated. While not all persons are actually autonomous, virtually all persons—with the exception of the irredeemably pathological or handicapped—possess the potential for a minimum level of autonomy.[7]

I understand feminism to be an intellectual and social movement with the goal of achieving justice for women in relation to all social institutions.[8] Feminism fundamentally seeks equality for women. It is premised on the view that women possess status and importance at least equal to men and hence deserve equal rights and opportunities. Given that there are many forms of feminism, however, and that some of these forms are at odds with one another, it is necessary to further specify that I am predominantly conceiving feminism at it has been developed in the liberal tradition, and specifically in the tradition of egalitarian liberal feminism.[9] The upshot of this conception is that women are entitled to the conditions that allow for full social equality as men, and that achieving this goal requires both that women are enabled to develop personal autonomy and that women are empowered to be coauthors of the social conditions under which they develop and live.[10] A natural concomitant of a commitment to feminism of this kind is the view that girls should be raised in such a way both as to secure the best chances for their personal autonomy enhancement and to be prepared to be vigorous social advocates for the equality and freedom of all women.[11]

---

[7] I assume that autonomy of this kind is metaphysically possible. See Catriona Mackenzie and Natalie Stoljar, "Introduction: Autonomy Refigured," in *Relational Autonomy: Feminist Perspectives on Autonomy, Agency, and the Social Self*, edited by Mackenzie and Stoljar (New York: Oxford University Press, 2000), 3–31; Friedman, *Autonomy, Gender, Politics*. This possibility involves the assumption that it is meaningful to speak of an authentic self and that it is possible to know one's authentic self (although it is not necessary to assume that it is possible to know it perfectly). I also assume that autonomy of this kind is not especially uncommon—that most people experience at least marginal increases in this kind of autonomy as they mature from childhood to adulthood.

[8] Sally Haslanger, Nancy Tuana, and Peg O'Connor, "Topics in Feminism," in *Stanford Encyclopedia of Philosophy* (Summer 2013), edited by Edward N. Zalta, http://plato.stanford.edu/archives/sum2013/entries/feminism-topics/.

[9] For an overview of the many forms of feminist theory, see Josephine Donovan, *Feminist Theory: The Intellectual Traditions* (New York: Continuum Publishing, 2012). For different feminist approaches to political theory specifically, see Noelle McAfee, "Feminist Political Philosophy," in *The Stanford Encyclopedia of Philosophy* (Winter 2011), edited by Edward N. Zalta, http://plato.stanford.edu/archives/win2011/entries/feminism-political/.

[10] For more details, see Amy R. Baehr, "Liberal Feminism," in *The Stanford Encyclopedia of Philosophy* (Fall 2012), edited by Edward N. Zalta, http://plato.stanford.edu/archives/fall2012/entries/feminism-liberal/.

[11] For the sake of economy, in what follows I will use the term *feminism* to refer specifically to egalitarian liberal feminism.

I understand gender to refer to the social roles, positions, behaviors, kinds of identity, interests, habits, and statuses that are considered as being associated with a person possessing a particular biological sex.[12] This characterization is intentionally ambiguous between accounts of gender that focus on characteristics that are typically associated with a biological sex and accounts that focus on characteristics that ought to be associated with the same. Importantly, this characterization of gender does not contain the idea that gender is principally a matter of occupying a subordinate or privileged social position.[13] Of course, gender relations exhibit a tremendous amount of inequality, but I take this to be a contingent fact about gender.[14]

I understand gender socialization as the process whereby children are instructed on how to understand the nature of, value of, and practices associated with gender as an institution in society and as a form of life.[15] The gender socialization process usually takes years, and its vehicles of instruction are manifold. In the present paper, as already emphasized, parental instruction will be the principal form of gender socialization under consideration.

2. The Coherence of Autonomy-Enhancing GS Geared toward Inculcating Feminist Ideals

Is autonomy-supportive gender socialization compatible with raising girls to view and value being female in a way that is supportive of egalitarian liberal feminism and its ideals? On the surface, it might seem as though it is not: for how could girls be raised for robust autonomy and at the same time be raised to view and value female gender in a particular, predetermined way? It might

---

[12] Cf. Kate Millet, *Sexual Politics* (London: Granada Publishing, 1971).

[13] Contra Catherine MacKinnon, *Toward a Feminist Theory of the State* (Cambridge, MA: Harvard University Press, 1989). It might be said that I am also arguing against Sally Haslanger, "Gender and Race: (What) Are They? (What) Do We Want Them to Be?" *Nous* 34:1 (2000): 31–55, insofar as she has defined gender with basic reference to facts of inequality. But this critique would be incorrect: Haslanger's work contains the caveat that she is defining gender to aid in the achievement of a particular practical purpose. Her conception of gender is pragmatic and ameliorative; she is not attempting to provide a real definition of gender.

[14] Although I deny strict gender realism, I assume that the category of *gender* is relatively unified insofar as it satisfies the demands of resemblance nominalism. See Natalie Stoljar, "Essence, Identity and the Concept of Woman," *Philosophical Topics* 23 (1995): 261–293; Stoljar, "The Politics of Identity and the Metaphysics of Diversity," in *Proceedings of the 20th World Congress of Philosophy, Vol. VIII*, edited by Daniel Dahlstrom (Bowling Green, OH: Bowling Green State University, 2000). I assume that sex and gender are distinct, contra Judith Butler, *Gender Trouble: Feminism and the Subversion of Identity* (New York: Routledge, 1999), 43. I assume that the sex–gender distinction is useful, contra Genevieve Lloyd, *The Man of Reason: "Male" and "Female" in Western Philosophy* (Minneapolis: University of Minnesota Press, 1984); Elizabeth Grosz, *Volatile Bodies: Toward a Corporeal Feminism* (Bloomington: Indiana University Press, 1994).

[15] Beauvoir, *Second Sex*; Millet, *Sexual Politics*; Sally Haslanger, "Ontology and Social Construction," *Philosophical Topics* 23 (1995): 95–125.

seem that we can have one ideal or the other but not both. We can raise girls to be autonomous (but then we can't predetermine key aspects of their value systems), or we can raise girls to view gender in a way that is supportive of feminism (but such inculcation seems to rob them of autonomy, at least on some accounts).

I believe, though, that this is a pseudo-problem. First, the objection may rest on a misunderstanding. It is not being suggested that girls ought to be raised in a manner that is autonomy supportive and will result in the inculcation of a particular value system no matter what. This would constitute a straw man of the theory being sought. The desire is rather to see if it is possible to have autonomy-supportive gender socialization coupled with instruction in the nature and value of gender that tends to be supportive of feminism or presents feminism in a reasonable, plausible light. Second, the incoherence charge is vulnerable to reductio problems. If the development of autonomy were incompatible with the teaching of any particular values, then no one would be autonomous, since everyone is raised (more or less by social necessity) to believe that some things are to be valued and that some things are not. But that can't be right: autonomy might not be automatically achieved by all, but it is achieved by many, to some degree at least. So it must be possible to raise someone in an autonomy-supportive way while teaching them that particular values are plausible or reasonable. What is required to have GS that is supportive of both autonomy development and feminism is a commitment to teaching the competencies that comprise autonomy and to presenting a feminist conception of gender as a plausible view that has a number of strong reasons in its support. Although young girls do not possess the autonomy capacities to reflect critically on the conception of gender they are being taught, these abilities grow with their autonomy competency, until they are able to decide for themselves whether to endorse feminist-supportive teachings. To deny that this is possible is, in effect, to deny the possibility of autonomy. Again, everyone begins life as entirely heteronomous and gradually obtains greater autonomy potential. People go on to actualize this potential to varying extents. The move toward greater self-government and independence of thought is difficult, but it does happen, even against the background of forms of upbringing that are stringent or stifling.

3. The Options

Even if we assume that autonomy-supportive gender socialization is compatible with teaching girls about the nature and value of gender in a feminism-supportive way, there are likely different ways to satisfy these two normative demands in a theory of GS. The challenge is to determine which GS strategy best satisfies both of these demands.

In what follows I examine three different forms of GS—by no means an exhaustive list—that can be differentiated according to the associated underlying views of the nature and normative importance of female gender:

1. Non-gendered socialization (NGS)
2. Traditional masculine gender socialization (TMGS)
3. Revisionary feminine gender socialization (RFGS)

The rest of this section is devoted to clarifying these positions. In the following section I analyze the positions to determine which one best satisfies the demands of autonomy enhancement and the promotion of feminism itself.

NON-GENDERED SOCIALIZATION

NGS has a classic standing in feminist studies. Gayle Rubin argues that feminists should seek to create a "genderless (though not sexless) society, in which one's sexual anatomy is irrelevant to who one is, what one does, and with whom one makes love."[16] According to Richard Wasserstrom, a properly "sexually assimilated" society would be one in which the gender system is repudiated. In such an ideal society, "persons would not be socialized so as to see or understand themselves or others as essentially or significantly who they were...because they were either male or female."[17] And Susan Moller Okin argues in *Justice, Gender and the Family* that a feminist reading of Rawls's *Theory of Justice* suggests that if those in the Original Position didn't know their sex they would probably opt for a genderless society: "A just society would be one without gender."[18]

Although various forms of NGS are possible, at present I wish to focus on a particularly robust form of NGS. According to this conception, NGS holds that gender has no normative importance of any kind. On this view, the psychological-social aspects of gender are nothing more than arbitrary social constructs, yet they have become infused with normative importance and have been used to promote unjust ends—most tellingly, the subordination of women. Recognizing this arbitrariness, this view holds that we should do away with the notion that the norms associated with gender generate any demands for maintenance, loyalty, or uptake of any kind. The very notion of gender difference is to be abolished. Some humans have different organs than others, but that is as far as the matter ought to go.

---

[16] Gayle Rubin, "The Traffic in Women: Notes on the 'Political Economy' of Sex," in *Toward an Anthropology of Women*, edited by Rayna R. Reiter (New York: Monthly Review Press, 1975), 204.

[17] Richard Wasserstrom, "On Racism and Sexism," in *Today's Moral Problems*, edited by Richard A. Wasserstrom (New York: Macmillan Press, 1979), 26.

[18] Susan Moller Okin, *Justice, Gender, and the Family* (New York: Basic Books, 1991), 171.

NGS holds that children's socialization should, as far as possible, be denuded of the notion that boys are (or ought to be) one way, and girls are (or ought to be) another way, in relation to the social-psychological roles associated with having a particular sex. It focuses on the idea that all children should be socialized in an extremely open, tolerant, broad way, with no reference to particular roles, duties, norms, or practices that attend membership in a gender group. Women who have been raised in accordance with NGS or who have subsequently embraced its values will have little patience for the notion that gender underwrites normative demands of any kind or has any intrinsic value. They will avoid attempts by others to normatively typecast them according to gender, and their self-conceptions will mirror this: "Forget about the category 'girl.' I am not to be identified with this arbitrary social construct that has been projected on to me. I have female organs—that's as far as the matter goes, or ought to go."[19]

TRADITIONAL MASCULINE GENDER SOCIALIZATION

TMGS holds that being a female is, as such, no less valuable than being a male but that the *traditional forms* that being female have taken are weak and invite just the sorts of oppressive treatment that women have historically received. On this view, women have been kept in a subordinate position throughout human history by two factors: male oppression and unwitting female complicity. Yes, women have been oppressed by men, but women have also wrongly accepted the view that their place in society is secondary, merely supportive (rather than dynamic and active), pliant, domestic, and weak. Yet being a woman need not come with such entailments. In all areas except the morally insignificant domain of physical strength, women can be the equals of men and ought to be. But actualizing this potential requires repudiating the notion that one should "act like a woman"—indeed, accepting that dictum is precisely one of the chief causes of women's oppression. On this view, the very notion of acting like a woman is tarnished: it is indelibly associated with the idea of self-constraint and subordination. Being female is just as valuable as being male, and hence females deserve equality with males. However, to realize this equality, it is necessary to deny the idea that female gender has a positive normative role to

---

[19] An example of NGS in action can be found at Egalia, a preschool in Stockholm, Sweden. Cordelia Hebblewaite, "Sweden's 'Gender-Neutral' Pre-school," *BBC News Europe*, http://www.bbc.co.uk/news/world-europe-14038419. The teachers there actively work against instilling in children expectations based on gender in several ways. They avoid using the pronouns "him" or "her" when speaking to children, instead referring to them as friends, by their first names, or as "hen" (a genderless pronoun borrowed from Finnish). The school's books are devoid of traditional presentations of gender roles. All the children are encouraged to choose from toys of all kinds, including those not traditionally associated with their gender. Boys are free to dress up and play with dolls; girls are free to play with toy tractors. Egalia is state funded and is proving popular in a country known for its passion for social equality.

play on women's behalf. Rather, women should seek as far as possible to live, think, and behave like men, for this is the path to empowerment, equality, self-expression, dynamic creativity, robust self-government, and flourishing.

In TMGS, girls are taught to be direct and willful, to play aggressively, to seek out and be comfortable in positions of social leadership, to be creative, to have social ambitions, and to expect to be part of the machinery of social power. In short, according to this approach all children should receive the same GS, both in terms of methods and content. This is the only way to provide all children, girls and boys, with the greatest chance of living the best life possible.

REVISIONARY FEMININE GENDER SOCIALIZATION

RFGS holds that being a woman is something that is distinctive, special, and worthy of being honored as such: female gender is a way of being in the world that is valuable and ought to be not only sustained but also celebrated and, in ways appropriate to women's life paths, fought for. The adjective *revisionary* is applied to this version of GS to indicate a split from traditional ways of conceiving gender roles, in at least two senses: (1) revisionary approaches do not rest on a sexist axiology that involves notions of an inherent value hierarchy between males and females; and (2) revisionary approaches are open to the possibility that *being a woman* is not necessarily associated with the traditional way of conceiving it—as a matter of being care oriented and the like. Rather, being a woman can take many different forms, some of which are considerable departures from traditional notions of femininity.

According to RFGS, almost all of the many different forms that being a woman can take are legitimate ways of being a woman, as long as they do not essentially involve accepting a sexist axiology. According to this view, certain general facts have characterized—and continue to characterize—the category *woman*. However, these facts do not constrain in any substantive way the possible legitimate ways of living that women can choose. On the basis of her writings, it is reasonable to hold that Judith Butler, for example, would endorse this form of GS. According to Butler, we should understand woman as "a term in process, a becoming, a constructing that cannot rightfully said to begin or end.... It is open to intervention and resignification."[20] It might also be surmised that those who espouse resemblance nominalism in relation to gender would espouse RFGS.[21]

On this view, being a woman certainly possesses value of its own sort: it is important for women to identify themselves as women and to engage in

---

[20] Butler, *Gender Trouble*, 43.
[21] Stoljar, "Essence, Identity and the Concept of Woman;" Stoljar, "Politics of Identity."

projects that speak to their gender. Living as a woman, it could be said, has definite prudential value for the women who do so. Yet on this view womanhood is not the most significant fact about a woman's normative status. More important still is the basic condition of being human, or of being a person, or of being a rational being. The normative grounding for women's basic rights to equality in RFGS is the stance that one would expect to be associated with feminists who espouse a "sameness approach" to feminism.[22] On this approach, women may be distinct in various ways, and embracing this distinctiveness can be important for the quality of women's lives. However, the ground of women's rights to equal opportunities and treatment is not to be found in the value of being a woman as such; it is to be found in a quality that women share with men alike. Girls raised in accordance with RFGS will acknowledge their gender but place deeper ethical import elsewhere: "Yes, I'm a woman, and this has a value of its own, but more importantly, I deserve equal treatment because I am a person [or, e.g., rational individual or autonomous agent]."

As we have seen, this approach allows for significant diversity amongst the life paths that particular women may take. As such, general commonalties among women are not conceived as binding on what a woman must be. In RFGS, a woman may choose to become just about whatever she wants. Following from this inclusivity, parents employing RFGS will raise their children to have skills, habits, and resources that have wide formal value, in facilitating the successful pursuit of as many different forms of life as possible.

Last, RFGS holds that girls ought to be taught—proudly—to be girls and ought to be trained to be effective advocates for women. This does not imply that all girls raised in RFGS should be taught that they must become public social figures leading the fight for equality, though, for this would run counter to the very inclusiveness of this approach to GS. Part of the inclusiveness of this approach is to teach girls that there are many ways to advocate for women. Certainly leadership in feminist social activism is one path, but there are others as well. The teacher or professor who is not intimidated by aggressive male students or a largely male administrative body, the businesswoman who does not laugh at misogynistic jokes from her coworkers, the aspiring carpenter who is not deterred by the absence of women in her chosen trade, or the homemaker who firmly insists that her unpaid work is at least as important as paid forms of labor—all of these are forms of advocacy for women. If there are general constraints associated with RFGS, they are only these: that girls will be raised to be widely competent and prepared for many different possible forms of life, that they will be taught that there are many valuable ways of being a woman and that they will be instructed in such a way as to foster the strength

---

[22] Cf. Martha Nussbaum, "Human Capabilities, Female Human Beings," in *Women, Culture and Development: A Study of Human Capabilities*, edited by Martha Nussbaum and Jonathan Glover (New York: Oxford University Press, 1995), 61–104.

and self-esteem to advocate for women in whatever fashion is appropriate to their natures and vocations.

This brings us back to the principal line of inquiry. We have seen that autonomy-supportive gender socialization is consistent with raising girls in a manner that is supportive of feminist values, but which approach to GS best satisfies the demands of autonomy and feminism?

4. Evaluating the Options

NON-GENDERED SOCIALIZATION

Is NGS supportive of girls' future autonomy? The answer depends on what autonomy development requires. As we have already seen, autonomy consists in the possession of internal authenticity and competency conditions. Authenticity conditions are those capacities that allow an agent to introspect, to accurately perceive her authentic self, and to form a coherent authentic self-conception (the *self* in self-determination). Competency conditions are those capacities that allow an agent to maintain and live according to this authentic self-conception in the face of various kinds of potential internal and external interference. Such conditions include, for example, self-control, logical aptitude, proactivity, and reasonable skepticism (to forestall easy acceptance of potentially undermining forms of external influence). Such conditions also arguably include self-reflexive attitudes such as a sense of self-worth or self-esteem, without which one would not feel oneself *worthy* of living according to one's lights.[23] Finally, autonomy requires the presence of external enabling conditions of various kinds. These include access to a range of options from which to choose, a minimum amount of security with which to prosecute one's life plan[24] as well as a number of close relationships through which one can better come to know oneself.[25]

One of the greatest strengths of NGS is in relation to the presence of a wide range of options from which to choose. Without predetermined gender roles, psychological profiles, or social associations, girls raised according to NGS would likely enjoy highly increased latitude in relation to the options open to them. Of course, at present many social institutions are influenced by established notions about what is proper for a woman to choose and would

---

[23] Paul Benson, "Free Agency and Self-Worth," *Journal of Philosophy* 91:12 (1994): 650–658.
[24] Marina Oshana, "Personal Autonomy and Society," *Journal of Social Philosophy* 29 (1998): 81–102.
[25] Charles Taylor, *Philosophy and the Human Sciences: Philosophical Papers 2* (Cambridge: Cambridge University Press, 1985), 187–210; Jurgen Habermas, "Individuation through Socialization: On George Herbert Mead's Theory of Subjectivity," in Habermas, *Postmetaphysical Thinking: Philosophical Essays*, translated by William Mark Hohengarten (Cambridge, MA: MIT Press, 1992); Anderson and Honneth, "Autonomy, Vulnerability."

bring their pressure to bear on women, but this could be mitigated by a consistent and systematic parental policy in support of diversity. Moreover, there is nothing in NGS that necessarily works against parental inculcation of competency conditions such as personal discipline, logical aptitude, moderate skepticism of outside influences, or proactivity in the prosecution of one's life plan. NGS is hostile to the system of gender roles, associations, and statuses that characterize traditional Western society, but this hostility does not essentially involve skepticism about the capacities mentioned. Indeed, it is likely that NGS would promote a more robust inculcation of the same, since girls raised in such a manner—one that radically opposes an entrenched aspect of social life—would require training in just these sorts of abilities to hold fast to their convictions against the potent general currents of gender conformity.

There are strong objections to NGS, however. For one thing, there is reason to believe that girls raised in NGS face dangers in relation to developing a strong sense of self-worth. Such girls run sharply against the conventional grain and would likely be belittled and combated on several fronts for their repudiation of the significance of gender roles and norms. There is empirical evidence to suggest that the distress caused by the experience of gender nonconformity can lead to self-doubt, which, if internalized, can prompt uncertainty about one's right to flaunt convention and can eventually lead in some children to a reduced sense of self-esteem.[26] And there is also evidence to suggest that girls whose behavior is not geared toward social approval will face reduced popularity.[27] If a sense of self-esteem or self-worth is important for autonomy possession, as many authors have argued, then such a result would likely undermine autonomy.[28]

However, the force of this objection should not be overestimated. First, on the plausible view that traditional forms of GS reliably lead to women having reduced autonomy capacity, forms of GS that may hold dangers for the development of self-worth but that also have resources for addressing the autonomy gender inequality problem might still be overall preferable, as containing better chances for girls to develop autonomy. Second, the influence of parental

---

[26] J. Block and R. W. Robins, "A Longitudinal Study of Consistency and Change in Self-Esteem from Early Adolescence to Early Adulthood," *Child Development* 64 (1993): 909–923; S. K. Egan and D. G. Perry, "Gender Identity: A Multidimensional Analysis with Implications for Psychosocial Adjustment," *Developmental Psychology* 37 (2001): 451–463; R. A. Josephs, H. R. Markus, and R. W. Tafarodi, "Gender and Self-Esteem," *Journal of Personality and Social Psychology* 63 (1992): 391–402; A. Thorne and Q. Michaelieu, "Situating Adolescent Gender and Self-Esteem with Personal Memories," *Child Development* 67 (1996): 1374–1390; Meenakshi Menon, "Does Felt Gender Compatibility Mediate Influences of Self-Perceived Gender Nonconformity on Early Adolescents' Psychosocial Adjustment?" *Child Development* 82:4 (2011): 1152–1162.

[27] Hunter College Women's Studies Collective, *Women's Realities, Women's Choices* (New York: Oxford University Press, 1983), 153.

[28] See, e.g. Benson, "Free Agency and Self-Worth"; Catriona Mackenzie, "Imagining Oneself Otherwise," in Mackenzie and Stoljar, *Relational Autonomy*, 124–150.

instruction should not be underestimated. Girls raised according to NGS by committed parents can be trained to be prepared for precisely such assaults on their sense of self-esteem. In full awareness of the likelihood of pushback from society, parents committed to NGS would be highly motivated to take special care to instill in their girls the inner fortitude required to maintain their sense of entitlement to cast off the traditional bonds of gender association. Indeed, there is empirical evidence to support the claim that strongly supportive parental involvement with children has a direct and positive bearing on children's self-esteem.[29]

The primary worry concerning the autonomy potential of NGS, however, is likely to come from those who hold that biology is destiny. Even if we assume, on the strength of research that supports social constructivism about gender, that this claim is false, a challenge might be raised by those who hold that biology has some influence on the shape of a woman's life. Empirical evidence for this thesis can be found. The sociologist Laura Lindsey, for example, has argued that "hormones predispose the sexes to different behavior" while still claiming that "societal factors will ultimately activate this behavior."[30] Sociologist Richard Udry has supported this claim by arguing that empirical research suggests that "humans form their social structures around gender because males and females have different and biologically influenced behavioral predispositions."[31] This and other research in the social and hard sciences does not debunk the social constructivist view of gender; indeed, both Lindsey and Udry call for an integrated theory of gender that combines biological determinism with social construction. The present concern is whether biology plays any role at all in gender development. If it does, the worry arises that at least some girls raised in accordance with NGS may feel alienated from themselves to some extent. Given their commitment to the idea that traditional gender associations are nothing more than arbitrary social constructs, some girls raised in accordance with NGS may come to feel conflicted and uncertain about womanhood or even about who they really are. And this could lead to a weakened ability to satisfy the authenticity conditions of autonomy, according to which autonomy requires that one have a firm, coherent, and committed sense of one's authentic self. The presence of empirical support for the influence of biology should be sufficient to undermine the worry that this is nothing more than a slippery slope fallacy masquerading as a real problem. If biology has any influence on gender dispositions, at least in some persons,

---

[29] M. H. Richards, I. B. Gitelson, A. C. Petersen, and A. L. Hurtig, "Adolescent Personality in Girls and Boys: The Role of Mothers and Fathers," *Psychology of Women Quarterly* 15 (1991): 65–81.

[30] Linda L. Lindsey, *Gender Roles: A Sociological Perspective* (Upper Saddle River, NJ: Prentice-Hall, 1997), 27.

[31] Richard Udry, "Biological Limits of Gender Construction," *American Sociological Review* 65:3 (2000): 454.

there is a real concern that raising children in a robust NGS manner—such as that practiced at Egalia preschool in Stockholm—may have the effect of sundering them from core, biologically grounded aspects of their identities, with concomitantly adverse effects on their potential for identifying with at least some aspects of their authentic selves.

Let us suppose that this challenge needs to be met. More specifically, let us assume, for the moment, that biology, while not absolute in its influence, does exert a pull in women toward certain traditional gender associations, especially those surrounding reproduction, mothering, and caregiving. Girls who are taught by NGS that gender associations are ultimately arbitrary may develop a damaging split in their self-conceptions that would undermine their ability to form a consistent self-identity, and this could lead to a weakening of their ability to be self-governing. If one isn't sure who one is, one cannot govern oneself effectively. This worry would not preclude the development of a consistent authentic self-conception in all women, of course, but it would likely undermine the formation of such conceptions in many women. And if biology in fact *is* destiny, then this concern is conclusive; in this event, NGS would fail the test of autonomy support, by severing women from a core component of their authentic selves. At this point, judging the strength of this challenge becomes an empirical matter on which I will not pass judgment. The empirical evidence seems to be conflicting, and I do not have the expertise to adjudicate the matter. If it is true that biology exerts even a reliable—if not absolute—influence on women, then many women will find it difficult to form a firm and consistent self-conception, thereby threatening their possibility of autonomy. If biology exerts no such influence, however, then this challenge disappears.

We come, then, to the question of the feminist credentials of NGS. It seems clear that at least one core aspect of NGS is favorable in this respect. NGS undermines the traditional system of gender associations that have been such a reliable vehicle of women's oppression. The traditional gender system views women as being of less worth than men in many important respects. NGS, by repudiating the gender system entirely, and by espousing the formation of a social order based on the equal worth of all persons regardless of sex, well satisfies the feminist project of overcoming women's subordination and creating a just and equal society. I would suggest that these considerations constitute the strongest specifically feminist argument that can be made in favor of NGS. It is precisely this virtue, it seems, that has led many feminists to support the eradication of the gender system—and, by implication, to support NGS for girls. There is, however, at least one objection that deserves mention.

It could be argued that there is a kind of practical value in maintaining the idea of a real difference between the genders. The practical value that I have in mind relates to the work on gender done by feminists like Sally Haslanger. According to Haslanger, one way to approach the normative problem of what ought to be done in relation to the gender system is pragmatic in character. The basic idea is that conceiving gender in particular ways might best support the feminist project. Haslanger holds that gender ought to be conceived primarily in terms of subordination. On this view—roughly—what it means to be a woman is to be in a subordinate social position in relation to men. Haslanger does not claim that this subordination constitutes a *real* definition of gender, however. She holds that conceiving gender in this way holds the best chance of furthering the practical aims of feminism itself, by motivating social action on behalf of justice for women.[32] This practical or ameliorative approach to conceiving gender can be taken in other directions, however, and that is what I have in mind here. The basic idea that I would like to tender is that the goals of feminism might best be supported by continuing to conceive the gender category *woman* as denoting a real difference from the gender category *man*. The justification for this claim is twofold. First, maintaining the category *woman* would have the beneficial effect of not alienating the many women who continue to accept the idea that this category is real and distinct. The majority of the world's women would likely consider the eradication of the gender system to be radically alien to their way of conceiving the world. If feminism begins with this very eradication, however, it risks the danger of alienating the great majority of the very constituency whose improvement constitutes the basic goal of feminism itself. In consequence, scads of possible allies to the feminist cause would likely find themselves at variance with the feminist movement itself. Since it is entirely possible to maintain the category *woman* without suffering this effect, it seems reasonable to do so and hence to avoid pinning one's hopes on such an alienating policy.

Second, maintaining the category *woman* could have the greatly beneficial effect of establishing a rallying point for the feminist cause. By maintaining the claim that the category *woman* is real and different from the category man, while continuing the focus attention on the problem of women's inequality—and, of course, while suitably modifying the conception of women in such a way as to fight the traditional (if often implicit) notion that women are in some normative sense inferior to men—the feminist movement could give women a "home" worth fighting for. Rather than being asked to fight to eradicate the very category of which most women consider themselves a member, women could be invited to fight for the rights of that very category. The emotional and social connotations of femininity are already exceedingly strong; with the proper modifications, the category *woman* could serve as an effective and motivating rallying call for women: fight for your rights *as a woman*! In accordance with the aforementioned considerations, I would submit that a

---

[32] Haslanger, "Gender and Race," 33, 36.

policy of this kind would have the best practical chance of securing wide consent and motivating women's action on a wide front.

It may perhaps be objected that enacting this suggestion might hurt the cause more than it helps. After all, in the face of widespread social injustice, sometimes it is best to buck even the deepest points of convention. Wouldn't the kind of reasoning tendered previously, applied, say, to slavery, suggest that we ought to maintain the category *slave* for similar reasons? Yet while I agree that a radical repudiation of conventional wisdom might be necessary in some circumstances, I am not convinced that this is appropriate here. For one thing, the analogy with slavery is strained at best. The category *slave* is *inherently* subordinate, while the category woman is not. Hence, maintaining the category *woman* would not entail the continuation of an inherently unjust social category. More broadly, decisions regarding the solution of social ills ought to be determined by the particulars of the case. In the case of social inequality toward women, I would argue, in accordance with the considerations given already, that the goals of the feminist movement are best satisfied by maintaining the category *woman* as real and distinct. Doing so would by no means require maintaining the traditional role associations, psychological profiles, or differential claims regarding status that have undermined the feminist cause, but it would increase the likelihood that fewer women would feel alienated from the movement devoted to their very liberation and that women could productively rally around their very gender identity in furtherance of their just aims. For these reasons, I conclude that NGS, while theoretically poised to support the feminist cause, holds considerable practical dangers for feminism and therefore fares poorly in relation to practical support for the feminist ideals that it was designed to facilitate.

Although these considerations are institutional in scope—relating as they do to the establishment of a policy for broad and effective feminist social activism—it should not be thought for that reason that they are unsuited to the far more local decision faced by parents regarding how to raise their daughters. If the practical arguments given already have bite, there is no reason to think that they would not inform parents' judgments about the best form of GS to apply when raising their daughters or the particular manner in which daughters are raised. Parents committed to the goals of autonomy and feminism wish for their daughters to flourish in the world as it exists, and this requires providing sound practical advice for understanding and interacting with the broad currents of social activism in which their daughters will live. It makes no small difference to the nature of a daughter's upbringing to be told that gender categories have no significance whatsoever—or, for that matter, that there is real practical value in maintaining that they do. Such instruction will certainly play a powerful role in how a girl understands and interacts with her peers and with gendered social conventions and norms and will influence a girl's judgments about what a commitment to feminist ideals demands of her and other women. Parents who wish for their daughters potentially to become strong advocates for feminism cannot afford to overlook broader considerations such as those given before when they will have a direct bearing, not only on how they raise their daughters but more importantly on what their daughters come to be.

In sum, then, I hold that NGS faces strong challenges as a feminist theory of GS, both because of concerns about its ability to be supportive of women's autonomy and because of concerns relating to its practical effectiveness in underwriting the desirable feminist goal of securing widespread and effective practical action in support of women's equality.

TRADITIONAL MALE GENDER SOCIALIZATION

Perhaps the most prominent advocate of TMGS as a feminist theory of GS is Simone de Beauvoir. Given the advantages associated with male socialization, de Beauvoir concludes that girls ought to be raised with the "same demands and rewards, the same severity and the same freedom, as her brothers, taking part in the same studies, the same games, [and] promised the same future."[33] De Beauvoir does not, it is true, think that this alone will solve the autonomy gender inequality problem. She is well aware that institutional changes must also be made in relation to education, employment, and financial independence for women. And she also implies that boys should be raised to see girls as equals: "To gain the supreme victory, it is necessary... that by and through their natural differentiation men and women unequivocally affirm their brotherhood."[34] But it is also clear that de Beauvoir viewed raising girls in a like manner as boys to be an essential instrument in the achievement of the goals of feminism. Diana Meyers, in support of this contention, argues that de Beauvoir held that "universal masculine socialization coupled with social and economic reform holds out the only hope of freeing women from immanence."[35] Following de Beauvoir, other feminists have supported the same conclusion. And one can well understand why this policy was formed. If women's subordination is best explained by the fact that men have been raised to be superior and women have been raised to be inferior, it would seem clear that the solution is to raise both sexes to be superior—that is, to raise girls in the same manner as boys.

How does TMGS fare in relation to the development of autonomy? As a start, it looks quite promising. Girls raised in accordance with TMGS will enjoy all of its benefits: they will be taught to be more assertive and proactive; they will be taught that they are fully entitled to direct their own life paths,

---

[33] Beauvoir, *Second Sex*, 681–682.
[34] Beauvoir, *Second Sex*, 687.
[35] Meyers, *Self, Society, and Personal Choice*, 190.

giving them a greater range of meaningful alternatives from which to choose; they will be raised to develop a stronger sense of entitlement to direct their lives, which should accordingly lead to a greater sense of self-worth; they will be taught to be more discriminating in their judgments, which may lead to an increase in logical aptitude; they will see themselves more as the rightful arbiters of their futures, which may lead to an increase in moderate skepticism in relation to others' plans for them; and they will be less concerned with the importance of their outward appearance, placing importance instead on the trajectory of their life plans, as determined by their own judgments. All of these features of TMGS will likely lead to an increased possibility for the development of autonomy.

Yet the autonomy-supporting benefits of TMGS ought not to be exaggerated. For one thing, TMGS places a premium on self-assertiveness and competitive success. While in moderation such a focus does not undermine future autonomy, excessive self-assertiveness can lead persons raised in accordance with TMGS to become too concerned with pushing through their own agendas despite the presence of external obstacles. As Diana Meyers argues, "The emotional isolation central to masculine socialization obliges boys to become independent, but it also heightens their aggressive tendencies because it makes them feel insecure."[36] From this point of view, TMGS could easily translate into closed-mindedness and obstinacy. Being autonomous requires a sensitivity to one's authentic self, yet this sensitivity could be lost if one trades careful reflection upon possible ways of living for a stubborn adherence to whatever one happens to will. Excessive self-assertiveness can close the doors to insightful introspection.

By contrast, traditionally feminine traits such as sensitivity and empathy can lead persons to be more introspective, more responsive to their feelings, and more adept at understanding themselves.[37] Such traits are also important for the ability to foster and flourish in interpersonal relationships, which, as autonomy theorists increasingly agree, is crucial for autonomy development.[38] According to Iris Marion Young, the trajectory of feminism since de Beauvoir has been excessively dismissive of the notion that traditional femininity contains anything of worth, and—what basically comes to the same thing—has been excessively supportive of the idea that valuable ways of living are to be found exclusively in the traditional male ideal.[39] Young and other gynocentric

---

[36] Meyers, *Self, Society, and Personal Choice*, 191–192.

[37] Beauvoir, *Second Sex*, 338.

[38] Taylor, *Philosophy and the Human Sciences*, 187–210; Evelyn Fox Keller, *Reflections on Gender and Science* (New Haven, CT: Yale University Press, 1985); Patricia Huntington, "Toward a Dialectical Concept of Autonomy," *Philosophy and Social Criticism* 21 (1995): 37–55.

[39] Iris Marion Young, "Humanism, Gynocentrism, and Feminist Politics," in *Theorizing Feminisms: A Reader*, edited by Elizabeth Hackett and Sally Haslanger (New York: Oxford University Press, 2005), 174–187.

feminists argue that traditionally female forms of life—centered on relationships of loving care, mothering, nurturing, and the like—ought in fact to be celebrated and should form one of the key bases for the feminist movement. Traditional female virtues form a highly desirable counterpoint to the overly aggressive, overly competitive, and often callous ways of interacting with others (and the world) associated with traditional masculinity. Instead of disparaging what is traditionally female, feminists ought to hold feminist virtues up as ideals of social interaction and emotional development. From this perspective, TMGS, by lionizing traditional masculine forms of life, both unjustly slights what is valuable in traditional femininity and does a disservice to feminism by undercutting the legitimate values that inhere within it.

Moreover, TMGS can reduce one's perceived life options as well. Raised to view oneself as a significant mover in social matters, one may come to disparage ways of life that are more focused on service or caregiving. Such ways of living may be lost on those raised in TMGS, even if those forms of life are actually more in accord with their authentic selves. Many males are raised to believe that it is fitting for them to be fighters, for instance, and this has doubtless led many to engage in acts of violence that are at odds with their real natures.

And there is a final potential problem, one that we have seen before. If biology exerts an influence—even if not absolute—on women's lives, then women raised in accordance with TMGS may find themselves alienated from aspects of womanhood, with the result that their ability to form clear and unified authentic self-conceptions may be undermined. As mentioned already, if it can be shown that biology has no such pull, then these issues dissolve, but if not they are considerable. In sum, then, TMGS presents mixed results in relation to autonomy support. It fares best in relation to the inculcation of the competency conditions of autonomy but presents problems in relation to the development of authenticity conditions, through its valorization of masculine traits that may actually undermine authenticity competency and its dismissal of valuable traditionally feminine traits that support those competencies. It also presents difficulties in relation to the presence of external alternatives considered as live options.

How well does TMGS stand in relation to support for feminism? In at least one key respect, it seems that it fares quite well. Girls raised in accordance with TMGS stand a greater chance of becoming women who are independent and powerful, and this is a notable attraction for parents raising girls in a sexist society. Secure in their conviction that women are equal to men in all key normative respects and raised to be assertive, forthright, aggressive in the prosecution of their life plans, and with a firm sense of self-worth, women who have been raised in accordance with TMGS will stand as strong advocates for the rights of women. They will take positions of social leadership and oppose social injustices on a broad front; they will not be cowed by spurious notions of "rightful" male authority or the overwhelming history of women's subordination. In short, TMGS will likely result in the development of strong leaders of social, political, and economic institutions and of feminism generally.

Yet there are some respects in which one might be reasonably critical of the extent to which TMGS supports feminism. Some of these issues have been explored already in relation to NGS. First, TMGS is premised on the idea that traditional notions of femininity are to be avoided. Lives devoted exclusively to mothering, or more generally to the loving care of others, or to homemaking, or indeed to any kinds of living that are characterized by what might be called quiet compassion are judged by the background normative commitments of TMGS as worthy of disparagement and even hostility, as precisely the ways of living that have historically worked to facilitate women's subordination to men. TMGS repudiates these ways of living as forms of collaboration in women's oppression. Yet while it cannot be doubted that these forms of life have contributed to women's oppression, values and practices based on the repudiation of traditional forms of femininity might work to undermine feminism by alienating broad swaths of women who associate with these ways of living. It is important to avoid understating the potential effects of propagating the view that the feminist movement is hostile to traditional forms of femininity. Told that their commitment to these forms of life constitutes an insidious form of unwitting collaboration with the forces of social injustice, many women may elect to keep their distance from—or even fight—the feminist movement out of a desire for ideological self-preservation.

Moreover, TMGS implies that women ought to assimilate their value systems, social expectations, and behaviors to traditional forms of masculinity. The implicit upshot of this recommendation is the idea that the category *woman*, while not empty of distinctive content, is empty of any desirable or commendable content. *Woman* becomes a symbol for an unworthy form of weakness that is to be avoided. By contrast, *man* becomes a symbol for forms of life and valuation that are truly valuable. Such a consequence contains the practical problem that women are deprived of basing possible activism on behalf of women in anything that is valuable about *being a woman*. One may still fight on behalf of the abstract claims of justice or perhaps on behalf of women qua individuals or persons; but the very category *woman* whose weal is sought through social action threatens to become little more than a symbol of an obstacle that needs to be overcome. In this way, a powerful potential resource for securing communal accession and social action is lost: the category *woman* is not a rallying point for women; rather it becomes a threat.

The upshot of these concerns is practical in character. A more effective conceptual practice in garnering wide and effective support for the feminist cause might be instead to maintain the notion that the category *woman* is distinctive and valuable in its own right. One is far more likely to fight effectively when one is fighting for one's kin and community, conceived as worthy of fighting for on its own merits.

In addition to practical worries, there is a second and related concern that TMGS would undermine feminist ideals by propagating a form of normative exclusion. Women who endorse traditional forms of femininity are judged by the value system within TMGS as not living lives that are valuable for women (properly conceived). Rather, their life choices and life experiences are viewed as being unworthy. This issue is a variant of the normativity argument made by Judith Butler.[40] The difference is that whereas Butler's argument is directed against feminist attempts to defend some form of gender realism, the current argument is directed against attempts to defend what might be called gender idealism: a view of what all women ought to be. The normative problem in the present case is that such a theory would delegitimize ways of being a woman that are not necessarily worthy of such condemnation. It is at least arguable that it is possible for a woman to be a committed feminist—with all the attendant normative commitments to equal status as men and a repudiation of gender injustice—yet autonomously and knowingly to choose a life that, in its outward character at least, adheres to more traditional feminine social roles. From this point of view, TMGS seems to propagate its own form of exclusion, and thereby to commit an injustice against some women. In this respect as well, then, TMGS seems to be potentially at odds with feminist ideals.

In sum, TMGS faces many strong challenges as a contender for a feminist theory of GS. While it doubtless satisfies the demands of autonomy support to a greater degree than traditional forms of female GS, aspects of TMGS undermine certain enabling conditions for robust autonomy, especially in relation to authenticity competency. Moreover, TMGS, like NGS, seems to hold practical problems for the possibility of establishing feminism as an effective and normatively inclusive social movement, and its disparagement of traditional femininity can be criticized as failing to do justice to the virtues of feminine ways of being.

REVISIONARY FEMININE GENDER SOCIALIZATION

RFGS is similar to NGS and TMGS in raising girls to be strong advocates for equality but differs from both in maintaining a clear commitment to the importance and positive value of the category *woman*. Living in accordance with a conception of womanhood can have great prudential value for women. Being a mother, for example, can be viewed as a significant source of felt satisfaction in a woman's life. In giving birth, or in breastfeeding a newborn baby, a woman takes part in an activity that binds women of all cultures and ages together; as such, it is an activity that enlarges and enriches a woman's experience of part

---

[40] Butler, *Gender Trouble*.

of what it can mean to be a woman. Moreover, as we have seen, RFGS holds that what it means to be a woman can differ depending on the social, familial, psychological, and political circumstances in which women find themselves worldwide. Although these different forms of womanhood will often share common features—such as widely shared histories, biological features, and challenges—the variability of women's experience and circumstances speaks against defending privileged conceptions of womanhood. Girls raised according to the tenets of RFGS will be taught that they are entitled to choose almost any life path they wish, as long as it does not essentially involve acceptance of a sexist axiology. And in accordance with this, they will be raised to be well equipped with skills and resources that will be of use to them in many different forms of life. In this way, RFGS is exceedingly flexible, especially in contrast to TMGS.

How does RFGS fare in relation to support for autonomy? I would argue that general indications are very positive. As we have seen, RFGS is premised on the idea that girls ought to be raised to be effective advocates for women's rights. A key part of this education is to raise girls to possess forms of self-control, logical aptitude, and reasonable skepticism toward attempts—especially by men—to impose their conceptions of what is proper. This suggests that girls raised in accordance with RFGS, like girls raised in accordance with NGS, will tend to receive an upbringing that well satisfies autonomy competency conditions. Moreover, girls raised in RFGS will be educated to take great pride in their status as women, which suggests that the condition of self-worth will be quite well satisfied.

Furthermore, RFGS has the virtue of not predetermining acceptable forms of life for women. The result of this inclusiveness is that girls raised in RFGS will experience a much wider array of live options in life from which to choose (assuming the proper supporting institutional conditions are in place, of course). As we have already seen, this is an important external enabling condition of autonomy. In accordance with this freedom, girls raised in RFGS will be open to explore different forms of authentic self-expression. In this way, a wider allowance for external options is matched by a wider allowance for internal expression of the kind that is important for authentic flourishing. This is a considerable advantage for RFGS as against TMGS especially. This flexibility also insulates RFGS from concerns stemming from the claim that biology has some influence on ways of being a woman. By remaining open to almost all possibilities, RFGS makes theoretical room for the possibility of choosing—and celebrating—ways of living that are in accordance with the influence of biology, if such influences are in play.

In general, then, RFGS seems to fare extremely well in relation to autonomy support. Girls raised in RFGS will tend to receive strong training in autonomy competency conditions, will tend to find parental support for largely unrestricted authentic introspection and the possibility of choosing from a wide variety of available life options, and will tend to develop a sense of self-worth grounded in an appreciation both of the value of their gender and their basic moral standing as persons.

RFGS has many advantages in relation to support for feminism as well. First, as mentioned already, one of the goals of RFGS is to produce committed, competent advocates for feminism (with the understanding, noted already, that this advocacy can take different forms, depending on a woman's nature and life choices). Second, RFGS maintains and celebrates the category *woman*—considerably broadened in its sense, of course—which serves the practical purpose of rallying support for feminism. RFGS favors as inclusive a home for women as possible, provided it is grounded in gender equality. As argued earlier, allowing for this has the considerable practical virtue of giving women a sense of kin and community that is seen as positive and worth fighting for.

However, unlike TMGS, RFGS will not introduce practical or normative worries associated with exclusion of conceptions of womanhood (beyond the exclusion of normative conceptions of womanhood that do not underwrite the basic commitment to women's equal worth and entitlements, of course). In its broad inclusive purview, women of many kinds and natures will be welcome. Of all of the forms of GS thus far considered, in fact, RFGS will have the broadest appeal and hence will have the potential for organizing and maintaining the widest base of support.

All of these advantages speak in favor of RFGS as a promising strategy in relation to engendering positive, broad, and sustained support for feminism.

However, the primary objection to RFGS relates precisely to its inclusiveness. It might be argued that this form of GS, in its broad acceptance of a wide variety of different valid conceptions of what it means to be a woman, lacks a unified conception of womanhood that delimits the parameters of womanhood itself. Feminism, it could be argued, has practical and theoretical need of a conception of womanhood that has a relatively clear and definable extension. Without this, the feminist cause loses its distinctiveness as a unified cause on behalf of women. From this point of view, RFGS engenders a degenerate form of feminism, one that collapses into a mealy, confused, and potentially contradictory congeries of "all of the above" that precludes coherent female self-understanding and diminishes the possibility of unified action on behalf of women.

This objection would be problematic, I believe, if RFGS had this effect. But it can be plausibly argued that it does not. RFGS has resources to provide the kind of unity to the category of womanhood that is necessary to ground a broadly encompassing understanding of what it means to be a woman and to motivate unified social action. The key here is to remember that RFGS contains and propagates the idea that women are to be understood as grouped together by general shared features, including biological similarities, a shared history of similar ways of living, and a shared experience of social oppression, largely at the hands of men. These identity conditions are specific enough to delimit the vast majority—if not all—of those who consider themselves women but, importantly, are general enough to allow for a wide variety of more specific ways one can conceive what women are or ought to be. In addition, the normative basis of RFGS serves as a unifying ground for social action: however various are the ways women live and experience the world, all women are clearly called to unite on behalf of resisting, in various ways, the social institutions that contribute to women's oppression. On the basis of these features of RFGS, then, I would suggest that the worry that RFGS is too inclusive can be met.

5. The Final Verdict

On the basis of these considerations, I conclude that RFGS stands as the most attractive option for a feminist theory of GS. RFGS fares exceedingly well both in terms of its potential for raising girls with the best chance for autonomy development and in terms of its worth as underwriting a broadly inclusive, practically effective, widely unified feminist movement. It supports a conception of what it means to be a woman that engenders solidarity while recognizing and celebrating difference and remains strong and unapologetic in its call for reform of the social institutions informed by gender conceptions.

6. Concluding Remarks

One of the most important tasks for any parent who espouses feminist ideals is the task of raising daughters. Although a proper upbringing is not perfect insurance against problems stemming from institutionalized gender inequalities, parental instruction is the beginning of a girl's experience of the world and has pride of place as the oldest root of a girl's theoretical and normative commitments. One of the most important parts of this upbringing is gender socialization itself. Improper forms of GS hold the risk, not only of damaging a girl's prospects for future autonomy but also of undermining, through the personal and social implications of its teachings about what it means to be a woman, feminist causes themselves. If we are to discharge our commitments to raising our daughters in a manner supportive both of their future autonomy and of feminism, we need a feminist theory of GS that pays due heed to both of these commitments and justifies its prescriptions in a manner that is both rationally compelling and realistic, given the state of the society as we find it.

In this chapter I have argued that both the goal of women's autonomy enhancement and the normative commitments and social goals of egalitarian liberal feminism are best satisfied by a form of GS that involves raising girls firmly in the commitment that women deserve equal treatment as men, that contains the notion that the category *woman* is to be maintained in its own right as identifying and celebrating a distinctive form of life and yet remains widely inclusive in terms of what it means to be a woman, and that locates the fundamental ground for gender equality in women's membership in a normatively significant category that is shared with men: the category of rational agents, or autonomous individuals, or simply persons. If this conclusion has merit, the remaining task assumes all the more importance: to apply theory to life, and raise our daughters conscientiously according to the theory's prescriptions, secure in the conviction that they deserve our best efforts to prepare them to advocate for a cause whose nobility and urgency cannot be reasonably doubted.

Acknowledgments

I would like to thank Andrea Veltman and all of the participants in the McGill University workshop Relational Autonomy: Ten Years On for their extremely helpful comments and feedback on this chapter. I would also like to thank my wife, Pia Antolic-Piper, for discussing these ideas with me, for giving birth to our daughter, and for being an amazingly devoted and inspiring mother.

{ 13 }

Autonomy and Oppression at Work
Andrea Veltman

A central aspect of autonomy, highlighted not only by feminist accounts of relational autonomy but also by other accounts of personal autonomy, is the exercise of reflective and agential capacities that develop in social and interpersonal contexts. Whereas theorists of relational autonomy often emphasize that capacities necessary for autonomy develop on account of our relationality, including our initial dependency on parents or other caregivers, theorists of autonomy rarely explore work as a social context that can support or stifle the development and exercise of autonomous capacities. In this paper I turn attention to the impact of work on autonomy and on related goods of self-respect and self-worth, which are required for full personal autonomy on some accounts. Drawing on empirical and philosophical literatures on work and well-being, I first draw together a case that eudemonistically meaningless work undermines autonomy and self-respect. By eudemonistically meaningless work, I mean work that does not develop or exercise human capabilities, permit independent judgment, integrate conception and execution, or otherwise facilitate expressions of agency.[1] These forms of work are not necessarily meaningless altogether, but working extensively at eudemonistically

---

[1] Some of the literature on meaningful work focuses on eudemonistic dimensions of meaningful work, that is, on the potential of work to contribute to human flourishing by developing or exercising capabilities or skills, by fostering independent judgment in performance of tasks, or by integrating conception and execution for a feeling of personal satisfaction at work. See, e.g., James Bernard Murphy, *The Moral Economy of Labor: Aristotelian Themes in Economic Theory* (New Haven, CT: Yale University Press, 1993); Adrian Walsh, "Meaningful Work as a Distributive Good," *Southern Journal of Philosophy* 32 (1994): 233–250. In a monograph I am now working on, provisionally titled *Meaningful Work*, I argue that meaningful work has several dimensions, and eudemonistic dimensions of meaningful work are integral but not exhaustive in an account of what makes work meaningful. In addition to being eudemonistically meaningful, work can be meaningful in serving a purpose, creating something of enduring value, reflecting personal life goals or values, or integrating otherwise disparate elements of a worker's life. Developing or exercising human capabilities in eudemonistically meaningful work exhibits agency, but as I understand it agency extends beyond developing or exercising human capabilities to encompass, for instance, expressions of values, principled commitments, character, personality, creativity, or individuality; agency at work stands in contrast with observation, passivity, merely following orders, or feeling like a cog.

meaningless work stifles the flourishing of a worker and, in particular, diminishes her drive toward self-determination and her sense of self-worth.[2]

I submit that eudemonistically meaningless work should be counted among other autonomy subverting social influences, which on feminist accounts range broadly from internalized oppressive norms to entanglements in abusive personal relationships to practices of childrearing that thwart development of autonomous skills. Although eudemonistically meaningless work is not alone in subverting personal autonomy, it merits particular attention in light of the impact that work has on a person, even outside the workplace. Work molds a person and stands to impart a cluster of moral and personal goods and virtues that are integral in a good life, including self-respect, honor, dignity, pride and intellectual development; work is also a primary avenue through which people achieve recognition for the exercise of skills, make contributions in communities, and achieve a sense of purpose and personal identity, among other goods.[3] With respect to autonomy and freedom, not only does an erosion of autonomous agency in work stand to damage skills and proclivities needed for full personal autonomy, as I focus on here, but escaping meaningless work also bears an intuitive association with achieving freedom. As E. F. Schumacher observes in *Good Work* of wanting to avoid the rat race, to not be enslaved by machines and bureaucracies, to avoid becoming a moron, a robot, a commuter or a fragment of a person, to do one's own thing, to deal with people, to respect that people, nature and beauty and wholeness matter and to care about what matters—these strivings are simultaneously a longing for freedom and a longing for an escape from work without meaning.[4]

Work also merits attention from feminist philosophers for whom oppression is a quintessential topic of interest and for whom an ideal of autonomy can serve as "a normative standpoint for critically assessing oppressive social conditions that suppress or prevent the emergence of autonomy."[5] Appreciating the ways women often lack autonomy in relation to work illuminates key elements

---

[2] In *Meaningful Work*, I am broadly interested in work in its relation to human flourishing, which requires the realization of human capabilities and the possession of a plurality of goods. My focus here is work in relation to autonomous agency, which I understand to be a component of human flourishing. For a good discussion of the components of human flourishing, see Douglas Rasmussen, "Human Flourishing and Human Nature," in *Human Flourishing*, edited by Ellen Frankel Paul, Fred D. Miller, Jr., and Jeffrey Paul (Cambridge: Cambridge University Press, 1999), especially 1–21.

[3] For a fuller list of goods that attach to work, see Andrea Veltman, "Is Meaningful Work Available to All People?" in *Philosophy and Social Criticism*, forthcoming. Consider also what one occupational psychiatrist writes: "It is possible that no single activity defines adulthood more specifically than work. To a large extent work influences how and where an individual lives, it affects social contacts and family activities, and it provides a title, role, and environment that shape and reinforce an individual's identity." Nick Kates, Barrie Greiff, M.D., and Duane Hagen, M.D., *The Psychosocial Impact of Job Loss* (Washington, DC: American Psychiatric Press, 1990), 185. See also the work of Al Gini, such as A. Gini and T. Sullivan, "Work: The Process and the Person," *Journal of Business Ethics* 6 (1987): 649–655.

[4] E. F. Schumacher, *Good Work* (New York: Harper and Row, 1979), 50.

[5] Marilyn Friedman, *Autonomy, Gender, Politics* (New York: Oxford University Press, 2003), 19.

of the oppression of women, particularly given the preponderance of time that oppressed women spend at work. A woman whose days (and nights—often enough) are spent slaving in a factory assembly line, a sweatshop, or a Foxconn plant may suffer several faces of oppression, but her oppression as a worker is paramount in her life and transcends mere exploitation as an underpaid employee. Her work may be oppressive first in respects of being heteronomous: she may enter work under conditions of constraint; her work may bear no part of reflectively held life goals; and she may not even have the freedom of bodily movement at work.[6] Her work may also fail to permit a meaningful measure of economic independence or to help her support herself or her family, which she identifies as the very purpose of her working. And her work may undermine her autonomy furthermore in the respect that her employer requires that she only mechanically follow goals set by others, in the precise manner in which others determine—a lack of autonomy in work that yet further erodes her well-being.

A central issue for those who value autonomy is that aspects of autonomous agency remain a privilege for those fortunate to work in enlightened workplaces that value employee decision making and promote the development of employee skills. Many current workplace management structures treat adult workers as though they lack competency to exercise intelligence, skill, and autonomous capacities, thus relieving employees of the need to make decisions, design goals, or determine methods by which to accomplish goals at work. Such ugly skepticism about the abilities of working people is a hallmark of the fairly influential principles of scientific management forwarded by Fredrick Taylor,[7] which stand in a basic tension with modes of working life that support autonomous development and self-realization. The Tayloristic assumption that employees enter workplaces with settled levels of intelligence and ability also merits rejection in light of more recent empirical literatures on work and well-being, which I discuss further herein and which indicate that work itself affects the development of a range of capabilities, including capabilities for self-direction, which can be nurtured or stifled by working conditions.

---

[6] Consider, e.g., what Ruth Cavendish, *Women on the Line* (London: Routledge & Keegan Paul, 1982), writes about her experience working in a car parts factory in England: on the assembly line "we couldn't do the things you would normally not think twice about, like blowing your nose or flicking hair out of your eyes; that cost valuable seconds—it wasn't included in the layout so no time was allowed for it. In any case, your hands were usually full" (41). "The women ran the line, but we were also just appendages to it. The discipline was imposed automatically.... We just slotted in, like cogs in a wheel. Every movement we made and every second of our time was controlled by the line..." (107).

[7] Taylorism is the idea that workplace managers increase efficiency, productivity, predictability, worker accountability, and control over working processes by extracting knowledge and skills from workers, subsequently reducing worker skill and knowledge to simple and discrete formulate so that production can be performed by "men who are of smaller caliber and attainments and who are therefore cheaper than those required under the old system." F. W. Taylor, *Shop Management* (New York: Harper & Brothers Publishers, 1912), 105.

In essence, a commitment on the part of a community to promoting human flourishing and autonomous agency entails a commitment to respecting the agency and dignity of people at work and a commitment to organizing work so that people can exercise agency and skills in occupational life. This goal does not necessarily entail Marxism, but it does entail opposing Taylorism and oppressive forms of work in which employers take dim views of the decision-making abilities of workers, in which workers consequently have scant opportunities to exercise thought, skill or judgment on the job, in which workers become effectively reduced from human agents into tools or appendages of machines, or in which workers are treated as cheap, expendable, interchangeable resources. Structuring working life around a goal of developing and exercising human capabilities harmonizes with a number of basic ethical principles and traditions, including eudemonistic ethical traditions originating with Aristotle and continuing with John Stuart Mill, which emphasize developing human capabilities as part of achieving happiness or flourishing. Outside of eudemonistic traditions, the Dalai Lama, for instance, expresses a principle of prioritizing people over profit with his typical simplistic elegance, writing that in modern life "human beings act like machines whose function is to make money. This is absolutely wrong. The purpose of making money is the happiness of humankind, not the other way round. Humans are not for money, money is for humans."[8]

In looking here at autonomy and work, I connect the development and exercise of human capabilities in work not only with eudemonistic ethics but also with the principle of humanity formulation of Kant's categorical imperative, which, as some scholars emphasize, requires treating the humanity in a person as an end and never as a mere means.[9] The imperative of never using humanity as a mere means is typically taken to mean that we should never violate the autonomy of rational human beings. But, as Thomas Hill observes, the imperative to treat humanity *in* a person as an end is more than a quaint way of saying that we must respect people or respect the ability of people to make their own choices concerning their lives.[10] Rather, in referencing the humanity in a person, the imperative means that we must treat the rational

---

[8] His Holiness the Dalai Lama, *How to Practice the Way to a Meaningful Life*, translated and edited by Jeffrey Hopkins (New York: Atria Books, 2002), 35. From the Catholic tradition, Pope Leo XIII gives a similar thought in writing that "it is shameful and inhuman, however, to use men as things for gain and to put no more value on them than what they are worth in muscle and energy." John Budd, *The Thought of Work* (Ithaca, NY: Cornell University Press, 2011), 59.

[9] Thomas Hill, *Dignity and Practical Reason in Kant's Moral Theory* (Ithaca, NY: Cornell University Press, 1992), 38–46.

[10] As Hill, *Dignity and Practical Reason*, 39, writes, "A review of Kant's repeated use of 'humanity in a person' in *The Metaphysics of Morals* and elsewhere strongly suggests that, contrary to the usual reading, Kant thought of humanity as a characteristic, or set of characteristics, of persons.... Humanity is contrasted with our animality; and it is said to be something entrusted to us for preservation.... Its distinguishing feature is said to be 'the power to set ends.'"

and autonomous *capabilities* of persons as ends. As Kant himself writes in *Groundwork for a Metaphysics of Morals*, "There are in humanity [Menschheit] capacities for greater perfection which form part of nature's purpose for humanity in our person." Failing to develop these capacities is not compatible with treating humanity as an end in itself; thus, there is a duty to develop one's talents.[11]

In the context of working life, this interpretation of the categorical imperative is nothing short of revolutionary, for it entails not merely that we have a duty to respect an individual's choice of employment but also that the development of human capabilities should be a goal of the provision of work. That is, if work were structured to treat the humanity in a person as an end and never as a mere means, then it would not be morally permissible to treat people as objects, machines, or appendages of machines, and diminishing the rational, autonomous and agential capabilities of a person for the sake of profit, productivity or efficiency would also run outside the bounds of the ethical. On the account I forward here, it is fundamentally a matter of ethics, and in particular a matter of respecting people as autonomous beings, to treat workers with dignity and to promote modes of working life that provide opportunities for people to flourish, develop agential capacities, and reinforce self-respect. I begin with some key distinctions concerning autonomy and work, pulling together a case that laboring extensively at eudemonistically meaningless work undermines workers' autonomous abilities and self-respect.

1. Work, Autonomy, and Self-respect

In considering elements of autonomy in relation to work, let us make a basic distinction at the start among autonomously chosen work, achieving autonomy as economic independence through work, and exercising autonomous agency in work. In the literature on work, some thinkers focus on the first concept, characterizing autonomous work as work that is freely entered into, or as work that is chosen because its end product constitutes a major life goal.[12] On this view, if someone reflectively determines that her personal well-being includes educating the young, creating art, or promoting health in her community, then choosing to teach, paint, or provide health care constitutes autonomous work. By contrast, heteronomous work has been characterized as work whose end

---

[11] Kant, *Groundwork of the Metaphysics of Morals*, translated by H. J. Paton (New York: Harper & Row, 1964), 97–98; 97– Hill, *Dignity and Practical Reason*, 40.

[12] John White, *Education and the End of Work: A New Philosophy of Work and Learning* (London: Cassell 1997), 48, defines autonomous work as "a form of activity whose end-product is chosen as a major goal of an autonomous agent"; cf. 5–10. A condensed version of the argument of this book appears in White, "Education, Work and Well-being," *Journal of Philosophy of Education* 31:2 (1997): 233–247.

product has not been chosen as a major goal; heteronomous work is work that one is constrained to perform for any number of reasons that do not stem from one's own personal goals, such as needing money for other life goals, satisfying others' expectations, or even following God's directive.[13] As John White observes, most work done in the world is heteronomous. People work because they must, and what most people do at work does not meet reflectively held personal life goals. In Section 2, I return to the concept of autonomously chosen work in addressing the notion—which I find dubious—that an autonomous choice to enter an agency-depriving occupation lends moral credence to the working arrangement.

Particularly for those whose work lacks internal rewards or whose work in itself is not a personal life goal, the hope of earning a livelihood or providing for a family provides purpose to work and a point to what one endures on the job. Although earning an income does not itself entail full economic independence, an income and associated benefits can provide a measure of independence and a source of pride, self-respect, and dignity. These virtues issue from work both in the respect that work represents a social contribution and in the respect that work enables a person to avoid relying on others, which places her under the will of others whose goodwill could potentially cease at any time. Among others, Paul Gomberg notes that lacking recognition as an economic contributor undermines personal dignity and self-esteem and that in the United States this moral and psychological pain has not been distributed equally across races: "In the United States for the past 50 years, black people have suffered twice the rate of unemployment as whites. The scars of this assault on people's dignity are deep in many neighborhoods."[14]

The concept of autonomy as economic independence is entangled with notions of autonomy no longer fashionable, as feminist philosophers have duly critiqued conceptions of autonomy as independence as drawn from male biographies and bound up with socially atomistic conceptions of human beings. Some also observe that an ideal of autonomy as economic self-reliance is manipulated in political rhetoric and used to justify denying welfare assistance to poor women, whose need to raise young children renders ideals of independence and self-sufficiency unattainable. Lorraine Code writes that "in the politics and rhetorics of social welfare...an assumed equality of access to social goods, that requires no advocacy, underwrites the belief that failure to achieve autonomy is a social sin…. Reliance on social services slides rhetorically into a weakness, a dependence on social advocacy that, paradoxically, invites—and receives—judgments of moral turpitude."[15] Insofar as a regulative

---

[13] White, "Education, Work and Well-being," 234.

[14] Paul Gomberg, *How to Make Opportunity Equal: Race and Contributive Justice* (Malden, MA: Blackwell, 2007), 70.

[15] Lorraine Code, "The Perversion of Autonomy and the Subjection of Women: Discourses of Social Advocacy at Century's End," in *Relational Autonomy: Feminist Perspectives on Autonomy, Agency*

ideal of autonomy as economic independence or self-sufficiency expresses a political ideology that is simultaneously oppressive and unattainable, the feminist thinker may be inclined to simply shelve the notion in a dustbin of dated ideas or to work to supplant the concept of self-sufficiency with one of supportive interdependence.

I will not spend much time here on the concept of autonomy as economic independence, but I would pause to note, first, that we should observe a distinction between personal autonomy and economic autonomy:[16] some feminist philosophers see economic autonomy as a dimension of personal autonomy that women have good reason to seek,[17] although others lay emphasis on morally problematic implications of a social ethos of financial independence.[18] I would also emphasize that in the present time, in which Wal-Mart, the most powerful corporation on the planet has been likened to a profiteering monster, it is not irrelevant to the oppression of workers that they toil at jobs that do not enable financial independence. At the same time that a purpose of work—deeply felt as such among many everyday people—is to achieve a measure of financial independence to support oneself and one's family, one of the major scandals of our time is that many employees of profitable corporations cannot manage a living above poverty lines. Some Wal-Mart employees require public assistance to survive,[19] and women work full-time in garment factories, assembly lines, call centers, and fast food operations and other restaurants, among other places, yet still cannot adequately feed their children because of low wages and diminishing benefits that exploit workers as human resources

---

and the Social Self, edited by Catriona Mackenzie and Natalie Stoljar (New York: Oxford University Press, 2000), 194.

[16] Diana Meyers, *Self, Society and Personal Choice* (New York: Columbia University Press, 1989), 12, distinguishes personal autonomy from economic autonomy, where the latter represents an ideal of financial self-sufficiency that people seek to prevent "the possibility that others might gain power over them through their needs. If one can take care of oneself, one is beholden to no one—neither to the state nor to any other individual. Thus, one is at liberty to live as one chooses." Friedman, *Autonomy, Gender, Politics*, 47–49, also writes that, although there is a "superficial resemblance" between philosophical conceptions of personal autonomy and conceptions of independence and self-sufficiency in popular understanding, personal autonomy and financial independence are distinct notions. On her account, financial independence is related to personal autonomy as a condition that can promote the realization of autonomy, but "financial independence is no constitutive part of autonomy," nor is it causally sufficient for it.

[17] Marina Oshana, *Personal Autonomy in Society* (Aldershot, UK: Ashgate, 2006), 87, identifies financial self-sufficiency as one of several social-relational properties of autonomy, arguing that a level of economic autonomy that enables a person to be independent of others is a requirement of personal autonomy. Simone de Beauvoir similarly acknowledges economic independence as a component of women's liberation.

[18] See Eva Feder Kittay and Ellen K. Feder (eds.), *The Subject of Care: Feminist Perspectives on Dependency* (Lanham, MD: Rowman and Littlefield, 2002), particularly Iris Marion Young, "Autonomy, Welfare Reform and Meaningful Work," 40–60.

[19] As given in social commentary such as Robert Greenwald (dir. and prod.), *Wal-Mart: The High Cost of Low Price* (Brave New Films, 2005).

in the most degrading sense of the term; that is, workers become tools of profit for others.[20] So it is not the case that a social sin of failing to achieve self-reliant independence falls on women or men who fail to work enough but rather that a social sin falls on corporations that net enormous profits and that can afford to pay adequate wages and benefits but instead place profit ahead of people. Finally, if the notion of autonomy as economic independence remains dated and problematic, it also remains perversely relevant in illuminating an appreciable dimension of oppression in relation to work—one distinct from autonomous work as freely chosen and from autonomous agency in work itself.

For a picture of work that permits neither economic autonomy nor autonomous agency in work, the reader may consider the work portrayed in *Fast Food Women*, in which filmmaker Anne Lewis records women employees whose nearly every move behind the counter and in the kitchen is predetermined by management, including the number of times a skillet is shook and the number of times pieces of chicken are rolled in batter. At KFC, the function of the female employee is to count to seven as she shakes a skillet and to count to ten as she rolls chicken in batter, on the assumption that it is best for quality control, and ultimately for company profit, that fast food women be relieved of the need to think or make judgments about cooking.[21] Managers of a Druthers restaurant in Whitesburg, Kentucky, comment in the film that the work is not the sort that a married man would seek out, in part because it does not pay a living wage and carries no benefits. Rather, the work is suitable for a woman who will derive a sense of accomplishment from completing a job while following orders and whose father or husband perhaps has good pay and benefits through his coal-mining occupation or other work.[22]

---

[20] Consider here the work of journalists such as Barbara Ehrenreich, *Nickel and Dimed: On (Not) Getting By in America* (New York: Henry Holt and Company, 2001).

[21] When interviewed in Anne Lewis, *Fast Food Women* (Appalshop Film, 1991), Barbara Garson contrasts the skill and flair exhibited in the work of a short order cook in a local diner of the 1950s with the Tayloristic principles of the late twentieth-century fast food industry—which essentially extract skills and knowledge from an original cohort of workers and transfers them into machines, systems, programs, and sets of rules for new employees, so that workers who are cheaper and more expendable need only follow beeps and buzzers, pull knobs, and turn cranks or perform other insignificant and mechanical movements of limbs. The short-order cook might whistle at work or swear at work but in any case exhibited a personality while at work; even if his or her work were largely routine, its details and execution were not predetermined and regimented by management. Similarly, in giving a portrait of his mother as a waitress, Mike Rose, *The Mind at Work: Valuing the Intelligence of the American Worker* (New York: Penguin Books, 2004), chap. 1, suggests that waitressing permits skill, flair, and judgment, as waitresses develop and rely on complex memory and navigation skills and create order amid lunchtime chaos. But in the chain restaurant of the twenty-first century, even flare itself can become regimented when the dialogue and attitudes used for taking customer orders becomes scripted and when waiters and waitresses are asked by management to select a dozen pins and buttons to wear at work to exhibit "flair."

[22] Lewis, *Fast Food Women*.

AUTONOMOUS AGENCY IN WORK

Work can also support or stifle autonomous agency in the respect that work itself permits opportunities for conceiving and carrying out projects, making decisions, exercising judgment, taking responsibility for decisions, forming goals, planning methods by which to accomplish goals, adjusting goals and methods in light of experience, and other aspects of autonomous agency. This aspect of autonomous agency in work is crucial to consider for a few reasons. First, empirical literatures on work and well-being indicate that the intrinsic features of work (i.e., what happens in work itself) have a more profound effect on worker well-being than the extrinsic features of work, such as wages, job security, and equality of opportunity for positions.[23] Opportunities within work to exercise abilities, learn new skills, take initiative, and make independent judgments have more influence on mental health and happiness than extrinsic aspects of work for the reason that, as James Bernard Murphy summarizes, "personal happiness and well-being are produced more by what people do than by what they possess: above a certain minimum income, differences in the enjoyment of work are more important than differences in income for overall happiness."[24] In examining the impact of full-time unskilled, routine occupations on mental health, Arthur Kornhauser writes in a classic study that "conditions of work and accompanying modes of life at lower skill levels do, in fact, impose more severe deprivations, frustrations and feelings of hopelessness.... Workers in better positions experience a greater degree of fulfillment of their wants and enjoy correspondingly greater feelings of satisfaction, adequacy, and self-regard."[25]

Second, as indicated in empirical and philosophical literatures on the impact of work on the person, a lack of opportunities for autonomous agency within work undermines the personal autonomy of workers *even off the job*. In a study identified as marking the beginning of the contemporary study of industrial-organizational psychology,[26] Kornhauser examines mental health among workers in the Detroit automobile industry, finding that

---

[23] Murphy, *Moral Economy of Labor*, 2.

[24] Murphy, *Moral Economy of Labor*, 4. According to recent empirical studies on income and happiness, in the contemporary United States $75,000 is the level of income above which increases in income cease to correlate with increased experiences of happiness. Below $75,000 (which is still quite high relative to what many workers earn), "a lack of money brings both emotional misery and low life evaluation," according to Princeton University professors Angus Deaton and Daniel Kahneman. See D. Kahneman and A. Deaton, "High Income Improves Evaluation of Life but not Well-Being," *Proceedings of the National Academy of Sciences of the United States of America* 107:39: 16489–16493.

[25] Arthur Kornhauser, *Mental Health of the Industrial Worker: A Detroit Study* (New York: John Wiley & Sons, 1965) 269.

[26] As characterized by M. J. Zickar, "Remembering Arthur Kornhauser: Industrial Psychology's Advocate for Worker Well-Being," *Journal of Applied Psychology* 88:2: 363–369; M. Tausig and R. Fenwick, *Mental Health in Social Context* (New York: Springer, 2011), 3.

individuals working extensively at routine production jobs tend to have poor mental health and, in particular, diminished drives toward accomplishing self-determined life goals. Kornhauser finds that this diminishing of personal autonomy occurs with respect not only to personal work or career goals but also to nonworking life:

> The general level of purposive striving and active orientation to life is relatively low among factory men and lower in the routine production groups than among those doing more skilled and varied work.... Factory employment, especially in routine production tasks, does give evidence of extinguishing workers' ambition, initiative, and purposeful direction toward life goals.
>
> Our own results present repeated illustrations; the unsatisfactory mental health of working people consists in no small measure of their dwarfed desires and deadened initiative, reduction of their goals and restriction of their efforts to a point where life is relatively empty and only half meaningful.[27]

In contrast with those whose jobs require skill and involve a variety of tasks and responsibilities—who have the highest mental health scores—factory workers whose jobs are automated, regimented, and repetitive tend to experience a debilitating grind, lower self-esteem and weakened personal ambition and initiative, among other mental health problems.[28] Insofar as extensive employment in routine unskilled work undermines purposeful direction toward life goals, not to mention deadening initiative and dwarfing desires, such work undermines an important aspect of autonomous agency. As Marina Oshana characterizes a basic intuition about autonomous personhood, "the autonomous person formulates certain goals as relevant to the direction of her life, and is able to pursue these goals and make them effective in action."[29] Kornhauser notes that it is not only factory workers who suffer from diminished drives to accomplish personal goals, as many types of jobs can damage workers psychologically and as mental health has many roots, ranging from personal background and upbringing to present life circumstances. But the evidence of his study shows genuine effects of job conditions on mental health, particularly with respect to opportunities to for workers to exercise skill and abilities on the job.[30]

---

[27] Kornhauser, *Mental Health of the Industrial Worker*, 252, 269–270.

[28] Kornhauser, *Mental Health of the Industrial Worker*, 266–268.

[29] Marina Oshana, "Personal Autonomy in Society," *Journal of Social Philosophy* 29:1 (Spring 1998): 82.

[30] As Kornhauser, *Mental Health of the Industrial Worker*, writes, "Many interrelated characteristics of jobs contribute jointly to the comparatively high or low average mental health of occupational groups.... By far the most influential attribute is the opportunity the work offers—or fails to offer—for use of the worker's abilities and for associated feelings of interest, sense of accomplishment, personal growth and self-respect" (263).

Additionally, in longitudinal studies of workers in a variety of occupations conducted over ten years, Melvin Kohn and Carmi Schooler show that dimensions of work not only reflect but also affect the personalities and intellectual abilities of workers, effectively overturning assumptions that personalities and abilities of workers emerge in final form before careers begin or that workers remain psychologically unaffected by what happens at work.[31] According to Kohn and Schooler, a reciprocal relationship between work and personality pertains both to levels of intelligence and to aspects of autonomous agency, including initiative and self-direction:

> In industrial society, where occupation is central to men's lives, occupational experiences that facilitate or deter the exercise of self-direction come to permeate men's views, not only of work and of their role in work, but also of the world and of self.... The conditions of occupational life at lower social-stratification levels...foster a narrowly circumscribed conception of self and society, and promote the valuation of conformity to authority. Conditions of work that foster thought and initiative tend to enlarge men's conceptions of reality; conditions of constraint tend to narrow them.[32]

In brief, complex work that permits self-direction fosters intellectual flexibility and autonomous self-conceptions among workers, whereas work that is routine, that is closely supervised, and that does not permit exercise of skill, intelligence, or self-direction encourages both conformity to authority and narrow conceptions of self among workers. Forms of work at lower social stratification levels often preclude autonomy in work in the respect that workers pursue goals determined by others, in ways that others deem appropriate, where often, as Adina Schwartz adds, "even the order in which [workers] perform operations, the pace at which they work, and the particular bodily movements they employ are largely determined by others' decisions."[33]

---

[31] Melvin Kohn and Carmi Schooler, *Work and Personality* (Norwood, NJ: Ablex Publishing, 1983), esp. 103.

[32] Kohn and Schooler, *Work and Personality*, 33. Rather than using the term *autonomous agency*, Kohn and Schooler use the concept of *self-direction*, looking at occupational self-direction in relation to several facets of workers' personalities and social positions. Although the central concepts and topics of Kohn and Schooler's work do not fit squarely into the philosophical literature on autonomy, I believe there is enough conceptual overlap that the work of Kohn and Schooler bears relevance to certain questions that concern philosophers of autonomy.

[33] Adina Schwartz, "Meaningful Work," *Ethics* 92 (1982): 634. I am indebted to Schwartz particularly for her work in drawing together a case that work bears a formative influence on the worker. As I discuss at length in my book on meaningful work, however, I disagree with Schwartz on the role that the state should play in creating opportunities for meaningful work. Schwartz argues that we should ask for government measures to effect rearrangements in industrial employment and to enforce a moral imperative that no one should be employed in purely routine occupations that stunt autonomous development. See, e.g., Schwartz, "Meaningful Work, 645. In contrast, I argue that the formative thesis need not entail that we call upon the state to minimize meaningless work or promote meaningful work, and I examine other ways social institutions can promote meaningful work.

WORK AND SELF-RESPECT

But why might a lack of autonomy in work foster a lack of autonomy in the worker herself? Some philosophers writing on work appeal here to connections among work, identity, and self-respect. For instance, in arguing that liberal political philosophers and recognition theorists owe greater attention to work, Beate Roessler highlights that work bears upon practical identity: work "has an influence on how we live, on who we are, and how we see ourselves."[34] Work affects our relations with others and with ourselves, and in light of the impact of work on identity it can hardly be pretended that "we can switch easily between different roles and forget... the sort of work we have been doing for hours. In a social context in which work dominates people's lives and plays a central role in identity formation, it is implausible to think that alienated work would have no impact on a person's self-conception and her relations with others in other spheres of life, and that she could simply choose, without cost, to undertake alienated work in order to autonomously pursue other interests."[35]

Some also argue that a lack of autonomy in work can undermine personal autonomy by undermining the self-respect or self-worth of employees. When workplaces preempt employee decision making, script employee attitudes, determine the precise ordering and pace of workplace operations, monitor employee activities, and subject employees to "close, intrusive supervision and constant correction (or the threat of it)," Richard Lippke writes, workplaces become inimical to "individuals developing and maintaining a sense of themselves as worthy of autonomy."[36] By contrast, workplace practices that convey trust for employees and that give employees latitude to make decisions—which entails giving employees a chance to make mistakes or do wrong—convey that employees are worthy of autonomy. And "encouraging an individual to believe he is *worthy* of autonomy may be, in the end, the most effective way of protecting his autonomy."[37]

Along similar lines, John Rawls notes that meaningful work provides a key source of self-respect, writing more than once in his later works that "the lack of... the opportunity for meaningful work and occupation is destructive... of citizens' self-respect" and suggesting for this reason that society serve as an employer of last resort.[38] Self-respect derives partly from the esteem of others

---

[34] Beate Roessler, "Meaningful Work: Arguments from Autonomy," *Journal of Political Philosophy* 20:1 (2012): 82.
[35] Roessler, "Meaningful Work," 83.
[36] Richard Lippke, "Work, Privacy and Autonomy," *Public Affairs Quarterly* 3:2 (April 1989): 44.
[37] Lippke, "Work, Privacy and Autonomy," 43.
[38] John Rawls, *Political Liberalism*, paperback edition (New York: Columbia University Press, 1996), lix. Rawls repeats the idea in *Law of the Peoples* (Cambridge, MA: Harvard University Press, 1999), 50. See also Rawls, *A Theory of Justice* (Cambridge, MA: Harvard University Press, 1971), 440ff. On the importance of self-respect and self-worth for autonomy, see, e.g., Paul Benson, "Free Agency and

and, in particular, from the judgments of our associates concerning the worth of our activities: "unless our endeavors are appreciated by our associates it is impossible for us to maintain the conviction that they are worthwhile."[39] Although in *A Theory of Justice* Rawls suggests that nonworking social life can provide social esteem for worthy endeavors, in turn providing a social basis of self-respect,[40] he shifts in *The Law of the Peoples* and in the introduction to the paperback edition of *Political Liberalism* to suggest that, in particular, opportunities for meaningful work are needed to provide a social basis for citizens' self-respect. As Jeffrey Moriarty interprets this shift, Rawls comes to reject an assumption at play in *A Theory of Justice* that meaningful work provides but one avenue for a social basis of self-respect, which presumably could be achieved in leisure activities for those whose work fails to provide a sense of self-worth; at the time of his later works Rawls instead believes that "we cannot merely hope that if people cannot find meaningful work, they can get self-respect from other activities, such as chess or softball."[41]

To be sure, work is not the only avenue by which a person can achieve self-respect, enjoy the exercise of realized capacities, or experience autonomous self-expression. It is possible that some people may acquire these basic goods in leisure activities, although the empirical literature indicates that such a possibility is slim: people tend to "apply the habit developed at work to their leisure: mindless work leads to mindless leisure whereas challenging work leads to challenging leisure."[42] But in any case a mere possibility that a person can live a richly autonomous life without eudemonistically meaningful work is hardly sufficient ground for an argument concerning questions of work and social justice, which beckon us to consider what social structures are likely to produce or encourage in human persons. The possibility—advanced by White—that rich self-centered fainéants can live autonomously and find personal fulfillment in a round of leisure activities avails very little in my mind.[43]

Self-Worth," *Journal of Philosophy* 91 (1994): 650–668; Joel Anderson and Axel Honneth, "Autonomy, Vulnerability, Recognition and Justice," in *Autonomy and the Challenges to Liberalism: New Essays*, edited by John Christman and Joel Anderson (New York: Cambridge University Press, 2005).

[39] Rawls, *Theory of Justice*, 440, cf. 544.

[40] Rawls, *Theory of Justice*, 442.

[41] Moriarty, "Rawls, Self-Respect, and the Opportunity for Meaningful Work," *Social Theory and Practice* 35:3 (July 2009): 450.

[42] Murphy, *Moral Economy of Labor*, 4. Likewise, Kornhauser, *Mental Health of the Industrial Autoworker*, 267, notes that the leisure activities of factory workers in routine jobs tend to be narrow and routine, with little indication of self-development and self-expression or devotion to larger social purposes: "many appear to be groping for meaningful ways to fill their spare time but with little conception of the possibilities and with inadequate preparation or stimulation."

[43] White, "Education, Work and Well-being," 241. On the whole, White advances an argument against writers like myself that autonomously chosen work is not a central element of the good life; he believes the possibility of living well without autonomous work should be reflected in social policy, which should "encourage a wide variety of ways of life in which autonomous work might—or might not—find a place" (241).

A life lived meaningfully in relation to others involves work, whether within or outside the home, and for most of us it is work that absorbs a predominance of productive energies and permits key opportunities for others' recognition and esteem, without which self-respect is liable to collapse.[44] For the reason that, as Rawls suggests, work provides an important source of social esteem that serves as a social basis of self-respect, those who perform work that does not merit esteem— such as work that is viewed as dirty, disgusting, or degraded—can in turn develop a sense of themselves as degraded and lowly people. Michael Walzer writes in conveying the work of sociologist Stewart E. Perry, "When a garbage-man feels stigmatized by the work he does...the stigma shows in his eyes. He enters 'into collusion with us to avoid contaminating us with his lowly self.' He looks away; and we do too. 'Our eyes do not meet. He becomes a non-person.'"[45]

2. The Dehumanization of Eudemonistically Meaningless Work

A lack of autonomous agency in work undermines the flourishing of a worker in yet another crucial respect, namely, that work is often experienced as dehumanizing when it fails to permit development or exercise of autonomous capabilities or skills, or expression of individual agency or identities. This experience occurs particularly—but not exclusively—in forms of automated, mechanized, or regimented work, which depletes the humanity of a person by making the person feel like an automated thing. At issue here is the Tayloristic outsourcing of thinking and skill that a person would otherwise put into working, thereby determining that workers will not act like thinking, skill-exercising human beings while on the job and thereby that workers are not valued as special and irreplaceable people but rather that people can be treated as interchangeable cheap human resources.[46]

---

[44] An integral connection between work and self-respect is argued for in a number of empirical and philosophical literatures. Moriarty, "Rawls, Self-Respect, and the Opportunity for Meaningful Work," 457n30, compiles a helpful list of literatures.

[45] Michael Walzer, *Spheres of Justice: A Defense of Pluralism and Equality* (New York: Basil Blackwell, 1983), 165. Walzer is here giving a point made by Stewart E. Perry, *San Francisco Scavengers: Dirty Work and the Pride of Ownership* (Berkeley: University of California Press, 1978), 7.

[46] For but one example, consider the words of a former McDonald's griddle man interviewed in Barbara Garson, *The Electronic Sweatshop* (New York: Simon and Schuster, 1988), 17, 20: "'They called us the Green Machine,' says Jason Pratt, recently retired McDonalds' griddle man, "'cause the crew had green uniforms then. And that's what it is, a machine. You don't have to know how to cook, you don't have to know how to think. There's a procedure for everything and you just follow the procedures.... You follow the beepers, you follow the buzzers and you turn your meat as fast as you can. It's like I told you, to work at McDonald's you don't need a face, you don't need a brain. You need to have two hands and two legs and move 'em as fast as you can. That's the whole system. I wouldn't go back there again for anything.'" For a classic critique of dehumanizing aspects of automated and unskilled work in the twentieth century, see Harry Braverman, *Labor and Monopoly Capital*, 25th anniv. ed. (New York: Monthly Review Press, 1998).

Some readers will see this point as Marxist since Marx critiques industrial forms of work as mutilating human persons into fragments and calls on the potential of work to offer a person an objectification of his individual humanness in the world. But the previous point would be better catalogued as a Kantian critique of Taylorism, and it is important to observe that the basic idea that work bereft of individual agency dehumanizes the person derives from a variety of intellectual traditions,[47] and one does not need to be schooled in Marxism to appreciate it. When Studs Terkel interviewed workers for his tome *Working*, he compiled a collection of experiences of dehumanization in jobs that diminish or restrict the potential of workers to conceive, plan, imagine, solve problems, or otherwise think creatively or constructively or move about freely at work:

> "I'm a machine," says the spot-welder. "I'm caged," says the bank teller, and echoes the hotel clerk. "I'm a mule," says the steelworker. "A monkey can do what I do," says the receptionist. "I'm less than a farm implement," says the migrant worker. "I'm an object," says the high fashion model. Blue collar and white call upon the identical phrase: "I'm a robot."[48]

I would argue that what is fundamentally at play here is not merely that workers are discontented, as Terkel himself suggests, but rather also that as a human activity working has a basic ambiguity of agency and utility, insofar as work simultaneously allows one to conceive and carry out projects, thus exercising agency, as well as to feel useful in serving needs and desires, thus exercising utility. When elements of human agency and freedom are taken from work, work degenerates from a meaningful experience of feeling oneself useful through an engagement of one's mind or body in the world, into an experience of feeling like a cog in a machine, or like a robot, an animal, or an implement.

Work can feel meaningless for several reasons—including a futile outcome, an apparent lack of purpose, or a failure to engage an individual's talents, intellectual capabilities, or artisan skills—but among the several facets of meaningless work, dehumanization and degradation stand out in undermining a meaningful experience of work. This dehumanization issues partly from a proliferation of automation in working life, which requires not that an employee act as a person exercising human capabilities but only that she use her voice, her hands, or her legs, as determined by a system.[49] But dehumanization and

---

[47] Consider the arguments of Adriano Tilgher, *Homo Faber: Work through the Ages* (Chicago: Henry Regnery Company, 1930); Schumacher, *Good Work*; or Pope John Paul II, *Laboren exercens*, Encyclical Letter, 1981.09.14.

[48] Studs Terkel, *Working: People Talk about What They Do All Day and How They Feel about What They Do* (New York: W.W. Norton & Company, 2004 [1972]), xi–xii.

[49] Even as automation creates jobs that are hardly set up for the exercise of individual worker ingenuity, pockets of ingenuity, creativity, and accomplishment can nevertheless emerge even in the context of performing automated work. Factory workers interviewed in Barbara Garson, *All the Livelong Day: The Meaning and Demeaning of Routine Work* (Garden City, NY: Doubleday, 1975), ix–xvi, report

degradation also occur outside of repetitive automated work in work in which people act or serve as implements, parts or objects, as when women are used in prostitution or pornographic films and other media, and when women or men serve as towel holders, toiletry dispensers,[50] or signposts. The employment of *people* to stand on street corners with signs reading "hot and ready" to attract consumers into pizza parlors (which is a standard marketing strategy of Little Caesar's in the area in which I live) does not cohere with human dignity. This kind of employment reduces the worker to functioning as a thing, makes a mockery of the human capacities of a person, and fails to permit virtues associated with work, such as honor or pride, on account of a lack of agency required for the work.

Some may argue that characterizing oppressed workers as tools is mistaken and overlooks an indelible element of autonomous agency exercised in an individual's choice to enter a particular employment. To be sure, choice of employment does represent a basic dimension of autonomy in relation to work and, more broadly, reflectively made choices figure prominently in many accounts of autonomy. But even if we often have reason to respect individual choices, we also have reason to be skeptical when appeals to the value of individual choice serve to justify the distribution of limited goods in competitive social and economic environments. In particular, we have reason to be skeptical of attempts to justify someone's working at an oppressive job by appeal to the fact of her having chosen to work at such a position. As a philosophical or rhetorical maneuver intended to sanctify an employment relationship, an appeal to individual choice or consent appears dubious if systemic inequalities limit available opportunities in the first place, and this maneuver flounders when the forms of work in question are inherently unchoiceworthy, such that a certain amount of coercion must be present to force workers with few or no alternatives into such occupations.[51]

---

on varied creative maneuvers they intersperse throughout the workday to achieve moments of ingenuity and feelings of purposefulness and fulfillment, such as allowing work to pile up to experience a few minutes of purposeful exertion in catching up, which creates opportunities for minor goals and fulfillments. But upsurges of worker creativity and purposeful exertion amid conditions of "speed, heat, humiliation, [and] monotony" likely demonstrates not that working on an assembly line provides meaning or fulfillment but, rather, that the human need for exercising agency, for reaching goals, for displaying some measure of individuality, and for feeling that one accomplishes a task creatively are basic enough in human well-being that workers find opportunities for these needs even on an assembly line.

[50] As in the job of a washroom attendant, whose function is to wait on people in restrooms and to dispense towels and toiletries. One washroom attendant employed for fifteen years at the Chicago Palmer House, Louis Hayward, describes the physical work of waiting on men in restrooms as "an automatic thing.... It doesn't require any thought. It's almost a reflex action. I set my toilet articles up, towels—and I'm ready." Terkel, *Working*, 106. In its social function, he believes his work serves to bolster the egos of bathroom visitors: when a man visits the restroom and receives an acknowledgment from the attendant, "it builds his ego up a little bit.... I'm building him up" (107).

[51] The point is suggested by Michael Walzer, *Spheres of Justice*, 165, who writes of jobs that are hard in the sense of being "harsh, unpleasant, cruel, difficult to endure" that they are like prison sentences

As Gomberg notes in criticizing Ronald Dworkin, asserting that a person occupies a social position as a result of past choices primarily serves an ideological purpose as "a moral sanctification of a social order," but there is a basic error in transferring moral concepts of praiseworthiness or blameworthiness into social contexts in which basic goods exist in limited supply.[52] As Gomberg has it, in a competitive economic system in which employment is a limited good, the functioning of state bureaucracies that handle unemployment depends on a large percentage of the unemployed living in a state of discouragement. In such a context, rhetoric to the effect that those who are unemployed choose to avoid the unemployment line—and thus have only themselves to blame for their condition—provides an appearance of justification of the state of things but obscures social forces, institutions and policies that cause a certain percentage of unemployment in the first place.[53]

Some readers may reach here for a stock distinction made in the context of Kantian ethics, wherein it is commonly noted that it is not wrong to treat a person as a means (as happens in work of all sorts) but wrong to treat him as a mere means, which disrespects his capabilities as an autonomous, rational agent, who as such must make his own decisions free from manipulation and coercion. In illuminating this notion, some ethicists quickly clarify that it is not morally objectionable, for example, to use a plumber to fix a broken pipe drain, as long as the plumber understands the situation and chooses, from his own will, to participate in the employment.[54] This clarification and illustration is, in fact, crafty in avoiding pervasive moral ambiguity, insofar as the worker in this example is one who uses intelligence and agency while on the job, making decisions and judgments in the context of exercising competency as a craftsman. The plumber who is employed freely and fairly and who exercises developed skills to solve problems, to install materials, or to make repairs is not exploited as a tool in the manner in which a factory hand or a sweatshop worker are oppressed as relatively expendable, interchangeable tools of production.[55] Even if all were to exercise agency in an initial choice of

---

in that people do not look for them and would not choose them if they face minimally attractive alternatives: "This kind of work is a negative good, and it commonly carries other negative goods in its train: poverty, insecurity, ill health, physical danger, dishonor and degradation. And yet it is socially necessary work; it needs to be done, and that means someone must be found to do it."

[52] Gomberg, *How to Make Opportunity Equal*, 23.

[53] Gomberg, *How to Make Opportunity Equal*, 23–24.

[54] As in the widely used ethics textbook James Rachels and Stuart Rachels, *The Elements of Moral Philosophy*, 7th ed. (New York: McGraw-Hill, 2012), 138–139.

[55] For a discourse on the intelligence and agency required for nonroutinized manual work, see Matthew Crawford, *Shop Class as Soulcraft: An Inquiry into the Value of Work* (New York: Penguin Press, 2009); Mike Rose, *The Mind at Work: Valuing the Intelligence of the American Worker* (New York: Penguin Books, 2004). For Crawford, the satisfactions of useful work accrue particularly to skilled practitioners of manual arts, like carpentry, plumbing, and motorcycle and car repair. Since these forms of work are necessarily situated in a particular context, they are inherently resistant to forms of external managerial or corporate control that undermine human agency and make work

employment, not all exercise agency in employment, and not all are equally exploited. And focusing on an exercise of autonomous agency in an initial choice of employment obscures ways work can itself undermine or enhance autonomous agency.

To be clear then, it is not the fact of being utilized as an instrument of production that is itself at issue. Being instrumental in producing, serving, creating, and fabricating lies in the nature of working—a fact also revealed through meditation on the meaning of *employment*—wherein one often finds satisfaction in making oneself useful, being purposeful, or being a means of achieving something of value. Rather, it is being used extensively as a tool, an implement, an object or a body, wherein a person is not also simultaneously expressing agency, which is dehumanizing. It is also dehumanizing to be treated as an expendable resource or to toil in a system as a nonthinking tool of production for several hours a day, which after time damages the body and mind and depletes intelligence and other human capabilities. When the working day is limited and one has opportunities to flourish outside of eudemonistically meaningless work, perhaps being a tool of production at work need not be felt as altogether dehumanizing. However, there are some for whom oppressive work effectively predominates life, as when one labors at eudemonistically meaningless work for sixteen hours a day, whether at one job or two, and here a person is likely to feel depleted of humanity or human vitality, and effectively transformed into a means for others. Oppression at work clearly comes in degrees.

It is also interesting to consider, as I mentioned above, that some interpreters of Kant argue that in giving an imperative to treat humanity as an end an never as a mere means, Kant himself lays emphasis on respecting the humanity in persons, that is, on respecting the rational and autonomous abilities within persons. Thomas Hill observes Kant repeating that respecting people as ends requires treating "the humanity in a person" as an end and never as a mere means.[56] The familiar dictum of treating persons as ends represents an abbreviation of treating humanity in persons as ends, Hill argues, and for Kant humanity represents a characteristic of persons, whose distinguishing features include the rational capabilities of setting ends and forming goals. In interpreting the principle of humanity formulation of the categorical imperative, Allen Wood also writes that the basic issue for Kant is that we disrespect

---

vulnerable to dehumanization and degradation. Building and fixing are embedded in a community in which the individual worker remains responsible for his or her own work and in which excellence at work comes with the exercise of judgment, the making of a social contribution, the feeling of pride in one's work, and the transformation of objective reality by one's own hands. Nonroutinized manual work demands intelligence; "the physical circumstances of the jobs performed by carpenters, plumbers and auto mechanics vary too much for them to be executed by idiots. One feels like a [person], not like a cog in a machine" (52–53).

[56] Hill, *Dignity and Practical Reason*, 38–46, 10.

humanity in placing things of lesser value ahead of our rational nature, which constitutes our humanity and which is an end in itself.[57]

What would it require of a human community to treat the humanity in a person as an end? In the context of work, it would entail that a goal of work be the development or exercise of the rational, autonomous, and agential capabilities of a person and that diminishing these gifts as a means for achieving economic values of profit or productivity or increasing efficiency is outside moral bounds. That is, the full realization of a moral imperative to treat the humanity in a person as a end would entail a revolution in modern economic life, which as presently structured often demands not that work serve the end of developing and exercising human capabilities but that "the worker adapt himself to the needs of the work—which means, of course, primarily to the needs of the machine."[58] It may be hard to fathom such a moral departure from present economic realities. But, as we know, implementing the categorical imperative can entail such radical transformations in human practices that, in a specific historical moment in which people are enveloped and enculturated in immoralities, meeting moral demands can appear bewilderingly near impossible. As Wood writes, the formula of using humanity as an end and never only as a means "is rather like the Sermon on the Mount...whose demands require such a radical departure from our customary practices and accepted attitudes toward ourselves and others that we are at first perplexed when we try to apply them."[59]

Some may see this call for ethical transformation in economic life as simply tantamount to rejecting capitalism and calling for communism or Marxism in its stead. In response, I note that Marx provides one rich source of criticism of meaningless work in capitalist economies, but pigeonholing criticism of meaningless work as Marxist overlooks a few facts. First, it overlooks the convergence of a plurality of philosophical and religious traditions around the importance of work in realizing part of the human good. Second, this pigeonholing overlooks the possibility for meaningful work in the context of capitalist employment relationships. The question of whether capitalism contains an inherent proclivity toward depriving people of autonomous agency depends partly on the ethical values paired with it and partly on whether the pursuit of profitability, productivity and efficiency is pure and unbridled, or limited and tempered by a respect for autonomy and other human values. Third, identifying meaningful work with communism overlooks the variegated realities of alienated labor under communist conditions: as James Bernard Murphy observes, in both capitalism and in communism "the worker is often treated as a mere instrument, a factor of production, rather than as the subject of his

---

[57] Allen Wood, *Kant's Ethical Thought* (New York: Cambridge University Press, 1999), 143.
[58] Schumacher, *Good Work*, 3.
[59] Wood, *Kant's Ethical Thought*, 139.

or her work.... When Charlie Chaplin satirized the mindless monotony of the assembly line in *Modern Times* (1936), he was denounced in the United States as an enemy of capitalism and in Russia as an enemy of socialism—and in a sense he was guilty on both counts."[60] In essence, promoting modes of working life that provide opportunities for people to flourish reaches beyond traditional bifurcations between capitalism and communism, implanting ethics at the seat of economic life and requiring respect for the exercise of agency in working life.

If it is bewildering to imagine economics structured around a goal of human development, I think it is also edifying to consider the bounds of moral progress that workplaces have already achieved in some quarters of the world in the twenty-first century. Consider, for instance, that it is now commonplace to maintain as workplace ideals—and to instantiate in practice in varying measures—rational and fair hiring processes, nondiscriminatory and harassment-free workplace environments, equitable wages and freedom from threats, and abuse and profanity while on the job. According to historian Stanford Jacoby, not one of these ideals was in place in the United States over a century ago, when the dominant mode of the production of commodities was the factory system, in which foremen used close supervision, abuse, profanity, and threats to motivate faster and harder work and in which work was highly insecure, very poorly paid, fraught with pay inequities and ethnic discrimination, and not uncommonly secured through nepotism, favoritism, and bribery.[61] Some of us live in a workplace utopia in comparison with the factories of the late 1800s, at which time it would have been difficult to see possibilities for the sort of change that is now a becoming reality, and it should not therefore be said in thinking about working life as we know it that work just is what it is. Appreciating moral progress in working life highlights abilities of human communities to transcend and reinvent workplace structures and leads us toward a position of open-mindedness in entertaining long-range

---

[60] Murphy, *Moral Economy of Labor*, 3–4. The prologue to Murphy, *Moral Economy of Labor* provides important clarification on the relationship between Taylorism and communism. Murphy notes, for instance, that "the detailed fragmentation of skilled labor into monotonous routine that once symbolized the horrors of capitalism became the basis of Soviet industry from Vladimir Lenin through Leonid Brezhnev. Indeed, Taylorism was more pervasive in Soviet Russia than it ever was in the United States" (3). Further, Murphy observes that the similar quality of the experience of work for the worker in both capitalist and socialist systems "leads apologists for both systems to emphasize distribution and exchange rather than the dignity of work. For example, one leading Marxist theoretician, John Roemer, says that if we were to focus on the labor process we would be forced to the bizarre conclusion that socialist countries exploit workers just as much as do capitalist countries" (3). See also Braverman, *Labor and Monopoly Capital*.

[61] Jacoby "The Way It Was: Factory Labor before 1915," in *Employing Bureaucracy: Managers, Unions, and the Transformation of Work in the 20th Century*, rev. ed. (New York: Columbia University Press, 2004).

possibilities for transforming elements of working life that stifle autonomous development or undermine human dignity.

Elsewhere, I further explore work and human flourishing, addressing additional ethical, social, and political implications of the formative influence of work on people.[62] In bringing this chapter to a close, I highlight that workplace structures and practices are not invariable elements of a natural order but rather change over time, and an understanding of the impact of work on autonomous development and self-realization can guide transformations of workplace goals and structures so that working can become more meaningful, or at least less oppressive, for more people. I also underscore in closing that an initial autonomous choice of occupation by no means exhausts the intersections between autonomy and work, and focusing only on autonomous choice of occupation constrains perceptions of ways Tayloristic forms of work undermine the development and exercise of autonomous capacities. Given that autonomous capacities are developed, or stifled, within social contexts including work, a democratic commitment to supporting the development and exercise of people's autonomous capacities entails an opposition to eudemonistically meaningless forms of work, which stifle worker autonomy and well-being.

Acknowledgments

I would especially like to thank Mark Piper and Erin Tarver for helpful comments on an earlier draft of this paper. This paper has also been enriched by discussions at the Relational Autonomy Workshop organized by Natalie Stoljar and Catriona Mackenzie, held in Montreal in September 2012, and at the conference on Work and Human Development organized by Nick Smith and Jean-Philippe Deranty, held in Sydney in September 2011.

---

[62] Veltman, *Meaningful Work*, manuscript.

{ 14 }

The Right to Bodily Autonomy and the Abortion Controversy
Anita M. Superson

1. Introduction

Laurence Tribe persuasively argues in his outstanding book, *Abortion: The Clash of Absolutes*, that abortion is not just about having control over one's body but also about having the choice to be a mother: "Pregnancy does not merely 'inconvenience' a woman for a time; it gradually turns her into a mother and makes her one for all time."[1] Being a mother goes well beyond gestating a fetus for nine months but involves being prepared to make many personal and financial sacrifices for the well-being of one's child to its development as a full and productive member of society—in short, motherhood is life-changing. Pregnancy for most women involves this choice, as only less than 3 percent in the United States put up their children for adoption.[2]

Tribe's powerful argument affirms the seriousness of enforced pregnancy brought about by strict antiabortion legislation that is trying to take hold in the United States. For example, Republican governor Jack Dalrymple of North Dakota recently enacted a law banning nearly all abortions once a fetal heartbeat is detectable, which could be as early as six weeks into pregnancy. Dalrymple also approved a statute, originating in Mississippi, requiring doctors who perform abortions to get admitting privileges at a local hospital, which could effectually shut down North Dakota's only abortion provider.[3]

---

[1] Laurence H. Tribe, *Abortion: The Clash of Absolutes* (New York: W.W. Norton & Company, 1992), 104.

[2] According to the Guttmacher Institute, 3 percent of unmarried white women gave up their babies for adoption from 1982 to 1988; fewer than 2 percent of unmarried black women gave up their babies for adoption during this time and earlier; and none of Hispanic women in the sample reported giving up their babies for adoption. Tamar Lewin, "Fewer Children Up for Adoption, Study Finds," *New York Times*, February 27, 1992, http://www.nytimes.com/1992/02/27/US/fewer-children-up-for-adoption-study-finds.html.

[3] "The Campaign to Outlaw Abortion," *New York Times*, March 29, 2013, http://www.nytimes.com/2013/03/30/opinion/the-campaign-to-outlaw.abortion.html?hp&_r=18.

Dalrymple signed a bill that bans abortions based solely on genetic abnormalities or on the gender of the fetus.[4] Personhood bills, which would extend legal protection to zygotes, have been introduced in Oklahoma and Mississippi. In Kansas, Republican governor Sam Brownbeck indicated that he would sign virtually any measure declaring that life begins at fertilization, and then he signed a personhood bill.[5] An abortion rights advocacy group, the Guttmacher Institute, which classifies states as *hostile, middle ground*, or *supportive* of abortion rights, reports that in the southern United States while only a handful of states were classified in 2000 as hostile there is now "a solid wall of hostility, from Virginia down to Florida and over to Texas and Oklahoma."[6]

Despite the power of Tribe's argument, if we argue in favor of abortion rights on the grounds he suggests alone, then it will be difficult to address the National Center for Men, for instance, which believes that men are entitled to some say over decisions that profoundly affect their lives—namely, the freedom to choose to be a father. In a 2007 court case, *Dubay v. Wells*, the Center backed Matthew Dubay, who sued his girlfriend after she became pregnant when the two had sex. Prior to the pregnancy, Dubay told her that he was not ready to have children, and she said that was fine, since she was infertile and using birth control just in case. When she discovered that she was pregnant, she wasn't willing to have an abortion. After giving birth to a girl in 2005, she obtained a court order requiring Dubay to pay $500 a month in child support. Dubay's lawsuit contended that men have a constitutional right to avoid procreation. Mel Feit, the Center's director, said, "There's such a spectrum of choice that women have—it's her body, her pregnancy. I'm trying to find a way for a man also to have some say over decisions that affect his life profoundly."[7] This Michigan case was called the *Roe v. Wade* for men. Although it was a case about whether child support laws violate Equal Protection by applying only to men, conservatives hoped to seize on it to gain control over abortion in both directions and to overturn *Roe v. Wade*. As things turned out, the judge dismissed the case in 2006. The National Center for Men appealed, but the appeals court said that "the 14th Amendment does not deny the State the power to treat different classes of persons in different ways."[8]

---

[4] Dave Thompson, "North Dakota Governor Signs 'Heartbeat' Abortion Ban," *Chicago Tribune*, March 26, 2013, http://articles.chicagotribune.com/2013-03-26/news/sns-rt-us-usa-abortion-northdakota.bre92pOua-20130326_1_heartbeat-bill-supporters-of-abortion-rights-restrictive-abortion-law.

[5] DeAnn Smith and Stephen Mayer, "Kansas Lawmakers Could Vote Friday on Tough Anti-abortion Bill," April 5, 2013, http://www.kctv5.com/story/21891968/Kansas-lawmakers-could-vote-Friday-on-tough-anti-abortion-bill.html. The bill states that life begins at fertilization and bans sex-selection abortion and was signed on April 5, 2013 (CBS Evening News).

[6] "Abortion Laws in the South: Cutting away at *Roe v. Wade*," March 16, 2013, *Economist* http://www.economist.com/news/United-States/21573594-rest-south-not-far-behind-strict-new-law-arkansas-cutting-away-roe-v.

[7] Judith Graham, "Unwilling Father Tests Men's Rights," *Chicago Tribune*, March 10, 2006.

[8] *Dubay v. Wells*, 506 F.3d 422 (6th Cir.; 2007); *Wikipedia*, "Dubay v. Wells," 506 F. 3d 422 (6h Cir.; 2007), http://en.wikipedia.org/wiki/Dubay_v._Wells.

Ironically, this case for so-called men's rights is not one prohibiting women's right to abortion but enforcing abortion when the father does not want children. Whatever the motive, and even though the lawsuit failed, the case makes clear the feminist objection that the state, through its institutions and practices, uses women's bodies as vessels for its own or men's ends.

Significantly, this case makes it very clear, or so I shall argue, that the right to bodily autonomy must be central in any argument for abortion rights. Tribe himself makes a great deal about bodily autonomy. But he seems to lean in the direction of nonliberal, or less individualistic, feminists, who advocate the centrality of motherhood, and away from liberal feminists, who advocate the centrality of bodily autonomy and other individualistic values.[9] One advantage of the nonliberal feminist view is that if parenthood is the supreme value, then a woman has a right to decide whether she is to become a parent even if her doing so does not involve her body in any significant way. Any argument about abortion rights would apply equally to in vitro development of a child as well as to the mother's rights over the child once it is born. But if bodily autonomy is the supreme value, then we will need a separate argument about a mother's right over the fetus in such cases. The key issue in the standard case of fetal development is the mother's rights over the fetus when the fetus is in her body. If we leave bodily autonomy out of, or make it secondary in, our arguments about abortion, we jeopardize its significance in arguments about rape, sexual harassment, female genital mutilation, woman battering, and fetal harm cases. Yet a significant part of our analysis of why these behaviors are wrong is that they deny women's bodily autonomy. It is important, then, for feminists to supplement the argument about the right to become or not to become a parent with an argument about the right to bodily autonomy.

Interestingly, if supporters of the "prolife"[10] or antichoice position really do oppose enforced abortion, *Dubay v. Wells* should force them to examine

---

[9] According to Martha Nussbaum, "Feminist Critique of Liberalism," in *Sex and Social Justice*, edited by Nussbaum (New York: Oxford University Press, 1999), "personhood, autonomy, rights, dignity, and self-respect" are the terms of the liberal Enlightenment (56). One of the charges cited by Nussbaum and made by feminist against the liberal tradition is that it is too "individualistic" in focusing too much on the dignity and worth of the individual and thereby diminishing the value of community and social entities such as families, groups, and classes (56, 58, 59). Nussbaum defends liberalism against this charge, arguing that "the separateness of persons is a basic fact of human life" (62), and is at the root of making the individual the basic unit for political thought: "each person has a course from birth to death that is not precisely the same as that of any other person.... Each person is one and not more than one.... Each feels pain in his or her own body...." (62)."

[10] I put this term in quotes because most people who claim to be prolife about abortion are not prolife about other issues. Only 11 percent of Americans hold a consistent ethic of life position, opposing legalized abortion and capital punishment, for example. Seventy-nine percent of prolife Republicans and 85 percent of prolife Tea Party identifiers who say abortion should be illegal in all or most cases also support the death penalty. See Robert P. Jones, "Like Perry, Most 'Pro-Life' Americans OK with Death Penalty," *Washington Post*, September 15, 2011, https://www.washingtonpost.com/blogs/figuring-faith/post/like-rich-perry-most-pro-life-americans-ok-with-death-penality/2011/09/15/

whether it is just the abortion part that they oppose (which makes this case no different from that of a woman willingly undergoing an abortion) or whether their opposition is also to the use of women's bodies in this way (which means that they actually do see the value of the right to bodily autonomy and that to be consistent they should acknowledge it in other cases as well). Tribe and many other feminists believe that the prolife position is really about controlling women and about race,[11] not about the rights of fetuses, since its advocates are more stirred up when women gain advances in society, or when women voluntarily have sex (i.e., are "guilty") and contraception fails,[12] and so on, or when more white women than black women have abortions.[13] This is because the prolife position is inconsistent on its position on the value of fetal life.[14]

What does it mean to say that someone has a right to bodily autonomy? What does this right consist in, and when does it trump other rights in conflict cases? These are difficult questions to answer, and in this paper I hope only to tease out a bit what this right might amount to, by taking as my starting point an account offered by Judith Jarvis Thomson in her famous article on abortion.[15]

It is noteworthy that standard accounts of personal autonomy or autonomy of the will tend to leave out discussion of the body and focus instead on conditions that are necessary and/or sufficient for self-determination. Sarah Buss

---

gIQA06XUIX=blog.html. The data come from the *Millenials, Religion, and Abortion Survey* conducted between April 22 and May 8, 2011, using a random sample of three thousand adults.

[11] In Nazi Germany, the Third Reich banned the production and distribution of contraceptives in 1941. By 1943 the penalty for performing an abortion on a woman who was "genetically fit" was death. But by 1938, Jews were defined as falling in the category of being "genetically defective," and the state readily granted abortions for women in this group. See Tribe, *Abortion*, 59–60.

[12] Tribe, *Abortion*, notes that some people believe that while abortion should be allowed in cases of rape, it should not be in cases of contraceptive failure because the woman "volunteered" in the sense that she chose to have sex and run the risk of pregnancy. He finds it curious that there is not a widespread sentiment among those who generally oppose abortion rights that abortion should be allowed in cases of contraceptive failure, since taking contraception means that the woman does not want to be pregnant. Tribe asks, "Does this not suggest that such opponents of abortion come to their views about the immorality of abortion not in response to the voluntary nature of the woman's *pregnancy* but in response to the voluntary nature of the s*exual activity* in which she has engaged? And does this not in turn suggest that such antiabortion views are driven less by the innocence of the fetus…than by the supposed 'guilt' of the woman?" (132).

[13] Tribe, *Abortion*, notes that in the 1800s there was an increase in abortion rates among married, white, middle-class Protestant women and that by 1860 the birth rate among white Americans of British and northern European descent declined significantly in comparison to new immigrants who were predominantly Catholic. Physicians who supported abortion restrictions warned of "race suicide," and fear of this was more widespread than religious antiabortion sentiment (32).

[14] Tribe, *Abortion*, 231, 232, 236–237, notes that virulent opponents to abortion such as Randall Terry, the originator of Operation Rescue, explicitly connect their opposition to abortion with their desire to put women back in traditional roles. He notes that our society is inconsistent in its thinking on fetuses and frozen embryos and on fetal development and child abuse.

[15] Judith Jarvis Thomson, "A Defense of Abortion," *Philosophy & Public Affairs* 1:1 (Autumn 1971): 47–66.

notes that most autonomy theories have in common the notion that autonomy consists in the agent's endorsing or identifying with her action.[16] Much of the current debate centers on the benefits and disadvantages of procedural and substantive theories of autonomy. Yet these theoretical debates emphasize the will, not the body. Discussions about bodily autonomy appear mostly, as one might expect, in the medical ethics literature (e.g., on reproductive technologies, organ donation and sale, euthanasia, and abortion), but we can also find them in feminist critiques of traditional autonomy theories (e.g., on deformed desires or adaptive preferences) and the feminist literature on rape, woman battering, and the like and how these acts stifle women's autonomy. In her feminist critique of notions of bodily autonomy found in the medical ethics literature, Catriona Mackenzie argues that this literature has overwhelmingly supported what she calls the *maximal choice view*, which in essence amounts to the view that autonomy reduces to choice, which is a matter of our subjective preferences, no matter their content.[17] This is an individualistic view of autonomy, one that favors maximizing control over one's body and having freedom to dispose of it as one chooses. This view, I would add, fits squarely into traditional accounts of autonomy by incorporating the body in terms of the agent's preferences and desires. Bodily autonomy, then, can be viewed as an extension of autonomy of the will through satisfaction of preferences and desires relating to the body.

But this conception of bodily autonomy might not satisfy feminists, who have critiqued traditional accounts of autonomy, and have developed what has been called *relational autonomy*. Relational autonomy theories are distinguished by their focus on the autonomous agent, in particular, on the rich and complex social and historical contexts in which the agent is embedded.[18] They aim to develop an account of autonomy that is characteristic of agents who are "emotional, embodied, desiring, creative, and feeling, as well as rational creatures."[19] Along these lines, Mackenzie develops an account of bodily autonomy that espouses the liberal and libertarian values found in the medical ethics literature yet grounds these values not in bodily ownership but in what she calls one's "bodily perspective." These values are (1) the right to noninterference

---

[16] Sarah Buss, "Autonomy Reconsidered," *Midwest Studies in Philosophy* 19 (1994): 95–121; Peter A. French, Theodore Ed. Uehling, Jr., and Howard K. Wettstein (eds.), *Midwest Studies* (Notre Dame: University of Notre Dame Press, 1994), 95.

[17] Catriona Mackenzie, "Conceptions of Autonomy and Conceptions of the Body in Bioethics," in *Feminist Bioethics: At the Center, On the Margins*, Jackie Leach Scully, Laurel E. Baldwin-Ragaven, and Petya Fitzpatrick, eds. (Baltimore, MD: Johns Hopkins University Press, 2010), 71–90.

[18] Catriona Mackenzie and Natalie Stoljar, "Introduction: Autonomy Refigured," in *Relational Autonomy: Feminist Perspectives on Autonomy, Agency, and the Social Self*, edited by Catriona Mackenzie and Natalie Stoljar (New York: Oxford University Press, 2000), 21. The workshop on relational autonomy for which this paper was written was held to celebrate the ten-year anniversary of this anthology.

[19] Mackenzie and Stoljar, "Introduction," 21.

(the right to be free from intrusion on one's body without one's consent), and (2) the right to bodily self-determination (the right to decide what happens in and to your body, which, Mackenzie notes, cashes out as a right to determine what you can do *with* your body—including sex selection, genetic enhancement, and organ sale—more extensively, and she believes incorrectly, on liberal and libertarian medical ethics accounts). Mackenzie, borrowing from Paul Ricouer, Maurice Merleau-Ponty, and Kant, argues that it is because my body is the medium through which I live my life that I must have a right to determine what happens in and to my body.[20] Our consciousness is not separate from our body; rather, we see the world from the perspective of our body.[21] I would add two points. First, our bodies as much as our minds shape who we are—often others react to us and treat us in certain ways because of some feature of our bodies, including our perceived gender, ethnicity, and ableness and whether we are obese or thin, attractive or unattractive, and so on, and we see ourselves in terms of how others see us and react to us because we often internalize social perceptions. Second, we come into the world and go out of it with our body. Because your body is yours alone in the sense that only you inhabit it,[22] there is a way your life and your death are necessarily and inevitably solitary events, no matter who surrounds you. Martha Nussbaum defends the individualism of liberalism on the grounds of the necessary separatism of persons and the fact that we each feel pain and pleasure in our own bodies only. These preliminary points speak to the significance of the body for morality in general and specifically for any full account of autonomy.

The account of the right to bodily autonomy that I defend here is relational in the sense that it is nuanced by feminist concerns. However, my starting point in defending this right is Thomson's article, and many of us would characterize her view of the right to bodily autonomy as falling squarely in the liberal or libertarian tradition that Mackenzie criticizes. I actually do not think these views are at odds with each other—indeed, liberalism/libertarianism and feminism share a concern for the body that seems to come from the same place. When many feminists discuss rape, woman battering, female genital mutilation, prenatal harm, and abortion, to name a few, they espouse a "hands-off" view that might be defended with the libertarian assumption of self-ownership of the body.[23] The underlying view is that women are not fetal containers, nor do men own women's bodies.

---

[20] See Catriona Mackenzie, "On Bodily Autonomy," in *Handbook of Phenomenology and Medicine*, S.K. Toombs (ed.) (The Netherlands: Kluwer Academic Publishers, 2001), 417–439.
[21] Mackenzie, "Conceptions of Autonomy," 80–81.
[22] I am going to avoid discussing controversial personal identity theories here.
[23] For a discussion of the libertarian principle of self-ownership, see, e.g., David Sobel, "Backing away from Libertarian Self-Ownership," *Ethics* 123 (October 2012): 32–60.

Since my interest is to explain what a right to bodily autonomy might consist in, I will take as my starting point Thomson's article, as it has insights on an issue near and dear to feminists and medical ethicists alike. Along the way, I will propose a few principles that tweak out the right to bodily autonomy sensitive to concerns raised by relational autonomy theorists. I intend for these principles to hold ceteris paribus. I do not believe that the right to bodily autonomy holds absolutely (nor does the right to self-defense). I leave for another occasion an exploration of the conditions under which it may be overridden.

Thomson appeals to and elucidates the right to bodily autonomy in at least four ways. First, she characterizes this right as a fundamental right, either grounded in, similar to, or the same as the right to self-defense. Thomson states, "My own view is that if a human being has any just, prior claim to anything at all, he has a just, prior claim to his own body... the woman has a right to decide what happens in and to her body."[24] A second and related point is that this right, for Thomson, is grounded in the fact that the mother owns her own body, making claims about it prior to other claims.[25] Ownership of one's own body grounds a right to defend one's body against things happening in and to it.[26] Third, the right to bodily autonomy also seems, for Thomson, to be tied up with the very status of being a person. Regarding what the mother may do as opposed to what a third party may do when it comes to abortion, Thomson says, "So the question asked is what a third party may do and what the mother may do, if it is mentioned at all, is deduced, almost as an afterthought, from what it is concluded that third parties may do. But it seems to me that to treat the matter in this way is to refuse to grant to the mother *that very status of person* which is so firmly insisted on for the fetus. For we cannot simply read off what a person may do from what a third party may do."[27] In other words, a person's right to bodily autonomy is connected to, and perhaps even stems from, her status as a person—that is, that someone's status as a person in the moral community forms the basis of at least some of the rights she has. Finally, Thomson asserts that no one has a right to use of your body unless you give him such a right,[28] suggesting that a right to bodily autonomy is so fundamental that only the bearer of such a right can legitimately waive it.

---

[24] Thomson, "Defense of Abortion," 54.
[25] Thomson, "Defense of Abortion," 53.
[26] Thomson, "Defense of Abortion," 53. Even though ownership of the body grounds a right to defend one's body against things happening in and to it, Thomson argues elsewhere that a right to self-defense is not absolute. For example, you cannot deflect a trolley heading toward you onto a bystander, nor can you shoot a bystander who will then fall on the trolley and stop it from killing you, nor can you do something that results in a bystander's death to spare your own life. All of these acts display a lack of respect for persons, treating them as if they were not there. Thomson, "Self-Defense," *Philosophy & Public Affairs* 20:4 (Autumn 1991): 289, 291. It is beyond the scope of this paper for me to argue when the right to bodily autonomy, as part of the right to self-defense, can be overridden.
[27] Thomson, "Defense of Abortion," 52. Emphasis added.
[28] Thomson, "Defense of Abortion," 53.

And strictly speaking, Thomson's view in this paper is that you do not waive the right to determine what happens in and to your body; rather, you just let someone use your body for a time.

The right to bodily autonomy plays a pivotal role in Thomson's three analogies about pregnancy, and she argues that in certain cases it trumps other rights, including even the right to life. In the violinist analogy, which compares enforced pregnancy resulting from rape to having to stay hooked up to a violinist who is attached to you without your consent, the mother's right to bodily autonomy overrides the right to life of the fetus. Because pregnancy was the result of rape, in no sense did the mother give the fetus a right to use her body. In the house analogy, which compares enforced pregnancy in cases where the mother's life is at stake to being trapped in a house with a rapidly growing child who will crush you to death, the mother's right to life overrides the fetus' right to life because the mother's prior existence and the fact that the fetus uses her body for its existence break the tie between the two innocent lives. The mother's prior existence and prior right to her body is decisive in just the same way that one's owning property is decisive over someone else's wanting it: an older brother who owns a box of chocolates that he does not share with his younger brother has a prior claim to them. In the people-seed analogy, which compares enforced pregnancy in cases of contraceptive failure to having to allow the people-seed that takes root in your upholstered furniture to develop in your house, the mother's right to bodily autonomy overrides the fetus' right to life even when the sex is voluntary but when the mother has taken precautions against pregnancy. Since she has done so, she does not give the fetus a right to use her body. Thomson concludes that in cases of rape, the mother's life being at stake, and contraceptive failure, abortion is morally permissible.

I find Thomson's analogies entirely persuasive, but I think that her reliance on the right to bodily autonomy allows her to draw even stronger conclusions than she does. Here I want to focus on the following two cases where I think that Thomson's conclusion is weaker than it need be: (1) the woman whose pregnancy lasts only one hour and is the result of rape; and (2) the woman who in her seventh month of pregnancy wants an abortion so she won't have to postpone a trip. These cases are Thomson's own, but I believe that her conclusions about them are weaker than the ones she can draw by invoking the same premise about the right to bodily autonomy. I believe that this right has more trumping power than Thomson defends. I use these cases as a springboard for developing further the right to bodily autonomy, though of course I cannot defend a full-fledged theory here. My aim is to put forward and then offer some precursory defenses of some principles about this right. Thomson herself does not defend this right but merely appeals to it in her paper, though elsewhere she argues that it is one of the fundamental rights that a plausible moral theory ought to acknowledge, since without such a right we are not even in the moral game.[29] I will return to this point later.

2. Case 1: When Pregnancy Lasts One Hour and Is the Result of Rape

Regarding case 1, Thomson says: "...suppose pregnancy lasted only an hour, and constituted no threat to life or health. And suppose that a woman becomes pregnant as a result of rape. Admittedly she did not voluntarily do anything to bring about the existence of a child. Admittedly she did nothing at all which would give the unborn person a right to use of her body. All the same...she *ought* to allow it to remain for that hour—it would be indecent in her to refuse."[30] And "...we should conclude that she is self-centered, callous, indecent, but not unjust, if she refuses."[31] Thomson's remarks about the mother's merely being indecent in refusing to let the fetus use her body show that whether the mother invited the fetus in isn't decisive in determining the permissibility of abortion. The mother's situation is compared to that of the older brother who owns a box of chocolates but does not share them with his younger brother. The older brother is indecent, but not unjust, in not sharing them, since the younger brother has no right to them. However, the older brother should, out of a sense of decency, share his chocolates because doing so doesn't present much of a hardship. Prior ownership makes it the case that the older brother has a right to the chocolates and that the mother has a right to bodily autonomy, but the degree of burdensomeness determines whether the brother is indecent in not sharing the chocolates and whether the mother is indecent in not letting the fetus use her body. In the case at hand, the length of time of pregnancy and the fact that this pregnancy doesn't pose a health risk to the mother make it indecent, though not unjust, for the mother not to carry the pregnancy to term.

But I think that when we examine what at least certain violations of the right to bodily autonomy involve, we will see that appeal to this right is sufficient to override even the indecency charge. Thomson believes that since the fetus is a person and pregnancy in this case poses no health risk, the mother should (in the sense that she'd be indecent not to) carry it to term, since one hour of her time is no big deal when another person's life is at stake. Of course, as Thomson admits, conservatives wrongly extend this logic to normal

---

[29] See Judith Jarvis Thomson, "Trespass and First Property," in *The Realm of Rights* (Cambridge, MA: Harvard University Press, 1990), 205–226.
[30] Thomson, "Defense of Abortion," 60.
[31] Thomson, "Defense of Abortion," 61.

pregnancies—they say that it's someone's life, it's no big deal to be pregnant for nine months, most women are fine during pregnancy, so you ought to do it. But consider what Thomson says in her Henry Fonda example, that if all I need to save my life is for Henry Fonda to touch his cool hand on my fevered brow, I do not have a right against him that he fly in from the West Coast to do this for me, though it would be "frightfully nice" of him to do so. But if all he has to do is walk across the room and touch my fevered brow, then it would be indecent of him to refuse.[32] Why would the mother's refusing to carry a fetus to term, even for an hour, *when it is the result of rape*, be self-centered, callous, and indecent, when Henry Fonda's refusing to hop on a plane and cross the country to touch my fevered brow not be indecent—in fact, it would be "frightfully nice" of him to do so? Surely carrying a fetus that is the result of rape even for one hour is much more onerous than flying across country. As Margaret Little perceptively argues, forced gestation is an evil of unwanted occupation, or an invasion of the self, which is neither reducible to the evil of medical risks of pregnancy nor merely a different way of talking about the evil of interference with the mother's plans.[33] Pregnancy, whether or not it is the result of rape, involves a sharing of one's very body, heart, and soul, whose sacrifices are measured not in degrees of risk but in degrees of intertwinement.[34] No such intimacy is involved in the Henry Fonda case, and forced intimacy is obviously not something it is indecent to reject. My first principle about bodily autonomy is this: You shouldn't be required to do anything with your body when the prior act that put you in the position you are in was against your will. I want to support this principle with a Kantian analysis of respect and degradation.

As is familiar, Kant believed that all rational, autonomous beings possess dignity and are deserving of respect, which for Kant means that they are to be treated as ends in themselves and never merely as means to an end.[35] Our rationality, or better, our capacity for rationality, is what makes us persons and distinguishes us from inanimate objects and nonhuman animals. Our capacity for rationality is marked by the fact that we have the ability to make plans and have goals, interests, and reflective desires. We ought to respect these in other rational beings by, for example, not putting our own interests and reflective desires ahead of those of others (e.g., by not aiding the needy when we are able to), or discounting the plans of others (e.g., by falsely promising to repay borrowed money and not letting the lender decide whether to give

---

[32] Thomson, "Defense of Abortion," 61.

[33] Margaret Olivia Little, "Abortion, Intimacy, and the Duty to Gestate," *Ethical Theory and Moral Practice* 2 (1999): 304.

[34] Little, "Abortion, Intimacy, and the Duty to Gestate," 305. Little rightly notes that her view is noticeably absent from the philosophical literature and urges the development of an ethic of intimacy.

[35] Immanuel Kant, *Grounding for the Metaphysics of Morals*, translated by James W. Ellington (Indianapolis: Hackett, 1981 [1785]), 36, AKA 428–429.

it to you in the first place), and the like. In virtue of our humanity, we ought to respect each person as a potential co-legislator of morality and engage in conduct only on which we could expect all reasonable people to agree. To do otherwise is to make an exception for yourself by treating another rational being as a mere means to your ends, behavior to which another would not autonomously consent.

Let's apply this analysis first to rape and then to enforced pregnancy. A common feminist analysis of rape explains rape as an act in which the rapist attempts to degrade his victim by considering her to be an inferior being, merely an object to be used for men's sexual pleasure or control.[36] According to Jean Hampton, rape conveys the attitude that women are even lower than chattel; they are mere "objects" that are there to be used whenever the male feels the need to do so but not beings with the capacity for rationality who ought to be respected as ends in themselves. Hampton classifies rape as a moral injury, which she defines as damage to the realization of a victim's value through behavior that diminishes, or, attempts to lower, the victim's value.[37] She agrees with Kant that a person's intrinsic value, the value she has as a person, cannot actually be lowered or degraded or for that matter raised—we are equal in virtue of our humanity, as ends in ourselves.[38] Rape is morally injurious not just to its direct victim but to all women. This is because rape sends the message to all women, that they are the kind of human beings who are subject to the mastery of people of the rapist's kind, namely, men.[39] Rape thus diminishes all women's value.

One way to parse this analysis of rape is along the lines of an individual account of autonomy. Kant ties respect for persons to their capacity for rationality and not anything bodily, but the body might factor in in terms of a person's having interests or reflective desires (e.g., not mere bodily appetites, but desires about whether to eat or drink and for which reason) relating to her body that are indicative of the capacity for rationality. Because rape is an act against a person's will, it disrespects her desires or interests having to do with

---

[36] See Jean Hampton, "Defining Wrong and Defining Rape," in *A Most Detestable Crime*, edited by Keith Burgess-Jackson (New York: Oxford University Press, 1999), 118–156; Susan Griffin, "Rape: The All-American Crime," in *Feminism and Philosophy*, edited by Mary Vetterling-Braggin, Frederick A. Elliston, and Jane English (Totowa, NJ: Littlefield, Adams, 1981), 313–332. Griffin says that rape is an act of aggression in which the victim is denied her self-determination and is a form of mass terrorism because the victims are chosen indiscriminately. See also Catharine MacKinnon, *Toward a Feminist Theory of the State* (Cambridge, MA: Harvard University Press, 1989), esp. chap. 9; MacKinnon, "Desire and Power," in *Feminism Unmodified: Discourses on Life and Law*, edited by Catharine MacKinnon (Cambridge, MA: Harvard University Press, 1987). MacKinnon says that "men have been knowers; mind; women have been 'to-be-known,' matter, that which is to be controlled and subdued, the acted upon" (55).

[37] Hampton, "Defining Wrong and Defining Rape," 132.
[38] Hampton, "Defining Wrong and Defining Rape," 127.
[39] Hampton, "Defining Wrong and Defining Rape," 135.

how her body is treated, specifically, her desires and interests about whether to have sex, with whom, and under which conditions.

Alternatively, we might parse this account of rape along the lines of a relational autonomy and make the Kantian case stronger, for it is not just interests you have regarding your body that are at stake, but bodily integrity. I want to suggest that all of your interests are interests of you as a person—your interests attach to you—and your person is housed in your body.[40] This is why you have bodily integrity. Rape is not just an act of ignoring or discounting or thwarting your interests about your body; rather, it is a violation of your very person, through your body, and as such it is a violation of your bodily integrity. This analysis explains in a better way than the earlier one why rape is an act against your will, specifically, using your body against your will. Rape is not just an act that goes against an interest you have regarding how your body is treated, but it is about how your whole person is treated.[41] It sends a message not just that a certain interest you have does not count but that you are the kind of being whose interests—any and all of them—do not count. This analysis allows for a deeper sense of the account of rape being "against your will."

Rape is a violation of the right to bodily autonomy in a way that attempts to degrade its victim. It seems that if rape attempts to turn a woman into an inferior being—nothing more than a body or body part or sex object to be used for men's pleasure or control—then a woman's right to bodily autonomy, if it means anything, allows her to affirm, through the right to abortion, that she is *not* such a being. It allows her to affirm what someone has attempted to take away from her. When someone uses your body against your will, he treats you as not being a member of humanity. Enforced pregnancy, some feminists have argued, treats women as if they were mere fetal containers, not full-fledged members of humanity.[42] If the woman does not want to carry to term a fetus resulting from rape, then she should not be required or deemed indecent if she does not subject her body to this intrusion against her will. By being free from morally bad judgment when she exercises her right to bodily autonomy through abortion, she is able to assert her bodily integrity, herself as a whole person, at base, her humanity. What's more, since rape sends a message of degradation to all women, when a woman asserts her humanity in this way, she is

---

[40] This account was inspired by Helga Varden's explanation of why, for Kant, from the point of view of justice we have to consider the relation between my person and my body as analytic, as a necessary unity. See Helga Varden, "A Feminist, Kantian Conception of the Right to Bodily Integrity: The Cases of Abortion and Homosexuality," in *Out from the Shadows: Analytical Feminist Contributions to Traditional Philosophy*, edited by Sharon L. Crasnow and Anita M. Superson (New York: Oxford University Press, 2012), 35.

[41] This analysis might reflect Catriona Mackenzie's account of relational autonomy.

[42] See Laura M. Purdy, "Are Pregnant Women Fetal Containers?" in *Reproducing Persons: Issues in Feminist Bioethics*, edited by Laura M. Purdy (Ithaca, NY: Cornell University Press, 1996), 88–105. Purdy's paper is mainly about whether and the extent to which women have duties to their fetuses, but presumably she would argue along similar lines about enforced pregnancy.

at the same time attempting to shrug off the degrading stereotypes associated with women: that they are nothing more than sex objects or mere bodies for men's use. The time that pregnancy lasts has no relevance to this argument: if someone uses your body against your will in ways that attempt to reduce your humanity, morality should allow you to reassert your humanity, to in effect send the message that neither you nor members of your kind are the kind of beings that can be treated this way.[43] This is true whether pregnancy lasts nine months or one hour. Thus, there is nothing indecent or callous about a woman who seeks to abort a fetus that reminds her of the rapist's attempt to degrade her. At best, the woman would be "frightfully nice" to carry the fetus to term.

3. Case 2: Late-Term Abortion for Morally Questionable Reasons

Regarding case 2 of the woman who, in her seventh month of pregnancy, wants an abortion to avoid postponing a trip, Thomson says, "...while I do argue that abortion is not impermissible, I do not argue that it is always permissible. There may well be cases in which carrying the child to term requires only Minimally Decent Samaritanism of the mother, and this is a standard we must not fall below... It would be indecent in the woman to request an abortion, and indecent in a doctor to perform it, if she is in her seventh month, and wants the abortion just to avoid the nuisance of postponing a trip abroad."[44] Again, Thomson is not saying that the fetus in this case has a right to use the mother's body and that the mother has a corresponding obligation to allow it to do so, so in some sense Thomson still protects the right to bodily autonomy. Yet this is another case where Thomson levels the charge of moral indecency on the woman who has an abortion in these circumstances, which supports her belief that abortion is not morally permissible in this case. The woman thus ought not to abort, but the "ought" is grounded not in the fetus' right to use the mother's body but in the woman's being indecent not to let it use her body.

In her paper, Thomson seems to set up a hierarchy of moral acts. At the top are the most morally onerous acts, ones in which a great deal of sacrifice is required of the agent. Thomson mentions "Splendid Samaritanism," in which the sacrifice is onerous, and "Very Good Samaritanism," in which the sacrifice is very large, in connection with this class of acts.[45] Good Samaritanism, ranking just below Very Good Samaritanism, also involves large sacrifices, where the

---

[43] We might even argue that you have an obligation, out of self-respect, to reassert your humanity. For this kind of view, see Thomas E. Hill, Jr., "Servility and Self-Respect," in *Dignity, Character, and Self-Respect*, edited by Robin S. Dillon (New York: Routledge, 1995), 76–92 (reprinted from *Monist* 57 (1973): 87–104).

[44] Thomson, "Defense of Abortion," 65–66.

[45] Thomson, "Defense of Abortion," 65, 64.

agent goes out of his way, at some cost to himself, to help one in need of it.[46] As an example, Thomson cites the Kitty Genovese case, where Genovese was murdered while twenty-eight people watched or listened without helping her—a Good Samaritan, Thomson notes. Then she immediately corrects herself and says that a Splendid Samaritan would have rushed out and assisted Genovese against the murderer.[47] Thomson's shift to what a Splendid Samaritan would have done is explained by the size of the sacrifice involved, which in this case is a risk of death for yourself.[48]

For any act involving Good Samaritanism or better, there is no requirement that the agent do it. Thomson notes that Henry Fonda would be a Good Samaritan, performing an act of kindness but not anything required that you can claim against him as your due, were he to fly in from the West Coast to touch your fevered brow.[49] She says the same about the violinist who needs to stay hooked up to your body to use your kidneys for his continued life: "it is a kindness on your part, and not something you owe him."[50]

Next on the hierarchy come acts that are indecent not to perform yet do not correspond to any rights violation and thus are not owed by you to another agent. These are acts of Minimally Decent Samaritanism. I understand moral requirements to rank just below acts of Minimally Decent Samaritanism in the hierarchy. I will address moral requirements first, since Thomson draws out their significance by comparing them with acts of Minimally Decent Samaritanism. Morally required acts, unlike the others so far mentioned, correspond to rights. One example of a morally required act comes in with the case of the two brothers who are jointly given a box of chocolates, but the older brother takes them all and refuses to give any to the younger brother. The younger has a right to them, so the older one is unjust and violates an obligation in not giving his brother his fair share.[51] Sharing the chocolates is morally required because the younger brother had a right to the chocolates. In contrast, you are not unjust if you unplug yourself from the violinist because he had no right against you to use of your body,[52] even if unplugging him means that he dies. Unless you gave him a right to use your body, you are not morally required to let him use it. Similarly, the woman who becomes pregnant from rape or due to contraceptive failure does not have an obligation to carry the fetus to term because she did not invite it in or give it a right to use her body, and it has no right against her for use of her body. Obligations corresponding

---

[46] Thomson, "Defense of Abortion," 62.
[47] Thomson, "Defense of Abortion," 62–63.
[48] Thomson, "Defense of Abortion," 63.
[49] Thomson, "Defense of Abortion," 55, 65.
[50] Thomson, "Defense of Abortion," 56.
[51] Thomson, "Defense of Abortion," 56–57.
[52] Thomson, "Defense of Abortion," 57.

with rights fall below acts that are indecent in you not to perform—you ought to perform the former; morality requires it.

Now consider Minimally Decent Samaritanism, acts that it should be morally indecent not to perform. Carrying a one-hour pregnancy to term, sharing your chocolates with your brother when they were given only to you and he wants some, Henry Fonda's walking across the room to touch your fevered brow, letting the violinist use your kidneys for one hour, and not requesting an abortion in the seventh month to avoid postponing a trip are cases of Minimally Decent Samaritanism.[53] Thomson says that you ought to perform such acts in the sense that it would be indecent to refuse.[54] Thomson distinguishes these cases, and this sense of "ought," from cases of moral obligations, which correspond with rights. She argues against those who believe that the "ought" of minimal decency generates a right: "…it seems to me to be an unfortunate loosening of what we would do better to keep a tight rein on."[55] Rights are generated differently, independent of the "oughts" of minimal decency, but on the basis of someone's having a clear entitlement to something (e.g., ownership of one's body or a box of chocolates).[56] The "ought" of obligation follows from this, whereas the "ought" of indecency follows from how easy it is to provide someone with something.[57] Thomson notes that, except where there is a right to demand it, nobody is morally required to make large sacrifices of health and other interests and concerns, even to keep another person alive.[58] Still, "oughts" of minimal decency are "oughts"—we cannot claim that the fetus who comes into existence from rape has a right to use the mother's body even for a one-hour pregnancy but only that the mother ought to let it use her body for this short time because she would be self-centered, callous, indecent to refuse. Thomson notes that "the complaints are not less grave; they are just different."[59] That is, they are both ways you ought to act, but the "ought" is grounded in a requirement in one case, and in minimal decency, in the other case. The "ought" of minimal decency is binding in a way that makes the act impermissible, but its impermissibility does not derive from its being a moral requirement or duty. Although Thomson is not explicit about this, we can discern from the cases that Minimally Decent Samaritanism is in the class of acts of Samaritanism whose degree of goodness depends on the amount of sacrifice involved. Obligations corresponding with rights do not: indeed "it's a rather shocking idea that anyone's rights should fade away and disappear as it gets harder and harder to accord them to him."[60] But since Minimal Moral Decency is

---

[53] Thomson, "Defense of Abortion," 60, 61, 59–60, 65–66.
[54] Thomson, "Defense of Abortion," 60.
[55] Thomson, "Defense of Abortion," 60.
[56] Thomson, "Defense of Abortion," 60.
[57] Thomson, "Defense of Abortion," 61.
[58] Thomson, "Defense of Abortion," 61–62.
[59] Thomson, "Defense of Abortion," 61.
[60] Thomson, "Defense of Abortion," 61.

farther down on the scale from the supererogatoriness of Splendid Samaritanism but closer to the moral requiredness of obligations that correspond with rights, Thomson assigns it the force of an "ought."

Return to Thomson's case of the woman who wants the late-term abortion to avoid postponing a trip. What drives Thomson's view that Minimally Decent Samaritanism means that the woman ought to carry the pregnancy to term is the amount of sacrifice involved in doing so.[61] Thomson must be weighing the sacrifice in postponing a trip against the value of the fetus' life. But I think the more apt comparison is the sacrifice in carrying the pregnancy to term versus the fetus' life. And here I am not convinced that Minimally Decent Samaritanism demands that the woman carry the pregnancy to term. Pregnancy is a risky undertaking. Tribe notes that as many as 30 percent of pregnant women have major medical complications and 60 percent have some kind of medical complication.[62] The Centers for Disease Control and Prevention (CDC) lists some of the common complications of pregnancy as anemia, urinary tract infections, mental health conditions (e.g., sad mood, problems concentrating, feelings of worthlessness), hypertension, preeclampsia (which occurs after the twentieth week of pregnancy and causes high blood pressure, problems with the kidneys and other organs, swelling of the hands and face, too much protein in the urine, stomach pain, blurred vision, dizziness, headaches, and seizures and whose only cure is delivery), gestational diabetes mellitus (which increases the risk of preeclampsia and having a big baby, which can complicate birth), obesity, infections, and hyperemenesis gravidarum (nausea and vomiting).[63] Amy Mullin, in her philosophical book on pregnancy, notes that vomiting two to three times a day in the first four months is considered normal, as is extreme fatigue.[64] It has been reported that 70 to 80 percent of pregnant women have some type of morning sickness and that although 60,000 cases of hyperemenesis gravidarum have been reported by hospitals, the numbers are much higher because many women are treated at home.[65] There is no prevention of this condition, and it causes severe dehydration, inability to keep down any food, extreme fatigue, headaches, confusion, fainting, low blood pressure, rapid heart rate, and secondary anxiety or depression. The CDC reports that in the United States 650 women die each year from pregnancy or delivery complications.[66]

---

[61] I do not take issue with Thomson's criterion for determining degrees of Samaritanhood.

[62] Tribe, *Abortion*, 103.

[63] Centers for Disease Control and Prevention (CDC), "Pregnancy Complications," February 5, 2013, http://www.cdc.gov/reproductivehealth/MaternalInfantHealth/PregComplications.htm.

[64] Amy Mullin, *Reconceiving Pregnancy and Childcare: Ethics, Experience, and Reproductive Labor* (New York: Cambridge University Press, 2005), 61.

[65] American Pregnancy Association (APA), "Pregnancy Complications," 2013, http://americanpregnancy.org/pregnancycomplications.

[66] CDC, "Pregnancy Complications."

In addition, Mullin notes that pregnancy exacerbates ongoing illnesses, and most health-care providers are unsure of how it affects such disabilities.[67] Some of the dozen or so preexisting health conditions listed by the CDC that can affect pregnancy include asthma (increases the risk of preeclampsia, Caesarean birth, and other complications), high blood pressure (causes preeclampsia, placental abruption, and preterm birth), and thyroid disease (causes heart failure).[68] Aside from these serious physical and psychological complications of pregnancy, Ann Cudd notes other harms, and jointly these dangers push pregnancy to the status of at least Very Good Samaritanism on Thomson's scale:

> Pregnancy is a dangerous and onerous task for a person. She may feel that she loses bodily integrity, freedom of movement, suffers physical pain and discomfort, and risks serious illness or death. If she is relatively wealthy, she must either submit herself to the frequent, often intrusive examinations by physicians and their restrictive instructions, or risk an alternative, less socially acceptable, kind of care. And if she is poor then she may not be able to afford the necessary care to lessen the risk of pregnancy. In any case she is likely to be discriminated against in employment and education, find it more difficult to be taken seriously, and be given unsolicited advice from all directions. All this suggests outstanding heroism but pregnant women are not accorded heroic status because it is expected of them, and what they really want anyway.[69]

Thus, factually speaking, I conjecture that Thomson underestimates the level of Samaritanhood in pregnancy. Since the sacrifices necessary to carry the pregnancy to term are great, the mother who would rather not do so, to take a trip or whatever, should not be deemed indecent if she opts to abort—she is nowhere in the league of Henry Fonda who has to walk across the room to touch your fevered brow.[70] For Thomson to say otherwise goes against her view that Minimally Decent Samaritanism does not require a lot of sacrifice.

I want to make a more general point about Minimally Decent Samaritanism. It has been objected that the "oughts" of decency should be even stronger than Thomson argues for. Peter Singer argues convincingly that we have an obligation to help the needy when we are able to do so without suffering any comparable harm to ourselves.[71] If we agree with Singer, the demands of morality

---

[67] Mullin, *Reconceiving Pregnancy*, 60.

[68] CDC, "Pregnancy Complications."

[69] Ann Cudd, "Enforced Pregnancy, Rape, and the Image of Woman," *Philosophical Studies* 60:1–2 (September–October 1990): 47–59, 53.

[70] To be clear, I am not saying that the indecency charge is overridden by competing moral claims but that it should not be leveled to begin with.

[71] Peter Singer, "Famine, Affluence, and Morality," *Philosophy & Public Affairs* 1:3 (1972): 229–243. Singer's principle is that "If it is in our power to prevent something bad from happening, without

are even more stringent than Thomson sets out. They would require both the woman in the seventh month of pregnancy who wants to take a trip and the rape victim whose pregnancy lasts only one hour to carry their pregnancies to term as well as other pregnancies when the mother does not suffer harm comparable to the fetus' death.[72]

Although many of us find Singer's general principle plausible, I believe that when it comes to using our bodies to carry out the prevention of something bad, the demands of morality are less stringent than this principle sets out. And the more intimately our bodies must be used, the less stringent the moral demand. Of course, pregnancy is exactly the kind of case where a woman's body is used most intimately in carrying out any moral demand made by the fetus' situation. As Margaret Little puts it, there are significant qualitative differences between gestating and giving money to Oxfam: "There are special facets to a decision about charity when the beneficence is a matter of sharing one's body, heart, and soul, not just one's pocketbook or general energies, when the sacrifice is measured, not in degrees of risk, but in degrees of *intertwinement*."[73] For this reason, pregnancy is more sacrificial than being hooked up to a violinist, which is more sacrificial than donating blood or getting vaccinated against contagious diseases.[74] Any of these is more sacrificial than donating money to Oxfam, simply because of the degree of bodily involvement.

Why does use of the body matter so much to the demands of morality? Thomson makes several remarks that speak to its significance:

> No doubt the mother has a right to decide what shall happen in and to her body; everyone would grant that.[75]
>
> If anything in the world is true, it is that you do not commit murder, you do not do what is impermissible, if you reach around to your back and unplug yourself from that violinist to save your life.[76]
>
> ...the mother *owns* the house.[77]
>
> Women have said again and again "This is *my* body."[78]
>
> My own view is that if a human body has any just, prior claim to anything at all, he has a just, prior claim to his own body.[79]
>
> For nobody has any right to use your kidneys unless you give him such a right...[80]

---

thereby sacrificing anything of comparable moral importance, we ought, morally, to do it" (231). I owe this example and the objection it makes to my view to Samantha Brennan.

[72] I do not know if Singer would say this because he does not address this in his paper.
[73] Little, "Abortion, Intimacy, and the Duty to Gestate," 305.
[74] Samantha Brennan and Heather Douglas provided the examples.
[75] Thomson, "Defense of Abortion," 48, 50.
[76] Thomson, "Defense of Abortion," 52.
[77] Thomson, "Defense of Abortion," 53.
[78] Thomson, "Defense of Abortion," 53.
[79] Thomson, "Defense of Abortion," 54.
[80] Thomson, "Defense of Abortion," 55.

Because you own your own body, have a just prior claim to it, and are the only one who can give some a right to use it, the right to bodily autonomy has high trumping power. Again, I believe that the significance of the body lies with the fact that you are your body: it is the vehicle through which you live your life.[81] Susan Brison cites Jean Améry, who claims that the boundaries of my body are also the boundaries of my self.[82] Both Brison and Laurence Thomas, in their work on bodily trauma experienced in rape or child abuse, further explain this insight. According to Thomas, a rape victim suffers the psychological scar of having a profound sense of diminished personal agency.[83] The sense of personal agency, which Thomas believes is acquired under favorable conditions in one's adult familial environment rather than at birth, "is absolutely central to being an adult, and at least partially captures the force of 'my' in 'my body.'"[84] It is the sense in which one has a great deal of control over things that happen to one's body in one's social interactions: "To have a sense of personal agency is to have the conviction that, well beyond cases of sheer bodily harm, there are things which a person ought not, and so will not, do to or with one's body, or observe one's doing with one's body, without one's consent."[85] According to Thomas, rape, childhood sexual abuse, and other similar bodily traumas shake the victim's sense of personal agency at its core in such a way that the victim's beliefs about her self become skewed, causing her to suffer a radical diminution of her self.[86] Although Thomas denies that the pain of rape is conceptually related to having suffered a bodily injury, the reality is that the diminution of the sense of self is carried out through an attack on one's body.

I would add to Thomas's account that having a sense of personal agency is to see oneself as a valid member of a moral community, a being who is owed a certain treatment including respect for her body. Along these lines, Brison argues that recovering from bodily trauma experienced in rape is a matter of being reconnected with humanity in ways that you value.[87] Physical trauma inflicted by another can change one's perception of one's own body, by

---

[81] Thomson speaks of owning your own body, but I think you are your body. She might agree, explaining that the fact that you are your body underlies your ownership of it. I leave aside the debate between being your own body and owning it. For a discussion of ownership, see Jennifer Church, "Ownership and the Body," in *Feminists Rethink the Self*, edited by Diana Tietjens Meyers (Boulder, CO: Westview Press, 1997), 85–103.

[82] Susan Brison, "Outliving Oneself: Trauma, Memory, and Personal Identity," in Meyers, *Feminists Rethink the Self*, 18.

[83] Laurence Thomas, "The Grip of Immorality: Child Abuse and Moral Failure," in *Reason, Ethics, and Society: Themes from Kurt Baier*, edited by J. B. Schneewind (Chicago, IL: Open Court, 1996), 144–167.

[84] Thomas, "Grip of Immorality," 152.

[85] Thomas, "Grip of Immorality," 152.

[86] Thomas, "Grip of Immorality," 153.

[87] Brison, "Outliving Oneself," 28–29.

reducing the victim to flesh or a mere object,[88] causing her to perceive her body as an enemy or a site of increased vulnerability,[89] to disassociate from her body or to have an intense awareness of her embodiment,[90] to experience traumatic memories through her body (e.g., racing heart, crawling skin, or being immobilized),[91] and to distance one's self from one's bodily self.[92] Victims of bodily trauma need to remake their selves, to reconnect their self that existed prior to trauma with the self they come to be through their trauma. This cannot be accomplished in isolation from others but only in a community of trustworthy persons, particularly those who are also survivors of trauma and who will listen to their story and engage in mutual empathy with them.[93] Through this process, the victim finds some aspects of her lost self in another person and is able to reconnect with it and remake her self as one, surviving as an autonomous self.[94] This process confirms the victim's humanity.[95]

I conclude from this discussion that the body is the vehicle through which you live your life, it plays a significant role in the identity of the self, and it is integrally bound up with having a sense of personal agency or being a member of humanity or the moral community. These factors give backbone to Thomson's belief that the body is so important that only you can give someone else a right to use your body and in turn to why the demands of morality are lessened accordingly with the degree of involvement of the body required to carry them out. I offer the following principle:

> The stringency of the demands of morality are dependent on the degree of the involvement of the body in carrying them out; an act that is otherwise a duty can be an act of at least Good Samaritanism commensurate with the degree of bodily involvement necessary to fulfill it.

Let's return to the indecency charge mounted against the woman who wants a late-term abortion to avoid postponing a trip, since this still needs defense. Perhaps it is not just the amount of sacrifice but also a kind of commitment the mother makes to the fetus that grounds Thomson's indecency charge.[96]

---

[88] Brison, "Outliving Oneself," 18.
[89] Brison, "Outliving Oneself," 16–17.
[90] Brison, "Outliving Oneself," 20.
[91] Brison, "Outliving Oneself," 17.
[92] Brison, "Outliving Oneself," 20.
[93] Brison, "Outliving Oneself," 29.
[94] Brison, "Outliving Oneself," 30. Since regaining autonomy involves dependence on others, Brison calls hers a relational account of autonomy.
[95] Brison, "Outliving Oneself," 28.
[96] Whether this is Thomson's view is unclear, and she certainly does not state it as such. The underlying issue is under what conditions the mother gives the fetus a right to use her body. We know that in cases of rape and contraceptive failure the mother does not give the fetus this right. We might infer, then, that when sex is consensual and when the woman (or couple?) does not take contraceptive measures because she intends to get pregnant, then if she does become pregnant, she gives the fetus a right to use her body. But the case at issue (which does not involve rape or contraceptive failure) is one

I think that it is odd to say that a person ever makes a commitment—an unbreakable commitment—to carry through with a bodily process, especially when it involves an intimate use of one's body. Suppose you agreed with your dentist to have a root canal or with your doctor to undergo chemotherapy, but during the course of the procedure you could no longer deal with the anxiety. Surely if you have a right to bodily autonomy, this right entails that you get to stop a medical procedure on your body at any point, even if doing so is not medically or practically wise. The maximal choice approach to health-care decision making, the predominant model in the medical ethics literature, would insist on it, as it endorses a right to refuse treatment, to die with dignity, to refuse experimentation, not to be sterilized, and even to commit suicide.

But maybe the maximal choice view does not apply when it comes to pregnancy because another life is at stake. Janet Gallagher discusses a number of cases in which fetal rights advocates use the viability line or cutoff point employed by the US Supreme Court in *Roe v. Wade* as part of its argument to show that once a woman decides to forgo abortion and the state chooses to protect the fetus the woman "loses the liberty to act in ways that would adversely affect the fetus."[97] Gallagher cites legal cases in which pregnant women were forced to undergo Caesarean sections despite their refusal or were detained or incarcerated to prevent harm to the fetus.[98] The assumption is that once a woman carries the fetus to the point of viability, she is committed or has contracted to carry it to term and not engage in behavior that might harm it, even when this entails severe restrictions on her liberty or bodily autonomy.

One wonders whether it is the fact that another life is at stake that makes the contract model override the maximal choice model or whether the maximal choice model really does not hold for women's bodies. It used to be the case that a woman's consent to marriage meant that she consented to sex with her husband at his discretion throughout the marriage. Indeed, there was a legal statute, which was finally repealed in all US states and Washington, D.C., since 1993 but still infrequently prosecuted, that denied the existence of rape of a wife by a husband on these very grounds.[99] Some people believe that women should not behave sexually unless they are prepared to carry through to intercourse, as if the woman's sexual behavior commits her to

---

of mere indecency, not one where the fetus can claim a right against the mother, so there is something else besides consent and intention that gives the fetus a right to use the mother's body.

[97] Janet Gallagher, "Prenatal Invasions and Interventions: What's Wrong with Fetal Rights," *Harvard Women's Law Journal* 10 (1087): 31, quoting John Robertson, "Procreative Liberty and the Control of Conception, Pregnancy, and Childbirth," *Virginia Law Review* 405 (1983): 437.

[98] Gallagher, "Prenatal Invasions," esp. 46–48, 9–10.

[99] See Sara Ann Ketchum, "Liberalism and Marriage Law," 264–276. In July 1998, the National Clearinghouse on Marital and Date Rape reported that in seventeen states there are no exemptions from rape prosecution granted to husbands under the law. But thirty-three states still have some exemptions from prosecuting husbands for rape usually with regard to the use of force, http://ncmdr.org/state_law_chart.html.

carry through in a way defined by her assailant in date rape.[100] The idea is that the woman forms a contract or makes an agreement through her behavior and that the contractor is entitled to demand that she uphold it. Lois Pineau argues against this view, noting that casual, nonverbal behavior, such as eye contact, smiling, and blushing are imprecise and ambiguous and can be misinterpreted and thus do not constitute a contract.[101] Such a contract, according to Pineau, is grounded in the myth that men cannot turn off their sexual arousal but women can, so it is women's responsibility not to provoke the irrational in men.[102] Men can rightly expect the contract to be fulfilled by using their natural aggression to see to it that it does. Pineau contrasts the sexual contract with legal contracts that are normally upheld only if the contractors are clear on what they agreed to and have enough time to think about whether this is what they want, the terms are usually written out or the expectations are well known due to tradition and are enforced only by the law, not private individuals. Consider, for example, the contracts we make when buying a car or a house.

Pineau is making two points here. First is an epistemological point, that behavioral cues should not constitute the basis of any contract—nodding your head doesn't mean you contract to buy this house, kissing doesn't mean you contract to sex, and carrying a fetus for seven months doesn't mean you contract to carry it to term. Second, a moral point, is that Pineau doubts whether sexual contracts—and, I would add, any bodily contracts—can even be made because behavior in fact does not entail a commitment but believes that even if they could, the terms would not be enforceable.[103] The right to bodily autonomy should protect against any such contract involving one's body. Pineau dislikes the contract model because it requires a strong act of refusal to overcome the presumption of consent, which essentially allows another person to decide what happens in and to your body. Pineau favors a communicative model that is based on the notion that there are noncommunicative sexual encounters that women would not find reasonable to consent to. Pineau's model puts the burden on the man to show that he got the woman's consent when the sex was of the kind that it would not be reasonable for women to consent to. It presumes the right to bodily autonomy because the man would have to get the woman's consent to further stages of foreplay and to intercourse by checking with her throughout rather than assuming that her consent to some sexual behavior entails a commitment or contract to have intercourse.

---

[100] Lois Pineau, "Date Rape: A Feminist Analysis," *Law & Philosophy* 8 (1989): 217–243.
[101] Pineau, "Date Rape," 229.
[102] Pineau, "Date Rape," 227.
[103] Pineau, "Date Rape," 230.

We can apply Pineau's objection to the contract model of sex—that it requires a strong act of refusal to overcome the presumption of consent—to the case of pregnancy. When it comes to sex, according to the contract model, once the woman displays certain behavior like kissing or smiling, she has contracted to intercourse, and the only thing that gets her out of the contract is a strong act of refusal on her part—the presumption is that contracts should not otherwise be broken. When it comes to pregnancy, according to the contract model, once the woman has carried the fetus to a certain point she has committed herself to carrying it to term (or, the longer she carries it, the stronger her commitment to carry it to term). The only thing that releases her from her commitment is a good and strong reason for terminating the pregnancy. The presumption is that once she becomes pregnant and does nothing to stop the pregnancy, she has committed to carrying it to term absent a good reason not to. Wanting to avoid postponing a trip is not a good reason for breaking her commitment. There are other bad reasons, like negligence and malicious deceit. George Harris discusses the fictitious case of Michelle and Steve, who have been married five years, and he wants children but she does not and does not tell him because confrontation is unpleasant.[104] Michelle allows Steve to believe that it is just a matter of time when they will have children but seeks an abortion when she becomes pregnant. Another case from Harris is that of Anne, the man hater who vents her rage about men against Mark, seduces him, and makes him give up his business and house for a family with her. She pretends at first to enjoy pregnancy but then has an abortion.

The first thing to be said is that these cases are probably the exception rather than the rule. Also, these cases assume that women use sex and pregnancy as a weapon, that they are evil, and that they have options about abortion. Even if some women do use sex or pregnancy for these reasons, doing so is likely out of desperation to have children to stay with a man or make a man want them, and the like, for lack of control over their bodies and from desires deformed by patriarchy. The reality is that women do not have the upper hand in abortion because, though legal in the United States, it is not widely available, its legality is constantly under attack, and it is still stigmatized.[105]

But more to the point about the right to bodily autonomy, the contract model gives another person determination of what happens in and to your own body. On the contract model of sex, the contract is in place absent the woman's strong act of refusal, which gives the man the right to continue onto

---

[104] George W. Harris, "Fathers and Fetuses," *Ethics* 96 (April 1986): 594–603.

[105] It has been estimated that in 87 percent of counties in the United States it is not possible to obtain an abortion because it is heavily restricted or banned in publicly funded facilities or because counseling for it is banned. Rachel Weiner, "No Choice: 87% of U.S. Counties Have No Access to Abortion Clinic," *Huffington Post*, July 3, 2009, http://www.huffingtonpost.com/2009/06/02/no-choice-87-of-us-counti_n_210194.html.

intercourse—the contract is the default position. On the contract model of pregnancy, the contract to carry the fetus is presumed to be in place absent the woman's giving a good and strong reason for aborting the fetus. But this gives a person other than her the right to determine what happens in and to her body by giving that person the power to assess her reasons. Certainly the right to bodily autonomy does not entail this. If a woman owns her body, and her ownership of her body is prior to anyone else's use of it, she, not someone else, should have the right to determine whether she consents to every stage in a process involving it. The right to bodily autonomy should protect against someone else's deciding on her behalf, which risks having her body used for someone else's ends.

Note that all of this is consistent with admitting that the woman in the pregnancy case has bad reasons for wanting to terminate her pregnancy. She might be morally indecent in virtue of her character, but I am arguing that her act of ending the pregnancy is not morally indecent in virtue of her violating some kind of commitment she makes about the use of her body. The contract model enforces pregnancy as punishment for a woman's bad moral character or irrationality and constitutes an illegitimate waiver of one's right to use of one's body. The right to bodily autonomy disallows this, given its significance to being a member of humanity.

In conclusion, I offer the following principle:

> Consenting to early stages of a process involving (especially intimate uses of) your body does not entail a commitment to the entire process; not consenting to the rest of the process, even if your reasons for not consenting are bad, is not morally indecent.

This principle and the others offered previously are intended to support and give substance to the right to bodily autonomy, which is a right that I believe is crucial to feminist positions on issues such as abortion, rape, obligations to fetuses, female genital mutilation, and woman battering, to name just a few. Much more needs to be said to articulate fully the boundaries of this right and its trumping power over other moral considerations. A full articulation and defense of this right will give feminists purchase against the current backlash against abortion rights.

Acknowledgments

For very useful comments, I thank the audiences at the following venues where I presented earlier versions of this paper: Society of Value Inquiry at the American Philosophical Association, Relational Autonomy Workshop held at McGill University, Society for Analytical Feminism conference held at Vanderbilt University, Southwestern Ontario Feminist Philosophers'

Workshop, graduate seminar at the University of California at Davis, and philosophy department at the University of Waterloo. I especially thank Mark Piper and Andrea Veltman for their very detailed comments and Catriona Mackenzie and Natalie Stoljar for inviting me to the Relational Autonomy Workshop where I benefited from comments from top scholars working on autonomy.

{ 15 }

Choosing Death: Autonomy and Ableism
Anita Ho

In recent decades, the values of autonomy and well-being have been very influential in western bioethics. Discussions regarding autonomy often focus on two moral dimensions: the internal capacity of the patient to form and make decisions consistent with her values and goals; and the freedom from external coercion and other undue interference in making such decisions. In discussions of end-of-life care, many have argued that a commitment to respect autonomy and to promote beneficence requires health-care professionals (HCPs) to facilitate the peaceful or dignified death of competent patients who find their terminal or disabling conditions intolerable. Since treatment refusal and withdrawal of life support can often hasten a patient's death but are legally and ethically acceptable when requested by competent patients, the more recent controversies focus on the question of allowing other forms of medically assisted death, such as physician-assisted suicide or active euthanasia, for similarly competent patients. Legalizing such procedures, proponents argue, would support or further patients' rights to make decisions about their lives and well-being in the most compassionate and benevolent ways.

Informed by feminist accounts of relational autonomy, this paper will argue that the individualist and minimalist conceptions of autonomy that are often used to support a right to medically assisted death often neglect the broader contextual factors contributing to people's loss of hope and may thus be inadequate in ensuring that end-of-life decisions truly promote their agency and well-being. In particular, this paper will examine how people's sociopolitical environment and interpersonal relationships affect or even frame the way they experience their impairments and related sufferings. While many bioethicists focus their concerns on third-party involvement in facilitating suicide, I will argue that we need to look at the broader societal assumptions about life with impairments and how these attitudes and our social structure may affect people's quality of life, their decision-making processes, and their desire to die. In examining various forms of professional assistance that would likely lead to the death of the person with impairment, this paper will explore how a society that has not yet overcome ableism should consider such socioenvironmental issues in determining people's potential right to medically assisted death. Even if lingering oppressive powers of an ableist society are not directly coercive, they can affect people's thoughts about their alternatives in such a way that certain options such as living with mechanical or human assistance are not considered as viable and other decisions about ending one's life must be made. In adopting an individualist and minimalist approach to autonomy, the common philosophical approach regarding medically assisted death may be prematurely neglecting many complex factors that contribute to people's decision-making process. In critically evaluating how the ableist ideology may impose various forms of oppressive influence that can restrict people's ability to reflect on their value system and choose their desired life-sustaining support and end-of-life treatments accordingly, this paper nonetheless cautions against treating people with impairments as a separate class of people who are categorically less capable to assess their situation.

1. The Centrality of Autonomy in Bioethics and End-of-Life Decisions

In western moral and political philosophy, particularly since the Enlightenment, there is an explicit acknowledgment of the importance of respecting the autonomy of moral agents. Personal independence and control have been held up as ideals, and conditions of dependency are often seen as misfortunes that should best be avoided. Immanuel Kant's principle of respect for autonomy and John Stuart Mill's principle of individualism, which have shaped the contemporary discussion of autonomy in bioethics and end-of-life care, focus on the inherent capacity and rights of self-determining agents to make their own decisions. For Kant, the capacity for rationally determining one's own ends or destiny is the locus and origin of one's unique and unconditional value.[1] Respect for autonomy requires that we recognize people's right to personal self-governance, that is, a right to be in control of themselves and to choose their own way. Adult autonomous moral agents presumably have the epistemic and moral privilege to determine their own good. Even if we may disagree with their decisions or believe that they are making mistakes, whether in relation to health care or other situations, we cannot coercively override their self-regarding decisions—we can only advise or persuade them to reevaluate their situation with more accurate information when they hold false views so that they are better equipped to reconsider their decisions accordingly.[2] To

---

[1] Immanuel Kant, *Foundations of the Metaphysics of Morals*, translated by Lewis White Beck (Indianapolis: Bobbs-Merrill, 1959).

[2] John Stuart Mill, *On Liberty* (Peterborough: Broadview, 1999).

coerce rational beings even for their own good is to paternalistically treat them as if they lacked the capacity to shape their own lives—it is to deny them their moral status as persons.

The primacy of respect for autonomy in Western bioethics was initiated as a response to research atrocities such as the Nuremberg experiments and the Tuskegee syphilis study, particularly in relation to how the individuals involved were subjected to harm without their knowledge, understanding, or agreement. The ideas of self-determination and well-being have subsequently been adopted in the literature on health-care delivery in the face of evolving individual/civil rights and rising consumer empowerment. Concerns have been raised regarding medical paternalism, where HCPs withhold information from or make value judgments and clinical decisions on behalf of patients allegedly for the latter's own good. The principle of respect for people's autonomy, particularly when expressed in terms of formal consent requirements and privacy regulations, establishes parameters and expectations for HCPs in their conduct with patients. As modern medical science and technology come with risks, limitations, and errors, these legal mechanisms structure HCP–patient relations and regulate what professionals can or cannot do to patients.

Protection of autonomy is considered particularly crucial in health-care settings because illnesses and injuries are physically and emotionally challenging for many patients, especially when the diagnoses are unexpected or grim or when the potential for adverse effect from medical treatment and abuse of power is high. Such protection ostensibly helps to promote patients' agency by ensuring that they understand the risks and benefits of available therapeutic options and have the freedom to choose between or refuse these interventions according to their own values.[3] As feminist bioethicist Susan Sherwin points out, patients are often worried about their situation and are ignorant of the particulars of various treatment alternatives, which generally make them dependent on the care and goodwill of others.[4] HCPs, on the other hand, are presumably more knowledgeable about their conditions, and their professional recommendations often determine whether patients would have (affordable) access to diagnostic and therapeutic procedures that can provide further information, minimize pain, restore health, or improve functioning and extend life. Given that HCPs are inadvertent gatekeepers of information and resources, there is an inherent power hierarchy in the HCP–patient relationship, making patients particularly vulnerable to manipulation or even coercion by their caregivers. While many conscientious HCPs would

---

[3] Leigh Turner, "Bioethics and End-of-Life Care in Multi-Ethnic Settings: Cultural Diversity in Canada and the USA," *Mortality* 7 (2002): 285–301.

[4] Susan Sherwin, "A Relational Approach to Autonomy in health Care," in *The Politics of Women's Health: Exploring Agency and Autonomy*, edited by Susan Sherwin (Philadelphia: Temple University Press, 1998), 19–47.

traditionally treat patients according to the clinician's judgment, with the benevolent assumption that patients who lack medical expertise would not know what clinical alternative is best for them, it is now generally acknowledged in Western bioethics that health-care decisions are not simply clinical decisions. They have important implications on various aspects of the patient's personal, professional, social, and family life. This is especially the case for patients who are terminally ill: that is, they are expected to die within six months from their conditions. For some of these patients, aggressive interventions may sustain or slightly prolong their life without restoring or maintaining their functioning or quality of life. In some situations, the interventions may even aggravate the patient's pain and suffering. As more medical options are now available, each with its own set of benefits and burdens for the patients and their loved ones, it is increasingly difficult for HCPs who have limited contact with patients under very specific circumstances to determine which available option is most compatible with the latter's value system and priorities. This is especially so in diverse societies, where patients may have different cultural values and beliefs regarding what causes illness, how it can be cured or treated, and who should be involved in the process. A strong principle of respect for patient autonomy is thus necessary to counter medical paternalism, particularly toward those who are most vulnerable or socially disadvantaged. Consent requirements for treatment, advance directives, and hospital policies regarding resuscitation and other aggressive interventions are formalized measures that allow patients more control in health-care and end-of-life planning.

2. Minimalist and Value-Neutral Approaches to Autonomy in Treatment Decision Making

One important aspect of the mainstream discussions and practices relating to respecting patient autonomy is that they focus on individual patients making specific decisions regarding their health care, that is, the making of autonomous choice, or the actual governance itself.[5] In contemporary health-care settings, particularly in Western countries that take individual rights for granted, respect for patient autonomy is often manifested in an individualistic manner by obtaining informed consent, one treatment or procedure at a time. Attending to separate and individual cases, respect for self-determination translates into using a primarily cognitive approach to assess that particular person's immediate capacity to make the relevant health-care decision,[6] providing that

---

[5] Tom Beauchamp and James Childress, *Principles of Biomedical Ethics*, 4th ed. (New York: Oxford University Press, 1994), 121.

[6] Catriona Mackenzie and Wendy Rogers, "Autonomy, Vulnerability and Capacity: A Philosophical Appraisal of the Mental Capacity Act," *International Journal of Law in Context* 9 (2013): 37–52.

patient relevant information regarding various available alternatives for his or her particular condition and then allowing the patient (or a substitute decision maker) to make decisions among these options according to his or her values, whatever those values may be. In fact, in most jurisdictions, a person is presumed to have the capacity and authority to make health-care decisions according to his or her own reasons and values, unless there are good reasons to question and formally assess such a capacity. Neither a person's rejection of the HCP's recommendation nor an unusual communication style proves incapacity. Such value-neutral and procedural approaches refrain from assessing the content of the motive behind the patient's decision—these approaches consider a choice to be autonomous if a sufficiently capable patient, construed as a "normal chooser," has and understands the relevant information about the available options and makes a reasonable and intentional choice without coercion from others.[7] The focuses here are on how HCPs may influence the patient's ability to make a particular decision and whether the patient temporarily fails to comprehend his or her situation because of illness or psychological affliction such as depression or severe anxiety in a particular moment. According to a minimalist notion of autonomy, if the patient had no serious cognitive or emotional impairment and was not subject to direct coercion by others, the person's health-care decisions, including choices regarding withdrawing life-sustaining interventions, should be considered autonomous.[8] Others are obliged to respect such decisions, even if these patients may not be exercising their autonomy wisely.[9] The minimalist notion of autonomy seeks to ensure that any potential power hierarchy that may exist between HCPs and patients is not used unjustly to pressure or coerce the latter in their decision making.

In the age of *patient-centered care*, this individualistic focus on each patient's decision-making process appears appropriate, given that patients in diverse societies have varying values and priorities. This approach underlies many mainstream discussions of end-of-life care, even though one's dying process often has tremendous familial and social impact, both in emotional and economic terms. Interestingly, such an approach also dominates discussions of life-sustaining supports and interventions for people with impairments who are not actively dying, particularly around continuing various interventions that may be considered by the patient or others to be physically burdensome. Most people are very concerned about pain and suffering that may accompany

---

[7] Sherwin, "A Relational Approach to Autonomy in Health Care," 26; Tom Beauchamp and James Childress, *Principles of Biomedical Ethics*, 123.

[8] Uma Narayan, "Minds of Their Own: Choices, Autonomy, Cultural Practices and Other Women," in *A Mind of One's Own: Feminist Essays on Reason and Objectivity*, edited by Louise Antony and Charlotte Witt (Boulder, CO: Westview Press, 1993), 429.

[9] Mackenzie and Rogers, "Autonomy, Vulnerability and Capacity," 39.

certain impairments and degenerative conditions as well as the experience toward the end of their lives. Many have a desire to retain dignity and control during this journey, and some find "the impairments and burdens in the last stage of their lives at some point sufficiently great to make life no longer worth living."[10]

Advances of modern medicine—in association with its overwhelming tendency to treat various conditions and symptoms aggressively—have engendered increasing fear among many of losing control over their own dying process. The right to forego "extraordinary" interventions or even requests for medically assisted death have been seen as potential means for patients of diverse values, experiences, and beliefs to maintain or regain power over their own life, their dying process, and their ultimate death.[11] Some patients may determine that their life is unduly burdensome or "wrongful," that is, it is "of sufficiently poor quality that it is worse than no further life at all."[12] Under the legal and moral right to informed consent, patients are presumably the rightful final decision makers to determine whether they want to start or continue life-sustaining measures either through direct consent or refusal or advance directives. These formal documents allow capable adults to give instructions regarding their desired health care, particularly in terms of what types of interventions they would not want, in the event that they are unable to make such decisions later on.

In acknowledging people's right to consider their wishes and well-being in the health-care decision-making process, court cases and legislations in various countries in the last few decades have considered the right of people who are terminally ill or have significant impairments not only to forego various treatments but also to seek physician-assisted suicide or euthanasia. While many people with impairments are not terminally ill, interestingly, several jurisdictions around the world have considered their requests to die by various assisted methods similarly as end-of-life cases. Some philosophers argue that the right to various forms of medically assisted death is a mere specification of the moral right to self-determination.[13] The Canadian examples of Sue Rodriguez in the early 1990s and Gloria Taylor in 2012, the American case of Dax Cowart in 1973, and discussions regarding Dr. Kevorkian from the late 1980s onward are often presented to demonstrate how it is sometimes morally permissible for HCPs to facilitate the death of competent patients who

---

[10] Dan Brock, *Life and Death: Philosophical Essays in Biomedical Ethics* (Cambridge: Cambridge University Press, 1993), 206.

[11] Tania Salem, "Physician-Assisted Suicide: Promoting Autonomy—Or Medicalizing Suicide?" *Hastings Center Report* 29 (1999): 30–36.

[12] Brock, *Life and Death*, 280.

[13] Ronald Dworkin, Thomas Nagel, Robert Nozick, John Rawls, Tim Scanlon, and Judith Jarvis Thompson, "The Philosophers' Brief," *New York Review of Books* 27 (1997): 41–47.

consider their lives to be not worth living due to the suffering brought on by their impairments or terminal illnesses.

The autonomy argument for medically assisted death generally appeals to patients' rights to refuse any procedure that counters their value system and priorities, even if that may result in the patient's death. Refusal of life-sustaining interventions, especially in situations where a person is terminally ill, is now generally considered noncontroversial and is widely accepted as a fundamental component of patients' rights to informed refusal. Taking such a position for granted, many now extend the autonomy argument to challenge the alleged moral distinction between actively killing a terminally ill or disabled patient and letting such an individual forego life-sustaining procedures, both of which can foreseeably lead to imminent death.[14] While withdrawing or refusing these interventions may facilitate a swift and painless death in some cases, it may not offer comfort for others with degenerative conditions who would have to endure a slowly deteriorating and dying process. Some argue that, when death is accepted or even desired by patients as a way to end their burdensome existence, whether due to their terminal illness or impairments, the autonomy argument that allows him or her to forego life-extending measures also supports giving them life-ending assistance. The assumption is that quality of life determination is subjective, such that only the patients themselves can determine if continued life in severely compromised and debilitated states is acceptable. According to this view, if people believe that their impairments or conditions are rendering their lives unbearable and if medical technology cannot cure their "defects" or halt their deterioration, they should be allowed to end their intolerable suffering and have control over the timing and circumstances of death in ways they see fit, including via assisted suicide or active euthanasia. While some have argued that these procedures require third-party involvement and thus are not simply matters of self-determination, they do not generally question the capacity of the person in forming such desires and the voluntariness of the decision itself, unless there are clear signs that the patient suffers from severe mental illness (e.g., depression).[15] They only question the claim that others have the obligation to assist in bringing on or hastening the dying process according to the patients' wishes.[16]

---

[14] Lance Stell, "Physician-Assisted Suicide: To Decriminalize or to Legalize, That Is the Question," in *Physician Assisted Suicide: Expanding the Debate*, edited by Margaret Battin, Rosamond Rhodes, and Anita Silvers (New York: Routledge, 1998), 225–251.

[15] Stell, "Physician-Assisted Suicide," 225–251.

[16] Daniel Callahan, "When Self-Determination Runs Amok," *Hastings Center Report* 22 (1992): 52–55.

3. The Impoverished Notion of Individual Autonomy in Bioethics

In the age of patient-centered care, respect for autonomy and privacy requires that we take the wishes of patients seriously in facilitating their decisions regarding life-sustaining interventions. It is often assumed that state sanctions and individual coercion are the main barriers to people's autonomy and that removal of such forces will allow people to freely reflect on their priorities and values, to form their own preferences, and to realize their life plans in ways they deem appropriate.

However, I wish to argue that the individualist and minimalist framework is too narrow and misses the significance of other external powers. It does not address how many subtle and yet powerful forms of influence—particularly the social structure and institutional framework that promote certain ideologies and reject others—determine people's available options and shape their decision-making processes. The individualist view tends to take restriction of autonomy as a dyadic matter between two individuals—one who is dominant (e.g., physician) and another who is subordinate (e.g., patient). It presupposes that decisions that are not unduly restricted by the dominant agent's actions are autonomous and thus should be respected. It also focuses on individual actions or interactions rather than social practices, unless those social practices have been formalized or codified by law, such as sanctions against euthanasia. In the context of medically assisted death, the individualist-minimalist framework focuses on whether people have all the information to make their end-of-life decisions rather than how various forms of medically assisted death may reflect larger structural issues such as health-care delivery, the professional–patient relationship, the ethos of the medical profession, and the definition of extraordinary care. In arguing for lifting prohibitions on certain forms of medically assisted death, many take it for granted that competent people with all the relevant information should be allowed to make their own decisions regarding whether or how to die.

The minimalist notion of autonomy is attractive in a liberal democratic society because it diminishes the possibility of paternalism, especially in situations where power hierarchy dominates the relational structure, such as health care. In respecting people's expressed choices as the default position, it adopts a relatively value-neutral position and prevents premature intervention in people's lives even when we disagree with their decisions. Nonetheless, in health care and other arenas, power and domination are not simply or always elements of individual actions.[17] Rather, they are also structural phenomena, the intended

---

[17] Iris Marion Young, *Justice and the Politics of Difference* (Princeton, NJ: Princeton University Press, 1990).

or unintended product of the actions of many people that are value laden and shape others' choices. The dyadic modeling of power and autonomy misses the impact of the larger social structure and ideology in determining patients' value frameworks and available options, including what constitutes quality of life, what technologies are considered mainstream, and what risks are deemed acceptable.

While the popular rhetoric regarding patient autonomy leads many to assume that patients determine their desired procedures, health-care systems are structured in such a way that patients do not have much control over their health-care pathway. Patients' diets, diagnostic or check-up schedules, access to specialists and technologies, and discharge plans are determined not based on patients' preferences or values but primarily on lab or bed availability, cost–benefit considerations, professionals' convenience, and insurance coverage.[18] It is often the accumulation of these quotidian decisions, about which permission is rarely requested, that predetermines the subsequent clinical options and outcomes wherein patient consent is finally sought under tight time constraints. Patients routinely behave as they do in the health-care setting partly because of how medicine is practiced or delivered, as determined by clinicians, administrators, politicians, funding agencies, and various regulatory bodies. They make decisions in various manners because of the presumed epistemic privilege and bureaucratic power that professionals hold and according to these clinicians' expectations, even though medical staffs generally do not do anything special to cause patients to adopt or change their actions. Patients recognize quickly that acting against professionals' recommendations even out of careful self-reflection can get one labeled as being noncompliant or difficult rather than being autonomous and acting in self-determining ways.

In other words, patients' actions and decisions are embedded within a complex set of social relations, practices, expectations, and policies that structure their selfhood and can significantly affect their ability to exercise autonomy with respect to their choices.[19] Given that patients' decision-making processes and considerations often incorporate intrinsically relational or social content, it is impossible to assess patient autonomy without critically evaluating how or whether the interconnected social, political, and health-care structural frameworks may foreclose or expand certain opportunities or predetermine how individuals approach various health-care situations.[20] Marilyn Friedman, for example, cautions that social conditions can affect a person's ability to act according to one's reflectively affirmed values and that the individualist view neglects how the collective action and ideology often shape the way people

---

[18] Richard Friedenberg, "Patient–Doctor Relationships," *Radiology* 226 (2003): 306–308.
[19] Sherwin, "Relational Approach to Autonomy in Health Care," 32.
[20] Catriona Mackenzie and Natalie Stoljar (eds.), *Relational Autonomy: Feminist Perspectives on Autonomy, Agency, and the Social Self* (New York: Oxford University Press, 2000).

evaluate their options by making some alternatives more costly than others.[21] The individualist and minimalist approach does not ask how the social system and our economic resources may need to be (re)organized and (re)distributed to ensure that people have meaningful opportunities to critically reflect upon their priorities, freely develop attitudes toward them, and make health-care decisions that would realize their life plans accordingly.

4. Seeking Medically Assisted Death: Sociorelational Contexts

Some notable cases may help shed light on how the individualist and minimalist approach to autonomy fails to capture the complexities of a patient's decision to seek medically assisted death. Larry McAfee and Kenneth Bergstedt, who became quadriplegic after a motorcycle accident and swimming accident in 1985 and 1969, respectively, sought court authorization to turn off their respirators years after their accidents.[22] Neither McAfee nor Bergstedt was terminally ill or experiencing abrupt physical decline, and they both could live for many more years with respiratory support that had become an integral part of their existence. Nonetheless, their respective courts presumed that the quality of life brought on by these individuals' impairments was poor and thus found that it was reasonable for them to think of their situation as hopeless, useless, unenjoyable, and frustrating. Since McAfee and Bergstedt were presumably competent adults who were not directly coerced by anyone to choose death, their respective courts appeared to have adopted the individualist-minimalist approach of autonomy and determined that the plaintiffs had the right to refuse artificial methods to extend their lives, which they presumed were full of suffering.

Another example, while not battled in court, brought up similar social issues around people's alleged desire to die. Dan Crews, an Antioch man who became quadriplegic from a car accident at age three, made national news in 2010 when he—in his mid-20s—asked his health-care providers to remove his ventilator. Despite having been paralyzed from the neck down for over twenty years, Crews reported having a happy childhood. The family won a lawsuit and received a $4 million trust to take care of Crews's medical expenses; they also built an accessible home.[23] Crews was an honors student in high school and

---

[21] Marilyn Friedman, *Autonomy, Gender, and Politics* (New York: Oxford University Press, 2003).

[22] Vicki Michel, "Suicide by Persons with Disabilities Disguised as the Refusal of Life-Sustaining Treatment," *HEC Forum* 7 (1995): 121–131; Anita Silvers, "Protecting the Innocents from Physician-Assisted Suicide: Disability Discrimination and the Duty to Protect Otherwise Vulnerable Groups," in Battin et al., *Physician Assisted Suicide*, 133–148.

[23] Susan Donaldson James, "Quadriplegic Dan Crews Swamped with Letters: Don't Die," *ABC News*, December 7, 2010, http://abcnews.go.com/Health/quadriplegic-swamped-letters-begging-pull-ventilator-die/story?id=12324809#.UWzodcpvAR9.

earned an associate's degree. However, the trust money ran out because he outlived his life expectancy. When his medical bills of more than $300,000 threatened foreclosure on the family's home, Crews feared he would be moved to a nursing home. Short of having someone generous enough to help pay his medical bills, he wanted help to die so that his family could sell the house and be settled financially.[24] Crews requested his health-care team to turn off his respirator, but he was deemed clinically depressed and incapable of making such a decision after he made threats toward his care team. He explained that anyone in his situation would be depressed. (There has not been further media report of his status in the last two years.)

A right to refuse life-prolonging interventions is important in modern health care and ought to be respected when demanded by competent individuals who have reflected on all their options and found such interventions too burdensome. Such requests by terminally ill patients and their families have become a routine part of discussions about the goals of care at the end of life. While many simply consider these situations matters of basic civil liberty, I contend that even these situations are often fraught with value-laden and stereotypical assumptions about life with impairments. Missing in these discussions are the larger social contexts that fail people with impairments and contribute to their suffering. In acknowledging people's despair and their desire to seek death, we need to explore the various factors that contribute to people's hopelessness. The desire to die on the part of McAfee, Crews, and Bergstedt was embedded within a complex set of social relations, policies, and circumstances that foreclosed preferred independent living options most people without impairment take for granted. While an altered life is presumably most difficult soon after one becomes impaired, it is important to note that none of these men sought to die soon after becoming quadriplegic. McAfee, Bergstedt, and Crews all lived with their impairments for years and wanted to die only when their support resources became so severely restricted that they had no feasible means to continue living what they considered to be a minimally decent life, making death appear the only plausible means to end their despair and suffering. With good nursing support covered under his insurance plan and a van customized with a lift and locks for his wheelchair, McAfee was able to rejoin society—he could ride to the grocery store, the occasional movie, or a basketball game. However, a few years later his insurance ran out and he was put into institutional care out of state and then shuffled into a hospital because of his restrictive Medicaid coverage. With no hope of ever living in the community and retaining some control over his life, McAfee wanted to die.[25]

---

[24] Christian Farr, "Quadriplegic Prefers Death to Nursing Home," *NBC Chicago*, April 12, 2011, http://www.nbcchicago.com/news/health/dan-crews-119740714.html.

[25] Peter Applebome, "An Angry Man Fights to Die, Then Tests Life," *New York Times*, February 7, 1990, http://www.nytimes.com/1990/02/07/us/an-angry-man-fights-to-die-then-tests-life.html?pagewanted=all&src=pm.

The Georgia Supreme Court granted McAfee's request presumably based on a right to refuse extraordinary interventions, but the state failed to facilitate what he really wished for and what was available to most people without impairment—his right to independent living and self-determination. What was more noteworthy in this case was McAfee's decision to keep living after the court ruled in his favor. When the publicity of his ordeal prompted advocates to help make it possible for McAfee to move into an independent care home and work toward getting occupational training so that he could use his engineering talents, he no longer wanted to die, even though his physical condition remained the same,[26] suggesting that it was not the impairment itself that caused his despair.

By contrast, Bergstedt's case had a different ending. Becoming quadriplegic as the result of a swimming accident at age ten, Bergstedt lived another twenty-one years of an apparently satisfactory life under his father's care and wrote poetry. However, when his father became terminally ill, he wanted to die, worrying that the society would "cast him adrift in a sea of indifference" and force him into a nursing home after his father's passing.[27] The Nevada court recognized that Bergstedt's desire to die was closely connected to his fear of lack of social support and that if there was an appropriate substitute caregiver he might not have wanted to die. Nonetheless, the court focused on the right to have his respirator disconnected rather than on facilitating his caregiving needs. They granted Bergstedt's petition, and before the Nevada Supreme Court reviewed the case his respirator was disconnected and he died.

Were these individuals' petitions for medically assisted death autonomous? An individualist notion of autonomy would likely render these petitions autonomous and thus respectworthy, even though such a minimalist view neglects how oppressive social conditions limit the availability of desired alternatives and might contribute to despair and low quality of life in the first place. The individualist model ignores the multiple ways one's autonomy and well-being can be compromised by existing institutional arrangements and practices in the health-care and social system. It mistakenly casts that respect for autonomy is mainly or even solely about complying with patients' isolated medical decisions. While some may consider the courts' willingness to consider withdrawing life-sustaining nourishment and interventions as the promotion of civil liberty and individual autonomy, the courts neglected to consider the possibility that the plaintiffs' desire to die was more of a symptom of other social problems rather than a true desire to end their lives. McAfee and Bergstedt went to court not because their impairments themselves imposed too much of a burden—rather, it was the lack of social support for independent living that

---

[26] Michel, "Suicide by Persons with Disabilities," 126.
[27] *McKay v. Bergstedt*, 801 P2d 617 (Nev. 1990), 628.

made their situation unbearable. There were no other desirable arrangements available, leading them to think that, even though they were not dying, death was the only option to escape suffering.

A relational approach to autonomy that pays attention to the impact of oppressive social conditions on agents' motivational structures and their formation can help to explain how the courts' decisions regarding McAfee and Bergstedt, while ruling in favor of the plaintiffs, may have failed to truly promote their overall agency. A relational approach to autonomy looks not only at the agent's expressed desires but also of the social and environmental contexts in which such desires are formed and considered. It examines how the intertwining contexts of social relationships, sociohistorical circumstances, and the range of options available to the agent may affect the reflective process and the development of the agent's capacity to engage in such a process. It also explores how these desires are labeled, interpreted, and responded to by others in social and legal contexts.

5. Ableism, Relational Autonomy, and the Alleged Desire to Die

A look at another court case, brought forth by Elizabeth Bouvia, can shed further light on how a relational approach to autonomy is more equipped in addressing the complexities around the formation of a desire to seek death in an ableist environment. In 1983, Bouvia, a twenty-six-year-old social work graduate student with severe cerebral palsy and degenerative arthritis, admitted herself to a psychiatric hospital in California as a suicidal patient—she wanted professional help to starve to death. Bouvia had lost her motor functions and was dealing with a miscarriage, financial hardship, and a failing marriage. Despite her graduate training in social work, she was told that she would never be employable.[28] As people with depression have a tendency toward global negative thinking, Bouvia's psychiatrist thought that the young woman was making "a bad decision at a very bad time" and that her wish to die could diminish or change with time and treatment.[29] When the hospital staff refused to abide by her wishes and threatened to force feed her, Bouvia went to court with the help of the American Civil Liberties Union (ACLU). The court determined that the state had viable interests in preserving life, preventing suicide, protecting third parties, and maintaining the ethical standards of the medical professions. It denied her judicial assistance to starve herself to death and authorized feeding via a nasogastric tube.[30] Bouvia checked out of the hospital

---

[28] Michel, "Suicide by Persons with Disabilities," 127.
[29] Mary Johnson, "Right to Life, Fight to Die."
[30] *Bouvia v. County of Riverside*, No. 159780 (Riverside Super. Ct. 1983).

to starve herself, but she changed her mind later after discussions with friends and was admitted to a county rehabilitation facility.

In 1986 Bouvia went to court again to have her feeding tube removed. The court denied her request, but the Appellate Court overturned the decision. While the latter court insisted that it did not assess the motive behind Bouvia's decision to refuse nourishment, it agreed that Bouvia, "lying helplessly in bed, unable to care for herself, may consider her existence meaningless."[31]

It is interesting to note that, while Bouvia expressed that she would "rather be dead than live like this," she also explicitly said she "never wanted to die."[32] She stated that physically she was "feeling all right, fine, OK," or that people "could say [she is] doing OK."[33] Nonetheless, the Appellate Court and mainstream commentators continued to consider Bouvia's assertions of a desire to die, albeit inconsistent, as evidence that the woman was making a reflective and autonomous choice. They expressed sympathy towards Bouvia, whom they thought was in a "pitiful state" and living a "life of helpless dependency."[34] There was no discussion of the social and relational contexts within which Bouvia formed her judgments, nor was there investigation of why or how Bouvia's wishes to die wavered at times. The Appellate Court determined that given Bouvia's low quality of life, her right to refuse life-extending interventions superseded the state's interests. Nonetheless, as was the situation a few years prior, after Bouvia was granted the right to starve to death she abandoned her plan, this time claiming that she could not stand the pain and was worried that her slow starvation would bring too much grief and guilt to the staff at her facility.

Bouvia's ultimate decision to continue living in her condition begs for the question of whether the rhetoric around respect for her autonomy is an ableist ideology in disguise. The Appellate Court and various commentators readily accepted her inconsistent desire to die at face value, perhaps because that desire harmonizes with "their own perception that the primary problem for such individuals is the unbearable experience of a permanent disability (and/or dependence on life aids)" and that death is the solution.[35] If Bouvia did not

---

[31] *Bouvia v. Superior Court*, 179 Cal. App. 3d 1127, 1135, 225 Cal. Rptr. 297, 299–300 (1986).

[32] Mary Johnson, "Right to Life, Fight to Die: The Elizabeth Bouvia Saga," *Ragged Edge*, January–February 1997, http: www.raggededgemagazine.com/archive/bouvia.htm; Beverly Beyette, "The Reluctant Survivor: 9 Years After Helping Her Fight for the Right to Die, Elizabeth Bouvia's Lawyer and Confidante Killed Himself—Leaving Her Shaken and Living the Life She Dreaded, *Los Angeles Times*, September 13, 1992, http://articles.latimes.com/1992-09-13/news/vw-1154_1_elizabeth-bouvia; Elizabeth Bouvia, "The Desire is Still There to Die," *Lodi News-Sentinel*, April 14, 1987, http://news.google.com/newspapers?nid=2245&dat=19870414&id=7BcoAAAAIBAJ&sjid=qDIHAAAAIBAJ&pg=6843,5967547.

[33] Beyette, "Reluctant Survivor."

[34] William Raspberry, "Quadriplegic's Life is Hers Alone to Live—And Also Hers to End," *Spokane Chronicle*, April 7, 1986, http://news.google.com/newspapers?nid=1345&dat=19860407&id=_vpLAAAAIBAJ&sjid=vvkDAAAAIBAJ&pg=2623,1367027.

[35] Gill, "Suicide Intervention for People with Disabilities."

have impairments but confirmed that her miscarriage, failing marriage, and employment and financial hardship contributed to her loss of hope in life, many would likely have taken her previous psychiatrist's testimony more seriously and considered her intent to die as signs of depression or social problems and thus potential grounds for support or intervention. The court's neglect of these considerations in its decision reflects the prevailing ableist attitude that having a disability is a sensible reason for committing suicide that requires no further investigation. Ironically, when Bouvia's own ACLU lawyer committed suicide a few years later, she said that she was "not convinced that he couldn't have gotten help." Like many others holding an ableist ideology, Bouvia also seemed to think that impairments were more legitimate than other reasons for one to desire death. She said she could understand if her lawyer had "tried everything and there was no way out" or "if he had cancer or some physical ailment. But he had a lot to live for."[36]

Bouvia's view of her own situation in comparison to that of her attorney's coincides with mainstream evaluations of life with and without impairments, respectively. Her different reactions to her and her lawyer's respective death wishes suggests that the young woman may have internalized society's rejection and devaluation of people with impairments, such that she did not recognize or resist the oppressive forces of ableist ideology.[37] Even as dependency is a natural and unavoidable part of the human condition, dominant social structure continues to espouse individual self-sufficiency as a norm and an ideal, such that technological and human assistance to daily living is often interpreted by HCPs and others to indicate an unacceptably low quality of life. McAfee and Bergstedt relied on respiratory support as part of their daily living—such mechanical assistance had become commonplace for them. Nonetheless, as Carol Gill points out, in a society where professionals attach words such as *radical, extraordinary,* and even *futile* to breathing and feeding supports people use each day, medical professionals and health-care administrators often decide themselves what people with impairments need and define what constitutes excessive needs.[38] International epidemiological measures that quantify the functional, financial, and other impact of various health problems, such as the disability-adjusted life years (DALY), incorporate as purported fact the view that disability and its consequences lower quality of life.[39] Not only do these quasi-scientific measures and HCPs' opinions influence intervention recommendations as well as resource and service eligibilities,[40] they also impact how

---

[36] Beyette, "Reluctant Survivor."

[37] Carol Gill, "Suicide Intervention for People with Disabilities: A Lesson in Inequality," *Issues in Law and Medicine* 8 (1992): 37–53.

[38] Carol Gill, "Disability, Constructed Vulnerability, and Socially Conscious Palliative Care," *Journal of Palliative Care* 22 (2006): 183–191.

[39] Jerome Bickenbach, "Disability and Life-Ending Decisions," in Battin et al., *Physician Assisted Suicide*, 123–132.

[40] Anita Ho, "Trusting Experts and Epistemic Humility in Disability," *International Journal of the Feminist Approaches to Bioethics* 4 (2011): 103–124.

the rest of us assess and in turn affect the quality of life of people with various kinds of impairment.

When such structural considerations frame the daily experience of people with impairments and their interactions with the health-care system, the rhetoric around autonomy in medically assisted death may not capture the full context of many people's decision-making processes, their subsequent choices, and social responses to such requests. The aforementioned court cases suggest that people's perceptions about their quality of life and their corresponding wishes regarding their preferred forms of end-of-life care are not isolated medical decisions. While many bioethicists and advocates for access to medically assisted suicide frame the debate as matters of clinical decisions that should fall under the rubric of informed consent and refusal, I contend that preferences regarding medically assisted death are not purely, or even primarily, medical decisions. They are part of broader evaluations and decisions determined in terms of people's general access to various opportunities to flourish, including their ability to maintain a multidimensional existence composed partly of significant relationships, goals, and values. As Tom Shakespeare points out, even individual choices are situated in social contexts, and a duty to promote autonomy requires assurance that those contexts are supportive of people's decisions in the widest possible sense.[41] McAfee and Bergstedt both fought to stay out of restrictive institutional care that further limited their social relationships and employment opportunities. Crews was worried that his family members would lose all their possessions. A right to discontinue life-sustaining interventions, especially when these individuals were not terminally ill, does not address these underlying issues of restricted opportunities that are essential to promote autonomy. Force feeding as a form of suicide prevention also did not address the social conditions and ableist ideology that contributed to Bouvia's belief that her life was so burdensome that death was perceived to be the only or best means to end suffering.

The intertwining social and relational factors that frame people's desire to die remind us that we need to clarify the cause of people's suffering to provide appropriate relief. Studies show that hopelessness is an essential element of unbearable suffering, and patients perceive their suffering to be unbearable not solely because of their medical conditions or symptoms. Nonclinical concerns regarding the loss of social significance, communicative problems, living arrangements, quality of care, being a burden on others, and loneliness also contribute to people's suffering.[42] The question is partly whether the larger

---

[41] Tom Shakespeare, "The Social Context of Individual Choice," in *Quality of Life and Human Difference: Genetic Testing, Health Care, and Disability*, edited by David Wasserman, Jerome Bickenbach, and Robert Wachbroit (New York: Cambridge University Press, 2005), 217–236.

[42] Marianne K. Dees, Myrra J. Vernooij-Dassen, Wim J. Dekkers, Kris C. Vissers, and Chris van Weel, "'Unbearable Suffering': A Qualitative Study on the Perspectives of Patients Who Request Assistance in Dying," *Journal of Medical Ethics* 37 (2011): 727–734.

system sees life with impairment and dependency as equally worthy and provides appropriate opportunities for people to flourish and retain or regain hope according to their particular contexts.[43] Even when patients are afflicted with terminal illnesses, hope and flourishing do not necessarily require reversing the medical conditions. In the context of mortal beings, hope and flourishing are also about being supported in various interdependent relationships and recognizing one's full humanity regardless of one's level of functioning. As Jerome Bickenbach points out, when an individual chooses death as the only viable way to escape an intolerable situation partly brought on by the social environment, it seems "perverse and unfair to say that this is an expression of self-determination or autonomy."[44]

6. Relational Autonomy and the Problem of Oppressive Socialization

The social context in which people make end-of-life decisions does not simply affect the feasible options available to them. It also affects the agent's development of her capacity to engage in a reflective process in which decisions are formed. As many feminists have noted, social relationships and historical conditions can either facilitate or stunt the development of autonomy.[45] When there is a lack of a supportive environment to facilitate and encourage such development, it is difficult to ascertain whether people's choices, including decisions to forego life-extending interventions or to seek assistance to die, are the results of oppressive socialization. Like oppressive gender socialization that can curtail some women's ability to develop the capacity for critical reflection, ableist ideology that treats a life with impairment as categorically worse off than one without impairment can impede some people's capacity to form the self-trust and self-confidence that are essential to possessing and exercising autonomy, especially if they do not have other strong social or familial support networks.[46] When people devalued by the mainstream society are also deprived of the opportunities to develop the necessary level of self-trust to gain and use their reflective skills effectively, they may not be able to exercise autonomy even when they are invited to make an uncoerced choice regarding their care goals. Such devaluation may hinder people's ability to critically explore their positive commitment to their particular beliefs

---

[43] Eva Kittay, *Love's Labor: Essays on Women, Equality, and Dependency* (New York: Routledge, 1999).

[44] Bickenbach, "Disability and Life-Ending Decisions," 128.

[45] Diana Tietjens Meyers, *Self, Society, and Personal Choice* (New York: Columbia University Press, 1989); Friedman, *Autonomy, Gender, and Politics*.

[46] Friedman, *Autonomy, Gender, and Politics*, 97; Carolyn McLeod and Susan Sherwin, "Relational Autonomy, Self-Trust, and Health Care for Patients Who Are Oppressed," in Mackenzie and Stoljar, *Relational Autonomy*, 259–279.

and value systems,⁴⁷ highlighting two related difficulties of determining whether we should accept at face value people's expressed desire to die, be it via assisted suicide or other means.⁴⁸

First, there are questions about whether one's commitment to a belief in itself affirms the autonomy of a decision made in accordance with that belief. Many proponents of legalizing various forms of assisted death, including mainstream commentators and the Appellate Court judge in Bouvia's case, assume that patients' consistent requests show that they identify with such desires after long reflection. However, even if we assumed for the sake of argument that Bouvia and other people with impairments never wavered regarding their desire to die, would that imply that their processes of reaching such a decision, and the decision itself, were autonomous? Harry Frankfurt, for example, famously argued that when an agent reaches inner equilibrium after reflecting on her first-order preferences and accepts them wholeheartedly, with no interest in making changes regarding them, the agent is choosing these preferences autonomously.⁴⁹

Many feminists have already explained how Frankfurt's ahistorical view neglects the context within which an agent considers her feasible options and forms desires, which might skew her vision of what options are realistic and desirable. I contend that even some historical approaches, such as that espoused by John Christman, do not fully appreciate the extent to which an oppressive environment can rob some people of the ability to form preferences in an autonomous manner. In his earlier works, Christman argues for an historical and counterfactual approach to examine if an agent's desire is authentic by examining whether the individual resisted the development of her preference or would have resisted it if she had attended to its development.⁵⁰ In his more recent work, Christman clarifies that if an agent would not be alienated from her desire if she were to critically reflect on the historical process, that is, if she would not hold a negative judgment or emotional reaction to that preference, the preference could be considered authentic.⁵¹

On the surface, Bouvia's preference to seek death could meet Christman's authenticity requirements. Bouvia had insisted that the real issue for her was the right to make an individual choice regarding her own future and that she

---

⁴⁷ Andrea Westlund, "Rethinking Relational Autonomy," *Hypatia* 20 (2009): 26–49; Paul Benson, "Taking Ownership: Authority and Voice in Autonomous Agency," in *Autonomy and the Challenges of Liberalism: New Essays*, edited by Joel Anderson and John Christman (Cambridge: Cambridge University Press, 2005), 101–126.

⁴⁸ McLeod and Sherwin, "Relational Autonomy, Self-Trust," 262.

⁴⁹ Harry Frankfurt, "The Faintest Passion," *Proceedings and Addresses of the APA* 66 (1991): 3–16.

⁵⁰ John Christman, "Autonomy and Personal History," *Canadian Journal of Philosophy* 20 (1990): 1–24; Christman, "Liberalism and Individual Positive Freedom," *Ethics* 101 (1991): 343–359.

⁵¹ John Christman, *The Politics of Persons: Individual Autonomy and Socio-historical Selves* (Cambridge: Cambridge University Press, 2009), 155–156.

reached her "personal and private decision" after "long and careful thought."[52] She did not claim to have resisted the process of forming her desire to die. She explicitly acknowledged an awareness of services and options available but stated that she did not want to utilize all of them. Nonetheless, even if Bouvia's choice was possibly rational given her dismal outlook or that she did not psychologically resist or struggle with her decision, it does not necessarily follow that her decision was autonomous. Her decision might have been an adaptive one, formed as a result of internalized oppression that was so deep-seated that it prohibited the agent to recognize its presence and force, let alone resist it. In other words, her wish to die might have been a "deformed desire."[53]

Echoing many feminists' focus on care and interdependent relationships in identity and character formation, many disability activists have attempted to counter the stereotypical mainstream view that dependency and vulnerability are abhorrent or undignified forms of living. Some of these activists believed that it was the social contexts that made death seem desirable to Bouvia when such an option would not have been preferable under circumstances of social equality.[54] Bouvia might have come to see the ableist environment as the limits within which she could make her choices or become accustomed to whatever she saw as her lot in life. The fact that her reasoning coincided with many ableist norms when she acknowledged feeling physically fine during the court battle demands a deeper exploration of her motivational system. Even if Bouvia truly had adopted such values as her own, we still need to ask if that might have been the result of her treating ableist norms as "natural" and formulating desires based on such norms. As Diana Tietjens Meyers argues, acting in a way that coincides with oppressive norms raises questions about the agent's autonomy but does not settle them.[55]

Carolyn McLeod and Susan Sherwin also remind us that members of oppressed groups are inclined to accept society's devaluing of their personal worth on an unconscious level and to doubt their own worth.[56] It is worth noting that various ableist norms seemed to be built into the workings of Bouvia's motivational system and sense of self-worth. Bouvia held many beliefs that conform to various stereotypical norms regarding life with impairments. More importantly, she did not appear to be fully aware of or have had critically evaluated such external norms and their potential impact on her own assessment of her life. She did not resist the thought of herself as being "trapped in a useless body" and found the "constant use of a machine or help from another person" at times "humiliating and disgusting."[57]

---

[52] Johnson, "Right to Life, Fight to Die."
[53] Ann Cudd, *Analyzing Oppression* (New York: Oxford University Press, 2006), 180–183.
[54] Cudd, *Analyzing Oppression*, 180.
[55] Diana Tietjens Meyers, "The Feminist Debate over Values in Autonomy Theory," in this volume.
[56] McLeod and Sherwin, "Relational Autonomy, Self-Trust," 262.
[57] Johnson, "Right to Life, Fight to Die."

In other words, the lack of resistance in the development of Bouvia's preference may not imply the autonomy of her desire to die, especially when such preference was developed within an ableist environment, one that she did not appear to resist. While Bouvia insisted that her decision to seek medically assisted death was made in a reflective manner, the fact that the young woman considered her life to be humiliating and disgusting suggests that she may have suffered from the indirect effects of oppression.[58] Bouvia apparently thought of her life not only as one full of suffering—she thought it had inferior worth and did not want to participate in society as a result. Her lack of resistance to the development of a desire to die could thus be the result of pervasive ableist ideology that robbed her of the power to defy such norms. She wholeheartedly identified her life as one with little value, but her attachment to such a belief makes her decision-making process even more questionable. Perhaps more importantly, the question is whether Bouvia recognized and resisted the process through which she arrived at her sense of estrangement and a loss of self-worth. Declining to talk with disability activists, Bouvia did not express an awareness of the oppressive norms around disability and how that might or might not have affected her evaluation of her options. By all appearances, she also did not acknowledge, assess, or develop alternative norms regarding living with impairments and in dependent conditions. Through her legal representative, she denied that other personal and relational factors played a role in her desire to die, emphasizing that her quality of life was poor due to the lack of control brought on by her impairments.

Bouvia's public statement released after refusing to meet with disability activists raises a second question about her autonomy in choosing death. What must answerable agents do to prove that their desires formed within an ableist environment are nonetheless autonomous, and what should the society and professionals do when these self-regarding desires may be deformed?[59] On one hand, in providing statements to respond to disability activists who reached out to her, Bouvia appeared to have not only internalized a disposition to answer for herself but also expressed a willingness to explain her reasons for her commitments. As Andrea Westlund argues, autonomy is tied to a commitment to hold oneself answerable to external, critical perspectives.[60] Such a disposition to answer for oneself, or what Westlund calls *self-representing* in justificatory dialogue, constitutes the self-responsibility that is required for genuine self-government of choice and action.[61]

---

[58] Cudd, *Analyzing Oppression*; Paul Benson, "Free Agency and Self-Worth," *Journal of Philosophy* 91 (1994): 650–668.
[59] Cudd, *Analyzing Oppression*, 180–183.
[60] Andrea Westlund, "Selflessness and Responsibility for Self: Is Deference Compatible with Autonomy?" *Philosophical Review* 112 (2003): 483–523.
[61] Westlund, "Selflessness and Responsibility for Self," 485.

On the other hand, the fact that Bouvia considered her life as one without dignity raises questions of whether her decision-making process demonstrated self-governance. Bouvia's responses expressed an attitude that appeared to deny or efface herself. Despite her legal quest, she did not appear to have a strong sense of trust in her own social standing as a person who should be treated with respect and dignity[62]—it was unclear that she respected herself as a moral agent. She seemed partly impervious to the disability activists' line of questioning regarding how life with impairments can still be fulfilling, only repeating her message that her life had little to no value. Bouvia appeared to derive no confidence or happiness from her identity. She lacked what John Christman called self-acceptance and viewed her life with disgust and contempt. She could not maintain a diachronic practical identity under which she considered her life as worthy of pursuit while negotiating through stultifying constraints. She fought through the psychological pain of her existence with resignation and bitterness and could not reflexively affirm her outlook on her options. Her responses thus seemed to undercut the self-affirmation that is inherent in autonomous action or a self-governing mode of existence.[63]

7. Choosing Death in an Oppressive Environment: Lessons for Public Policy

The context within which Bouvia came to see her life as one without dignity raises questions about the autonomy of her requests to seek medically assisted death. Bergstedt's decision to remove his respiratory support due to his worry of having no means to live outside of an institutional setting may be reasonable given his wish to remain in the community, but it did not represent his true values, goals, and desires. Their respective situations remind us that people's desire for medically assisted death is shaped by broader familial, social, economic, historical, and cultural contexts, some of which have reinforced the idea that a life with impairments is burdensome or even not worth living. An ableist social context and its associated environmental barriers contribute to an inequality of autonomy among people,[64] suggesting that a minimalist approach to autonomy may neglect various relational and systemic factors that can contribute to people's alleged desire to die. There is no sufficient statistical evidence to suggest that impairment and low quality of life are inevitably linked or that a life with impairment is globally worse than one without impairment. In fact, when asked about their quality of life, people

---

[62] Mackenzie and Rogers, "Autonomy, Vulnerability and Capacity," 45.
[63] John Christman, "Coping or Oppression: Autonomy and Adaptation to Circumstance," in this volume.
[64] Bickenbach, "Disability and Life-Ending Decisions," 126.

with impairments often report a quality much higher than that projected by people without impairments.[65] As our examples have shown, some people with impairments who seek assisted death would want to live if social support and opportunity-enhancing arrangements were available, even if their physiological condition were to remain unchanged, suggesting that factors beyond one's physical conditions can have significant impact on one's quality of life. Granting their request to die may end their suffering, but it does not necessarily respect their true desire or deal with the social causes of their despair.

Despite these ableist concerns, the question remains as to whether we should treat people with impairments differently from people without impairments regarding their life-ending preferences. In discussions of medically assisted death, some prominent philosophers reject the application of the autonomy argument specifically for people with impairments, arguing that these people constitute a vulnerable group that requires special protection.[66] While people without impairment are presumed to have had the appropriate environment to develop the capacity to make their own reasoned choices regarding end-of-life care, those with impairments are presumed to be vulnerable. They are believed to be at an increased risk of harm to self and others and thus allegedly require special procedural safeguards. As a lawyer representing the Canadian federal government warned the British Columbia Court of Appeal in March 2013 regarding physician assisted suicide, people with impairments and other vulnerable patients may be at risk of being coerced to kill themselves. The federal lawyer appeared concerned that people with impairments are, as a class, incompetent to assess and protect their own well-being.

Putting aside the issue of whether it is always possible clearly to distinguish between two classes of patients, particularly in end-of-life cases, there are questions about whether correcting an ableist sociocultural framework requires special protection for all people with impairments regarding medically assisted death. As I have argued elsewhere,[67] we need to acknowledge the impact of an ableist social structure on people's despair, and to ensure that the autonomy language used in support for medically assisted death does not mask various barriers of oppression. McAfee and Bergstedt did not want to die—they simply did not want to live with severely restricted social support. The ableist sociocultural framework often precludes certain options from being considered and reshapes a person's value system. Any autonomy-based argument for supporting medically assisted death must consider such complexities.

---

[65] Ron Amundson, "Disability, Ideology, and Quality of Life: A Bias in Biomedical Ethics," in *Quality of Life and Human Difference: Genetic Testing, Health Care, and Disability*, edited by David Wasserman, Jerome Bickenbach, and Robert Wachbroit (New York: Cambridge University Press, 2005), 101–124.

[66] Ronald Dworkin, Thomas Nagel, Robert Nozick, John Rawls, Thomas Scanlon, and Judith Jarvis Thomson, "The Philosophers' Brief," *New York Review of Books* 27 (1997): 41–47.

[67] Ho, "Individualist Model of Autonomy," 204–205.

In addressing systemic issues contributing to people's despair and decision-making framework, we need to lift social barriers and promote a motivational system within which people can make informed and voluntary treatment decisions, including those regarding life-sustaining procedures. At the system level, increased availability of home support and personal care, assistive devices (e.g., ceiling lifts, electric wheelchair), and accessible transportation services can help to maximize people's functioning, provide respite, and allow them to live integrated lives to the greatest extent possible. These services generally cost less than hospital stays and can contribute to people's psychological well-being. At the individual level, clinicians also need to go beyond a cognitive test in determining whether a person's decision to seek medically assisted death is autonomous. Given the finality of such decisions, which may be processed in a depressive state or within an internalized oppressive state, it is important for clinicians to fully explore the context within which patients assess their clinical and overall situations and to offer any resources and support that can foster autonomy and well-being. In addition to the aforementioned system resources, referral to peer support, advocacy groups, or psychological counseling may help patients get more information about living with impairments and navigating the system to access various services.

My suggestions of paying attention to the impact of oppressive social structure on people's identity and decision-making framework do not imply that people with impairment are inherently incapable of self-government. It would be extraordinary to contend that oppression destroys the status of all individuals with impairments as moral agents, rendering them categorically disqualified to evaluate their overall situations and exercise judgment accordingly, when their nonimpaired counterparts have the right to make many unwise decisions that may also have significant and irreversible consequences. The disability movement, the feminist movement, and other similar civil rights movements are prime examples of how, under the right circumstances and when given the opportunity to explore various factors of oppression, many people in historically marginalized positions can critically reflect on their social surrounding and adopt or even promote alternative norms. They can also empower each other and educate those in dominant positions of the unjust situations and motivate change. Prevention of medically assisted death particularly for people with impairment, through denial of self-determination based on speculation about social manipulation, treats the targets of protection as less than persons. It violates their moral agency, isolates them, and perpetuates their inferior status by allowing dominant nondisabled agents to override their expressed wishes and act paternalistically toward them.[68] Behind the façade of the care paradigm, such protective measures may ironically reinforce

---

[68] Silvers, "Protecting the Innocents," 135.

yet conceal epistemic oppression and self-serving relationships of power and domination.

When the concern of an individual's autonomy is partly a problem of the oppressive impacts of the social environment, respect for autonomy should focus on removing such barriers or empowering all through social restructuring rather than paternalistic protection. Instead of giving people with and without impairment different treatment regarding medically assisted death, which reinforces the symbolism of otherness and perception of vulnerability, it is more important to carefully assess the cultural framework that defines and shapes people's life experiences. To ensure that we do not further marginalize or patronize people with impairments, we should collaboratively examine the context within which they assess their quality of life, attend to our hidden and explicit assumptions about living with impairments, develop and explore alternative norms, provide additional information and resources as appropriate, and advocate for removing systemic barriers that may negatively affect people's life experiences. However, after such comprehensive exploration, respect for people's agency requires that we accept their subjective interpretation of their own situation. It is only when a system acknowledges the input of people with impairments and guarantees a fair process to determine adequate access to effective and affordable palliative, home-care, and hospice services that people can be genuinely free to construct their own identity and make health-care and other decisions according to their value system.

Acknowledgments

For critical and constructive feedback on prior versions of this paper, I thank participants from the Relational Autonomy: 10 Years On workshop organized by Natalie Stoljar and Catriona Mackenzie. In particular, I would like to express my deepest gratitude toward the coeditors of this volume, Andrea Veltman and Mark Piper, for their insightful comments and suggestions. All remaining errors are mine and mine alone.

{ INDEX }

ableism, 338–342
abortion: bodily autonomy and, 10, 301–309; late-term, 313–324; length of pregnancy and, 309–313; pregnancy complications, 316–317; rape, 309–313
Abortion: The Clash of Absolutes (Tribe), 301
abstract individualism, 80
accountability, 19, 35–36, 38
ACLU (American Civil Liberties Union), 338–339
active self, 77, 81
adaptation: defined, 206; oppression, 207–215
adaptive preferences: deformed desires as, 229; Double Axis Thesis and, 128, 131–132; internalized oppression and, 137–138; Khader's theory of, 9, 132, 140; in oppressive circumstances, 5, 9, 201–203
adaptive preferences formation: bad options, choosing among, 243–248; coercion, 248–252; freedom to do otherwise model, 238–243; overview, 9, 227–233; psychological processes model, 233–238
adoption, 301
affective states, 167
affiliation, defined, 34
agency: adaptation and, 202, 249; authentic, 211–212; authority and, 93, 106, 108, 140; autonomous, 8, 11, 89, 93–96, 99–101, 103–106, 108, 112–113, 128, 132, 138, 140, 152, 178, 180, 189, 195, 205–206, 213–215, 217, 220, 249, 251, 281–284, 287–290, 293–298; brainwashing and manipulation and, 214; capitalism and, 298; care and, 182, 191; control over one's body and, 319; dialogic interaction and, 211; distinguished from autonomy, 249; emotions and, 8, 170–172, 178, 180, 184–185, 189, 214; end-of-life decisions and, 326, 348; environment and, 214; epistemic, 172; feminist scholarship and, 4, 62, 87, 95, 201; free, 179, 232; full-fledged, 165, 171, 176, 212, 281; gender socialization and, 94; general account of, 173; global characteristics of, 92, 250; human flourishing and, 214–215, 283; local characteristics of, 92; membership in a moral community and, 319–320; moral, 348; oppositional, 114; oppression and, 2, 4–6, 9, 88, 93, 103, 201, 211, 214, 231, 244, 249–250, 338; passivity and, 214; of patients, 328; practical, 142, 172; rational, 59, 245; of rape victims, 319; reason-responsiveness and, 178; reflective, 36, 217; respect for, 5, 10, 99, 101, 106, 231, 349; self-constitution account of, 218; self-creative, 65; self-respect and, 3; self-writing and, 192; social and relational character of, 1, 4, 6, 75, 89, 93, 96, 181, 195, 208, 338; successful, 145; women's, 96, 111–112, 114, 138, 211, 244, 249; work and, 280–285, 287–290, 293–297, 299; unified across time, 187
agential ownership, 118–119
Agential Virtue Account, 172–177, 179
agential voice and authority, 105–112
agentic skills, 121–124, 126, 131, 139
akrasia. *See* weakness of will
alienation, 213, 217, 219, 222, 235–236
Ali, Hirsi, 81
American Civil Liberties Union (ACLU), 338–339
American Enterprise Institute, 147
Améry, Jean, 319
analytical skills, 121
Anderson, Elizabeth, 28
Anderson, Joel, 19, 37
answerability, 9, 19, 32, 35–36, 109–112, 115, 119, 124–126, 134–140, 188–190, 192, 196, 221, 345
applied ethics, 2
Aristotle, 255, 283
Arjomand, Homa, 148
Astell, Mary, 71
attitudes, 184–187
authentic self, 3, 32, 95, 106, 164, 257–258, 265, 267–268, 272–273
authenticity: conditions of, 17–18, 21, 92, 103, 257, 265, 343; conditions of autonomy, 183, 206, 233, 235, 246, 257, 267; conditions of self-governance, 24, 30–32, 40; honesty with oneself and, 196; mental freedom and, 187–190
authority, 8, 90–94
autonomous agency in work, 288–290
autonomous personhood, 44, 59, 90, 216–217, 289
autonomously chosen work, 284–285
autonomy: in bioethics, 333–335; of body, 10; care-based analyses, 18; choices and, 8; competency, 122, 126, 139, 260, 276; concept of, 39, 61, 164–165; defined, 1–2, 45, 78, 141, 257, 265; dimensions of, 5–6; economic independence,

autonomy: in bioethics (*Cont.*) 10, 285–286; in end-of-life decisions, 327–329; as finding one's own law, 44–45, 47–48, 59; free will and, 165; gender inequality problem, 256; government's role in, 54; human development and, 153–156; independence and, 57; individualistic aspects of, 42–43; internalized oppression, 94–96; levels of, 19; in medical decision making, 329–332; minimalist notion of, 333, 335; multidimensional, 15–16, 39–41; negative liberty, 25; normative commitments, 8; oppression and, 207–215, 224–226; overview, 6–7; philosophical conceptions, 5; philosophical interest, 2; role of, 2; self-governance conditions, 31; social capacity, 19; social-relational power and authority, 90–94; thick autonomy, 151; value-neutral, 5–6; value-saturated, 5–6. *See also* feminism commitments; relational autonomy; *specific types of autonomy*

"Autonomy and the Feminist Intuition" (Stoljar), 88, 94–96, 104–105, 114–118, 120, 125

autonomy-based conception of justice, 24–25

baad (Afghan method of justice), 149, 153
Babbitt, Susan, 116, 129, 132
Baber, Harriet, 243–248
bad options, choosing among, 243–248
Bakan, David, 66, 67
bargaining with patriarchy, 243
Bartky, Sandra Lee, 3, 228
Beauchamp, Tom, 18
Benjamin, Jessica, 62, 69, 79
Benson, Paul: oppressive norms, 236; relational autonomy, 7–8, 18, 87; on self-authorization, 220–221; social agents, 36; on value axes, 118–120
Bergstedt, Kenneth, 335–338
Berlin, Isaiah, 72–73
Bickenbach, Jerome, 342
bioethics: autonomy in, 333–335; commodification of body parts, 26; end-of-life decisions and, 327–329; facilitating suicide, 326, 331–332, 335–338, 341; local autonomy, 20; reproductive freedom, 26
biological influences, 267–268, 273
bipolar disorder, 215
bodily autonomy, 10, 301–309
borderline personality syndrome, 68
Bouvia, Elizabeth, 338–341, 343–346
Bouyeri, Mohammed, 147
Bowery, Charity, 209
Bratman, Michael, 184
Brison, Susan, 319
Brownbeck, Sam, 302

Brown, Wendy, 63
Bruckner, Donald, 234–235
bundles of options, 244–245
Buss, Sarah, 213–215, 304–305
Butler, Judith, 263, 275

Canadian Council of Muslim Women, 148
capabilities theory, 28–30
capacity and capabilities: approach to human and moral development, 154–156; conditional environment for, 101; independence and, 58–59; relational autonomy, 20–21, 33–34, 81, 131, 280; work and, 280, 282–284, 292–295, 297–298, 300
capitalism, 7, 42–43, 49, 55, 298–299
care-based analyses of autonomy, 18
care of the self, 190, 192–194, 197
cares and caring, 178–180, 182–187
"Caring and Internality" (Jaworska), 184
categorical imperative, 72, 283–284, 298
Centers for Disease Control and Prevention (CDC), 316–317
Chaplin, Charlie, 299
character: abortion and, 324; altered in response to oppression, 201, 203; as a component of gender, 259; formation of, 82–83, 344; John Stuart Mill on, 82–83; of autonomous agents, 98, 214, 216, 218; of self-made men, 52; planning, 233, 239
childrearing, 10, 69–70, 80, 122, 126, 230, 234, 239, 255–279
Childress, James, 18
Chodorow, Nancy: men's relationship with women, 66; object relations theory, 79; on psychoanalysis, 70; relational autonomy, 61, 67, 69; women's basis for empathy, 68
choices, 1, 8, 17, 25, 62, 73–75, 77–79, 81, 90, 97, 105–108, 115–116, 191, 206, 241–244, 295–296, 333–334, 341–342
Christman, John: authenticity, 32; autonomous decision making, 343; changing life circumstances, 9; consent confers legitimacy on governments, 134; nonalienation analysis of critical reflection, 18, 223; nonrelational theories, 88–89; Oshana's response to, 157; self-acceptance, 346; socio-historical self, 235–237
Code, Lorraine, 163, 285
coercion, 212, 229, 248–252, 295, 326–328, 330
coercive desires, 212
collective norms, 46–48
commitments: to autonomy, 6, 35, 151–153, 156–159, 283, 326; to fetus, 320–324; identity-defining, 2, 18, 24, 35, 37, 59, 97, 123–125, 206, 218; normative, 7–8, 88–90, 96, 99, 105–106, 108, 215–216, 278; to oneself, 44–45;

Index 353

to promoting human flourishing, 283, 300; to respecting agency of workers, 283; social, 96–102; tonal, 185, 186; transitional, 185, 186; of the will, 190. *See also* feminism commitments, religious commitments.
commodification of body parts, 26
communal self, 67
communication skills, 121
communism, 298–299
compassion trait, 274
competence conditions: for autonomy, 103, 110, 188, 196, 205, 216, 227, 233, 235, 246, 251, 257, 265–6, 273, 276; of self-governance, 17–18, 21–22, 24, 30–34, 40
competency skills, 121, 205–206
constitutive relationship, 56
Constitutivity Axis, 8, 120, 129, 133–140
content-neutral conceptions of autonomy, 96, 98–99
contractarian theory, 154
contract model of pregnancy, 322–324
conversion experiences, 132
Cornell, Drucilla, 63
corporations, , 286–287
Cowart, Dax, 331
Crews, Dan, 335–336
critical reflection, 1, 18, 32–35, 48, 78, 81, 165, 171, 178, 180, 217, 231, 235–238, 257, 260, 335, 342–343, 348
Cudd, Ann, 3, 228–229, 238, 242–243, 317
cultural beliefs, 251
cultural images of independence, 58–59
cultural opportunities, 27–28, 46
cultural patriarchy, 146–150

Dalai Lama, 283
Dalrymple, Jack, 301–302
Damasio, Antonio, 185
Darwall, Stephen, 36, 196
date rape, 322–324
day-wage laborers, 145
death. *See* end-of-life decisions
de Beauvoir, Simone, 271–2
decision making in medical treatment, 329–332
deference, 5
deformed desires, 9, 228–232, 243–245
degradation of persons, 287, 293, 295, 310–311
dehumanization of work, 283–300
deliberate character planning, 233–234
democratic participation, 102–104
dependence, 21, 24, 31, 44, 54, 56–59, 63, 78–79, 144–145, 154, 182, 244, 280, 285, 327, 339–340, 342, 344. *See also* independence
deprivation, 230, 241–242, 288
de-Shalit, Avner, 155

designer babies, 26
desires: coercive, 212–213; conflicting, 73, 211; critical evaluation of, 77–78, 136; deformed, 2, 9, 211, 228–234, 237, 242–245, 248–249, 305, 323, 345; deliberate adjustment of, 233; determined by character, 82; dwarfed, 289; first-order, 183–184, 213; historical formation of, 236; as non-autonomous, 235, 249; as one's own, 75, 127, 136, 211, 213; oppressive norms or conditions and, 114;¹¹⁸, 211, 228–230, 234–238, 243–245, 249; irrational, 72–75; as socially constructed, 73, 76; as reasons, 37; reflective, 1, 101, 213, 310–311, 343
dialogical accounts of autonomy, 6, 33, 36, 135
dialogical answerability, 109–110, 195, 197
dialogical rationality, 138–139
dialogical skills, 33
Dickens, Charles, 247
Dinnerstein, Dorothy, 62, 69
Directivity Axis, 8, 116–120, 129
disability activists, 344, 345
DiStefano, Christine, 61, 67
dogmatism, 36
Döring, Sabine, 172–174
Double Axis Thesis, 8, 127–133
Douglass, Frederick, 52–53
Druthers Restaurant, 287
Dryden, Jane, 4
Duality of Human Existence, The (Bakan), 67
Dubay, Matthew, 302
Dubay v. Wells (2007), 302–304
Dworkin, Gerald, 17, 78, 87, 236–237, 296

Ebadi, Shirin, 91, 93, 112
economic (or financial) independence, 10, 56–57, 208, 271, 282, 284–287
economic security, 8
egalitarian liberals, 43
Ehrenreich, Barbara, 143
Ekstrom, Laura, 178
Elster Jon, 229–230, 233–234
emotional actions, 176–177
emotional agents and autonomy: autonomy theories, 178–180; overview, 8, 163–166; reason responsiveness, 8, 165–166, 171–177; value perceptions, 166–170
emotional skills, 33
emotions, defined, 34
employment. *See* work
end-of-life decisions: ableism and, 338–342; autonomy in, 327–329; autonomy in treatment decision making, 329–332; bioethics and, 327–329, 332–335; medically assisted death, 335–338; oppressive socialization, 342–346; overview, 10–11, 326–327; public policy and, 346–349

epistemic values, 120, 125–126, 127, 135
equal pay for equal work, 157
equality: in capabilities theory, 29; disability activism and, 344; gender, 29, 142, 157, 159, 255, 258, 262, 264, 271, 275, 279; as a goal of liberalism, 43, 45; moral, 157; of opportunity, 27, 30, 285, 388; value of, 5, 43
ethical theory, 2
eudemonistically meaningless work, 280–281, 293–300
evaluative identity categories, 219–220, 224
exploitation: bioethics and, 26; economic or financial, 145, 282; feminism and, 153
external critical perspectives, 131

Fast Food Women (Lewis), 287
Feeling Theory, 168
Feit, Mel, 302
feminine model of relational autonomy, 67
feminine psychoanalytical development, 7
feminism: autonomy and, 2, 7–10, 83, 141–143, 150–153, 156–159, 270, 278; embodiment and, 306; defined, 142, 258; liberal, 258, 278; sameness approach to, 264; relational autonomy and, 7–8, 62, 77
feminism commitments: agential voice and authority, 105–112; autonomy, 150–153; cultural and religious patriarchy, 146–150; democratic participation, 102–104; gender socialization, 9, 255–261, 265, 270–4, 277; human development, 153–156; internalized oppression, 94–96; objections to, 157–158; overview, 7–8, 87–89, 141–143; social commitments to inclusion, 96–102; social-relational power and authority, 90–94; wage labor, 143–146
feminist intuition, 94–95, 116–118
financial insecurity, 144–145
first-order cares, 191, 193, 195
first-order desires, 183, 213
Flathman, Richard, 80
Flax, Jane, 61, 67, 68
flourishing, 116, 132, 214–215, 230, 240–242, 263, 276, 281, 283, 293, 300
Forbes Magazine, 51
Foucault, Michel: care of the self, 190, 192–194, 197; on freedom, 76–77
Frankfurt, Harry: autonomous decision making, 343; autonomy and, 87; commitment of the will, 190; hierarchical model of free will, 165; identification of will, 18; personhood and freedom of the will, 182–184
freedom: concept of, 62; conditions of self-determination, 17, 25–27; defined, 76; of international movement, 25; negative liberty, 26; relational autonomy and, 7, 76–78; role of, 71–76

freedom to do otherwise model, 232, 238–243
free will and autonomy, 165, 185
Freudian psychoanalysis, 70
Freud, Sigmund, 63
Friedman, Marilyn: autonomy, defined by, 77; concept of autonomy, 7; on emotions, 167; financial insecurity, 145; limitations of opportunities, 2; nonrelational theories, 88–89; oppressive norms, 129; personal autonomy, 95; philosophical conceptions of autonomy, 4–5; relational autonomy and independence, 42; self-made men and women, 83; social conditions and reflective values, 334; women as capable of own rights of full moral agency, 156
Frye, Marilyn, 3
full-fledged or full-blooded agency, 165, 171

Gallagher, Janet, 321
Gates, Bill, 51
gender conformity, 117
gender, defined, 259
gendered socialization: autonomy-supportive, 259–260; defined, 259; definitions and assumptions, 257–259; evaluation of options, 265–278; forms of, 260–265; gender norms and, 227–233; non-gendered socialization, 261–262, 265–271; overview, 9–10, 255–257; revisionary feminine gender socialization, 263–265, 275–278; traditional masculine gender socialization, 262–263, 271–275
gender identity, 64–66
Gender in the Mirror (Meyers), 5
gender oppression, 2, 4, 5, 20, 24, 227, 229. *See also* oppression
gender psychology, 70
gender-specific discipline of boys and girls by mothers, 68
gender system, 268–270
Genovese, Kitty, 314
Gill, Carol, 340
Gilligan, Carol: on care, 182; moral maturity, 190–193, 197; object relations theory, 61; relational autonomy, 69
global autonomy, 19–20, 23–24, 249–250
global self-esteem, 213
Globe and Mail (Canadian newspaper), 148
Gomberg, Paul, 285, 296
Good Work (Schumacher), 281
government, role of, 50, 54
Groundwork for a Metaphysics of Morals (Kant), 284

habitual actions, 176
Hampton, Jean, 311
Harding, Sandra, 61–62, 67, 69
harm principle, 251

Harris, George, 323
Hartsock, Nancy, 61, 67, 69
health care providers (HCPs), 326, 328–331, 340
health-care system structures, 334, 340
Helm, Bennett, 184, 185
heteronomous persons, 258
heteronomous work, 284–285
heteronomy, 72
hierarchy of moral acts, 313–316
higher-order desires and attitudes, 183–184
Hill, Thomas, 283, 297
Hirschmann, Nancy, 7, 61
Hirsi Ali, Ayaan, 143, 146–148, 153
Ho, Anita, 10, 326
Hobbes, Thomas, 71
Hogben, Alia, 148
honesty with oneself, 196
Honneth, Axel, 37
Huckleberry Finn example, 172–173, 174, 176
human agency. *See* agency
human development, 153–156
human flourishing. *See* flourishing
Humean tradition, 68, 165

identifiable self, 74–75
identification of will, 18
identity formation, 291
imagination skills, 33, 121
impaired persons: ableism and, 338–342; oppressive socialization and, 342–346; public policy and, 346–349
implied contracts, 322–324
In a Different Voice (Gilligan), 61, 190
inappropriately adaptive preferences (IAPs), 212–213
inclusion, 96–102
independence: as an aspect of autonomy, 42, 44, 46, 56–60, 65, 158, 240, 260, 285; defined, 44, 56; dependence as a degree of, 56–7; ideal of, 7, 57–9, 327; as faulty ideal, 58–9, 158, 285–287; of mind, 59, 236; normative, 35; procedural, 90, 208, 214, 232, 236–8, 248, 251–2; relational autonomy and, 7, 42–43–44 56–60; and self-made persons, 56, 60. *See also* economic independence
independent-mindedness, 59
interdependence of human lives, 44, 79, 286
individualism: relational aspect of, 7, 43–49; social ontology of persons, 21
inequalities, 22–23, 243, 255, 259, 269–270, 295, 346
injustice: autonomy and, 111–112; function of, 22; social, 105, 110
inner self, 73–4
intellectual abilities, effect of work on, 290
intentional action model, 218

internalized oppression, 3, 31, 94–96, 111–112, 120, 137–138, 152, 201, 215, 223–224, 227, 252, 266, 281, 340, 344, 348
introspection skills, 121, 272
intuition, 94–95
Islamic culture, 146–149

Jacklin, Carol, 68
Jacoby, Stanford, 299
Jaggar, Alison, 163
Jaworska, Agnieszka: authenticity and, 188; on care, 182, 183, 184; first-order cares, 191, 193; mental freedom, 194–195
Jones, Karen, 170, 171–172
judgment, 78, 191–192, 204–207
Judgmental Theory, 168
justice: autonomy-based conception of, 24–25; and inequalities, 22–23
Justice, Gender and the Family (Okin), 261

Kant, Immanuel: on autonomy, 61, 66, 72, 79; bodily autonomy and, 306; categorical imperative, 283–284; conception of persons, 154; on degradation, 310–311; on ethical theory, 2; individualistic morality, 70; on respect, 310–311, 327; responsiveness to reason, 129; rule-governed autonomy, 67; Taylorism and, 294; treatment of workers and, 296–297
Keller, Evelyn Fox: object relations theory, 62, 67, 79; reactive autonomy, 65; relational autonomy, 69; true self, 66
Kevorkian, Jack, 331
KFC, 287
Khader, Serene: adaptive preferences, 9, 132, 140; coercion, 248–251; deformed options, 237–238; desires for oppressive conditions, 230; inappropriately adaptive preferences, 212–213
Klein, Melanie, 67
Kohn, Melvin, 290
Kolodny, Niko, 173
Kornhauser, Arthur, 288–289
Korsgaard, Christine, 17, 206, 218
Kymlicka, Will, 43

labor: division of, 69–70; financial independence and, 10, 56–57; low-wage labor, 150; stigmatized by feelings toward, 3; wage labor, 143–146. *See also* self-made men and women; work
Lapham, Mike, 50, 54
late-term abortion, 313–324
Law of the Peoples, The (Rawls), 292
laws, one's own, 44–45, 47–48, 59
Law's Relations (Nedelsky), 7, 42, 43, 79
legislative bills on personhood, 302
levels of relational autonomy, 19–20
Lewis, Anne, 287

liberal democracies, 2
liberal individualism, 43–49
liberal justice, 154
liberals and liberalism, 43, 59–60
liberal self, 82–83
life circumstances, responding to changing in, 9
Lindsey, Laura, 267
Lippke, Richard, 291
Little Caesar's, 295
Little, Margaret, 310, 318
local autonomy, 19–20, 249
Locke, John, 71
"Love and Knowledge" (Jaggar), 163
lower-order motivational states, 189, 217
low-wage labor, 150
Ludicrous Argument, The, 163–164, 180

MacIntyre, Alistair, 79
Mackenzie, Catriona, 6, 42, 87, 208, 251, 305–306
Macoby, Eleanor, 68
Mahler, Margaret, 63, 68, 69
manic depression, 215
Marx, Karl, 294, 298
McAfee, Larry, 335–338
McKay, Brett, 53, 55
McKay, Kate, 53, 55
McLeod, Carolyn, 19, 344
meaningless work, 280–281, 293–300
medical ethics, 305
medically assisted death and suicide, 326, 331–332, 335–338, 341
memory skills, 121
mental freedom, 187–190, 194–195
mental health, effect of job conditions on, 288–289
Merleau-Ponty, Maurice, 64, 306
Meyers, Diana Tietjens: autonomous decision making, 344; on autonomy, 77, 95; male socialization, 271–272; relational autonomy, 69; self-discovery, 246; values in autonomy theory, 5, 8, 114
Miller, Brian, 50, 54
Mill, John Stuart, 71, 82–83, 283, 327
minimalist notion of autonomy, 333, 335
model of intentional action, 218
Modern Times (film), 299
Mohmand, Fraidoon, 149
moral acts, hierarchy of, 313–316
moral maturity, 190–193
moral perspective of women, 154
Moriarty, Jeffrey, 292
Müller-Lyer illusion, 169
Mullin, Amy, 316–317
multidimensional autonomy, 15–16, 39–41
Murphy, James Bernard, 288, 298
Myatt, Mike, 51

Narayan, Uma, 151, 152–153, 211, 243–244
National Center for Men, 302
Nedelsky, Jennifer: choices, 78; independence, 56–60; liberal individualism, 7, 43–49; relational autonomy, 77; on self, 79–80; self-made men and women, 49–55
negative liberty, 25, 26–27, 72–76
New York Times (newspaper), 149
Nickel and Dimed (Ehrenreich), 143
Noddings, Nel, 182
nonalienated self-affirmation, 219
nonalienation analysis of critical reflection, 18, 223
nonautonomous agents, 137
non-gendered socialization (NGS), 261–262, 265–271
non-ideal theory, 23
normative authority over values, 209
normative commitments, 7–8
normative individualism, 20, 21
Nozick, Robert, 80
Nuremberg experiments, 328
Nussbaum, Martha: on abortion, 306; adaptive preferences, 239–240; capabilities theory, 21, 28, 33–34, 154–155; human and moral development, 154–155; self-authorization, 35; severe deprivation and, 230, 249

objective reasons, 173–174
object relations theory, 61–71
obligations corresponding with rights, 314–315
"Of Liberty and Necessity" (Mill), 82
Okin, Susan Moller, 261
O'Neill, Onora, 57
open-mindedness, 9, 38, 135, 182, 188–190, 196–197, 262, 276, 299
opportunity conditions of self-determination, 17, 27–30
oppression: adaption and autonomy, 207–215; by choice, 242–243; circumstances of, 5, 9, 201–203; defined, 2–3; dynamics of autonomy attribution, 224–226; female complicity in, 262–263; feminine norms, 117–118; internalization of, 94–96, 111–112; internalized, 94–96, 111–112, 137–138; judgment and, 204–207; procedural autonomy and, 215–224; psychological dimensions of, 3; psychological harms of, 228–229; self-affirmation, 215–224; social oppression, 31
oppressive socialization, 342–346
options theory of self-determination, 27–28
orthonomy, 96
Oshana, Marina: authority over choice, 8; autonomous agency, 104; autonomous personhood, 289; autonomy and feminism, 141; coercion, 250; freedom and opportunity, 17, 134; honesty with oneself, 196; liberal self, 82;

personal autonomy, 105; relational autonomy, 88–89; self-authorization, 35; socio-relational account of autonomy, 28, 90–94, 208

parents and parenting: inculcation of competency conditions, 266; responsibilities for autonomy of children, 26; sexual division of labor and, 69–70. *See also* gendered socialization
paternalism, 38, 134–135, 329
patient-centered care, 330
patriarchal norms, 221
patriarchal social relations, 77–78
patriarchy, autonomy and, 151
Perceptual Theory of Emotions, 168–170, 179
Perry, Stewart E., 293
personal autonomy: agential voice and authority, 105–112; critical reflection and, 164–165; democratic participation, 102–104; economic autonomy and, 286; feminism and autonomy, 158; internalized oppression, 94–96; social commitments, 96–102; social-relational theory, 90–94
personalities, effect of work on, 290
personal liberties, 26
personhood: freedom of the will and, 182; legislative bills, 302
persons: conception of, 21, 154; threats to, 60. *See also* respect for persons
Phelan, Shane, 235
philosophical moral psychology, 18
physician-assisted suicide, 331–332
Pineau, Lois, 322
Piper, Mark, 1, 9, 157, 255
Political Liberalism (Rawls), 292
political liberties, 25
Politics of Persons, The (Christman), 24
positive liberty, 72–73, 75
power, 90–94
practical identity, 206–207, 210
practical rationality, 173–174, 206
practical reason, 34, 35
preferences. *See* adaptive preferences; desires
pregnancy, complications of, 316–317. *See also* abortion
primary emotions, 184–185
procedural accounts of autonomy, 5–6, 9, 47, 88, 94, 96, 102, 108, 110, 112, 203, 207–208, 212–224, 230–232, 236–238, 243, 248, 251–252, 305, 330
procedural independence, 232, 236
programmatic level of autonomy, 19
psychoanalytic theory, 7, 61–66
psychological processes model, 232–238
psychosexual development, 63–66
public policy and medically assisted death, 346–349

rape, 309–313, 322–324
rational choice theory, 120
rational guidance, 171, 173
Rawls, John: concept/conception distinction, 15; contractarian theory, 154; gendered socialization, 15; meaningful work, 291–292
Raz, Joseph: choices, 78; coercion, 250; on freedom, 77; liberal individualism, 43; opportunity conditions, 17; self-determination, 27–28
reactive autonomy, 65–66, 81
reason responsiveness, 8, 165–166, 171–177
reason tracking, 171–174
reflective acceptance, 217
reflective endorsement, 91–92, 97–98
reflexive insightfulness, 136–137
reflexive self-affirmation, 9, 203, 216–218, 222, 224
regulative guidance, 172
relational accounts of autonomy, 208
relational autonomy: feminine psychoanalytical development, 7; freedom and, 7, 76–78; gender oppression, 20; independence and, 7, 42–43, 56–60; levels of, 19–20; liberal individualism, 43–49; normative commitments, 7–8; object relations theory and, 61–71; oppressive socialization and, 342–346; origins of, 63–66; overview, 4–5; self-authorization, 35–39; self-care and, 195–197; self-determination, 23–30; self-governance, 31–35; self-made men and women, 7, 42–43, 49–55; social character of human agency, 4; unitary conception, 16–19; vulnerability, 21. *See also* autonomy
Relational Autonomy (Mackenzie & Stoljar), 5, 42, 87–88
relational freedom, 63
religious commitment, 35, 36
religious patriarchy, 146–150
Reproduction of Mothering, The (Chodorow), 61, 68
reproductive autonomy or freedom, 26
resistant slaves, 209–211, 237
respect: for autonomy and autonomous choices, 2, 8, 15, 99–102, 107, 153, 156, 159, 201, 231, 250–251, 283–284, 295, 297–298, 310–311, 326–328, 333, 349; for the body, 319; for feminism, 153, 159; for oppressed women, 5, 95, 114, 139, 150–151, 141; for patient autonomy, 21, 329–330, 333–334, 336–337; for persons, 37, 39, 99, 102, 210, 281, 283–4, 297, 310–311, 346; for preferences formed in adaptive contexts, 5, 96; for rights, 156; for agency in working life, 10, 283, 299. *See also* self-respect
responsibility: for action, 134; for aspects of oneself, 9, 36, 129, 137, 150, 189, 191–193, 195, 197, 345; for childcare, 69, 255; for others' needs,

responsibility: for action (*Cont.*) 108; for oppression, 249; for social change, 133; moral, 2
reversibility of preferences, 246–248
revisionary feminine gender socialization (RFGS), 263–265, 275–278
Richardson, Henry, 246–247
Ricouer, Paul, 306
rights: to bodily autonomy, 306–308; of full moral agency, 156; obligations corresponding with, 314–315
Robeyns, Ingrid, 28
Rodriguez, Sue, 331
Roessler, Beate, 291
Roe v. Wade (1973), 302, 321
Rousseau, Jean-Jacques, 72
Rubin, Gayle, 261
Ruddick, Sarah, 182

Schooler, Carmi, 290
Schumacher, E. F., 281
Schwartz, Adina, 290
secondary emotions, 185
second guessing, 72, 73, 75
second-person standpoint, 36
Seidman, Jeffrey: autonomous agency, 189; on care, 182–183; first-order cares, 191, 193, 195; valuing and caring, 185–187
self: active self, 77; dialogical conception of, 33; inner self, 73; liberal self, 82–83; outer self, 73; responsibility for, 189; role of, 79–82
self-acceptance, 217, 346
self-affirmation, 215–224
self-answerability theory, 134–139, 189
self-assertiveness, 272
self-authorization: accountability, 35–36; for autonomy, 122, 220–221; defined, 18, 35; self-evaluative attitudes, 35–37; social recognition, 35, 37–38
self-care: care as attitude towards others, 182–187; concept of, 190–195; mental freedom and, 187–190; overview, 8–9, 181–182; relational autonomy and, 195–197
self-conception, 265
self-confidence, 37, 119
self-constitution account of agency, 218
self-deception, 246–247
self-defense, 307
self-definition of self, 57
self-determination: autonomy as, 1; autonomy-based conception of justice, 24–25; capabilities theory, 28–30; cultural opportunities, 27–28; defined, 17, 25, 257; freedom conditions, 17, 25–27; global analysis, 23–24; opportunity conditions, 17, 27–30; options theory, 27–28; as relational concept, 23–30; structural constraints on, 24
self-direction, 290
self-discovery, 246
self-esteem, 3, 37
self-evaluative attitudes, 19, 38
self-governance: authenticity conditions, 31–32; autonomy conditions, 31; capabilities, 33–34; competence conditions, 17, 32–33; defined, 16–17, 31; honesty and, 196; relational conception of, 31–35; unitary concept, 17, 32
self-identities, 74–75
self-knowledge, 33, 137
self-made men and women, 7, 42–43, 49–55, 83
"Self-Made Men" (Douglass), 51–53
Self-Made Myth, The (Miller & Lapham), 50
self-nurturing skills, 121
self-reflexive attitudes, 265
self-representing, 345
self-respect, 3, 10, 34–37, 116, 125, 151, 208, 222, 247, 280–281, 284–285, 291–293
self-responsibility, 150–151, 195–197
self-transformative activities, 33
self-trust, 37, 203, 209
self-worth, 37, 119, 181–182, 203, 208, 211–212, 216, 219, 222, 224–225, 228, 265–266, 272–273, 276–277, 280–281, 291–292, 344–345
Sen, Amartya, 29, 154–156, 230
senses, defined, 33
Sermon on the Mount, 298
severe deprivation, 230
sexual contracts, 322
Shafiqzada, Nasima, 149
Shakespeare, Tom, 341
Shakila story, 149, 153, 156
Sharia law, in Canada, 148
Sherwin, Susan, 328, 344
Shoemaker, David, 165, 179
Singer, Peter, 317
Single Axis Thesis, 128, 130
skills: for autonomy, 17, 20–22, 31–34, 205, 207, 227, 246, 281, 342; cognitive, 188; damaged by meaningless work, 281; developed by infants and children, 64, 264, 276; exercised at work, 10, 281–283, 288, 294, 296. *See also* agentic skills
slaves, 209–211, 237, 270
social capacity, 19
social commitments to inclusion, 96–102
social conditions, 22
social constructivist and constructivism, 73–78, 81, 82–83
social injustice, 105, 110
social ontology of persons, 21
social oppression, 23, 31, 227
social recognition, 37–38

social-relational theory of personal autonomy, 90–94
social skills, 33
socio-historical self, 235–237
socio-relational account of autonomy, 28, 90–94, 208, 335–338
sour grapes, 229–230, 233–234
Srey Mom, 248
Stoljar, Natalie: adaptive preference formation, 9, 227; autonomous agency, 104; feminist intuition, 116–118; personal autonomy, 87–89, 94–96, 105; social relations, 42; value axes, 116–118, 120
structural accounts of autonomy, 207–208
structural conditions of autonomy, 17, 23–25, 28, 31–32, 208–209, 224
structural constraints on self-determination, 23–4
structural injustice and inequality, 133, 210, 243
subjective reasons, 173–174
Submission (television film), 146
subordinate persons, 58
subservience, 5
substantive autonomy, 8–9, 88, 90, 94–96, 98–100, 103–104, 111, 114–115, 128, 130, 152, 208, 230–2, 240, 243, 252, 305. *See also* weakly substantive views
successful agency, 145
suicide, medically assisted, 326, 331–332, 335–338, 341
Superson, Anita, 10, 211, 229
System of Logic (Mill), 82

Tale of Two Cities, A (Dickens), 247
Tappolet, Christine, 8, 163
Taylor, Charles: dialogical conception of self, 33; internalized recognition, 211; responsibility, 36; second guessing, 72
Taylor, Fredrick, 282
Taylor, Gloria, 331
Taylor, Harriet, 71
Taylorism, 283, 293–294, 300
Terkel, Studs, 294
"The Art of Manliness" (website), 53
Theory of Justice (Rawls), 261, 292
thick autonomy, 151, 157
Thomas, Laurence, 319
Thomson, Judith Jarvis: on abortion, 10, 304; on late-term abortion, 313–324; on rape, 309–310; on right to bodily autonomy, 306–308
tonal commitments, 185, 186
traditional masculine gender socialization (TMGS), 262–263, 271–275
transitional commitments, 185, 186
Tribe, Laurence, 301, 303–304, 316
Tuskegee syphilis study, 328

"25 of the Greatest Self-Made Men in American History" (McKay & McKay), 53
two value axes, 116–121

Udry, Richard, 267
"Understanding and Overcoming Pathology" (Nedelsky), 79–80
unitary concept, 16–19, 39

value-neutral autonomy, 5–6, 88, 114–122, 125–140, 329–330
value-saturated and value-laden autonomy, 5–6, 96, 98, 101, 104, 114–122, 126–133
values: agential skills and, 121, 126; alienation and, 219; of autonomous agents, 2, 17, 54, 97–8, 103, 106–10, 114–122, 152; constitutive, 116, 120, 122–124, 126–127, 129–130, 134–140; distinctions in, 6, 8, 114–115, 122–128; double axis thesis, 8, 127–133; emotions and, 166–170, 175; liberalism and, 43–45; overview, 8, 114–115; supported by autonomy, 2; two value axes, 116–121
"Valuing and Caring" Seidman, 185
van Gogh, Theo, 146–147
Vasanti (Indian woman), 239–241, 244–246, 249
Velleman, David, 134, 174, 177
Veltman, Andrea, 1, 10, 280
virtues: agential, 166, 172, 175, 177–178; of autonomous agents, 190; female, 273; feminist, 273; social, 158; work and, 281, 285, 295
voice: authentic, 107; of autonomous agents, 89, 105–112, 203, 226; internal, 210–211; silencing of, 130
volitional skills, 121
vulnerability, 7, 21, 41, 57–58, 133, 144, 150, 185, 208, 320, 328–329, 344, 347, 349

wage labor, 143–146
Waldron, Jeremy, 43
Wallace, Jay, 171
Wal-Mart, 286
Walzer, Michael, 3, 293
Wasserstrom, Richard, 261
weakly substantive views, 94, 114, 116, 119, 121–122, 128, 130, 215–216
weakness of will (akrasia), 33, 101, 166, 172
welfare programs, 54, 55, 285–286
Wente, Margaret, 148
Western values, 150–151
Westlund, Andrea: accountability, 18; feminist view, 152–153; Meyers' critique of, 134–139; relational autonomy, 88–89; relational capabilities, 131; responsibility, 36; self-care, 8–9, 181; self-representing, 345; self-respect, 150–151; self-responsibility, 150–151
White, John, 285, 292

will: commitment of, 190; freedom of, 182–184; free will, 165, 185; identification of, 18
Winnicott, D. W., 67, 68, 69
Wolff, Jonathan, 155
Wollstonecraft, Mary, 71
womanhood: NGS view of, 267; RFGS view of, 264, 275; TMGS view of, 273, 274–275; value system of, 114
women: harm suffered by, 60; Ludicrous Argument and, 163–164
Wood, Allen, 297, 298

work: autonomous agency in, 288–290; autonomy and, 280–284; dehumanization of, 283–300; equal pay for, 157; heteronomous, 284–285; identity and, 291; impact on autonomous capabilities, 10; as key to success, 52–53; meaningless, 280–281, 293–300; self-respect and, 291–293; social recognition, 38

Young, Iris Marion, 272

Zerilla, Linda, 63